ESSAYS ON KELSEN

Essays on Kelsen

EDITED BY

RICHARD TUR

AND

WILLIAM TWINING

CLARENDON PRESS · OXFORD

1986

Oxford University Press, Walton Street, Oxford ox2 6dp

Oxford New York Toronto
Delhi Bombay Calcutta Madras Karachi
Petaling Jaya Singapore Hong Kong Tokyo
Nairobi Dar es Salaam Cape Town
Melbourne Auckland
and associated companies in
Beirut Berlin Ibadan Nicosia

Oxford is a trade mark of Oxford University Press

Published in the United States
by Oxford University Press, New York

British Library Cataloguing in Publiction Data
Essays on Kelsen.
1. Kelsen, Hans   2. Jurisprudence
I. Tur, Richard   II. Twining, William
340'.109   K215
ISBN 0–19–825470–9

Library of Congress Cataloging-in-Publication Data
Essays on Kelsen.
Includes index.
1. Law—Philosophy.   2. Kelson, Hans, 1881–1973.
I. Tur, Richard.   II. Twining, William.
K339.E87 1986   340'.1   86–6878
ISBN 0–19–825470–9

Set by Hope Services, Abingdon
Printed in Great Britain
at The Alden Press, Oxford

CONTENTS

PART FIVE: JUSTICE

PART SIX: INTERNATIONAL LAW

ABBREVIATIONS

WORKS BY KELSEN

HPS[1]	*Hauptprobleme der Staatsrechtslehre* (Tübingen, 1911).
HPS[2]	*Hauptprobleme der Staatsrechtslehre*, 2nd edn. (Tübingen, 1923).
ASL	*Allgemeine Staatslehre* (Berlin, 1925).
RR[1]	*Reine Rechtslehre* (Leipzig and Vienna, 1934).
PTL-IMFC	'The Pure Theory of Law. Its Method and Fundamental Concepts', tr. Charles Wilson, 50 *LQR* 474 (1934) and 51 *LQR* 517 (1935).
GTLS	*General Theory of Law and State*, tr. Anders Wedberg (Cambridge, Mass., 1945).
WIJ	*What Is Justice? Justice, Law and Politics in the Mirror of Science. Collected Essays* (Berkeley and Los Angeles, 1957).
RR[2]	*Reine Rechtslehre*, 2nd edn. (Vienna, 1960).
TPD	*Théorie Pure du Droit*, tr. Charles Eisenmann (Paris, 1962).
ASL (Sp.)	*Allgemeine Staatslehre* (Spanish translation: L. Lacambra, *Teoría General del Estado* (Barcelona, 1934; Mexico, 1948)).
PTL	*Pure Theory of Law*, tr. Max Knight (Berkeley and Los Angeles, 1967).
ELMP	*Hans Kelsen: Essays in Legal and Moral Philosophy*, tr. Peter Heath, ed. Ota Weinberger (Dordrecht, 1973).
ATN	*Allgemeine Theorie der Normen* ed. K. Ringhofer and R. Walter (Vienna, 1979).

WORKS BY KANT

CPuR	*Critique of Pure Reason*, tr. F. Max Müller (London, 1881); tr. Norman Kemp Smith (London, 1929).
MEJ	*The Metaphysical Elements of Justice*, tr. John Ladd (Indianapolis, 1965).

OTHER WORKS

Ebenstein	William Ebenstein, *The Pure Theory of Law* (New York, 1969).

WRS I/II   H. Klecatsky, R. Marcic, H. Schambeck, eds. *Die Wiener rechtstheoretische Schule*, Volumes I and II (Vienna, 1968).

CONTRIBUTORS' WORKS

Works by contributors are referred to in the conventional way except that reference to an essay included in this volume is by way of the contributor's surname together with a page number in this volume.

EDITORS AND CONTRIBUTORS

RICHARD TUR *Oriel College, Oxford.*

PROF. WILLIAM TWINING *University College, London.*

PROF. JOSEPH RAZ *Balliol College, Oxford.*

PROF. ROBERTO VERNENGO *University of Buenos Aires.*

DR ALIDA WILSON *University of Aberdeen.*

DR HILLEL STEINER *University of Manchester.*

DR IAIN STEWART *University of Hull.*

PROF. OTA WEINBERGER *University of Graz.*

DR J.W. HARRIS *Keble College, Oxford.*

PROF. STANLEY L. PAULSON *Washington University, St Louis.*

DR INÉS WEYLAND *Polytechnic of North London.*

DR JES BJARUP *University of Aarhus.*

PROF. PHILIP PETTIT *Australian National University.*

THE LATE PROF. HEDLEY BULL *Balliol College, Oxford.*

INTRODUCTION

RICHARD TUR AND WILLIAM TWINING

HANS KELSEN was born in 1881 and died in 1973. In the view of some he is 'the jurist of our century'.[1] His seminal work. *Hauptprobleme der Staatsrechtslehre* was published in 1911[2] and his *Allgemeine Theorie der Normen* was published posthumously in 1979. His major works in English include *General Theory of Law and State* (1945), *What Is Justice?* (1957), *Pure Theory of Law* (1967), and *Essays in Legal and Moral Philosophy* (1973). He is the author of innumerable articles and his works have been translated into many languages.[3] Kelsen's disciples may be found in many countries. His range, too, is impressive and the insights into the works of others are frequently revealed only in footnotes not always available to an anglophone.[4] His writings include contributions on constitutional law, international law, and legal theory; his interests in political philosophy include the nature of the state, democracy, and liberalism as well as more polemical pieces on Bolshevik, Communist, and Marxist theories of law and state. His life, too, is a fascinating study: born in Prague, he spent his youth in Vienna, where later he taught, drafted the Austrian Constitution of 1920, and sat as a member of the Constitutional Court.[5] Subsequently he taught in Cologne, Geneva, Paris, and in America, at Chicago, Harvard, and Berkeley.

[1] Weinberger, *ELMP*, ix. 'the jurist of our century'; Pound, 'Law and the Science of Law in Recent Theories', 43 *Yale Law Journal*, 532, 'unquestionably the leading jurist of the time'; Ebenstein, xi; 'the most influential juristic movement of the twentieth century'; ix, 'the most important theory of law in our century'.

[2] Nearly everyone cites this work as having been published in 1911, but Métall, *Hans Kelsen; Leben und Werk* (Wein, 1969) and Golding, *The Encyclopedia of Philosophy* (New York, 1972) cite it as published in 1910. The edition consulted by the editors is dated 1911.

[3] Métall, *Hans Kelsen*, lists over 600 items in his bibliography and more has been published since 1969. He also lists 24 different languages into which some works have been translated.

[4] The English edition of the *Pure Theory of Law* omits all the major footnotes and one must look to the French or German editions for Kelsen's comments. A fine example from *ATN* is note 164 which is one of many offering comment on the criticism of the moral philosophy of R. M. Hare.

[5] See Métall, *Hans Kelsen* and Moore, *Legal Norms and Legal Science: A Critical Study of Kelsen's Pure Theory of Law* (Honolulu, 1978), p. viii.

Many have praised him. Thus Laski wrote of his 'profound philosophic mind, quick, agile and widely read'.[6] Gulick referred to him as 'probably the outstanding political scientist of central Europe of the twentieth century'.[7] Lauterpacht thought that the concluding pages of *Vom Wesen und Wert der Demokratie* 'belong to the best that political literature has produced'.[8] Hart has called Kelsen 'the most stimulating writer on analytical jurisprudence of our day'.[9] Though widely regarded as a, if not the, pre-eminent modern legal philosopher, English-speaking, and especially English, commentators have generally been ambivalent, hailing Kelsen as a leader in his field yet contriving to dismiss much of his contribution as irrelevant or marginal to English legal theory and practice. Some, perhaps most, of this criticism is misconceived, turning upon misunderstandings begotten of the radically different philosophical traditions of England and Europe. Ebenstein catches the point exactly: 'If a Morris Cohen or a Roscoe Pound attributes to the Pure Theory of Law, in the person of Kelsen, views which at no point correspond with its doctrines, it is not surprising that many thinkers of lesser stature should be led into condemning the Pure Theory of Law.'[10]

To coincide with the centenary of the year of Kelsen's birth, the United Kingdom Association for Legal and Social Philosophy devoted the whole of its 1981 annual conference to the theme: 'Law and State: *in memoriam* Hans Kelsen (1881–1973)'. The event attracted to Edinburgh leading Kelsen scholars, devotees and critics alike, not only from the United Kingdom, but also from Austria, Denmark, the Netherlands, Mexico, Argentina, and the United States. The favourable reaction of those attending the conference suggested that the event was significant both by exposing a critical and professional audience to the best in Kelsen scholarship, and because the issues raised and discussed were apparently new to some English-speaking Kelsen scholars as well as to non-specialists.

The coherence and quality of the symposium persuaded us, as

---

[6] *Holmes-Laski Letters* (Harvard, 1953), vol. ii, p. 1376 (17/4/32).

[7] Gulick, *Austria from Habsburg to Hitler* (Berkeley, 1948).

[8] Lauterpacht, 'Kelsen's Pure Science of Law', in Jennings, ed., *Modern Theories of Law*, p. 137 n. See Kelsen, 'Foundations of Democracy' LXVI *Ethics* (supplementary Volume) 1–101 (1955).

[9] Hart, 'Kelsen Visited' 10 *UCLA Law Rev.*, 728 (1963).

[10] Ebenstein, 205, n. 135.

officers of the Association responsible for the conference, that the papers would be of interest to the international community of Kelsen scholars, to braver spirits among students of jurisprudence, and to specialists in several disciplines upon which Kelsen's work impinged. This volume is based upon the conference proceedings but goes beyond them in several respects. All the papers have been thoroughly revised by their authors and some, for example, Professor Stanley Paulson's, extensively rewritten.[11] In addition this volume includes a reply to Dr Joseph Raz's Austin Lecture by the distinguished South American scholar, Dr Roberto Vernengo and a new translation of Kelsen's own paper, 'The Function of a Constitution', which contains the fullest account of his revision of his conception of the basic norm. Dr Inés Weyland (formerly Ortiz) has contributed an essay on norm conflicts which considers the issues raised in the papers presented to the conference by Dr J. W. Harris and by Professor Ota Weinberger of Graz. In his contribution, Professor Weinberger deals briefly with the Brno School, comparing and contrasting it with the better-known Vienna School, thereby highlighting some refinements and divergences within pure theory. Professor Paulson's analysis shows that there are also important divergences as between the several phases of Kelsen's own thought at least as regards the *lex posterior* rule. This in turn suggests, though it does not discuss, that the exegesis of Kelsen's works generally requires a more sophisticated differentiation than the popular division into an 'earlier' or 'classical' period and a 'later' or 'revisionist' period, with 1960 or thereby being taken as the watershed. Finally, the volume commences with this Introduction for which Richard Tur is primarily responsible; William Twining has assisted throughout and contributes increasingly in the second half of it, engaging Tur in debate as to the alleged 'sterility' of Kelsenism and its relevance for the jurisprudential enterprise. Despite our different perspectives we think that we have achieved what is perhaps a surprising measure of agreement.

The purpose of this volume, then, is to present a series of discussions and debates about central issues of interpretation and

---

[11] We acknowledge the kind permission of the editor of the *Liverpool Law Review*, Professor Jackson, to republish Professor Paulson's paper in its slightly amended form. Since the paper originated as a presentation to the Kelsen Conference in 1981 we are particularly pleased to be able to include it, albeit much reconstructed.

substance in Kelsen scholarship. Most, but not all, of the contributors have a specialized knowledge of Kelsen. They represent a diversity of backgrounds, perspectives, and concerns, but they all share the view that Kelsen's ideas are central to legal philosophy and that, whether or not one accepts those ideas in whole or in part, they deserve sustained critical scrutiny. Naturally we hope that this collection will not be perceived merely as a contribution to Kelsen studies, but that it will also demonstrate to the non-specialist the depth and the range of Kelsen's work and its centrality to legal philosophy, if not to all areas of jurisprudence and legal scholarship.

No brief comment can or should attempt to do justice to the scope, the sophistication, the rigour, the insight and, above all, the systematic quality of Kelsen's theorizing. Many have discovered that criticizing Kelsenism is like stamping on quicksilver. Understanding is a necessary prerequisite of informed criticism and some of the contributors to this symposium are at pains to defend Kelsen against criticisms which they see as resting upon misconceptions of or deviations from Kelsen's works. The responses of Steiner, Vernengo, Tur, and Pettit to Wilson, Raz, Stewart, and Bjarup, respectively, are illustrative. Criticism may also take the form of exposing inconsistencies in Kelsen's thought together with an attempt to repair the defect, thus presenting a more or less reconstructed version of Kelsenism which may remain substantially faithful to Kelsen's own presentation. The essays by Vernengo, Tur, and Weyland, though critical, present themselves as remaining substantially faithful to their Kelsenian roots. However, some such reconstructions may deviate so decisively and some criticisms may be so radical as to suggest that the critic has substituted concerns of his own for those of Kelsen. Of course, no one is under an obligation to share Kelsen's concerns and such critics by reconstruction or transcendence of Kelsenism may still reveal its relevance for current jurisprudential controversies and issues. The essays by Wilson, Raz, Stewart, Weinberger, and Harris, though in very different ways, are all of this type in that by repudiating some fundamental aspect of Kelsenism they lead on to issues either beyond the central core of Kelsenism or raised, but not resolved, within it. It should be noted, however, that Kelsen scholarship involves difficulties of exegesis as Paulson brings out in his provocative analysis of Kelsen's thought into four distinct phases, at least so far as the *lex posterior* rule is concerned. All the essays in this collection are 'critical', in some of the senses of that term outlined above, even where they seek to defend rather than to attack.

Those who perceive depth and rigour in Kelsen's theorizing might turn to the words of Sassoon for comfort in the face of the blank non-comprehension which vitiates some comments on their hero: 'small talk about great men . . . Fools! How can they speak such names and not be humble?' This catches the awe and reverence in which Kelsen is held by those who have tried and tried again fully to comprehend his message and its method. Raz writes of the 'haunting quality' of Kelsen's work and of the sensation of a mind wrestling with the most complex problems of legal philosophy. He also writes of the exasperation caused by the almost impenetrable obscurities and contradictions of Kelsen's system of thought. This difficulty is sometimes put down to problems of translation, but in truth it flows from the difficulty faced by almost any philosopher who is genuinely original. He may, perhaps must, devise a new terminology to express new thoughts. It is extremely difficult to give an adequate summary of Kant or Hegel in any vocabulary other than their own. The Kelsen scholar faces similar problems. The best translations in the world do not make Kant or Hegel easy and the same is true of Kelsen. It is not so much the language, but the philosophy that is difficult, a difficulty all the greater for the English reader whose modes of thought and language are likely to reflect an altogether more simple empiricism and who views metaphysical system-building with suspicion or antipathy. Even so, there are notorious difficulties in Kelsenian exegesis which flow from the apparent and real contradictions that characterize his work. Indeed, as Kelsen himself remarks, in a different context: 'More intensely than ever does one perceive that behind each "book" there is a man with his conflicts'.[12]

That Kelsen's jurisprudence is rooted in the critical philosophy of Kant is, it might be thought, beyond serious dispute.[13] None the less, the claim that Kelsen consciously intended to *apply* Kant's philosophy to law is controversial; 'It is historically true, however, that Kelsen's first principal work, *Hauptprobleme der Staatsrechts-*

---

[12] *GTLS*, 430.
[13] Ebenstein, Ch. 1; Moore, op. cit. note 5 above, p. 7; Weinberger, *ELMP*, 1.

lehre (1911) was an intuitive creation, written with no profound knowledge of Kant and with no knowledge at all of [Hermann] Cohen [of the Marburg School of neo-Kantian thought]. It was a philosophical review of his first book which showed to Kelsen the far-reaching parallels between his thinking and the philosophy of Kant and Cohen.'[14] Further there were two Immanuel Kants; the epistemological relativist and the ethical absolutist. Moreover, critical philosophy did not come to a full stop with the publication of the *Critique of Pure Reason* in 1781. Neo-Kantian schools of thought developed in both ethics and epistemology. In jurisprudence, Del Vecchio and Stammler were, in a sense, neo-Kantian. Both, in different ways, developed sophisticated theories of law as 'justice' contemplating the historical realization of a community of rational, autonomous agents in a 'kingdom of ends'. From the beginning Kelsen's preoccupation with 'purity' in the sense of the exclusion of 'justice' from the cognition of law flows from his conscious opposition to such neo-Kantian jurisprudence. For these reasons simply to classify Kelsen as a Kantian without further qualification is potentially misleading.

Wilson, in a penetrating and scholarly analysis, calls Kelsen's Kantianism into question. She challenges his account of imputation as analogous to the Kantian category of causality and stresses that Kelsen's formal 'ought' finds no basis in Kant's ethical philosophy. She argues, further, that Kelsen's account of causality distorts Kant's analysis of it as an a priori category. Steiner reasonably points out that the case is weighted rather heavily against Kelsen if, as Wilson assumes, his neo-Kantianism is to count as evidence *against* a Kantian influence. Steiner neatly reverses the question, asking just how Kelsenian Kant's theory of law is and comes to the conclusion that, apart from intractable problems concerning their respective basic norms, the two theories of law are remarkably similar.

The issue of Kelsen's Kantianism reappears in several of the other essays; briefly in those of Bjarup, Paulson, and Stewart, more fully in Tur's contribution which analyses the similarities and the major differences between Kelsen and Kant. It is possible to treat Kant's ethics as definitive of Kantianism or to seek, as Kant himself did, to present his ethics and epistemology as a unified and

[14] Kunz, 'The "Vienna School" and International Law', 11 *New York University Law Quarterly Rev.*, p. 372, n. 9 (1934).

consistent philosophy. On the basis of such definitions of Kantianism it is not too difficult to be persuaded that Kelsen is no true Kantian. If, however, one accepts Kelsen's own assessment that Kant himself abandoned his critical philosophy and maintained a pre-critical rationalism in his ethics, then one can classify Kelsen as Kantian. Indeed, Kelsen's enterprise might be summarized as a sustained attempt to rectify the defect he detected in Kant's philosophy by applying Kant's critical epistemology, as refined by the Marburg School of neo-Kantianism, to the normative sphere. It was Kant's claim that he 'found it necessary to deny *knowledge*, in order to make room for *faith*'.[15] Kelsen's enterprise is to reassert knowledge in order to make room for normative science.

Tur is wholly in agreement with Steiner's analysis of the structural parallels in the legal theories of Kant and Kelsen, but he proceeds to an account of their respective basic norms in order to demonstrate that the difference between Kant and Kelsen on this one point is of the first importance. Kant, as Steiner observes, defined law as part of morals. Consequently, his is an impure, material 'ought' from which normative conclusions may be drawn by logical deduction. This conflicts not only with the Kelsenian formulation of the basic norm as a logical, formal 'ought' providing no inference ticket to material normative conclusions, but also Kant's own critical philosophy. For Kant that knowledge is 'pure' which contains 'no admixture of anything empirical'.[16] The distinction between form and content is central to Kant's critical enterprise. Kant holds that his formal category cannot tell us a priori what effects causes actually have in empirical reality; 'that in order to exhibit the objective reality of the pure concept of understanding we must always have an intuition [sense-perception], is a very noteworthy fact'.[17] Kelsen holds that his formal category cannot tell us what consequences conditions have in the normative sphere. In both cases, therefore, it is a contingent matter of fact which provides the content of judgments, be they causal or normative. If one regards the Kantian epoch in the history of ideas as the critical synthesis of empiricism and rationalism then it is the absolutist, natural law ethics which falls to be discarded and the relativist epistemology, retained. This is Kelsen's option. Tur uses it to define the Kelsenian enterprise as an attempt to show that if

---

[15] *CPuR*, B xxx.   [16] *CPuR*, B 3.   [17] *CPuR*, B 288.

natural science is epistemologically valid for the reasons advanced by Kant then normative science, too, is epistemologically valid.

Steiner concludes his survey with unanswered questions about the basic norm. Four of the essays deal directly with such questions; those of Raz, Vernengo, Stewart, and Tur. Faced with the difficulties flowing from unfamiliar philosophical assumptions and from the obscurities in Kelsen's presentation of his thought, a Kelsen scholar may, as Raz proposes, elegantly reconstruct Kelsen and thereby tame him. This, in turn, may show how the reconstructed concerns and solutions of Kelsenism relate to current jurisprudential controversies. Raz turns to the familiar jurisprudence of Hart as a backdrop against which to explain his own reconstructed version of Kelsenism. This is not, however, without a price, as Vernengo sharply reminds us, namely the risk of falsifying or trivializing Kelsen's thought. Persuasive and ingenious as Raz's account of detached and committed statements is, Vernengo argues that it does not make sense within Kelsen's own framework and that it is difficult to believe that Raz's notion of being morally committed to the basic norm would have found answering sympathy from Kelsen. All the contributors differ as to what Kelsen meant on crucial issues and as to how one should study and use Kelsen's works. This is revealed very clearly in the debate between Raz who is willing to reconstruct Kelsen and Vernengo who demands an account which is exegetically defensible. It is also revealed in the debate between Wilson and Steiner and joined by Tur. Kelsen scholars may differ radically as to the Kantian strains in Kelsenism and as to their relevance. Perhaps Kipling's 'Disciple' fits Kelsen's disciples:

> He that hath a Gospel
> For all earth to own—
> Though he etch it on the steel
> Or carve it on the stone—
> Not to be misdoubted
> Through the after-days
> It is his Disciple
> Shall read it many ways.[18]

The *Grundnorm* has been the butt of much ill-informed criticism

---

[18] *Rudyard Kipling's Verse* (Definitive Edition, London, 1940), p. 774.

revealing too often a lack of understanding rather than any defect in Kelsen's theory. It has been stigmatized as a great mystery, as wholly superfluous, as a completely unwarranted *deus ex machina* and as the Achilles heel of pure theory. Commentators have explored the splitting and the fusion of the *Grundnorm* and experienced *Grundnorm*-watchers have charted its disappearance and reappearance, transmogrified, in revolutions and devolutions. Most of these issues seem quaintly out of touch with Kelsen's central concern of seeking a basis for normative science. The normative science which Kelsen's theory leads to, however, strikes many, especially contemporary moral philsophers, as altogether too conventionalist, too formalist, or too descriptive of prevailing social mores to be taken seriously. What Kelsen sees as necessities —the inability of a science to go beyond its subject-matter and the impossibility of obtaining material, practical precepts of morality through science—they would see as defects. Moral philosophy, unless prepared to abandon itself to social psychology, insists that there are reasons for action independently of the law and, on occasion, even directly contrary to law.

At first blush, Raz's distinction between detached and committed statements seems to offer the prospect of a *rapprochement* between morals and pure theory. The fictitious 'legal man', too, seems a useful means to this end. No actual human being approves of each and every law within a legal system. None the less, it may be the case that within a given system enough people enough of the time either do approve on moral grounds or, at least, do not morally disapprove of, with sufficient passion, a significant proportion of the laws. Such people may be dupes, as Stewart suggests, but the conformity of conduct and norm is sufficient both to found normative science and to justify individuals taking account of laws as reasons for action in their moral deliberations. There is an obvious danger that Raz's committed statements might run the practical and the formal 'ought' together, offending thereby against the Kelsenian requirement of purity. Tur emphasizes that Kelsen's normative science, as science, has no practical pay-off in that it cannot prescribe how one ought to behave but merely describes how one ought to behave according to prevailing norms. Such a science is constrained by descriptive accuracy and science is forsaken should the scientist, *qua* scientist, go beyond his method to offer practical guidance. Raz, however, has made it clear that, in his view, there is no obligation to obey the law.[19] Consequently, it is open to Raz to claim that his 'legal man' does not threaten the purity of Kelsenism but merely makes vivid Kelsen's notion that legal science should describe law from its own immanent point of view.[20]

The basic norm is thought to be so important that any change in its formulation by its author requires a reassessment of the entire theory. The dispute between Raz and Vernengo does not reach to the issue of the redefinition of the basic norm, though Vernengo might argue that his pragmatic analysis is consistent with this redefinition. Others may perceive difficulties in understanding Raz's proposal that the 'legal man' is morally committed to the basic norm if, as Kelsen says, the basic norm is to be characterized as a fiction. The major article by Kelsen expressing the change of definition has been retranslated by Stewart.[21]

Stewart regards the change as enormously important for jurisprudence and sociology. To him it reveals the pure theory as fallacious and a sham because it is now evident, he thinks, that the basic norm implies untranscended assumptions of an absolute subject and of objective idealism and thereby continues the apologetics of the exegetical tradition. The pure theory of law, Stewart argues, must now be superseded in order to establish a thoroughly relativized science of law which does not connive at objectivity or illusion. Such a concept of 'law' would be sociologically valid. In so interpreting Kelsen, Stewart seeks a *rapprochement* of pure theory and the kinds of social theory currently espoused by members of the critical legal studies movement.[22]

In responding, Tur develops the thesis that far from destroying the pure theory from within or being, as Harris claims, but a minor readjustment, the redefinition of the basic norm reveals even more precisely the Kantian basis of Kelsen's normative science. Drawing on Vaihinger and the neo-Kantian tradition, he refines the Kelsenian analogy between natural and normative science in order

[19] Raz, *The Authority of Law* (Oxford, 1979), p. 233.

[20] *PTL*, 104.

[21] We are grateful to the editors of *Neues Forum* and *Juridical Review* for permission to publish this new translation which is included in order that English-speaking Kelsen scholars may more readily assess for themselves the significance of the redefinition.

[22] Unger, 'The Critical Legal Studies Movement', 96 *Harvard Law Rev.* 563 (1983) and see Hunt, 'Critical Legal Studies: A Bibliography' 47 *MLR* 369 (1984).

to reveal the basic norm as a Kantian regulative idea or methodological maxim. He thereby attempts to acquit Kelsen of the charges, brought by Stewart, of objective idealism, of commitment to and participation in the exegetical tradition and of a belief, albeit subconscious, in an absolute subject. Kelsen evidently anticipated the types of criticism exemplified by Stewart's, but argues that such criticism depends upon the erroneous attribution to the pure theory of an absolute value immanent in its category of the 'ought' whereas the 'ought' of pure theory 'has the meaning of a special functional connection'.[23] Thus Tur claims to present an account which is exegetically defensible. None the less, for all the differences between the symposiasts, Tur agrees with Stewart that it is possible to achieve a *rapprochement* between pure theory and sociology, though he differs as to the nature of the sociology involved and as to the need significantly to transcend, modify, or reconstruct Kelsen in order to realize that objective. Again, Kipling's 'Disciple' seems to fit Kelsen's disciples:

> It is His Disciple
> Who shall tell us how
> Much the Master would have scrapped
> Had he lived till now—
> What he would have modified
> Of what he said before.
> It is His Disciple
> Shall do this and more. . .

Though both refer to the issue of custom, neither Stewart nor Tur significantly address the problems it raises for an unreconstructed Kelsenism. Weinberger, however, in rejecting a central element in the later writings of Kelsen, namely the impossibility of normative inference, draws support from the inconsistency between Kelsen's observations on custom as a source of norms and the 'act-relative positivism' which Weinberger attributes to the later Kelsen. 'Act-relative positivism' is the phrase used by Weinberger to refer to Kelsen's apparent late commitment to a one-to-one relationship of act of will and norm. It is this commitment, so Weinberger argues, that leads Kelsen to deny the validity of normative inference from general norm to particular decision though not, as Weinberger observes, from and to norms of

---

[23] *PTL*, 101–3; 'The Denial of the "Ought"; the Law as Ideology'.

different degrees of generality. Although it may appear to follow from the general norm, 'Thieves ought to be punished' (as major premiss) and the factual statement, 'Smith is a thief' (as minor premiss) that 'Smith ought to be punished' (as conclusion), according to Kelsen this is invalid because without an act of will corresponding to it, there can be no individual norm. Thinking, as Harris remarks, cannot kill a cat nor can thinking alone, according to Kelsen, create norms.

Weinberger's solution is to reject 'act-relative positivism'. It is, he argues, inconsistent with the Kelsenian account of custom; it also destroys the pure theory, for it dismantles the ingenious dynamic and hierarchical 'steps and stairs' account of the concretization of law. Further, he argues, derogation necessarily presupposes normative inconsistency which is denied by act-relative positivism. Therefore act-relative positivism is inconsistent with the role of derogation in Kelsen's thought, as Weinberger understands it. Stewart may take some comfort from Weinberger's opinion that the fiction characterization of the basic norm, too, flows from Kelsen's embracing act-relative positivism, which commitment ultimately destroys the pure theory. Weinberger helpfully contrasts the Vienna and Brno Schools, explaining that the latter, through the works of Weyr, rejects the sanction theory of Kelsen and the Vienna School, and treats as law any norm imputed to the state as author irrespective of sanctions. It appears, therefore, that Tur's reinterpretation of Kelsen, rejecting as it does the sanction theory of the specificity of the legal moves him in the direction of the Brno School. Weinberger's main point, however, is to dissociate himself from the sanction theory and from act-relative positivism in order to secure the validity of a logic of norms, because he regards Kelsen's rejection of normative inference as unacceptable and as detrimental to jurisprudence. The solution which Weinberger canvasses is that we should conceive of norms as ideal entities which, though produced by acts of will, have their own independent ideal existence. Once norms are ideally existent (valid), normative inference can, so Weinberger maintains, proceed to particular normative conclusions which are valid without the requirement of a related act of will.

Harris is no less an opponent of norm irrationalism than is Weinberger. He rejects outright one of the most problematic aspects of Kelsenism, namely the alternative character of the norm, that is the proposition that norms authorizing legal organs authorize either decisions in conformity with the authorizing norm or authorize any decision whatsoever. Harris insists that if legal science is to be possible at all the principles of exclusion, subsumption, derogation, and non-contradiction and the practice of normative inference are essential. The main thrust of his argument, nicely illustrated by a series of discussions between a Student and a Tutor, is that the earlier Kelsen who adopted all five criteria of legal science is preferable to the later Kelsen who apparently abandoned three of the five criteria thereby, contributing to an unusual instance of an undergraduate besting an Oxford tutor three times out of five.

What Weinberger does once, Harris does fourfold; not only is derogation denied by norm irrationalism, as Weinberger maintains, but also, according to Harris, norm irrationalism denies exclusion, subsumption, and norm-consistency. There is substantial agreement, therefore, between Weinberger and Harris on norm irrationalism and even partial agreement as to the explanation of why so apparently bizarre a view was ultimately embraced by Kelsen, namely, his conviction that norms and acts of will stand in a one-to-one relationship. It is surprising, therefore, that the ideal existence of norms which Weinberger sees as a necessary device to overcome norm irrationalism is, for Harris, precisely what distorts Kelsen's view of the principles of legal science. The reification of norms as ideally existing things is, says Harris, an 'obsession' which led Kelsen astray. For Weinberger, Kelsen's alleged denial of such independent ideal existence commits him to this unacceptable norm irrationalism.

If, conjoining Weinberger and Harris, norm rationalism is consistent with both the denial and the assertion of the ideal existence of norms, such norm rationalism is defensible irrespective of the existence (validity) of norms and correlated acts of will. The act of will for both, and even the norm for Harris disappear; for both, the norm-sentence of legal science becomes central. This, as Weyland points out, is to mistake the ideology of legal science for the object of legal science. She notes the possibility of detaching Kelsenism from its Kantian roots in order to present the legal system not as a necessary structure determined by categories of thought but merely as a conception based on a particular ideology shared by jurists and legal officials. This, Weyland believes, is precisely what Harris does, characterizing the official ideology in terms of legality and constitutionality.

Vernengo does not specifically comment on either Weinberger or Harris but his comments, both in the text of his essay and in an important footnote, on a tendency to assimilate erroneously the modality of norm-sentences and the function of norms are relevant here. In such an assimilation the independent existence (validity) of norms disappears and law and science of law are also assimilated. This, in turn, suggests that by norm rationalism both Harris and Weinberger contemplate legal science as providing a rational method for the creation of norms, a position which conflicts markedly with Kelsen's separation of law and legal science and his repeated attempts to distinguish norms and norm-sentences. Perhaps Kipling's 'Disciple' fits here as well:

> He that hath a Gospel
> To loose upon Mankind,
> Though he serve it utterly—
> Body, soul and mind—
> Though he go to Calvary
> Daily for its gain—
> It is His Disciple
> Shall make his labour vain.

None the less, norm rationalists such as Harris and Weinberger can draw support for their position from Kelsen's works. That they can is brought out, indirectly, by Paulson although he supports norm irrationalism. Paulson identifies four different phases in Kelsen's thought on the *lex posterior* rule and on his attitude to logic and law. These phases are as follows: first, up to about 1918, Kelsen regarded the *lex posterior* rule as a logical postulate; secondly, under Merkl's influence, from 1918 to the mid-twenties, Kelsen regarded *lex posterior* as a contingent rule of positive law; thirdly, from the mid-twenties to about 1960, Kelsen, in his long neo-Kantian phase, justified *lex posterior* transcendentally as a logically necessary presupposition of legal knowledge; fourthly and finally, in the post-1960 phase, Kelsen returned to the positivistic conception of *lex posterior*. Thus, as Paulson observes, Kelsen held three different views on logic and law, the first and third of which might reasonably be supposed to give some support to norm rationalism.

Paulson is unconvinced by all three positions but he evinces more sympathy for the positivistic conception than for either of the logical versions. He suggests that the distinction between 'non-contingent' and 'positivistic' is inappropriate and that one might proceed on the model of Duhemian holism, with the legal system conceived of as a sphere, such that some norms, and *lex posterior* is an example, are 'well entrenched . . . towards the centre', whereas other norms, more readily subject to alteration, are 'out towards the periphery'. Paulson admits that his view is highly metaphorical and requires considerable working out but he believes it to offer a happier conceptual framework than the traditional distinction between the arbitrary, positivistic conception and the necessary, logical conception of the *lex posterior* rule. Be all that as it may, Paulson's article is an important and interesting attempt to bring some order into the conflicting views expressed by Kelsen in the various phases of his thought. The article is also important for its argument against norm rationalism. Those who rely upon Kelsen's neo-Kantian transcendental deduction of *lex posterior* as a logically necessary presupposition of legal science inherit the defect in Kelsen's reasoning which Paulson points out, namely that whereas *some* rule for the resolution of norm conflicts is necessary if there is to be knowledge, that it be the *lex posterior* rule is merely a possibility and not a necessity.

Weyland seeks an account of logic and law which is exegetically defensible. She links Kelsen's treatment of norm-consistency and the alternative character of the norm on the one hand with Kelsen's treatment of interpretation in the final chapter of the *Pure Theory of Law*, on the other. In a perspicacious survey she identifies and rehearses the various positions offered by Kelsen and considers the solutions offered by other writers, notably Harris and Paulson. Although she regards none of the solutions offered as wholly satisfactory, Weyland considers that the point of departure must be Kelsen's ideal conception of a legal system. However that is only the point of departure. By a subtle process of reinterpretation Weyland seeks to move Kelsen's theory in the direction of the decisionist emphasis of such writers as Gray or Holmes. Such an approach allows for the inclusion of non-rational as well as rational elements as determinants of decisions. Thus, for Weyland, extra-legal norms and custom have a role in judicial decision-making. This reworking of Kelsen's account of the concretization of legal norms allows of a middle way between perfect norm rationalism and capricious norm irrationalism and preserves the main tenets of Kelsenism even though Kelsen himself vacillated on many of the issues involved. None the less, the Kelsenian aphorism, 'every law-applying act is only partly determined by law'[24] and the explanation which unpacks it might offer support even beyond that which Weyland cogently presents in her essay.

Norm rationalism suggests the possibility of a cognitive method for the creation or discovery of norms. Such a view has obvious affinities with natural law thinking and rationalist theories of justice. Kelsen has been a consistent and persistent critic of all such doctrines. He classifies theories of justice as either metaphysical-religious or pseudo-scientific. Whether presupposing an absolute subject or a practical, norm-creating reason, both types of theory are, according to Kelsen, incapable of solving the eternal riddle of mankind; 'What is Justice?' Absolute justice is beyond human cognition; it is an 'irrational ideal'.[25] This does not mean that there is no justice, only that justice is a relative value;[26] one does not throw to the dogs all that is not fit for the altars of the Gods.

Bjarup analyses Kelsen's theory of justice and, on his interpretation, finds it to be vitiated by serious inconsistencies. He concludes that Kelsen is not an ethical relativist but an ethical absolutist in disguise. Pettit, responding, identifies three main charges brought by Bjarup: alleged inconsistencies between ethical relativism and (i) epistemological relativism; (ii) the doctrine of the basic norm; (iii) Kelsen's personal commitment to the value of tolerance. Bjarup's first argument is that Kelsen, as an epistemological relativist, is not entitled to the distinction between subjective value-judgments and objective statements of fact. His second argument attributes to Kelsen the presupposition of an absolute value, 'legality', necessarily common to all legal systems as immanent in the presupposition of the basic norm. Thirdly, Bjarup claims that by deriving tolerance from a theory of relative values, Kelsen involves himself in manifest self-contradiction.

In his admittedly charitable reading of Kelsen, Pettit rallies to Kelsen's defence, not because he is particularly sympathetic to

[24] *PTL*, 349.   [25] 'What is Justice?' in *ELMP*, 1–26.
[26] 'On The Pure Theory of Law', 1 *Israel Law Rev.* 1, 3–4 (1966).

Kelsenism but because he considers Bjarup's reading of Kelsen to be extremely uncharitable and contrary to Kelsen's own statements. The alleged inconsistency in Kelsen's joint commitment to ethical and epistemological relativism is defused by reading the former as culture-relativism and the latter as species-relativism. This, Pettit claims, is exegetically defensible. The suggestion that, in presupposing the basic norm, Kelsen is committed to presupposing an absolute value is met by a neat distinction between the formal idea of 'orderedness' and the substantive value of 'orderliness'. Further, Pettit argues that there is support in Kelsen's writings for the view that it is not the legal scientist but the legal agent who presupposes the basic norm. Pettit concedes that there is some force in Bjarup's third charge if one takes Kelsen's statements literally. None the less, by adopting a distinction which probably did not occur to Kelsen, namely that between evaluations and prescriptions, Pettit argues that even here Kelsen's position can be salvaged. Thus Pettit concludes that Kelsen's theory can be legitimately interpreted in such a way as to immunize it from Bjarup's criticisms.

Kelsen wrote extensively on international law and the volume concludes with an assessment of his contribution by Professor Hedley Bull who has elegantly expounded his view of international society and international order in *The Anarchical Society*. Bull remarks that Kelsen, uniquely in modern analytical jurisprudence, had a great deal to say on the subject. The extent of Kelsen's contribution is brought out in Bull's first paragraph. Bull sees in Kelsen's approach a variant of the Grotian tradition in international law, complicated by Kelsen's commitment to coercion as the criterion of law and his opposition to iusnaturalism. Further, Bull regards Kelsen's thinking about international relations as a product of the 1930s and 1940s rather than already prefigured in the seminal *Hauptprobleme der Staatsrechtslehre* of 1911.

Bull's assessment addresses five points: first, whether international law is really law; secondly, the relation of force and international law; thirdly, 'positivism' in international law; fourthly, change in international law; fifthly, the relation of international law and power politics. This assessment produces more brickbats than bouquets for Kelsen. Bull argues, first, that Kelsen is vulnerable because of his coercive definition of law; secondly, that Kelsen's insistence on a monopoly of force in the international community 'strains against the facts', being at least 'premature' and a product of 'wishful thinking'; thirdly, that positivism in international law has been under considerable attack both from natural law writers such as Brierly and Lauterpacht and from sociological writers led by McDougal and therefore that Kelsen's positivism, for all its admirable scientific rigour, is overly narrow in its concerns and that, in any case, Kelsen does not restrict himself as his own methodology requires; fourthly, that in admitting change in international law Kelsen moves from his 'strict positivism', thereby contradicting himself, and that such a move is independently appropriate because of the development of 'soft law' in the international arena as a response to the alienation of new states towards strictly defined positivistic rules; fifthly, that Kelsen himself goes beyond positivistic legal science and in so doing tacitly adopts the idealist and progressive assumptions common in the period when Kelsen wrote so extensively on international law.

We find it interesting that many of the criticisms raised by Bull in the particular context of international law are isomorphs of criticisms brought against Kelsen's general theoretical stance in jurisprudence. Bull's specific criticisms remain unanswered in this volume but we now address ourselves to some of the general criticisms frequently brought to bear on Kelsenism. This introductory survey, itself, illustrates some of the range of concerns within Kelsenism and the essays themselves illustrate the depth to which such concerns may be pursued. It is remarkable, therefore, that a common charge brought against Kelsenism is its 'narrowness' or 'sterility'. Llewellyn, for example, remarks that 'Kelsen, in law, offers the closest approach to a truly courageous logical system, with, in my view, a consequent almost complete sterility—save in his by-product remarks'.[27] Others might see a remarkable similarity between the map of a legal system offered by Kelsen and the Bellman's map:

> 'Other maps are such shapes, with their
> islands and capes!
> But we've got our brave captain to thank'

---

[27] Llewellyn, *Jurisprudence: Realism in Theory and Practice* (Chicago, 1962), p. 90, fn. b.

(So the crew would protest) 'that he's brought
us the best—
A perfect and absolute blank!'[28]

It is also remarkable that a jurist who wrote widely on topics such as democracy, justice, natural law, constitutional law, international law, science, politics, philosophy, and sociology and who, moreover, devoted energy and insight to refining his theories and defending them against the works of other thinkers should have attracted such a reputation.

Part of the reason for this is the emphasis in Kelsen studies upon 'purity'. Though Kelsen understandably laid great stress upon 'pure' theory it was not his view that it is the sole or chief concern of jurisprudence. The pure theory is a methodology, a recipe for doing legal science. In order to have legal knowledge the method must be applied to the data. Consequently the Kelsenian legal scientist is no mere manipulator of formal, legal concepts but one who soaks himself in the details of the law. Further, and this distinguishes the Kelsenian legal scientist from much contemporary textbook writing, the law is to be presented without any admixture of values proceeding from the legal scientist himself or from the conceptual frame of reference used to describe the law. This is clearly a requirement of any presentation of law which seeks to be accurate and yet it is extraordinarily difficult to achieve in practice and, indeed, on some accounts of law it is quite impossible. Some theorists go so far as to insist that merely to describe something as 'law' is necessarily to adopt the values immanent in the system and they may conclude that the only way to be 'scientific' about law is to abandon normativity and to present 'law' as a factual matter based solely upon power relationships.[29] At the other extreme, some argue that law is necessarily and irreducibly 'moral' and that any legal theory which ignores or rejects that circumstance inevitably distorts its subject-matter. To maintain a middle position between the absolute values of the natural lawyer and the unimpeachable facts of the causal sociologist is no easy task and the tensions within pure theory itself reveal how difficult it is to avoid one extreme without falling into the other. Consequently the

---

[28] Carroll, *The Hunting of the Snark*, Fit the Second (London, 1916), p. 16; cf. Twining, 'The Great Juristic Bazaar', 14 JSPTL (N.S.) 185, at 194 (1978).
[29] *PTL*, 101–3.

pursuit of Kelsenian legal science requires determination, dedication, and a refusal to settle for either soft, ideological option.

The charge of sterility may be directed towards the kind of legal science that would emerge if the pure theory were interpreted as a working theory or guide for expositors. Some writers approach the ideal of purity of method more closely than others and such descriptive works serve a useful expository function. Criticism of such works as 'sterile' is misconceived in so far as such works do not even purport to go beyond the 'humble' task of the 'Expositor'.[30] Writings of this kind may also supply material for other jurisprudential activity. This is to reassert the Benthamite point that expository jurisprudence is independent of censorial jurisprudence. However a Kelsenian legal scientist might make larger claims than that legal science is an ingredient within the discipline of law. He might claim that a knowledge of law is a necessary prerequisite to its criticism. Kelsen himself holds that normative jurisprudence is prior to sociological jurisprudence.[31] A Kelsenian legal scientist might also claim that the pure form of legal knowledge is a necessary element immanent in all legitimate legal knowledge. These are important claims which should not be obscured from view by the vague and pejorative term 'sterile'.

Such claims are highly controversial in that they maintain the positivist commitment to law as a product, that is, as a body of rules which can be known, stated, and learned. These presuppositions are challengeable. Dworkin has stated that he

did not mean, in rejecting the idea that law is a system of rules, to replace that idea with the theory that law is a system of rules and principles. There is no such thing as 'the law' as a collection of discrete propositions, each with its own canonical form. People have legal rights, and principles of political morality figure in deciding what legal rights they have.[32]

Simpson contrasts 'the "school-rules concept" of law' (which he sees as the 'predominant conception today') with 'the idea that the common law is best understood as a system of customary law, that is, as a body of traditional ideas received within a caste of experts'. He doubts the utility of the model of rules because 'the common

---

[30] Bentham, *A Fragment on Government: Collected Works*, ed. Burns and Hart (London, 1977), pp. 397–8; 404.

[31] *GTLS*, 175; 178; 183.

[32] Dworkin, *Taking Rights Seriously* (Third Impression, London, 1981), p. 344.

law is more like a muddle than a system'.[33] Like Bentham, Simpson argues that 'As a System of general rules, the Common Law is a thing merely imaginary.'[34] But unlike Bentham who disqualifies common law as 'unlaw' because it does not fit his theory of law, Simpson, holding the common law to be 'law', rejects the theory of law which would disqualify the common law and presents a different theory, that of law as a customary activity, process rather than product, which includes the common law.

From such points of view Kelsenian legal science is a misconceived activity not merely because such a science would be narrow but also because, if possible at all, such a science is possible only at the price of distortion. Such perspectives challenge Kelsenism in other ways. Law, it might be argued is not a datum which projects itself into the mind of the legal scientist who can present it, as a product, in a series of value-neutral descriptive sentences.[35] Rather the legal scholar is seen as necessarily *participating* in the legal enterprise.[36] It may not even be appropriate to define an area of study by reference to its subject-matter at all; 'We are not students of some subject matter but students of problems.'[37] In the activity of problem solving one might turn from law to logic, psychology, statistics, sociology, moral philosophy, economics, history, and so on. Further, the problems themselves may not emerge from a consideration of the law as it is. There is a legitimate place in legal study for the jurisprudential pioneer, the scholar who perceives an issue as problematic long before any 'law' has come to bear upon the matter. All these considerations suggest that it would be difficult for a Kelsenian legal scientist to maintain his strong claims about the priority of legal science. If he retreats to the weaker claim that legal science is an important ingredient within the discipline of law, the Kelsenian legal scientist is on stronger ground and the charge of 'sterility' would stick only if he claimed that what was an end in itself for the legal scientist could not be a point of depature for other scholars. These claims

[33] Simpson, 'The Common Law and Legal Theory', in Simpson ed., *Oxford Essays in Jurisprudence (Second Series)* (Oxford, 1973), pp. 77–99; at pp. 82, 80, and 99.
[34] Bentham, *A Comment on the Commentaries: Collected Works*, ed. Burns and Hart (London, 1977), p. 119.
[35] Fuller, *The Morality of Law* (revised edn., London, 1970), pp. 149; 156; 192.
[36] Simpson, loc. cit, n. 33 above, p. 97.
[37] Popper, *Conjectures and Refutations* (London, 1974), pp. 397–8.

and counter-claims involve important areas of disagreement within the jurisprudential enterprise.

A book describing as exactly as possible the law as it is for the time being according to Kelsen's recommended method, observing the canonical form of normative sentences and exhaustively detailing all the conditions of validity in the antecedent clauses would not be merely dry, but repetitious and monumentally boring, if indeed such a project were possible at all. The individuation of normative sentences and doubts as to the relationship of acts of will to norms as well as the comprehensiveness of such a book of Kelsenian legal science raises serious doubts as to the feasibility of the project at least in practice if not in principle. The Kelsenian method of legal science remains programmatic—an ideal unfulfilled in practice. No one, not even Kelsen himself, has made the pure theory practical. His own major work on the content of the laws of a positive legal system, *Principles of International Law* (1952), is not and does not purport to be an application of the rigorous method argued for in the methodological works. Consequently, there are some grounds for doubting whether Kelsen saw himself or can legitimately be seen by others as offering a working theory for the exposition of law. The charge that books of legal science faithfully constructed according to the Kelsenian prescription would be dry, bloodless descriptions of no philosophical or jurisprudential merit and of no sociological relevance is hypothetical. But even if one concedes the point without evidence, the broader charge of the 'sterility' of Kelsenism would have force only if the critic could show that for Kelsen and for Kelsenites 'legal science' is exhaustive of 'jurisprudence'. It is difficult, however, to prove that a commitment to rigorous legal science entails the proposition that legal science is exhaustive of the jurisprudent's concerns.

Far from ever holding that legal science is exhaustive of the jurisprudent's concerns, Kelsen was at pains to deny it; 'The pure theory of law leads only to a division of labour . . .'.[38] Thus 'science of law' is concerned with as exact a description of law as it is possible to achieve and (on Tur's interpretation) 'pure theory' seeks to provide a recipe for doing this. 'Philosophy of law' concerns itself with the question of justice and therefore with legal

---

[38] 'On The Pure Theory of Law', loc. cit. n. 26 above, p. 4.

politics, law reform, and visions of the good, rather than with questions of legal knowledge. Even 'sociology of law' is not excluded from the Kelsenian perspective but it contemplates 'certain parallel phenomena in nature',[39] which stand in a causal relationship to events which, from a normative point of view, also feature as the content of norms as condition or consequence. Of course, not all sociology is causal but in so far as it is normative Kelsen has no argument with it at all and indeed, if one accepts Tur's interpretation, there may be very little difference between Kelsenian legal science and normative sociology, though Kelsen, primarily by way of his commitment to the sanction theory of law, resisted generalizing his concerns from legal to social norms. Consequently, Kelsenism is a rather broad church and not the barren wilderness popularly imagined.

Kelsen's alleged 'sterility' is sometimes argued for on the basis that Kelsenism has no place for empirical data such as actual human conduct nor for morality. But Kelsen's observation that the legal scientist is not concerned with human conduct but is only concerned with norms may have obscured from view the important point that so far as human conduct features in a norm as condition or consequence such conduct falls foursquare within the concerns of the Kelsenian legal scientist. Kelsen remarks that 'the definition of law as a system of norms would seem too narrow . . . [but it is] . . . incorrect to say that law consists of norms and acts. It would be more nearly correct to say that law is made up of legal norms and legal acts as determined by these norms'.[40] When one considers the legal system in a state of rest one notices chiefly the norms; when one considers the process through which law is made and implemented one notices chiefly the acts.[41] There is a tendency among commentators on Kelsen to give disproportionate weight to general hypothetical norms and to ignore particular categorical norms emanating, for example, from legal transactions or judicial decisions. If acted upon, a statement describing the norm is simultaneously a description of actual conduct. For Kelsen, even general norms are, in a sense, descriptive of actual human conduct.[42] Questions relating to effectiveness as a condition of validity, whether at the level of legal system, legal rule or legal decision, and about desuetude are discussed no further in this

[39] *PTL*, 102.   [40] *GTLS*, 39.   [41] *GTLS*, 39, 110 ff.
[42] *GTLS*, 163.

Introduction. Even if it is conceded that the Kelsenian frame of reference accommodates actual human conduct, the gap between words and what actually happens suggests that Kelsenism stops short of as full an account of actual human conduct as some legal scholars demand. None the less, Kelsen permits of a greater degree of reference to actual human conduct than is sometimes perceived by those who would label his contribution as 'sterile'.

As to morality, those who see in 'purity' a denial of its relevance fail to distinguish the critical morality which the impure legal scientist may improperly import into his account of law and the positive morality which may influence the legal organ in reaching his decision, and to which he may, indeed, be specifically authorized to turn. Kelsen insists that 'every law-applying act is only partly determined by law'.[43] It follows that the moral beliefs of the legal organ or his interpretation of the moral values of the community may feature as an element in his determination of an issue. Other factors may well influence the outcome. Consequently the charge of 'sterility', if it is based upon the alleged exclusion of actual conduct and of morality, appears exaggerated.

However, accusations of 'sterility', especially against some followers of Kelsen, are not so readily disposed of. At this point a possible fundamental divergence between the two editors needs to be brought into the open. Tur, as a disciple of Kelsen, is at most critical from within the Kelsenian camp, refining and explaining what he takes to be Kelsen's contribution to jurisprudential endeavour. Twining, who is more firmly identified with the mainstream of Anglo-American jurisprudence as represented by Hart, Llewellyn, and Bentham, is a somewhat sceptical outsider. Collaboration has been possible only by one curbing his enthusiasm and the other suspending his disbelief. So far what has been said expresses the views of the disciple. Up to this point the sceptic has not found any reason for registering a strong dissent from Tur's self-referring Kiplingesque interpretation of what Kelsenian discipleship involves. Twining readily concedes that Kelsen is a major figure in legal theory who (in common with other such figures) has too often been misrepresented or criticized on the basis of caricature or misunderstanding;[44] that his writings are rich

---

[43] *PTL*, 349.

[44] Kant, *Prolegomena To Any Future Metaphysics*, ed. Beck (Indianapolis, 1950), p. 9;, 'It [the *Critique of Pure Reason*] will be misjudged because it is

in particular insights and *aperçus* and that the central tenets of pure theory address some important issues in legal philosophy. Conversely, on Tur's interpretation, crucial concessions are made to those with different concerns. In particular, if one accepts that it was Kelsen's view that pure theory 'is not the sole or chief concern of jurisprudence'[45] and that 'the pure theory of law leads only to a division of labour',[46] the way may be open for a much closer *rapprochement* than either of us had originally contemplated. For this suggests a broader and more catholic view of jurisprudence than some interpretations of Kelsen allow and, even more important, that Kelsenian 'legal science' is not coextensive with the discipline of law or 'legal scholarship'.

Such concessions by no means exhaust the most important grounds for scepticism about pure theory not least of which are objections to the notion of 'autonomous disciplines' and to the tendency to lump together all empirical questions about legal phenomena in the real world under the loose heading of 'sociology'. There is also the resultant narrowness of vision which disregards human conduct in so far as it does not feature in the content of a legal rule or decision as condition or consequence. Even if it is conceded that actual human conduct is not totally ignored by a Kelsenian legal scientist and that positive morality, too, fits into his scheme of things, not all inheritors of Kelsenism are so catholic in their interpretation, nor would the broader interpretation of Kelsenism arrived at here be broad enough to embrace the concerns of all legal scholars. On Tur's interpretation it may be possible to defend Kelsen himself, arguing that pure theory was never presented as a comprehensive prescription for legal education, still less as a descriptive account of the enterprise of legal scholarship. None the less Kelsen frequently claimed merely to be making evident 'what most legal scientists do'.[47] The catholic interpretation presented here can also be supported:

we . . . delimit law from nature and the science of law, as a normative science, from all other sciences which aim at explaining causal, natural processes. In particular, we delimit it from one science which sets itself the

misunderstood, and misunderstood because men choose to skim through the book and not to think through it—a disagreeable task, because the work is dry, obscure, opposed to all ordinary notions, and moreover long-winded.'

[45] See above nn. 38 and 49.
[46] 'On the Pure Theory of Law', loc. cit. n. 26, p. 4.   [47] *PTL*, 204.

task of examining the causes and effects of those natural processes which, receiving their designation from legal norms, appear as legal acts. If such a study be called sociology, or sociology of law, we shall make no objection. Neither shall we say anything here of its value or prospects.[48]

Kelsen insists that such 'sociology' cannot replace a normative science of law because the two disciplines deal with quite different problems. He adds that, 'the rank of this discipline [normative legal science] in the general system of sciences is another and secondary question. What is needed is not at once to exalt this [normative] science of law . . . but to limit it to its subject matter and to explain its method critically.'[49] Exegetically defensible as the catholic interpretation of Kelsenism may be, it represents so considerable a revision of the received wisdom about Kelsen as to raise doubts about its authenticity. Is this, once again, an instance of Kipling's 'Disciple'?

> It is His Disciple
> (Ere Those Bones are dust)
> Who shall change the Charter
> Who shall split the Trust—
> Amplify distinctions
> Rationalise the Claim
> Preaching that the Master
> Would have done the same.

It is even more difficult to exonerate some of Kelsen's disciples from the charges which are most commonly levelled against Kelsenism. The pure theory is widely perceived and used as a theoretical basis for general approaches to law that have at least one salient feature in common: they appear to treat the study of law as being coextensive with something approximating to a Kelsenian 'science of law'. There are many legal scholars who are deeply committed to keeping legal education, legal scholarship, legal philosophy, and legal discourse 'pure' or 'scientific' and who insist upon rigorous method as the touchstone of intellectual respectability. Twining remains committed to the view that such scholars have a lot to answer for. Much legal discourse is contaminated as well as impoverished by aspirations towards Kelsenian 'purity'. Such uses of the pure theory to justify narrow approaches to the study of law may be an example of the 'overspill

---

[48] *PTL-IMFC*, 480.   [49] *PTL-IMFC*, 490.

effect', that is the misuse of a theory for purposes for which it was neither intended nor well suited.

Even if it is possible to disassociate pure theory from narrow approaches to the discipline of law, it fails to address some of the central concerns of many legal scholars and teachers about the nature and direction of their enterprise. This failure itself may be perceived as giving some theoretical support to the proposition that legal scholarship is exhausted by pure legal science, thereby sterilizing legal scholarship by removing most of the impurities which are the lifeblood of any actual legal system. It is difficult to see how the failure of pure theory to address central concerns really offers support for either side in such debates. Kelsenian pure theory prescinds from such debates and the defect is in the misperception of the theory and practice of legal science as a comprehensive philosophy of legal education and scholarship. The corrective is to subsume legal science within such a philosophy rather than, absurdly, to equate the two. The equation of science and general philosophy and the prejudice that the only knowledge worthy of the name is scientific knowledge is an aspect of recent human thought which goes far beyond the limits of jurisprudence (if such limits there be) in that the recent history of ideas in western culture has elevated science to the status of an idol and dismissed all other forms of intellectual activity as nonsense and metaphysics.[50] It is an irony that Kelsen, who devoted so much energy and ingenuity to resisting the claim that natural science is the only legitimate form of knowledge, is misused within academic law in support of the proposition that legal science is the only legitimate form of intellectual activity for the legal scholar and that all else is nonsensical or irrelevant, or, at best, fit for the pages of the colour supplements but not for the academies of the learned.

No less ironical is the oft-repeated charge that pure theory ignores the impurities which are the lifeblood of any legal system. Here a distinction is in order. The book entitled *Pure Theory of Law* 'ignores' these impurities. It is concerned with what Kant referred to as the pure *part* of knowledge, that from which all admixture of empirical elements have been removed. As a

---

[50] Popper, *Objective Knowledge* (Oxford, 1974), p. 108: 'Epistemology I take to be the theory of *scientific knowledge*.' The success of logical positivism in contributing to this 'scientific' world view owes much to the seductive clarity and force of Ayer, *Language, Truth and Logic* (London, 1936).

methodology it is 'absolutely pure'.[51] As such it can have no empirical content just as logic or pure mathematics have no empirical content. Yet logic and mathematics may be used to model the 'real world'. It is a remarkable feature of pure mathematics that it can be applied to the 'real world' in which we live. In applying it, of course, we bring together the empirical data of the real world and the formal structure of pure mathematics. Such applied mathematics is not devoid of empirical content and it is indeed empirically true that such mathematical modelling of the real world is useful. That mathematics therefore gives us access to ultimate reality is, however, a further and unwarranted claim. Ultimate reality may be beyond the reach of any discipline but such disciplines may, none the less, have great explanatory power in that they aspire to produce cosmos out of chaos. 'Legal science', that is, the conjoining of the actual facts of the real world in which we live with the formal structure of law as explicated by the *Pure Theory of Law* does not ignore and cannot plausibly be regarded as ignoring the impurities which are the lifeblood of any actual legal system. What is ironical is that, arguably, no theory of law (as opposed to reductive theories of 'law' which seek to explain it away as fact, be the facts psychological, economic, historical, or whatever) goes as far as Kelsenism in its emphasis that law is and must necessarily remain impure.

In Weyland's essay we find an explanation of how, in Kelsen's theory, irrational, informal, spontaneous elements combine with rational, formal, predetermined elements in the concretization of norms within any actual legal system. Far from excluding impurities from legal study, Kelsenian legal science elevates them to a position of great significance for our understanding of law. This is most clearly revealed in Kelsen's denial of a logic of norms and in his insistence upon the alternative character of the norm, that is, the proposition that the law-applying organ is authorized either to decide according to the content of the higher norm or in any other way.[52] This surprising doctrine flows directly from the primacy granted in Kelsen's thought to the principle of delegation

---

[51] See *CPuR*, A 9–11; B 19–23; 'Every kind of knowledge is called *pure*, if not mixed with anything heterogeneous. But more particularly is that knowledge called *absolutely pure*, which is not mixed up with an experience or sensation, and is therefore possibly entirely a priori'.

[52] *GTLS*, 157–62.

over the principle of subsumption and his commitment to
dynamism as the essential feature of positive law. The sterilization
which many have perceived and some have tried to practise is
immanent not in Kelsen's thought itself but in the interpretations
of such disciples as attempt to establish a watertight logic of norms
by which may be derived actual legal decisions without the need to
identify in actual human society any such empirical fact or
'impurity' as an actual act of will corresponding to the norm. The
'purity' of pure theory relates not to the subject-matter of legal
science but to the manner in which legal science is to be carried on.
There are suggestions in the literature that 'pure knowledge' exists
and is attainable and that such works as the *Pure Theory of Law* or
the *Critique of Pure Reason* are books containing 'pure knowlege'.[53]
However neither Kant nor Kelsen would claim that *knowledge*
could be other than a synthesis of form and content; rather so-
called 'pure knowledge' is merely an indispensable *part* of
knowledge.

If this be conceded the prospects of some *rapprochement* are
indeed good. However the point has been made that together with
the imperialism of the inheritors of pure theory in regarding it as a
complete account of legal scholarship one finds a tendency to lump
together, dismissively, all empirical questions under the loose and
even pejorative term 'sociology', thus excluding such elements to
the impoverishment of legal scholarship. The point has been met
in part by the discussion of 'purity'. However it may be helpful to
explore further facets of the question by way of an example.
Consider a society in which, together with what is called
substantive law, there is also a highly developed and detailed body
of legal rules about evidence. A Kelsenian legal scientist could,
consistent with his method, present as legal knowledge these rules
in a textbook entitled, *The Law of Evidence*. Consider now
another society in which 'free proof' obtains. Now, it appears,
there is nothing about which a Kelsenian legal scientist could write
his textbook. He is reduced to stating that there is no law of
evidence just as Horrebow, writing of Iceland, and, having
entitled a chapter 'concerning snakes', could state only, 'There are
no snakes to be met with throughout the whole island.'[54] But in
such a society the practices of decision-makers as regards

---

[53] See Ebenstein, Ch. I, especially, pp. 35–9.
[54] *Boswell's Life of Johnson* (London, 1904), VOL. II, 212.

evidence, their attitudes to 'the provable and the probable' and their conception of what counts as a good reason for belief in a proposition of fact would not disappear and a legal scholar could justifiably be heard to say that such matters were both interesting in themselves and useful to those whose business it was to argue for and secure decisions in the tribunals of such a society. To call the study of such questions 'sociology' is very odd.[55] That the Kelsenian legal scientist folds his tent and steals off into the night in such circumstances is condemnation indeed.

It is true that Kelsen acknowledged the legitimacy of legal sociology but it is also true that he believed that such legal sociology as he had experience of was programmatic and could not begin even to approximate to the articulation and detail of normative legal science.[56] In this Kelsen may have been less than fair. The method of the legal scientist cannot, by definition, apply

[55] The study of proof in adjudication includes, for example, the logic and psychology of proof. An example of a very unkelsenian view of what is involved in the study of legal proof is offered by Michael, *The Elements of Legal Controversy* (1948): 'since legal controversy is conducted by means of words, you need some knowledge about the use of words as symbols, that is, some grammatical knowledge. Since issues of fact are constituted of contradictory propositions, are formed by the assertion and denial of propositions, and are tried by the proof and disproof of propositions, you need some knowledge of the nature of propositions and of the relationships which can obtain among them, and of the character of issues of fact and of proof and disproof, that is, some logical knowledge. Since the propositions which are material to legal controversy can never be proved to be true or false but only to be probable to some degree and since issues of fact are resolved by the calculation of the relative probabilities of the contradictory propositions of which they are composed, you need some knowledge of the distinction between truth or falsity and probability and the logic of probability. Since propositions are actual or potential knowledge, since proof or disproof is an affair of knowledge, since, if they are truthful, the parties to a legal controversy assert, and witnesses report, their knowledge, and since knowledge is of various sorts, you need some knowledge about knowledge, such, for instance, as knowledge of the distinction between direct or perceptual and indirect or inferential knowledge. Since there are intrinsic and essential differences between law and fact, between propositions about matters of fact and statements about matters of law, and between issues of fact and issues of law and the ways in which they are respectively tried and resolved, you need some knowledge about these matters. Since litigants and all those who participate in the conduct and resolution of their controversies are men and since many of the procedural rules are based upon presuppositions about human nature and behaviour, you need some psychological knowledge. Finally, of course, you need such knowledge as is necessary to enable you to understand the tangential ends which are served by procedural law and to criticize the rules which are designed to serve them.' See, further, Twining, 'Taking Facts Seriously', 34 *Journal of Legal Education* 22 (1984).

[56] *GTLS*, 162–78.

to such circumstances and such a body of 'knowledge' as one may develop need not be discounted simply because it is not as precise or as clear as the deliverances of normative legal science. In any event it is easy to exaggerate the precision and clarity of the deliverances of normative legal science which cannot, while remaining true to its method, go beyond its subject-matter which may itself be unclear and inexact. None the less, a Kelsenian legal scientist can admit that decision-making in our hypothetical 'free proof' society is a significant phenomenon and that it is susceptible of scholarly study. What the scholar who takes such decision-making as his subject-matter cannot legitimately do, according to Kelsen's theory, is to appropriate the term 'law' in the sense associated with Kelsenian legal science for the body of knowledge he produces, nor can he turn to the epistemological basis of Kelsenian legal science to warrant the knowledge claims he makes. That does not preclude the legal scholar offering a different epistemological basis for his study.

The Kelsenian legal scientist would also be suspicious that moral impurities might enter at this point and that the deliverances of the legal scholar purported to state what ought to be or, at least, were understood by the scholar's audience to do so, even though the method employed was necessarily non-normative. Of course, if custom and practice are sources of norms in our hypothetical society or if our hypothetical tribunals are authorized to determine their own procedures, their practices may crystallize into a body of norms which are susceptible to the method of the Kelsenian legal scientist, just as the Praetor's Edict or the Chancellor's Equity came in time to be sufficiently fixed for scholars to write learned commentaries, that is, books purporting to describe a body of norms. The only real difference between the Kelsenian legal scholar and our hypothetical scholar is that the latter should not appropriate the term 'law' for his deliverances and that he should offer some warrant for the knowledge claims he makes.[57]

Different aspects of society call for different methods of study. Differences of method for neo-Kantians and Kelsenians determine different 'sciences'. Given different forms of knowledge there will be different 'autonomous sciences'; 'different' because the method differs—'autonomous' because one cannot legitimately incorporate

[57] In Twining's view, whether or not the word 'law' is used, our hypothetical scholar is involved in the activity of *legal* scholarship.

two distinct methods within one science. That leads to what Kelsen called 'methodological syncretism'[58] and what Kant called 'antinomies of reason'.[59] If, for example, causal social science presupposes determinism and normative social science presupposes freedom, any mixing of such sciences calls into play the contradictory claim of the same phenomenon that it is both caused and free. Formal logic tells us that from any pair of contradictory propositions any proposition whatsoever may be proved.[60] Consequently, methodological syncretism denies the possibility of knowledge in any form. That being so, different forms of intellectual activity needs to be kept separate and distinct. It does not follow, however, that any individual must ignore all but one form of intellectual activity and it is arrant epistemological imperialism to claim that one's own favoured activity produces the only true and legitimate form of knowledge. Kelsen's epistemology allows equally legitimate status to a variety of methods and perspectives. That is brought out by his oft-repeated, but equally often ignored, comment that a normative interpretation of human conduct is a possible, not a necessary, interpretation and that a causal interpretation, too, is possible but not necessary. Consequently objections to Kelsenism solely on the grounds of its commitment to 'autonomous sciences' require careful unpacking.[61] What may be at play, once again, is the 'overspill effect'. There is a tendency for those who have mastered a method and a related field of knowledge to imagine that they have found the philosopher's stone and that all other alleged disciplines deliver pseudo-knowledge. This attitude indeed generates a narrowing effect which taken to its extreme produces the narrow 'scientism' of that style of legal discourse which (as Twining puts it) has a lot to answer for.

The issues canvassed above beg the question, 'What is jurisprudence?' Both editors have published views on that issue.[62] Tur

---

[58] *PTL*, 1. [59] *CPuR*, A 405–567; B 432–595.

[60] Popper, *Conjectures and Refutations*, 5th edn. (London, 1974), Ch. 15, especially p. 317.

[61] Tur and Twining disagree fundamentally about the notion of an 'autonomous science' but the issue is not pursued here.

[62] Tur, 'Legal Education Again!' 20 *JLSS* 343–49 (1975); 'Jurisprudence and Practice', 14 *JSPTL* (N.S.) 38–47 (1976); 'What Is Jurisprudence? *Phil. Quarterly*, 149–61 (1978). Twining, 'Some Jobs for Jurisprudence' 1 *Brit. Jo. L. Soc.* 149 (1974); 'Academic Law and Legal Philosophy' 95 *LQR* 557 (1979); 'Evidence and Legal Theory' 47 *MLR* 261 (1984).

believes that it would be a scandal in the enterprise of legal education and legal scholarship if we could truthfully say without further qualification, as has been said, that jurisprudence is 'a chaos of approaches to a chaos of topics, chaotically determined',[63] or that it means 'pretty much whatever anyone wants it to mean'.[64] He believes that if such propositions are literally true we who practise jurisprudence could not begin to tell our students what the activity of jurisprudence was about or how they might aspire to it. In his view such anarchy gives interdisciplinary study a thoroughly bad name. The apprehension that as thus defined 'traditional jurisprudence' itself (rather than 'pure theory') might be a 'perfect and absolute blank'[65] led him to equate it with legal epistemology.[66] Having adopted a pluralist epistemology he now accepts that it was wrong to define jurisprudence as epistemology but he still believes that epistemology is a central element within jurisprudence. Under the benign influence of his co-editor he sees that an account of jurisprudence as activity, not product, is preferable but, under Tur's reciprocal influence, Twining acknowledges that within the activity of jurisprudence there is a legitimate place for pure theory and possibly for 'legal science' as indeed there is for all forms of knowledge that can assist us in the enterprise of knowing, understanding, and evaluating social and legal phenomena.

It is not possible to pursue these issues further in this Introduction. They re-emerge at various points throughout this symposium. As to Kelsen's alleged 'sterility' we agree that, first, if the charge is that Kelsen has nothing important to contribute to any significant issue in jurisprudence, this is clearly nonsense. Secondly, if the charge is that the pure theory is largely irrelevant to many central concerns about the nature of legal scholarship and what is involved in understanding actual legal systems, much depends on one's interpretation of Kelsen. Thirdly, if the charge is that the search for purity in legal science impoverishes legal

---

[63] Stone, *The Province and Function of Law* (London, 1947), p. 16; cf. the same author's rather less astringent criticisms in *Legal System and Lawyers' Reasonings* (London, 1964), Ch. 1.

[64] Dias, *Jurisprudence*, 4th edn. (London, 1976), p. 1.

[65] Carroll, *The Hunting of the Snark*, Fit the Second; cf. Twining 'The Great Juristic Bazaar', 14 *JSPTL* (N.S.) 185, at 194 (1978).

[66] 'What Is Jurisprudence?' loc. cit. n. 62 above, p. 159; 'Jurisprudence is part of epistemology . . .' It would have been better to have written, 'Legal epistemology is part of jurisprudence'; cf. Tur, 'Jurisprudence and Practice', loc. cit., p. 39, where jurisprudence as 'an activity' is discussed.

scholarship by unduly restricting it, this is valid against at least some versions of Kelsenism whether or not it can be pinned on Kelsen himself. To conclude (as Tur does) that jurisprudence is wider than Kelsenian legal theory and that legal scholarship is wider than a form of legal science that aspires to purity is to concede more than enough for the present purpose, which is to seek a better understanding of Kelsen, and to explain his contribution to the jurisprudential enterprise. The disciple who concedes so much may have to face one more charge of Kiplingesque discipleship:

> He that hath a Gospel
> Whereby Heaven is won
> (Carpenter or cameleer,
> Or Maya's dreaming son),
> Many swords shall pierce him
> Mingling blood with gall;
> *But His Own Disciple*
> *Shall wound him worst of all*

PART ONE

KELSEN AND KANT

CHAPTER I

IS KELSEN REALLY A KANTIAN?

ALIDA WILSON

MY aim in this paper is, first, to examine how far Kantian principles direct Kelsen's theory and how far it is also informed by anti-Kantian ideas, and second, to look at one aspect of the philosophical infrastructure of the Pure Theory, *Zurechnung*.[1]

In 1925 Kelsen identifies the directing principles of his work in the Preface to *Die Allgemeine Staatslehre*:

I feel myself . . . in harmony with . . . [the] line of enquiry into the theory of the state which aspired to build a theory of positive law, as of social reality (sociology). Its method was influenced, more or less consciously . . . by the Kantian critique of reason: dualism of 'is' and 'ought'; substitution of transcendental categories as conditions of experience for hypostasis and metaphysical postulates; transformation of absolute, because qualitative and transystematic, antitheses into relative, quantitative intrasystematic differences; passage from the subjective sphere of psychologism to the field of logical-objective validity. Here are . . . the directing principles of my theoretical work.[2]

DUALISM SEIN/SOLLEN[3]

Let us consider this dualism, introduced by Kelsen in *Die Hauptprobleme*, and alongside it, that other great dualism whereby Kelsen sunders our being into cognition on the one hand and disposition on the other.

---

[1] *Zurechnung* is normally translated as 'imputation'. Since 'imputation' has a definite meaning which is challenged by Kelsen and since the connotation and denotation of *Zurechnung* are problems discussed at length here I prefer to retain the original throughout.

[2] *ASL* vii.

[3] For the purposes of this paper I shall use the original German terms *Sein* and *Sollen*. Translators have noticed the difficulties involved in rendering *Sollen* as 'Ought'. The connotation and denotation given by Kelsen to *Sollen* is itself one of the major problems in his writings.

Already in 1923, as if to signalize his Kantian pedigree, Kelsen had declared in the Preface to *Die Hauptprobleme*:

[this book] starts from the fundamental antithesis between *Sollen* and *Sein* that Kant was the first to discover in and through his endeavour to establish the independence of the practical reason over against the theoretical reason, of value over against reality, of morality against nature.[4]

This disjunction, as he puts it a little later in the book, is absolute:

the question why anything ought to be can invariably only lead back to an ought; just as the question why anything is invariably finds an answer only in the being of something else.

In the second dichotomy Kelsen sees us as radically divided in our being. That is, for Kelsen our rationality is theoretical only, with a restricted range and with restriction on its modes of operation. Cognition apart, that is, in the physical, instinctive, and emotional aspects of our being, in our willing and our valuing, we are involved in processes into which rationality cannot enter; these processes feed material to our rationality but are not fundamentally understood by it nor affected fundamentally by its operation. Reason is thus essentially the 'slave of the passions', there is no practical reason in a philosophical sense. This dichotomy will be indicated hereafter as 'cognition/disposition'.

In the second dichotomy rationality has as subject to it, examinable by it:
(*a*) what can be observed empirically and understood in terms of cause and effect;
(*b*) what individuals, groups, and societies assert in terms of norms and values; in examination of these reason can only describe; having no objective criterion it cannot evaluate or subject to judgment schemes of value or normative systems;
(*c*) what can be understood and determined a priori. I include (*c*) here because one of the basic elements of Kelsenism—*Zurechnung* —is allegedly an a priori category; and for the more general reason that inclusion of the a priori must be attributed to one claiming to regard the power of thought as effectively active to the point of

---

[4] *HPS*[2], VI. This and other passages from Kelsen's early works are my own translations.

creating its own objects in cognition.[5] Yet as will be seen, Kelsen's attitude to the a priori is problematic.

The two dichotomies stand in an uneasy relation to each other. (i) In Kelsen's account of what we are and what we can know, understanding of the *Sein/Sollen* dichotomy itself has no clear provision made for it. He should on the basis of this account—though he does not try to define with precision the limits of experience and empirical knowledge—dismiss any suggestion that in some way or other we *experience* the *Sein/Sollen* distinction. He could not legitimately find it in his examination of normative systems, for, as he himself would have said, the distinction is presupposed in any normative system and its concepts. (ii) The two dichotomies—*Sein/Sollen* and cognition/disposition—correspond, respectively, to Kelsen's aim to locate law exclusively in the normative world and his other aim, to build his theory on the basis of ethical relativism. As a moral relativist he was drawn towards the cognition/disposition dichotomy, since it seemed to give theoretical support to that view by debarring cognition, on good psychological/epistemological grounds, from authoritative establishment of norms or standards. But he did not see clearly the full consequences of what he was doing in isolating the will and disposition altogether from cognition and thus excluding the workings of the will—the source of normativity—from what is understandable except in a purely superficial way.

Kelsen desired his theory to be seen as an appropriate application of Kant's transcendental method to law, and he was successful in getting it seen as such:

. . . a review of [*Die Hauptprobleme*], which appeared in *Kantstudien* in the year 1922, in which this work received recognition as an attempt to apply the transcendental method to legal science . . .[6]

In fact, there is hardly the beginning of such an application, even if we make a synthesis of Kelsen's writings. He rejects piecemeal, tacitly or explicitly, the essential elements of that method: the belief in the powers of pure reason; the possibility of a priori knowledge of the world; Kant's concern with reason's

---

[5] *GTLS*, 434; 'Cognition itself creates its objects out of materials provided by the senses and in accordance with its immanent laws.'

[6] *HPS*[2], VI.

examination of its own powers; the thing-in-itself; the categories, save causality.[7] The rejection will be examined later.

The structure of Kant's thoughts about morals and men is such that Kelsen could find no real footing there for his eclectic outlook. In particular, it is difficult to understand Kelsen's professed acceptance of the Kantian distinction *Sein/Sollen*, since the notion of *Sollen* in Kant has as its core freedom of will and 'practical reason',[8] whereas Kelsen, after an apparent endorsement of this notion,[9] goes on to rule out freedom and practical reason in so far as he postulates the causal determinability of man's will by the idea of a norm.[10] There is no room for conscious thinking affecting the willing. The idea of a norm, and the evil consequences of its violation are not, for Kelsen, alternatives for man to choose from. They are 'motives' which 'cause'[11] man's will to act with an 'irresistible compulsion'.

Kant's philosophical doctrines are remote from Kelsen, whichever dichotomy we consider.

Kant believed that there is in man, from one standpoint, determination by causes in the sensible world, and, from another, independence from determination by such causes. But the term 'standpoint' should not mislead us into thinking that we perceive something merely apparent in either case. Human determination and independence are both realities, jointly aspects of the complete man as he is and lives. A man belongs both to the *mundus sensibilis* and to the *mundus intelligibilis*, that is, to the order of nature with its pervasively operating causality, and to that intelligible world where he is subject, as to laws, to rational principles inescapable in their demand for recognition.[12] As part of nature, man's actions are bounded by the various laws of nature. As part of the intelligible world—to which he belongs *qua* rational being—man cannot conceive his actions as blindly

---

[7] Causality, as will be seen, was accepted by Kelsen, but distorted at his hands into a non a priori category of the mind.

[8] From Plato's time to Kant it was a widespread belief among philosophers that man's power of rationality had a part to play in human conduct, determining or influencing the choice of actions, especially moral actions, and shaping man's character. Rationality displayed in action is called 'practical reason' as opposed to theoretical or discursive reason.

[9] Cf. *HPS*[2], VI.   [10] *PTL*, 95 and 92.

[11] The confusion between motives and causes is Kelsen's; cf. *PTL*, 97.

[12] Kant, *Groundwork of the Metaphysic of Morals*, tr. Patron as *The Moral Law*, 107 (51).

determined by the causality of the sensible world; on the contrary, the very source of his actions, his will, appears now as free. This is the meaning of Kant's assertion: 'man belongs to the intelligible world'. But man is not drawn into a conflict of elements within himself which he can never, even in principle, resolve. For rational beings have, in their 'will', 'the power . . . to act in accordance with their conception of laws, i.e. in accordance with principles.'[13] These principles are not alien to their rationality, but inhere in it.

In Kant's doctrine there is no 'unbridgeable gulf' in man and the life of man between the *mundus intelligibilis* and the *mundus sensibilis*: since the practical reason, identified by Kant with the 'will', wills certain actions because of the principles or maxims which can be the real grounds of our actions. Man, as a rule, does not respond blindly to impulses.[14] He knows the quality of his actions. His theoretical reason apprehends the concept of the principle of his act. His practical reason, or rational willing, determines the choice of actions on the grounds of the principle which each action embodies. Even if the principle is not necessarily universalizable it is wider than a mere 'motive'. Kant distinguishes aspects of man— his natural and his moral aspect—as wholly disparate, yet brings them together in the individual, integrates the individual even in terms of his human duality.

Kelsen's position is wholly different. We see, thus far, that his account of *Sein/Sollen* is remote from Kant's because he severs one aspect of Kant's account—the non-inferrability of each from the other—from context, gives an account of *Sollen* alien to Kant, allowing man neither freedom nor rational apprehension of duty, and denies man the practical reason essential in Kant's view to performance of duty.

Kelsen follows Kant in so far as he denies the ability of reason to infer a judgment in the 'ought' mode from a judgment in the 'is' mode. This by itself does not render Kelsen a Kantian. Kelsen claims to be a Kantian—in so far as this first 'guiding principle' is concerned—because of his endorsement of the *Sein/Sollen* dichotomy. But this dichotomy, in Kant, does not merely mean a belief in a distinction between the intelligible and the material worlds. The Kantian *Sollen* necessitates both freedom and practical

[13] Kant, op. cit., 76 (36).
[14] The exactly opposite doctrine, as expounded by Kelsen, can be seen in *PTL*, Ch. 3, Section 23.

reason. If there were only rational—purely rational—beings there would be no need for a *Sollen* since reason, on its own, can but act in a rational manner. If, on the contrary, there were only causally determined beings, there would be no *Sollen* either; an 'ought', arises because volition and disposition have tendencies alien to the course of action that, rationally, 'ought to be'. If there were no possibility of following the latter course, via its apprehension by reason and a movement towards it by will, there would be no *Sollen*. Kant's dichotomy is founded upon freedom and practical reason; if they are removed, as they were by Kelsen, the Kantian character of the dichotomy is lost; and *Sollen* needs to be redefined entirely—as Kelsen did not do—for it to make sense.

That Kelsen rules out apprehension by reason of the course of action someone 'ought to take' and a movement towards it by the will, is quite clear when we consider his determinism. Whilst in various discussions Kelsen turns the general notion 'causality' over and over, inclining now to one definition, now to another, he adopts in *The Pure Theory*, with little argument and in a very simple formulation, a determinism embracing inanimate, animate beings, and human nature in a comprehensive sense. This determinism drives him in a direction akin to that in which the cognition/disposition dichotomy already drives him. Whereas that dichotomy compels him to deny, in principle, any kind of objective criterion making choice or purpose right, good, or rational, his determinism compels him to deny real and distinct meaning of the terms 'choice', 'purpose', and the like, as used in common parlance and by many philosophers: the denial is glaring in the statement in *The Pure Theory*:

man always acts under irresistible compulsion, because his actions are always causally determined; and causality, by its very nature, is irresistible compulsion. That which is called 'irresistible compulsion' in legal terminology actually is only a special case of irresistible compulsion . . .[15]

This determinism makes nonsense of the occasional apparent claim by Kelsen to take *Sollen* seriously as moral reality. For it is clear, at the beginning of any thought about *Sollen*, that 'I ought to do X' presupposes 'I can do X or refrain from doing X'; and that it is senseless to say 'I ought to do X' if I cannot do X, or if I am 'irresistibly compelled' to do X.

[15] *PTL*, 97.

The following is the operative statement by Kelsen about the determinability of the human will in our establishment and acceptance of law:

The establishment of a normative, behaviour regulating order, which is the only basis of imputation, actually presupposes that man's will is causally determinable and therefore not free. For it is the undoubtable function of such an order to induce human beings to observe the behaviour commanded by the order. But this means that the idea of a norm commanding a certain behaviour becomes the cause of a norm-conforming behaviour.[16]

Kelsen seems here to see causal determination as a straightforward fact about human behaviour; he is not speaking in the terms of Kant's moral philosophy, or even applying the approach of Kant's *Critique of Pure Reason* to the field of human behaviour. For he is not saying that the causal determinability of the human will is a mode inherent in our thinking about human behaviour but that it is something inherent in human behaviour. In fact the weakness of the opening statement—to the effect that the establishment of law presupposes the causal determinability of a man's will—is at once apparent if we notice that 'presupposes' attempts, by its specious vagueness, to make acceptable what is altogether controversial: how controversial, we see if we substitute for 'presupposes', 'proves'. Of course, to anyone interested, in detail, in the development and functioning of human society, the establishment or extension of a legal system presupposes a measure of predictability in the response of men to varying circumstances, but—apart from the complication that it presupposes more than *responses*—such a measure of predictability does not entail, does not even make probable, the 'causal determinability of the human will'. One may, if one so wishes, adopt this as an assumption made dogmatically, in advance of any close consideration of human behaviour; or one might regard the 'causal determinability of human will', as a hypothesis that will never perhaps be finally verifiable but will become progressively more and more acceptable with the progress of the social and psychological sciences. What one should not assume is that any one human institution points, simply by its existence, to the 'causal determinability of the human will'. Common experience seems, in the case of law, to point the

---

[16] *PLT*, 94 (abridged).

other way. People often defy or disregard legal norms no less than moral norms.

Were we to suppose a closed compartment of life within which each legal norm, with its sanction, is understood by the subject and obeyed by reason of the sanction contained in it, we might think of causal determinability as operating, from norm to subject, within that compartment; but there would be no good inference to general determinability of the will. However, we cannot reasonably suppose such a closed compartment for the operation of law; if Kelsen seems at times to assume it, at others he does not. For example, in *The Pure Theory* he allows that not only a moral or religiously determined order, but a legal order may carry with it a 'psychic coercion' distinct from fear of punishment in the individual. Such psychic coercion is surely something not to be defined in narrowly legal terms. But a view that ascribes to a legal order a not precisely defined 'psychic coercion', comparable with the psychic coercion exercised by a moral order, seems to enter a field quite beyond *The Pure Theory*, and here it would be hard to show how the idea of the norm determines behaviour.

In an essay of 1941 it appears that Kelsen is going to offer an escape from his determinism and its consequences. We read in the essay that 'there is no contradiction between so-called determinism and so-called indeterminism. There is nothing to prevent the human mind subjecting human behaviour to two different schemes of interpretation.'[17]

An expectation aroused by this remark might be: Kelsen, following Kant, intends to describe man in one aspect of his being as strictly subject to causal determination, in another as having freedom of choice, but none the less as a unity. But Kelsen is not about to present man as a unity with sharply distinct aspects. For him man has not two different aspects, since in his view man belongs exclusively, so far as his conduct is concerned, to the *mundus sensibilis*. It is Kant's merit to have posed the question, how can freedom be compatible with the causal law which prevails in nature, and in man as part of nature? It is this question which Kelsen neglected, after accepting, not only the *Sein/Sollen* dichotomy of Kant's doctrine, but also the possibility of subjecting human will to normative injunctions.

[17] 'Causality and Imputation', in *WIJ*, 345.

Nothing prevents the mind from entertaining two or even more schemes of interpretation as concerns man, as Kelsen envisaged. Indeed, *pace* Kelsen and his purity of method, we may have to do so if we are not to work for ever in isolated compartments. But the two or more 'interpretations' need to be brought together—as far as intelligence can attain this—in their bearing on the common object, and to be related to one another. *The Pure Theory* does not bring together, let alone reconcile or explain, the relationship between determinism and freedom, for the only 'freedom' Kelsen is prepared to allow man is not freedom but a label given to his actions: 'Man is not held to account because he is free: he is free because he is held to account.'[18]

In Kelsen's theory, then, X is 'free' in so far as he is held to account—and no further; the legal norm is what establishes accountability, and—most important—the legal norm, as such entirely conventional and arbitrary, establishes this accountability in a wholly and unavoidably contingent manner: this accountability 'has a purely formal character . . . It is applicable no matter what the content of the circumstances which it links together, no matter what character of the acts to which it gives the name of law.'[19]

It follows, therefore, that, on Kelsen's premises, X can stand for, not only a man, but any object, animate or inanimate. Whatever is held to account is, he tells us, free. If the law (as in some periods) holds an animal or even some inanimate object accountable for damage done, then the Kelsenian formula would run (just as for a man): 'X, (e.g. an ox or a stone), is not held to account because it is free; it is free because it is held to account.'[20] But it is absurd *ab initio* to speak, in the case of animals and inanimate objects, in terms of freedom or the reverse.

Is Kelsen more convincing when we pass from his determinism stated in rather a general way to more specific statements about the will and willing?

I contend that rationality, predicated of conduct, means the choice by thought of a goal and the movement of the will to extricate itself from all obstructive inclinations in order to pursue the goal. Where there is no such guided movement towards a goal or goals, this indicates absence both of rationality as applied to conduct, and of will. Now, rationality and will, in this sense, had

---

[18] *PTL*, 98.   [19] *PTL-IMFC*, 485.
[20] The 'Kelsenian formula' can be seen in *PTL*, 98.

already been dismissed by Kelsen when he defined 'willed conduct' as: 'such actions or omissions as can be imputed to the person under a legal norm';[21] and when he declared: 'that A wills an action means that such an action is imputed to A'.[22] Thus defined 'a willed action' ceases to have the meaning attached to it by psychology, moral philosophy, or common parlance. Yet, despite such a definition, Kelsen gets himself into a position where he needs the real, psychological will of real man if the system he posits is to operate: for, as he declares, it is acts of will in man, as the addressee of the norm, that *cause* the commanded behaviour.[23] There is present to man, as addressee of the system, a 'representation' of the norm, and the convergence of this with other factors—unspecified by Kelsen—bends man's will; the working of those factors—social, psychological, physiological, normative, etc.—acts as a *cause* of the 'willing'. Kelsen assumes the representation of the norm to be, as a rule, strong enough to overcome resistance from any quarter, so that the content of the 'willing' is determined—as an effect—by the representation of a norm—which acts as a cause.[24]

The determinability Kelsen posits operates, as I have shown hitherto, to bring into line the content of this 'willing' with the different factors converging in the formation of the 'act of will'.

There is, however, another link in the cause-effect chain in relation to human behaviour: once man has 'willed' an action, says Kelsen, he can but perform the willed behaviour. This assertion—that the passage from a 'willed' action to its performance is causally determined—does not endure reflection or introspection.

This pattern of human behaviour, as sketched out by Kelsen in these passages of *The Pure Theory*, seems wrong. Yet, there appears room for another criticism: seemingly unaware of the difference between motives, reasons, and causes, Kelsen plunges into yet another attempted explanation of human behaviour especially the 'law-conforming behaviour':

the causal connection [between the norms and the behaviour intended to be brought about by them] exists only if the behaviour is actually motivated by men's ideas about the intention of the law-creating acts, *a motivation* which by no means is always the case because obedience to the law is frequently caused by other motives.[25]

---

[21] *ASL*, 64.   [22] *ASL*, 85.   [23] *PTL*, 97.
[24] *PTL*, 97.   [25] *PTL*, 103 (emphasis added).

Setting aside for a moment the 'causes' *vis-à-vis* 'motives' issue, I want to concentrate on the inconsistency between that passage and the following:

children and mentally ill adults are not held responsible . . . [on] . . . the assumption that children and the mentally ill (because of the condition of their consciousness) can not, or not sufficiently be caused, by the idea of legal norms . . .

If a mentally sane individual, Kelsen maintains, i.e., 'an average human being', acts causally determined by an 'average set of external circumstances' and so acting 'exhibits a conduct that the legal order prohibits, then this human being is responsible for his conduct and its effects according to this legal order'.[26]

This passage would be perverse, if it were not incoherent: (*a*) an insane person is not responsible, says Kelsen, because he cannot be 'sufficiently caused' to obey the norms; but a mentally sane adult who—due to circumstances stronger than the idea of the norm—is not 'sufficiently caused' to obey the norms, is held responsible; (*b*) this happens notwithstanding the fact that he acted under 'irresistible compulsion' to follow a conduct 'prohibited' by the legal order; since, however, as Kelsen never tires of repeating, wrong-doings, criminal acts, misdemeanours, etc., are *not* prohibited by the legal order, the only class of people who can perform acts 'prohibited' by the system is law-officials: these, in this context, will be penalized when, under 'irresistible compulsion', they refuse to apply sanctions.

Man is causally determined—so Kelsen's basic contention runs—to obey law because the representation of the norm and its sanction operates within him as a 'cause' for his 'willing' a law-abiding behaviour.[27] However, this motivation is 'by no means always the case . . . obedience to the law is frequently caused by other motives'.[28] But man does not always obey the law; his disobedience is explained in terms of motives 'stronger than the idea of the norm': motives which 'cause' man's willing in another direction.[29] This array of motives bending man's will and actions now in one way, now in another would have led any other writer to consideration of the choices presented to man. But not Kelsen:

[26] *PTL*, 97.   [27] *PTL*, 97.   [28] *PTL*, 103.
[29] *PTL*, 97.

'. . . man, as part of nature, is not free . . . his behaviour . . . is caused by other facts according to the law of nature'.[30]

Kelsen's contentions about determinism in general and freedom of the will in particular reveal the rift between his conception of man—and consequently of *Sollen*—and that of Kant.

Kelsen's view of human behaviour as causally determined brings him close to the empiricist philosophers who 'until recently have not only claimed that their assumptions about the ubiquity of causal determination were compatible with our everyday views about moral responsibility, but have claimed that these assumptions were actually required by these views.'[31]

In his turn, Kelsen had asserted that 'causality is not only not incompatible with imputation implying freedom and that means with regulation of human behaviour by norms connecting reward with merit and punishment with crime—but indeed the principle of causality is presupposed by such regulation.'[32]

If the empiricist line of thought appears no less strange than Kelsen's about imputation and freedom, both the argument in its support and its crucial flaw at once remind us of Kelsen. The argument 'was essentially that predictability was presupposed by such practices as punishment',[33] since punishment is predicated, universally, upon some degree of predictability in the individual's reaction to punishment. The flaw is that in such arguments there is ignored 'the notion of *desert* which does not seem to be causally analysable'.[34] When we praise (or reward) or blame (or punish) someone for what he has done we are not merely doing what we think, on the basis of causal determination, will affect his future conduct. On that basis praise or reward, being calculated simply to affect the individual's future conduct, would not be what we understand by praise or reward; blame or punishment might be assigned not in such fashion as to make these fit the fault but simply with a view to achieving the best social results on an utilitarian calculus. Kelsen assumes—and assumes without unease —that punishment and reward are provided in society in precisely these terms: 'punishment and reward are provided for only because it is assumed that the fear of punishment can causally

---

[30] *PTL*, 91.
[31] Ryan, *The Philosophy of Social Science*, 1970, p. 120.
[32] 'Causality and Imputation', in *WIJ*, 346.
[33] Ryan, *The Philosophy of Social Science*, p. 120.
[34] Ibid.

determine men to refrain from committing a crime and that the desire for reward can causally determine men to perform a heroic deed.'[35]

The second of Kelsen's directing principles is the 'substitution of transcendental categories as conditions of experience for hypostasis and metaphysical postulates'. What he saw as metaphysical postulates was not only religious or philosophic suppositions about the order of the universe and our world, affording support to natural law, but any attempt to find, in human nature or reason, anything determining law and our view of it in a sense not merely formal but substantial. One might well see Kelsen as barred from both the metaphysical and the empirical path, and taking up the only other road he could see ahead; but then it is puzzling why, in his use of Kant, he is scarcely more than allusive.

Let us look, firstly, at the general gulf between Kant and Kelsen; secondly at the aspects of Kant particularly invoked by Kelsen, and at the ways in which he invokes these.

(i) Kant is a rationalist, in the full sense, in as much as philosophy, science, moral thought, and action are for him predicated upon the great powers of reason. Kelsen is an eclectic who sketches only in a slight way his own view of the mind and reason and sees in recent and contemporary German *Wissenschaft* one great movement capable in its various branches of providing him with material to be worked into legal science.

(ii)(*a*) Kant, in examining the a priori element found by him in our thought about nature, is pursuing in this field his concern with the a priori in general. He is pursuing the same concern when he asks what we can say a priori about morals. He does not divorce moral philosophy from theory of knowledge. To Kelsen, by contrast, the power of the mind to think rationally independently of experience was an alluring prospect that captivated him for a comparatively brief spell. During this he posited the mind as active, in determinative fashion, in the process of cognition; the object as 'created' by that process; and truth and objectivity as dependent upon the conformity of that process to the immanent laws of reason. Eventually he abandoned such idealism and, falling back upon empiricism, demanded verification by facts before he could grant truth or objectivity, without seeing the awkwardness of this position for the normative approach to law.

---

[35] 'Causality and Imputation', in *WIJ*, 346.

(ii)(*b*) For Kant, nature and natural man is one theme for enquiry, man as rational and moral agent another. Yet the two themes have their connection, as man is one being and must ultimately be seen as such. The early Kelsen thinks quite otherwise: it has already been noticed how for him the world of man falls apart into the fields of *Sein* and *Sollen* and the being of the individual into 'cognition' and 'disposition'.

(ii)(*c*) There supervenes later, with Kelsen, on this disjunctive view of man's world and of man, something else which conflicts with the pair of dichotomies, without bringing him closer to Kant. That is to say, he tends more and more to adopt a dogmatic materialist determinism.

To Kant in the crucial stage of his philosophic development, metaphysics, as long pursued, seemed an impasse. That sort of metaphysics, as he saw it, transcended the limits imposed by our experience precisely where it ought not to transcend them—in those fields where securely based sciences could establish and had established knowledge about the natural world. It reasoned a priori about matters on which it had no right so to reason, in particular the general nature and order of the universe. But neither could he believe that our awareness receives the given as if it were a *tabula rasa*, or that our picture of the world and ourselves represents merely associative habit and its results. He thought that there must be a priori elements in our scientific knowledge, already present in our daily understanding of the 'natural world'. He therefore saw as necessary and decided to pursue an enquiry which was metaphysical in a new way and which would search out the a priori elements within that very knowledge unsuccessfully transcended by traditional metaphysics; this enquiry would not be 'transcendent', but, in Kant's term of art, 'transcendental'.

Thinking in the first place of physics and certain natural sciences, Kant opens the Introduction to the *Critique of Pure Reason* with the words: 'There can be no doubt that all our knowledge begins with experience'; and continues with the great question of his enquiry: whether our empirical knowledge may not be a combination of that which we receive through impressions and of that which the faculty of cognition supplies from itself. This latter, though an element present in even 'wholly unphilosophical' human intellect, is seen as something 'which we cannot distinguish from the original element given by sense until long practice has made us attentive to it and skilful in separating it'. In striving to separate out this element, Kant passes from a general explanation of 'cognition a priori', to the notion of space and time as 'necessary representations a priori', serving as the foundation for the intuitions of sense; from this he passes to the presupposed unity of consciousness necessary for any exercise of understanding; and thence to an account of those a priori elements that he terms the 'categories'. The categories function as a priori conditions for the possibility of all experience, and are grounded in 'categorial principles' that are both a priori and synthetic. Thus, in the case of *causality and dependence* the principle 'there are no events without causes' is synthetic since the notion 'event' (distinct from the notion 'effect') is not contained in the notion 'cause'; the a priori character of the principle is clear since we do not derive it from our observation of phenomena, yet have to use it in our organization of observed phenomena. In handling our physical experience, we are continually involved in application of both this and the other categories; the application of the categories pervades science but they are not derived from science. Because the phenomenal is equally given for all and the a priori is involved equally in all thinking about the phenomenal, there is an actual world common for all and we have a progressive understanding of its organization.

Here we come to that aspect of Kant's philosophy entitling him to be called from one aspect 'realist' and from the other 'idealist'. The 'order and regularity', Kant declares, 'in the appearances, which we entitle *nature*, we, ourselves introduce. We could never find them in appearances, had we not, ourselves, or the nature of our mind, set them there.' What follows is even more important, both in itself and for our theme:

this unity of nature has to be a necessary one, that is, has to be an *a priori* certain unity of the connection of appearances; and such synthetic unity could not be established *a priori*, if there were not subjective grounds of such unity contained *a priori* in the original cognitive powers of our mind, and if these subjective conditions, in as much as they are the grounds of the possibility of knowing any object whatsoever in experience, were not at the same time objectively valid.[36]

Turning now to Kelsen's epistemological claim that he substitutes for 'hypostasis and metaphysical postulates', 'transcendental cate-

[36] *CPuR*, A 125.

gories as conditions of experience', there are three matters to look
at: (*a*) his early attempt to find an epistemological definition for
Sein and *Sollen*; (*b*) his preoccupation with causality, its relevance
or otherwise for his transcendental approach; (*c*) the coupling of
causality and *Zurechnung*.

The most detailed account of *Sein/Sollen* is found in Kelsen's
early writings. The references in his later writings are based on this
but are less articulated.

In 1916 Kelsen considered that the early nineteenth-century
philosopher J. F. Herbart had revised Kant's conception of *Sein*
and *Sollen* for the better, in presenting these in terms of a
'fundamental awareness'. Apparently basing himself on Herbart,
Kelsen defined *Sein* and *Sollen* as two forms of understanding
determining what comes to us as indeterminate and dividing the
understanding itself in logically different ways. Thus he declares:

> The purely formal character of the concepts *Sein* and *Sollen* . . . cannot be
> expressed too emphatically . . . [with them] we are concerned only with
> forms of understanding under which the given becomes sometimes reality,
> sometimes value . . . In so far as the given is ordered through causality'
> . . . we see it in terms of '*Sein*'; in so far as it is ordered under the unity of
> a norm it is '*Sollen*'.[37]

I have rendered Kelsen's term *Erkenntnisformen* as 'forms of
understanding', not using the more emphatic words 'knowledge'
or 'cognition'. Whichever be the best word, understanding,
knowledge, or cognition are, for Kelsen, purely theoretic. Thus, in
apprehending the given under the form of *Sollen* (and the same
would hold *mutatis mutandis* for *Sein*) we are receiving and
determining it in terms purely of theoretical understanding, the
kind of knowledge that eventually establishes 'normative science'
whether moral, legal, or social. But what then is the place for the
practical import of *Sollen*? On Kelsen's premises, human actions
which implement the 'conditioning event' and the 'legal consequence' in the legal norm are also cause and effect. Such actions
are understood in primary experience in terms of causality, hence
as *Sein*. If they can also be understood as *Sollen*—via the
knowledge of the norm to which they correspond—it follows that
the form of understanding *Sollen* is less basic than *Sein*. Only
through legal system can the form of understanding *Sollen*

---

[37] *WRS* I, 37–9.

operate. *Sein*, on the contrary, following this scheme, is the basic nexus imposed by the mind upon external objects and events. As causality is not, for Kelsen, an external link among objects and events themselves, and as the elements of any norm are wholly arbitrary and conventional, a certain action such as the behaviour on the part of law officials after a crime could be seen as the effect of a cause and/or the embodiment of a 'legal consequence'. This discretion in the choice of forms of understanding renders these useless in the determination of *Sollen*. As to the 'conditioning fact' of the norm, it is impossible to perceive or to understand an act of murder, let us say, as 'linked by the unity of a norm' to any other human action, since (i) the second action may never happen; (ii) the changing nature of the legal commands will transform the same action into an irrelevant action, legally speaking, so soon as the legislator changes the norm itself; (iii) not even Kelsen's scheme, within which the legal norm is based on the contravention of the 'secondary, unwritten norms', does the conditioning fact ever acquire the status of what 'ought to be'.

'Forms of understanding', in the citation, are meant to reflect Kant. But of what element of Kant's doctrine precisely is Kelsen thinking? Kelsen's phrase seems to point to Kant's categories, but the token explanation given by Kelsen of his forms of understanding reveals nothing in their nature and functions parallel to the Kantian categories.

Sein and *Sollen* are conceived by Kelsen, not only as two different worlds, the Platonic or Kantian *mundus intelligibilis* and *mundus sensibilis*, but also as methods of cognition: 'in so far as it is the method or form of understanding through which the object (the given) is determined, the antithesis of causal and normative sciences rests just as much on a difference in the direction of understanding as on a difference in the object of understanding.'[38]

The emphasis on the two 'standpoints' is such that Kelsen seems to be slipping into a form of idealism hard to accept. For it seems to follow from Kelsen's view of *Sein* and *Sollen* as *determinative* forms of understanding that, given the one standpoint there is one reality, and given the other, another reality. This, for me, involves *inter alia* the difficulty of the status of reality prior to its apprehension through these two forms of understanding.

[38] Ibid.

This attempt by Kelsen to explain *Sein* and *Sollen* as epistemological tools is, to me, unsatisfactory and obscure. It is also, undoubtedly non-Kantian.

The second guiding principle of Kelsen's work, i.e. the substitution for hypostasis and metaphysical postulates of transcendental categories as conditions of experience, takes the form, first, of replacing deliverances from God, reason, or nature— supposed to convey the idea of duty and make clear our particular duties— with the Basic Norm; and, second, of replacing the notion of responsibility—which founded the notion of sanction or punishment in traditional jurisprudence—and any moral or political value attached to it, with the new notion of *Zurechnung*.

ZURECHNUNG

Since *Zurechnung* is seen by Kelsen as analogous to the Kantian categories of reason, such a substitution should start from a clear grasp of Kant's doctrine of the categories. In fact, this aspect of Kelsen's theory has either been accepted uncritically or quite overlooked.

One weakness that affects Kelsen in this context is that he ignores his own general remoteness from Kant. Prepared as he was for brief consideration of Kant in morals, where he was hostile to him, he is allusive, not explicit, in his treatment of the Kantian theory of knowledge and seems hardly conscious of the frame wherein Kant brings together his theory of knowledge and his moral philosophy.

The a priori character of the categories involves a high degree of generality and logical necessity. This, together with the fact that they apply solely at the empirical level, is of special relevance for the comparison of Kant's epistemology with *The Pure Theory*, which is based, so Kelsen claims, on Kant's transcendental logic. In fact, we cannot find in Kelsen's allusions to Kant and Kant's method or in his own procedure anything amounting to a carefully worked out plan to transplant and adapt to legal theory Kant's epistemological scheme of thought. Consider, for instance, the alleged analogy between *Zurechnung* and 'causality' in the Kantian scheme: in the end, it is unclear whether Kelsen has in mind 'causality' as understood by Kant, by Hume, by neo-Kantian thought, by Cassirer, or in some not clearly defined 'common-sense' way. Here my point is: if Kelsen really wished to rest his case on the *Zurechnung*/causality analogy, he should have explained why he passes over silently that concatenation of argument in the *Critique of Pure Reason* of which the categories, and among them causality, are but a part; and further, whether or not he thinks the rest of Kant's argument comparatively unimportant or wrong and how causality can stand on its own as a 'transcendental category'.

The relevance of the comparison between *Zurechnung* and the Kantian categories is twofold: it resides, first, in Kelsen's insistence on presenting legal science as involving the 'epistemo-logical creation' of law. Had he tried to demonstrate the creation of law on some other basis, his theory would be appropriately judged on the validity of his own arguments, but since we are offered, in its justification, simply allusion to the power of Kant's transcendental method, this must be examined for its bearings on *Zurechnung*.

Second, *Zurechnung* is presupposed, says Kelsen, in the existence of any normative social science, in so far as only *Zurechnung* can transform a mere multitude of men into society.[39] As to legal science, Kelsen wants us to believe that legal materials are ordered and unified in a system because we have, contained a priori in the original powers of our mind, the principle of *Zurechnung*.

If the analogy between *Zurechnung* and causality is to be valid *Zurechnung* has to be an a priori mental category in virtue of which law is ordered and unified. But if the alleged analogy does not endure analysis, Kelsen's claim as to the creation of law by legal science fails.

When we consider Kelsen's attempt to present *Zurechnung* as a Kantian category implicit in our understanding of every normative order of human behaviour several difficulties arise which may have more telling joint impact if first set out summarily.

(1) Kelsen, as a matter of method, ought to have begun by considering whether the notion 'category' as propounded by Kant with our understanding of the phenomenal world in view was equally relevant in the different context involving our understanding of the normative.

(2) Kelsen speaks of *Zurechnung* as 'a Kantian principle for

---

[39] 'Causality and Imputation', in *WIJ*, 325.

the understanding of a normative system moral or legal'. As a Kantian a priori principle, it ought to be either regulative of empirical enquiries or constitutive of experience. But it is neither, as will be seen.

(3) Kelsen changes repeatedly, without signalling these changes, his view of *Zurechnung per se*, his understanding of the analogy *Zurechnung*/causality, and his view about causality, in itself and as viewed by Kant.

I shall now examine these difficulties:

(1) Considering nature and our knowledge of natural phenomena, Kant was concerned to establish the character and basis of that knowledge and what we mean by 'nature' in terms of that knowledge. Considering what cannot be understood in terms of natural phenomena, he saw himself confronted with a different set of issues. Though in each field he strove to establish the basis of our thought and came to see a priori elements as an essential element in it, he rejected decisively any notion of transferring beyond the phenomenal realm that precise technique of investigation, 'the transcendental method', which he saw as suitable for disentangling the a priori elements in our understanding of nature. His refusal (*pace* Kelsen) to carry the method beyond this field was no blunder or inadvertence; Kant thought that a quite different approach was required. Kelsen, in his statement of objectives, also purports to discern a sharp line between the phenomenal and what he calls the normative, and to draw like consequences. So, when he attempts to apply Kant's method beyond that line, the charge against him is not merely that he endeavours to use the Kantian intellectual instrument and fails; not merely that he overlooks a prime fact about Kant's categories, that is, their definition in terms adapted to our understanding of natural phenomena; but rather that he supposed it possible to employ Kant's method on intellectual ground where he had debarred himself from so doing. For, if we bar argument from the 'is' statement to a statement or prescription in terms of 'ought', it is hard to see how any useful connection could be found between such concepts as are involved a priori in our knowledge of what is and the type of concepts involved a priori in the normative view of the world. That is to say, talk of *analogy* between causality and *Zurechnung* is of no help with morality and law, if we insist that the essence of each of these is its normative character.

So long as Kelsen is concerned with 'general' legal norms, the reference made in the prescription is to 'antecedent' (the 'if' clause) and 'consequent' (the 'then' clause) in terms of *type* of action or event. To say this is only to point out an aspect of the normative as seen by Kelsen; in considering such a norm we are considering a prescription issued in terms of a possible action of a legally defined type. The actions and/or events constituting the elements of the 'if/then' clause are conceptual, and are conceptually or ideally linked, not empirically so. It is only in the particular norm—the decision by the judge—that there is reference to an actual and experienced example of the antecedent action. The point in my allusion to this difference between general and individual norms is to underline the difficulty of applying, to a general prescription couched in ideal terms, a mental category— such as Kelsen claims *Zurechnung* to be—which can connect only empirically perceived actions or events.

(2) In Kelsen's account law belongs to the realm of meaning and values. On that basis, if its essential character is to be understood, we have to define what it is we wish to signify when we refer to the 'normative meaning' of the human words and actions constituting law. Those words and actions to which we ascribe legal character do not convey this character to us *per se*; if not interpreted as belonging to a legal context, they appear as meaningless. But to say this, as Kelsen does, is to say that *Zurechnung*, the all-important category, does not, by itself, infuse legal meaning into words and actions. If the normative meaning is to be present, indeed if there is to be a legal norm at all, we require the attachment of the normative pronouncement to a valid system. Without that attachment there is no valid norm, therefore no *Zurechnung*; in other words, *Zurechnung* exists and functions only within a valid norm; a valid norm requires the validity of the normative system to which it belongs, and this validity—according to Kelsen—can only be bestowed upon the system by the basic norm: thus *Zurechnung*, referred to by Kelsen as 'the *a priori* category for the comprehension of the empirical legal material',[40] is not enough to give us the legal meaning of the events and actions which make up the elements of the 'if-then' clause. It is not necessary for their perception either because the actions or events which make up that clause are not to be *perceived* as conjoined,

[40] *PTL-IMFC*, 485.

because they are not empirically linked. The typical example, that is, the criminal deed and the punishment which ought to follow are not two events whose conjunction can be *perceived* through our senses. Their link is ideal or conceptual.

(3) A further difficulty about seeing *Zurechnung* as a Kantian category lies in the disparity of the formulations given to its notion—and that of causality—by Kelsen in the course of his career.

At the beginning of his career Kelsen offered nothing more specific by way of definition of *Zurechnung* than the link obtaining between the two elements indicated by the norm. Any norm, Kelsen maintained at this stage—grammatical, logical, or aesthetic, not only legal or moral—exhibits this link.[41] It is only later that Kelsen offers his definition in Kantian-transcendental terms: *Zurechnung* is presented as a category in the Kantian sense, and thus the necessity of the link in *Zurechnung* is seen as 'logical'.[42] But in offering this account of *Zurechnung* Kelsen now confines himself to norms of social character, either legal or moral, having eliminated from consideration grammatical, logical, or aesthetic norms. It was at this stage that Kelsen should have explained more clearly—if he wished this thought to be taken as genuinely Kantian—the scope and application of *Zurechnung*.

At the start of Kelsen's work the context in which *Zurechnung* is discussed is difficult to make precise; it seems that Kelsen was applying the concept to the legal norm and only later to the legal rule. The confusion results from the fact that the clear-cut distinction between *Rechtssatz* and *Rechtsnorm* emerges only in the 1945 edition of *The General Theory*; and also from Kelsen's view of the legal norm as a hypothetical judgment. This has led Kelsen's commentators to believe that the distinction did not exist during the first period. Kelsen has answered that criticism in categorical terms.[43] Despite his denial there seems room to believe that the original distinction was drawn between law and legal science, not between legal norms and legal rules.

The difference is relevant as an aspect of Kelsen's idea of the 'creative' role of legal science in relation to law. For Kelsen believes this science, with its synoptic view and its organizing principles, introduces order and regularity into its matter, makes it

---

[41] *HPS*², V–VI.   [42] *PTL-IMFC*, 485; *WIJ*, 331.
[43] 'Reply to Stone', 17 *Stanford L. Rev.* 1128 (1965).

knowable as law, even, 'in an epistemological sense', creates law. To articulate this idea more fully, he has to regard legal science as made up of general statements about law—'laws' about law which are to be comparable with the 'natural laws' forming natural science in its various branches. This comparison requires him, in its turn, to see the principle of *Zurechnung*, presupposed in his general statements about law, as corresponding to causality in the case of the general statements making up natural science: that is, to see *Zurechnung* as a category in the Kantian sense.

In Kantian terms it is only through a 'synthesis' that natural science creates its object, that is, nature. A synthesis needs the workings of a priori principles capable of organizing experience. In the critical philosophy these principles are the twelve categories. In the Pure Theory the principle is *Zurechnung*. What is established on the basis of *Zurechnung*, that is, the legal rules, constitute for Kelsen synthetic judgments precisely comparable with the general statements of natural science.

In all this Kelsen becomes so preoccupied with legal science that he forgets law: in explaining the principle upon which legal science works, he no longer has eyes for the object upon which it works.[44]

It was not at one leap that he reached his final, extreme position; as late as 1953, he tried to combine his allegedly Kantian approach with a vestigial direct concern with the legal norm. The attempt in question is in the article of that year: 'What is the Pure Theory of Law?' Here the Pure Theory is seen as starting with logic and the 'fact of legal science'. Legal science 'subjects the statement in which this science describes its objects to a logical analysis, that is, it establishes the presuppositions under which statements about legal duties, legal rights . . . are possible'; and by this route 'arrives at the fundamental concept of all legal knowledge, the concept of the norm'. Legal science, that is,

investigates the specific sense in which—in the hypothetical judgments to be described as *Rechtssätze*—the condition is coupled with the consequence; and meanwhile it compares these *Rechtssätze*—in which it describes its object, the *Rechtsnormen* and the relations constituted by these norms— with the hypothetical judgements in which natural science grasps its specific object . . .   [45]

This sounds fine: but where is the primary *Zurechnung*, in the

----

[44] *PTL*, 75.   [45] *WRS* I, 612.

Rechtssatz or in the *Rechtsnorm*? Or is *Zurechnung* to be understood in one sense in the *Rechtsnorm* and in another in the *Rechtssatz*?

It is not difficult—given the 'epistemological' creation of law by legal science postulated in the Pure Theory—to perceive why Kelsen wished to find a principle or principles in terms of which law could be said to be 'created'. He wishes it to be accepted that 'the science of law, as cognition of law . . . creates its object in so far as it comprehends its object as a meaningful whole.'[46] Such a view of legal science and what it achieves, he thinks, will gain in acceptability if we are convinced that it is parallel to Kant's view of our understanding of nature. Kelsen wishes us to think that he is saying, for law and legal science, precisely what Kant said for nature and natural science: 'Our understanding is itself the lawgiver of nature; it imposes rules on appearances, which exists only in our sensibility, and in so doing *creates* nature in one sense of the term.'[47] But for a reasonable comparison of *Zurechnung*, as organizing principle, with Kant's causality, it had to be made clear, at the start, what *Zurechnung* was to organize; and this Kelsen did not make clear. Thus in the 1969 edition of *The Pure Theory* what is seen as connected in terms of *Zurechnung* is not only legal antecedent and legal consequence, but also—an addition not at all justified—the 'law-creating act' and the 'law-obeying act'[48].

Kelsen's changing terms as to *Zurechnung* seem connected with an ambiguity in his conception of what Kant meant by *category*; and this ambiguity is the third obstacle to the construction of a successful analogy between *Zurechnung* and the Kantian categories of the mind.

Sometimes he refers to causality as if it were a connecting link among events, the evidence of the link residing in past experience.[49] In doing this Kelsen is thinking of one presupposition of the scientific law stated in the form: 'if X then Y, for any specific value of X'. But he takes no account of the fact that causality for Kant is only one of a number of presuppositions or modes of thought involved in our examination of the phenomenal world. Once Kelsen had instituted the comparison with the Kantian scheme of the categories he should have considered whether any support for *Zurechnung* could be obtained by reference simply to one of the

[46] *PTL*, 72.   [47] *CPuR*, A 126.   [48] *PTL*, 103.
[49] *PTL*, 88; *PTL-IMFC*, 485.

Kantian categories: for these operate in conjunction in determining our view of the phenomenal world.

Sometimes Kelsen chooses to think about the categories rather in terms of 'schemes of interpretation'. Thus he can say, apropos of determinism and indeterminism and their application to human behaviour: 'causality . . . and imputation . . . [do not] exclude each other. There is no contradiction between so-called determinism and so-called indeterminism. There is nothing to prevent the human mind's subjecting human behaviour to two different schemes of interpretation. . .'.[50]

Here Kelsen with his 'scheme of interpretation' is thinking of some all-embracing view of human behaviour. An all-embracing view is very different from a Kantian category.

The final difficulty about seeing *Zurechnung* as a Kantian category arises from the fact that during his career Kelsen abandons the Kantian view of causality: which means abandoning the creative power of causality. When Kelsen moved towards the Humean, the neo-Kantian or even the 'common-sense' view of causality, he may have been getting nearer to or further from the truth, but he has certainly lost the attribute Kant attached to *his* causality *qua a priori category of the understanding*, i.e., its creative power—the power Kelsen so badly needed for his *Zurechnung*.

Kelsen's causality now not only *links* events, it belongs to science and depends on experience:

The individual legal norms, created by judicial decisions or administrative acts, are described by the science of law as a concrete experiment is described by natural science by referring to a law of nature that manifests itself in the experiment.[51]

But Kant's categories—causality among them—

. . . are not co-ordinating concepts . . . in the way in which some scientific concepts are. They do not serve directly to link phenomena, as for example the notion of a field of force does . . . it is because they have this formal character that they can form part of . . . philosophy rather than belong to general science.[52]

As early as 1939 Kelsen adopts Ernst Cassirer's notion of causality as 'a methodological principle' or a mere rule of inquiry. Commenting on this version of causality Ernest Nagel has this to

[50] *WIJ*, 345.   [51] *PTL*, 80.
[52] Walsh, *Kant's Criticism of Metaphysics* (Edinburgh, 1975), p. 42.

say: 'When formulated in this general way the principle is admittedly vague . . . Indeed, unless the formulation is understood in the light of certain additional . . . stipulations, the principle is reduced to triviality.'[53]

Kelsen accepted Cassirer's formulation of causality because it provided causality with a 'historical beginning' as a mode of thinking that Kelsen needed given his beliefs about the 'emergence of causality'.[54]

There is no evidence that Kelsen went into Cassirer's version of the problem of causality beyond the point where it suited his own needs, i.e., to deny that causality was 'an innate concept of the understanding'. In his own words:

causality is not, as has been supposed, a form of thought necessarily given to human consciousness, an innate concept of the understanding, but rather there have been periods in the history of the human mind in which causal thinking had not yet come about . . .[55].

This crossing over from Kant's to Cassirer's causality ought to have been impossible for Kelsen; Cassirer's causality does not carry with it the consequences or applicability of Kant's causality and is not a concept to which *Zurechnung* may be related in terms of analogy, if *Zurechnung* is to be implicit in all thought about law.

After a bow to Kantian and neo-Kantian thought on causality Kelsen ends up with a mere form of words, a half-hearted attempt to paper over the crack in his own ideas:

Imputation, like causality, is a principle of order in human thinking, and therefore just as much or just as little *an illusion or ideology* as causality—which to use Hume's or Kant's words—is only a thinking habit or category of thinking.[56]

If *Zurechnung* is to work as 'a transcendental-logical condition

---

[53] Nagel, *The Structure of Science* (London, 1961), p. 320.

[54] It was Kelsen's doctrine that what he called the 'principle of imputation' was *the* mode of thinking dominant from the beginning of civilization up to approximately the fifteenth century AD, when the discoveries of natural science and the theories of Kepler, Bacon, and Galileo helped to rid the interpretation of natural and social occurrences of this quasi-religious approach. Kelsen's treatment of the historical origin—or what he takes as such—of causality cannot be dealt with in the scope of this paper.

[55] 'The Emergence of the Causal Law', in *ELMP*, 166.

[56] *PTL*, 103 (emphasis added).

of experience',[57] with Kant's causality as its analogue, words should not be used ('just as much . . . ideology') suggesting that a precise definition is unimportant. It should not be suggested—against the truth—that there is little important difference between Hume's perception of cause and effect in terms of association of ideas—'thinking habit' Kelsen calls it[58]—and Kant's of causality as a category of reason.[59]

To assert that there is in Kelsen no real commitment to Kantianism may cause surprise but this can be proved from his writings:

> If causality is no objective bond between cause and effect, but a mere habit of thought evoked by the observation of regular sequences, we have done away with that element to *which alone* an absolute necessity or inviolability can attach: the transcendent will which institutes this objective conjunction. Kant, indeed, endeavoured to salvage something of this inviolability by explaining causality as an innate concept of the understanding, an a priori category, without which knowledge of any kind would be impossible. But in this *we should see a retreat from rather than an advance over Hume*. For the assumption that causality is an absolute necessary condition of knowledge has no foundation in the facts.[60]

> A causal law of nature . . . functions primarily as an explanation of an event that already took place . . . in this respect it refers to the past . . . Laws of nature *are based on experience* and our experience *lies in the past*, not in the future.[61]

This is empiricism in accordance with Hume. By observing, Hume argues, that two kinds of event are repeatedly conjoined in nature one comes to elevate this constant conjunction to a 'law'. But, he adds, the basis of such a law is our observation, and the principle itself is but a mere habit of thought. In the Humean understanding of the question there is no a priori necessity in the operation of causality. By contrast, in *The Critique of Pure Reason* Kant had aimed to show that there can be, nay, that there is a priori knowledge of the world; we are not led by experience and observation of empirical reality to discover that events are causally determined, but rather know it a priori.

---

[57] *WIJ*, 363; *PTL-IMFC*, 485; *Rechtswissenschaft und Recht* (Leipzig, 1922), pp. 194 and 197.

[58] *PTL*, 103.   [59] *PTL*, 103.

[60] 'The Emergence of the Causal Law', in *ELMP*, 199.

[61] *PTL*, 88 (emphasis added).

Kant's critical idealism rejects the empiricist view of causality precisely on the grounds that the connection between events is presumed a priori; the connection does not depend on our experiencing the association repeatedly, albeit the connection could not be established had we no experience at all of the conjunction of events.

In wholly anti-Kantian fashion Kelsen wants to derive the objectivity and necessity of causality from experience and observations:

> by an extension of Hume's arguments Kant arrives at his doctrine, that a mere observation of reality is incapable of justifying the necessity of the connection of two facts as cause and effect and that causality, as the necessity of this connection, is an innate concept of the understanding, an a priori category of our knowledge by means of which we order the material of sense-perception empirically given to us. But then, whence do we derive this idea, that the necessary connection of cause and effect is objectively grounded and thus immanent in the causal process, that the cause brings about or draws after it the effect, that between the two there is not only a 'post hoc', but a 'propter hoc'?[62]

Yet he insists elsewhere: first, that causality and *Zurechnung* are forms of connection which tolerate no exception:

> The *Rechtssatz* unites one fact as condition with another as consequence . . . whilst the law of nature connects cause and effect with the necessity of a must that endures no exception.[63]

and second, on *Zurechnung* as a necessary and universal principle: a necessity and universality typical of a priori concepts. But, if *Zurechnung*—as Kelsen's causality—is not a pure concept of the mind, whence do its objectivity, necessity, and universality come?

Eventually, Kelsen founders upon his distrust of the a priori, even where *Zurechnung* is concerned. When he makes his criterion of propositional truth 'verification by facts',[64] how is he to prove, on that criterion, that *Zurechnung* is a necessary principle of thinking? or that the alleged connections of *Zurechnung* really work? Unable to prove either of these things, he talks about *Zurechnung* in terms of 'ideology' or 'illusion'.[65]

---

[62] *ELMP*, 185.

[63] *HPS*², VII; *PTL*, 80–1.

[64] Cf. 'Science and Politics', in *WIJ*, 350.

[65] I would like to thank Dr M. Dalgarno, Professor G. D. MacCormack, and Dr P. Gorner who helped me in the course of preparing this paper.

CHAPTER 2

KANT'S KELSENIANISM

HILLEL STEINER

THE learned and meticulous scholarship which Alida Wilson has brought to bear, in delivering a negative answer to the question posed by her title, prompts me into two opening confessions. First, it has not proved possible, within the scope conventionally allowed to commentaries, to deal with all the major points she raises. And in that respect, I have certainly done less than justice to a most impressive paper. But second, and even apart from these limitations, it seems as well to acknowledge at the outset that the largely dissenting arguments registered in what follows do not, in the final analysis, add up to a sufficient reason for rejecting Dr Wilson's general conclusion. Hence my execution of the respondent's traditional task—that of providing a coherent set of critical comments—has proved difficult, inasmuch as it involved navigating a course between the Scylla of redundant consonance and the Charybdis of eclectic nit-picking. I fear that the voyage has not been altogether successful and that Charybdis has claimed another victim.

The burden of Dr Wilson's paper is that Kelsen should be prosecuted under the Trade Descriptions Act for advertising his theory of law as a Kantian one. In this connection, the sentencing judge may wish to take into consideration the interesting fact that this kind of misdemeanour has become increasingly common in recent years and currently threatens to reach near epidemic proportions. Why is this? Almost one hundred years ago, the English translator of Kant's *Philosophy of Law* reported that

The very cry of the hour is, Fichte and Schelling are dead, and Hegel, if not clotted nonsense, is unintelligible; let us go back to Kant. Within the last ten years many voices have been heard, both in this country and in Germany, bidding us *return to Kant*, as to that which is alone sound and hopeful in Philosophy.[1]

[1] Kant, *Philosophy of Law*, tr. W. Hastie (Edinburgh, 1887), p. xvii.

Arrivals on the Kantian shore have, in the event, proved a more varied lot than merely the shipwrecked survivors of Fichte-Schelling-Hegel. But what is more to the point is the fact that their respective conceptions of this secure haven have been very nearly as diverse as the perils they managed to avoid or escape.

Thus Dr Wilson suggests that Kelsen's assumption of Kantian citizenship should be voided because his Kantian principles are compromised, not only by anti-Kantian ideas, but also by notions derived from neo-Kantianism. Evidently, space and our present interests permit neither an examination of the differences between Kantianism and neo-Kantianism nor, therefore, an assessment of the neo-Kantians' claim to have made good certain deficiencies in the teachings of the Sage of Königsberg, while remaining faithful to his philosophical method. Nevertheless, counsel for Kelsen clearly labours under a forensic handicap in attempting to vindicate his client's Kantianism, if the case is to be conducted on the presumption that the latter's *neo*-Kantian credentials count as evidence for the prosecution rather than the defence.

It is certainly indisputable, as Dr Wilson acknowledges, that Kelsen was strongly influenced by neo-Kantian thinking. But it is also true that the neo-Kantians saw their task as one of overcoming certain perceived contradictions in the *Critique of Pure Reason (CPuR)*, and of reconciling its central philosophical doctrines with several subsequent discoveries (particularly in mathematics) which are inconsistent with some of its more specific claims. Moreover, an important project of many later neo-Kantians was to extend *CPuR*'s account of the epistemological foundations of natural science to a corresponding account of the basic structure of the social and behavioural sciences, about which Kant himself had said little. Taken together, these facts constitute at least prima facie grounds for not entirely discounting the possibility that a theory of law, informed by neo-Kantian (and even some anti-Kantian) ideas, might none the less qualify as a coherent Kantian one.

So much by way of preliminary, and inconclusive, generalities. What is the basis of the case against Kelsen's Kantianism? I suggest that the heart of the matter lies in the question of whether there can be a *theory*—in Kant's sense of the term—of law, as such. Do laws inhabit the phenomenal or the noumenal world? Can we have knowledge of laws, as distinct from practical reasons for affirming laws? Can we describe without prescribing, in the field of law? For a Kantian, the answer to these questions must await the answer to the more general question of whether it is possible to describe or refer to a statement as a norm without endorsing it, without assenting to its appropriateness as a standard for conduct.

On the face of it, the answer to this latter question seems to be, 'Obviously, yes'. If the answer were 'No', a good deal of social and behavioural science would lack any foundation; nor is it certain that any sense could still be given to such concepts as 'institution' and 'practice'. And yet there are those who would say that a statement like 'One ought to cause as much suffering as possible' is not so much wicked, as strictly meaningless. To say this is a norm would, on this view of the matter, be like saying that centimetres are lazy. That is, persons taking this view would claim that the *meaning* of 'ought' and related terms is such that they cannot have, as their (primary) object, the causing of suffering. And it would follow from such a position that, although the statement in question has the grammatical form of a norm, it is nevertheless not a norm and cannot intelligibly be described or referred to as one. The factual judgment that 'action A causes gratuitous suffering' is sufficient to imply the normative judgment that 'action A ought not to be done'. In short, this view holds that the form and content of norms cannot be entirely dissevered one from the other.

Our present concerns clearly preclude any extensive consideration of this all too familiar metaethical issue. Nor, of course, can the validity of any particular resolution of it be determined by the implications it might have for the foundations of the social and behavioural sciences. But what *is* of importance to this discussion is whether the distinction between the form and content of norms—and with it, the possibility of non-committal reference to norms—possess a basis in Kantianism. For it is obvious that Kelsen heavily relies upon just this distinction, and that on it rests much of his account of the structure of one subject of our normative discourse—the legal system.

Let us begin, somewhat hazardously and obliquely, with that part of Kant's teaching that looks to be—and according to Dr Wilson, is—the least propitious for Kelsen's view of law. It is also the aspect of Kant's work that least interested those neo-Kantians whose doctrines so influenced the development of the Pure

Theory. I refer, of course, to Kant's moral philosophy. There are a number of good reasons for taking this as a starting-point, not the least of which is the fact that the *Metaphysics of Morals* and specifically, the first half of it entitled the *Metaphysical Elements of Justice*[2]—constitute Kant's only systematic writing on the subject of law. What I hope to show is that both the general moral philosophy and this text (which does not figure in Dr Wilson's paper) suggest that a Kantian view of law might pose many of the same difficulties, for the Kant of Dr Wilson's paper, that she acutely raises with regard to Kelsen.

Kant divides the field of moral judgment into two areas: the realm of virtue or ethics (*Tugend*) and the realm of justice (*Recht*). His credentials as a natural law thinker—d'Entrèves describes him as 'the most forceful exponent of natural law theory in modern days'—arise from his insistence (i) that legal norms must be governed by the requirements of justice, (ii) that there is a single and objective standard of justice—the Universal Principle of Justice (UPJ), and (iii) that the content of this principle is a deliverance of reason. Kelsen, as a legal positivist and ethical relativist, is committed to denying all three of these propositions. How, then, can he possibly be a Kantian?

To identify the affinity we must first explore a distinction. In differentiating justice from virtue, Kant is *not* doing either of two things. He is not distinguishing justice from only some particular virtue, for example, benevolence. And he is not denying that just conduct can be virtuous. Rather, he is saying that the requirements for an action to be just are different from those which qualify an action as virtuous—whether through its benevolence, prudence, courage, or whatever—though some actions may satisfy both sets of requirements. What qualifies an action as virtuous or ethical is the conformity of its intention with the first formulation of the Categorical Imperative (CI1), as set out in the *Foundations of the Metaphysics of Morals*;

Act only according to that maxim by which you can at the same time will that it should become a universal law.[3]

---

[2] Kant, *Metaphysical Elements of Justice*, ed. J. Ladd (Indianapolis, 1965); a modernized and abbreviated edition of *Philosophy of Law*; hereinafter *MEJ*.

[3] Kant, *Foundations of the Metaphysic of Morals*, ed. L. W. Beck (Indianapolis, 1959), p. 39; also entitled *Groundwork of the Metaphysic of Morals*; hereinafter *FMM*.

What makes an action just is its compatibility with UPJ:

Every action is just that in itself or in its maxim is such that the freedom of will of each can coexist together with the freedom of everyone in accordance with a universal law.[4]

Unlike the requirements of virtue, however,

The concept of justice does not take into consideration the matter [content] of the will, that is, the end that a person intends to accomplish by means of the object that he wills . . . Instead, in applying the concept of justice we take into consideration only the form of the relationship between the wills insofar as they are regarded as free, and whether the action of one of them can be conjoined with the freedom of the other in accordance with a universal law.[5]

UPJ, or the Law of Equal Freedom, appraises an action by reference *not* to the intention with which it is done but, rather, to its effect on the liberty of others—that is, by reference to its *distributional* effect on (external) liberty.[6] And thus, as one commentator has remarked, 'contrary to much traditional inter- pretation of Kant, some of the *unintended consequences* of one's actions are clearly of moral relevance in determining the rightness of those actions—at least with regard to perfect duties.'[7] That is, at least with regard to duties of justice. An action may be ethical or virtuous—may conform to CI1 by proceeding from a universalized intention—and yet be unjust, by encroaching on another's equal external liberty. Conversely, an action may be vicious, and yet infringe no one's rights under UPJ.

The aspect of human conduct governed by UPJ is, then, the effects of actions on the interpersonal distribution of external liberty, and the set of norms which are to embody and apply UPJ is the legal system. Legal rules, for Kant, thus pertain to the *phenomenal* aspects of actions, constitute essentially a liberty- allocating or *coercive* order and, thereby, forcibly restrict the range of performable actions including the range of performable virtuous actions. An action's conformity to CI1 is neither necessary

---

[4] *MEJ*, 35.   [5] *MEJ*, 34.

[6] Cf. Hart, 'Are There Any Natural Rights?', 64 *Philosophical Review*, 175–91 (1955); reprinted in Quinton, ed., *Political Philosophy* (Oxford, 1967), p. 36; also Hillel Steiner, 'The Natural Right to Equal Freedom', *LXXXIII Mind*, 194–210 (1974).

[7] Murphy, *Kant: The Philosophy of Right* (London, 1970), p. 104; see, also, R. C. S. Walker, *Kant* (London, 1978), p. 160.

nor sufficient to imply either its immunity from legal interference
or, therefore, the illegality of the norm which mandates that
interference.

It follows that there is a fundamental difference between legal
and ethical duties:

All [moral] legislation . . . consists of two elements: first, a law that
objectively represents the action that is to be done as necessary, that is,
makes the action a duty; second, an incentive that subjectively links the
ground determining will to this action with the representation of the law
. . . all legislation can nevertheless be differentiated with regard to the
incentives. If legislation makes an action a duty and at the same time
makes this duty the incentive, it is *ethical*. If it does not include the latter
condition in the law and therefore admits an incentive other than the Idea
of the duty itself, it is *juridical*. As regards juridical legislation, it is easily
seen that the incentive here, being different from the Idea of duty, must
be derived from pathological grounds determining will, that is, from
inclinations and disinclinations and, among these, specifically from
disinclinations.[8]

Unlike ethical rules, legal rules necessitate the performance of an
action by implying, of its non-performance, *not* that it violates CI1
but rather that it is penalized. The normativity of legal rules, the
mode in which they govern human conduct, lies—for Kant—*not* in
their being justified prescriptions addressed to free-willing agents,
but in their constituting cognitive (negative) stimuli which act
upon deterministically motivated subjects.

For Kelsen, the link between the antecedent and the consequent
of a legal rule is akin to the notion of causality which connects
antecedents and consequents in the laws of natural science. Dr
Wilson shows admirably how Kelsen's conception of this link—
Zurechnung or imputation—has taken several different forms in
his writings, though it is always conceived of as analogous to
causality in the Kantian scheme[9]—an analogy which she vigorously
contests. Is there, then, no Kantian warrant for thus linking non-
compliance with punishment? Kant's own words are:

Imputation (imputatio) in its moral meaning is the judgement by which
someone is regarded as the originator (*causa libera* ['free cause']) of an
action. . . . If this judgement also carries with it the juridical consequences of

---

[8] *MEJ*, 18–19.
[9] Wilson, p. 54; objecting *inter alia*, to 'the *new* notion of *Zurechnung*'
(emphasis added).

this deed, it is a judicial [*rechtskräftig*] imputation (*imputatio judiciaria s. valida*); . . . The juridical effect of demerit is punishment (*poena*).[10]

More generally, Dr Wilson maintains that

The structure of Kant's thoughts about morals and men is such that Kelsen could find no real footing there . . . In particular, it is difficult to understand Kelsen's professed acceptance of the Kantian distinction *Sein/Sollen*, since the notion of *Sollen* in Kant has as its core freedom of will and 'practical reason', whereas Kelsen . . . goes on to rule out freedom and practical reason in so far as he postulates the causal determinability of man's will by the idea of a norm. There is no room for conscious thinking affecting the willing. The idea of a norm, and the evil consequences of its violation . . . are 'motives' which 'cause' man's will to act with an 'irresistible compulsion'.[11]

Does endorsement of the cognition/disposition dichotomy rule out practical reason, as well as freedom? Beck offers the following view of what Kant means by 'practical reason':

Reason determines the action by which impulse is to be satisfied; when it does so, it is called 'practical reason' . . . [Kant] mentions the danger of taking the words 'practical reason' as if the 'object' of practical reason were comparable to an object of theoretical reason, i.e. an epistemological object and not as an object of desire or volition . . . [Practical reason] provides the cognitive factor in the guidance of action whose *dynamis* is impulse.[12]

More prosaically, in my faculty at the University of Manchester we have a Department of Decision Theory. Decision theorists, one may suppose, are in the business of discovering and elaborating various forms of practical reasoning. No doubt many of my colleagues in that department have, from time to time given some thought to the question of whether human beings are possessed of free will. But I should be surprised if any of them were to imagine that their jobs depend upon the truth of an affirmative answer to that question. (I shall return to this general problem further on in my commentary.)

Notwithstanding the absence of any clear conceptual relation between practical reason and free will, it might still be objected that the suggested affinity between Kelsen and Kant is unwarranted

---

[10] *MEJ*, 29. [11] Wilson, p. 40.
[12] Beck, *A Commentary on Kant's Critique of Practical Reason* (Chicago, 1960), pp. 39–40.

inasmuch as it overlooks the fact that, for Kant, law must be governed by UPJ. The objection is correct, but its force is uncertain. In what sense of 'must' must the law be just? Law governs the external aspects of actions—their consequences—and, in so doing, effects some interpersonal distribution of liberty. In what sense *must* this distribution be an equal one, as UPJ requires? Anterior to this question is the one which asks for the sense in which UPJ is itself a necessary element in our normative thinking.

It is clear that, for Kant, CI1 *is* such a necessary element. But as we have seen, it is not the case that an action which violates UPJ necessarily violates the requirements of CI1. My doing A may have the effect of infringing your equal liberty, but my intention in doing A—my maxim—may (and I would argue, must) have nothing to do with this effect, and may be one which I am perfectly able 'at the same time to will that it should become a universal law'. (An example frequently invoked by Kant himself is paternalistic rights-violation.) It is, I think, true that *if* actions are appraised in terms of their liberty-distributing effects, then UPJ presents itself as rationally necessary and its contradiction as inconsistent with CI1. But it is not rationally necessary that actors' intentions be informed by a concern with these effects. Therefore Kant's elsewhere apparent belief, that its consistency with UPJ is a necessary condition of an action's normative necessity or permissibility, reflects his own ethical priorities and commitments and not any conceptual truth. And the same, of course, is true of legislators and the norms they create.

That I adopt as a maxim the maxim of acting justly is a requirement that Ethics (rather than jurisprudence) imposes on me. . . . Admittedly, this law imposes an obligation on me, but I am not at all expected, much less required, to restrict my freedom to these conditions for the sake of this obligation itself. Rather, reason says only that, in its very Idea, freedom is restricted in this way and may be so restricted by others in practice. Moreover, it states this as a postulate not susceptible of further proof.[13]

That the legal system is a set of coercive, i.e. freedom-distributing, rules is insufficient to imply that it must be governed by what is, admittedly, the one specifically freedom-distributing principle that is consistent with CI1. (An alternative argument for ascribing rational necessity to UPJ—and, thereby, for construing justice as a condition of legality—has been that UPJ is an implication of the *second* formulation of the Categorical Imperative (CI2): 'Act so that you treat humanity, whether in your own person or in that of another, always as an end and never as a means only.'[14] But while there are persuasive grounds for holding that UPJ is indeed an implication of CI2, the same argument that worked against a CI1–UPJ implication also negates a CI1–CI2 implication. That is, I may do an action which has treating another only as a means as one of its effects, and yet do it with an intention which I am not merely able but also happy to universalize.)

Closely related to the foregoing discussion is the matter of how distant the ethical relativism and non-cognitivism, which Dr Wilson correctly attributes to Kelsen, actually remove him from Kant. Again, as with the more specific subject of legal rules, the case for fundamental divergence seems to rest more on a traditional construction of Kant's broad outlook—and on an assumption of Kantian consistency—than on what Kant's basic premisses actually entitle him to say. For it is difficult to see, and more recent moral philosophy offers no grounds to suppose, that there is any necessary tension between the ethical *formalism* with which Kant is indissolubly identified and ethical non-cognitivism and (at least some forms of) relativism. Kant's own belief, that CI1 can be made to yield material moral conclusions about the rectitude of such things as suicide, promise-breaking, cultivating one's talents, and beneficence, is now acknowledged as incapable of withstanding analysis and—as with his ascription of priority to justice—as reflecting his own ethical commitments.[15]

Where does all this leave us? We have found that even on the least favourable of Kantian terrains—the moral philosophy—the following Kelsenian positions receive fairly firm support:

(1) what determines the will to comply with a legal duty is a sanction and not the content of the duty itself;

(2) juridical legislation presupposes that willed conduct is 'externally' determined, rather than 'internally' freely chosen;

---

[14] *FMM*, 47.
[15] Cf. Wolff, *The Autonomy of Reason* (New York, 1973), pp. 157–73; Walsh, *Hegelian Ethics* (London, 1969), ch. IV; Ross, *Kant's Ethical Theory* (Oxford, 1954).

(3) a legal norm expresses a (kind of) causal relation between its condition and its consequence;

(4) rationality in normative willing does not necessitate a regard for the requirements of justice;

(5) justice is not a necessary condition of legality;

(6) the content of normative standards is independent of their form.

Although Kant does register some claims which are not compatible with (5), (6), and perhaps (4), his so doing is neither consistent nor well supported.

One might, therefore, feel entitled to conclude that a Kantian account of law which took seriously items (1), (2), and (3)—as well as Kant's insistence on the distinction between justice and virtue—would not end up looking so very different from at least some of the more salient features of the Pure Theory. If legal norms pertain to the external aspects of human conduct—if they connect temporally ordered events in the phenomenal realm—they are fit objects for scientific study and it is possible to have a *theory* about them, in the Kantian sense of that word. The normative (as distinct from descriptive) character of these norms would consist in their being addressed to discursively rational beings whose compliant conduct would be construed as the effect of (i) their being deterministically motivated to minimize harm to themselves, in conjunction with (ii) the operation of practical reason in calculating how to achieve (i). In short and, not inappropriately, as Hobbes did, legal norms could be construed as 'assertoric hypothetical imperatives',[16] which govern the behaviour of beings whose wills are, in Kant's own phrase, 'pathologically determined'.

Discussing Kant's 'two completely different views of the relationship between reason and desire in men', Wolff has argued convincingly against the traditional interpretation that desire is seen as a limitation or condition upon the will.[17] On this view, the rational will, as the author of moral duty, is locked in a constant struggle with the lure of inclination. Kant's own remarks to this effect are familiar enough:

And yet, strange as it may seem, if the central argument of the *Critique of Pure Reason* is correct, then such a conflict as Kant describes is absolutely

[16] Watkins, *Hobbes's System of Ideas* (London, 1965), ch. 5.
[17] Wolff, *The Autonomy of Reason*, pp. 119 ff.

impossible! In order for it to take place, the real, or noumenal, self would have to step into the temporal order of appearances and do battle with phenomenally determined inclinations. . . . But no coherent account can be given of such a struggle within the framework of the Critical Philosophy, as Kant from time to time reminds himself in the *Groundwork*. Any conflict about which we could speak significantly or whose episodes we could witness internally would have to be fought between mere appearances. It could only be a conflict of inclinations of the sort described by Hobbes and Hume.[18]

The more plausible view, and the one consistent with *CPuR*, is that 'desire selects the ends of our action, and reason identifies the most efficient means'. Adapting Kant's *CPuR* formulation of the relationship between concepts and intuitions, Wolff summarizes this view as 'Reason without desire is impotent; desire without reason is blind'.[19]

And yet, as I mentioned at the outset of this commentary, I am unable entirely to reject Dr Wilson's general conclusion. For although, as I hope I have shown, the distance between Kant and Kelsen may not be as great as she has suggested, there remains a deep problem for the sort of account of law intimated in the preceding paragraphs—a problem having to do, as best I can judge, with the concept of the Basic Norm and one the intractability of which may well be sufficient to undermine any such account. It is not inappropriate, therefore, to have this problem stated by Kant himself:

Among external laws, those to which an obligation can be recognized a priori by reason without external legislation are *natural laws*, whereas those that would neither obligate nor be laws without actual external legislation are called *positive laws*. Hence it is possible to conceive of an external legislation which contains only positive laws; but then it would have to be preceded by a natural law providing the ground of the authority of the legislator (that is, his authorization to obligate others through his mere will.)[20]

My concluding contention, then, is simply that if this is a problem for Kelsen, it is also one for Kant.

---

[18] Ibid., p. 2.   [19] Ibid., p. 119.   [20] *MEJ*, 26.

PART TWO

THE BASIC NORM

CHAPTER 3

THE PURITY OF THE PURE THEORY*

JOSEPH RAZ

KELSEN'S range of interests and creative impulses were prodigious. In constitutional law, international law, moral philosophy, political theory, and the philosophy of law he kept a lively interest throughout his life. To all those areas he made valuable contributions, bringing to them the fruits of his incisive and uncompromising reflections. On many issues his contributions are of lasting value and will continue to stimulate students and scholars for many years to come.

Some commentators have expressed exasperation in face of what they regard as Kelsen's obscurities and have dismissed some of his central doctrines as confused. I myself have not escaped the occasional feeling of despair in struggling to fathom the meaning of some of his theses. But I have always had the sense that he was a philosopher grappling with some of the more difficult problems of legal philosophy, problems the complexity of which he often understood better than anyone. All too often I have discovered that my sense of puzzlement at some of his doctrines was due to my failure to grasp the difficulties which Kelsen tackled and was striving to solve. His central doctrines have acquired for me a somewhat haunting character. Every time I return to them I discover new depths and new insights which had escaped me before. It is, therefore, as a personal tribute to his work's continuing fertilizing influence that I have chosen to return once more to review some of Kelsen's fundamental doctrines.

I

Kelsen's reputation for obscurity contrasts with his reputation for logical rigour. Logical rigour he certainly respected and aspired to achieve. There is a fascinating sense of great austerity about his

* This paper was first published in 138 *Revue Internationale de Philosophie* 441 (1981).

work. Of course this austerity did not remain a matter of personal style. It became the cornerstone of his legal theory, the purity of it.

Kelsen's theory is, as is well known, doubly pure. It is free of sociological and psychological investigations and it separates law from morality.[1] The first purity has attracted much criticism and is generally regarded as having been completely discredited. The criticism is based on one or the other of two quite separate objections. First is the objection that the content of the law cannot be established without regard to the actions and intentions of legal institutions be they legislative or adjudicative.[2] Second, there is the objection that the law and its significance cannot be appreciated unless one studies it in its social context, with an emphasis on its actual effects in practice. Both objections are familiar and I will not discuss them in detail. Let me, though, make a couple of observations about the second one.

It is beyond doubt part of the task of legal philosophy to explain the methods by which the existence and content of the law are ascertained. If it is true that they cannot be ascertained without regard to the practices and manifested attitudes of legal institutions then the first objection is—as I believe it to be—an important valid objection to Kelsen's theory. It is less clear that the second objection is an objection at all. Kelsen did not deny the possibility of sociological jurisprudence. He was content to maintain four theses. First, that beside sociological jurisprudence there is also an independent enquiry, normative jurisprudence, whose subject is different. Normative jurisprudence is the study of legal norms, that is, the study of how people ought to behave according to law. It is not an enquiry into how they actually do behave. Second, normative jurisprudence is no less empirical than sociological jurisprudence, since it is concerned exclusively with *positive* law, that is, law as the product of the activity of social custom and of legislative and adjudicative institutions. Thirdly, normative jurisprudence enjoys in an important way a logical priority over sociological jurisprudence. The very definition of the subject-matter of sociological jurisprudence presupposes an understanding of law as provided by its normative study, since sociology of law is the study of those aspects of human behaviour which are related to the law. Here 'the law' must be normatively interpreted. Fourthly,

---

[1] Cf. e.g. *PTL*, 1.
[2] Cf. Hart, 'Ķelsen Visited' 10 *UCLA Law Rev.* 109 (1963).

normative jurisprudence is presupposed by sociology in another important way as well. The explanation of human behaviour related to law has to take account of the way people's beliefs about the law, normatively understood, affect their behaviour.[3]

I think that Kelsen was essentially right in all four theses. They show that he was not hostile to sociological jurisprudence, though admittedly his own interests did not take him that way. Though these views have since been independently explored and developed by both social scientists and philosophers, I do believe that Kelsen has anticipated many of the arguments used by other thinkers and that we can still benefit from his explanation of the relations between the normative and the sociological study of the law. Both his emphasis on the explanatory importance of people's beliefs concerning what they are normatively required to do and his insistence on the autonomy and distinctness of normative concepts are a valuable and lasting contribution to a subject which has been for years dominated by reductive attempts to provide eliminative definitions of normative terms in favour of non-normative, descriptive ones.

II

Kelsen's semantic anti-reductivism is of course intimately connected with the other purity of Kelsen's theory: its being free of moral elements. Here the antagonists were not the sociological theorists but the natural lawyers. The opposition to natural law was a major preoccupation of Kelsen and he wrote extensively on the subject throughout his life. His views place him in the historical tradition of legal positivism.

Three major theses have been traditionally associated with legal positivism.[4] First is the reductive semantic thesis which proposes a reductive analysis of legal statements according to which they are non-normative, descriptive statements of one kind or another. Second is the contingent connection thesis according to which there is no necessary connection between law and moral values. Third is the sources thesis which claims that the identification of

---

[3] See, for a detailed discussion, *GTLS*, 162–78.

[4] Cf. my discussion of these problems in *Practical Reason and Norms* (London, 1975), Section 5. 3 and *The Authority of Law* (Oxford, 1979), essay 3. See also, Hart, 'Positivism and the Separation of Law and Morals', 71 *Harvard Law Rev.* 593 (1958).

the existence and content of law does not require resort to any moral argument.

The three theses are logically independent and one is free to accept any one of them while rejecting the others. They were, however, collectively endorsed by many leading positivists such as Bentham, Austin, Holmes, and Ross among others. Where does Kelsen stand on these issues? The question is of the utmost importance to the understanding of his theory of law. In many ways it is the most important set of problems that any philosophy of law has to face since it raises the problem of the double aspect of law, its being a social institution with a normative aspect. The supreme challenge for any theory of law is to do justice to both facets of the law.

Kelsen's solution is to reject the reductive semantic thesis and to embrace the contingent connection and the sources theses. Kelsen regards the law as positive law. It is based on social sources identifiable without any reference to moral argument. On this Kelsen never had any doubt. He never wavered in his endorsement of the two aspects of the thesis. The existence or non-existence of a legal system as a whole is a matter of social fact. It depends entirely on its efficacy in the society in question. Moreover, the test determining for every individual rule whether it belongs to a legal system in force in a certain country is equally a matter of social fact. It turns on whether or not it was posited in the appropriate way: whether or not it can be traced to an authorized social source.

Equally firm is Kelsen's belief in the contingent connection thesis. Kelsen insists that (1) to claim that there is a necessary connection between (the content of) law and morals either presupposes absolute moral values to which the law necessarily conforms or assumes that all the divers relativistic moralities have some values in common and that the law conforms to those. He further argues that (2) there are no absolute moral values and there is no common content to all the relativistic moralities. Hence he concludes that there is no necessary connection between law and morals.[5]

Kelsen's departure from the traditional positivist view is in his rejection of the semantic reductive thesis. Reductive positivists

---

[5] Cf. *PTL*, 63–5.

have variously argued that legal statements are statements about commands, or predictions of the likelihood of sanctions or of courts' decisions, etc. Kelsen is adamant in rejecting all reductive analyses of legal statements. He holds that that 'a norm . . . is "valid" means that it is binding—that an individual ought to behave in the manner determined by the norm.'[6] Kelsen regards legal statements as fully normative statements. This view of his, as has been often noted, is difficult to reconcile with his acceptance of the sources and of the contingent connection theses which leads him to say at the same time that 'juristic value judgments are judgments which can be tested objectively by facts'.[7] It is in his handling of the tension between his non-reductive semantic views and the sources and contingent connection theses that one finds his most original contribution to the general theory of law. It is this tension which leads directly to his best known doctrine, that of the basic norm.

III

Before we turn to an examination of this aspect of Kelsen's contribution it has to be conceded that Kelsen's own espousal of the two positivist theses leaves a lot to be desired. Kelsen's defence of the sources thesis is largely dependent on the view that the 'scientific' study of law would not be possible if the identification of law turned on moral argument.[8] But this argument is clearly fallacious. The study of law must be adjusted to its object. If its object cannot be studied 'scientifically' then its study should not strive to be scientific. One can learn from the nature of an object how it should be investigated but one cannot postulate that the object has a certain character because one wishes to study it in a certain way.

Nor is Kelsen's defence of the contingent connection thesis more convincing. Not only has he failed to establish that there are no absolute values nor even that there is no common ground to all relativistic moralities, he has failed to perceive the nature of the problem and addressed himself to the wrong question. Four elements contribute to this failure. First, from a relativistic point of view the right question for a person to ask is whether the

[6] *PTL*, 193.   [7] *WIJ*, 227.   [8] Cf. *GTLS*, 5.

morality which he shares does lead to the conclusion that there is a
necessary connection between law and *this* morality, that is,
whether *this* morality is such that all legal systems whatever they
may be do necessarily enshrine some of the values which it
proclaims. For a relativist this question is of practical and
theoretical importance. Clearly an affirmative answer to it does
not require an affirmative answer to Kelsen's question whether
there are common values to *all* relativistic moralities which are
respected by all legal systems.

Second, the question whether the law by its content necessarily
conforms to moral values is not the only pertinent question to ask.
Another is whether obedience to law is always morally required
regardless of the content of the law. Possibly it is required because
it is expected by others or because it will reciprocate their
obedience. After all, Kelsen regards law as existing only if
efficacious. I do not wish to maintain that this fact gives rise to any
moral obligation. But it must be acknowledged that if it does, this
will show a necessary connection between law and morals which
does not depend on the content of the law.

Third, Kelsen's discussion is coloured by his conception of
natural law as a theory which maintains that unjust laws are not
valid laws at all. But many natural law theories do not conform to
this view. Consider three prominent recent examples. Fuller,
Dworkin, and Finnis maintain that there is a necessary connection
between law and morality. But none of them denies that there may
be valid unjust laws.[9]

Finally, Kelsen here as elsewhere considers only conclusive
moral force and neglects the possibility of a connection between
law and morality which lends the law a prima facie moral character
which may be overridden by conflicting moral considerations.

When we examine the views of the three authors I mentioned,
we find that they tend to emphasize a connection between law and
morality resting on various content-independent features of the
law which does not exclude the possibility of valid unjust laws and
which endows the law with only a prima facie moral force.

[9] Fuller, *The Morality of Law* (New Haven, 1964); Dworkin, *Taking Rights
Seriously* (London, 1977); Finnis, *Natural Law and Natural Rights* (Oxford, 1980).
Incidentally while all three reject the contingent connection thesis only Dworkin
rejects the sources thesis. Fuller's and Finnis's writings are consistent with a weak
version of the sources thesis. For a distinction between a weak and a strong version
of this thesis see my *The Authority of Law* (Oxford, 1979), essay 3.

Kelsen's arguments for the contingent connection thesis are inadequate against such theories. The inadequacy of Kelsen's arguments does not, of course, mean that the views he thus tried to justify are themselves misconceived. But it is not my intention here to examine these theses.[10] Instead let us return to the question of their compatibility with a non-reductive semantic view of the analysis of legal statements. The question is crucial to the success of the second purity of the pure theory, its purity from moral elements. This purity seems to be guaranteed by the sources and contingent connection doctrines. But isn't that purity undermined by the views that legal statements are ordinary normative statements just like moral statements?

IV

I have already mentioned that Kelsen's rejection of semantic reductivism was a departure from traditional positivist views. Another legal philosopher who shares his anti-reductivism is H. L. A. Hart, and it may help clarify Kelsen's position briefly to describe Hart's first.

As is well known, Hart distinguishes two kinds of statements standardly made by the use of deontic sentences, which he calls internal and external statements.[11] External statements are statements about people's behaviour and attitudes and need not concern us. Hart's notion of internal statements is fraught with difficulties. I will outline without detailed textual argument my understanding of it when applied to the law and I will refer to such statements as legal statements.[12] The law is for Hart an immensely complex social practice or set of practices. In part the meaning of legal statements can be given a truth-conditional analysis. Legal statements are true if and only if certain relations obtain between

[10] In *The Authority of Law* I have defended the sources thesis. Regarding the contingent connection issue one has to be more specific. I have argued that whatever moral character the law has it is not enough to establish a prima facie obligation to obey the law. This leaves open the possibility of a necessary connection between law and morals of a lesser force.

[11] Cf. Hart, *The Concept of Law* (Oxford, 1961), pp. 56–8, 86–8, 244. For a discussion of Hart's anti-reductivism see Baker, 'Defeasibility and Meaning', in Hacker and Raz, eds., *Law, Morality and Society: Essays in Honour of H. L. A. Hart* (Oxford, 1977), p. 26.

[12] A similar analysis can be applied to his views of moral statements of duties but not to other normative statements.

them and the complex legal practices. But it would be wrong to say that legal statements are just statements about the existence of those practices. The truth-conditional analysis does not exhaust the meaning of legal statements. To understand them one must also understand their standard uses and what they express. Their typical use is to provide guidance by criticizing, commending, demanding, advising, approving, etc., and they express acceptance by the speaker of standards of behaviour towards conformity with which the statement is used to guide its addressee.

This view of legal statements is meant to accommodate both their social-factual and their normative aspects. The factual aspect is captured by a truth conditional analysis. The normative one is accounted for by an explanation of the illocutionary force of the statements and by the fact that they express not only the speaker's beliefs but also his practical attitude, his willingness to be guided by certain standards.

One would expect Kelsen to propound a view of legal statements rather like Hart's since Hart's account shares three of the most important features of Kelsen's doctrine of the law and of legal discourse. First, the existence of law can be objectively ascertained by reference to social facts. Hence Hart says, and one would expect Kelsen to agree, that legal statements are either true or false and that their truth conditions are their relations to complex social practices. Second, Hart, like Kelsen, regards legal statements as having a normative dimension which cannot be reduced to an assertion of any social facts. Third, Hart's account of the normative dimension in terms of the illocutionary and expressive force of legal statements avoids any reference to moral facts and does not presuppose the existence of moral values. Since Kelsen denies the existence of absolute moral values one might have expected him to provide an analysis of legal discourse along lines similar to Hart's.

Despite these similarities Kelsen's view of legal statements is radically different from Hart's, because Kelsen advances a cognitivist interpretation of all normative discourse. He rejects expressive explanations such as Hart's. For him a normative statement, be it legal, moral, or other, expresses a practical attitude only in that it expresses a belief in the existence of a valid norm, and a norm constitutes a value.[13] Hence the normative

[13] *WIJ*, 179.

aspect of legal statements is not to be explained by their illocutionary force nor by the fact, taken by itself, that they express an acceptance of a standard of behaviour. It has to be explained by the fact that such statements state or presuppose the existence of a value or a norm, that is, a normatively binding standard and not merely a social practice.

This understanding of Kelsen's position is not without its difficulties. He says, for example, that '[t]here is not, and cannot be, an objective criterion of justice because the statement: something is just or unjust, is a judgment of value . . . and these value judgments are by their very nature subjective in character, because based on emotional elements of our mind, on our feelings and wishes. They cannot be verified by facts, as can statements about reality. Ultimate value judgments are mostly acts of preference. . .'[14] This passage suggests a non-cognitive interpretation of moral statements. But for the most part Kelsen adopts a cognitive view and regards every normative statement, legal or otherwise, as a statement of a binding norm or of the value it institutes. Such a semantic view is of course consistent with value-scepticism. It will merely lead the sceptic to the belief that all normative statements are false. Kelsen, however, is not a sceptic. He is a subjectivist or a relativist. Normative statements can be true or false. It is merely that their truth depends on the existence of relativistic rather than absolute values: 'relativistic . . . positivism does not assert that there are no values, or that there is no moral order, but only that the values in which men actually believe are not absolute but relative values.'[15]

Unfortunately Kelsen's version of relativism is the familiar and incoherent one by which relativism is the non-relativist position that each person's values apply only to himself and each society's values to itself.[16] It is, of course, Kelsen's semantic doctrine rather than his theory of morals than I am concerned with. But the troubles with this kind of relativistic morality infect the interpretation of moral statements. It seems to suggest the oddity that sincere moral statements of a person about his own conduct are always true. Since he believes that there is a norm that he ought to perform a certain action, there is, in virtue of the relativistic morality, such a norm and his statement is true. Insincere moral statements about

[14] *WIJ*, 295.   [15] *WIJ*, 179.   [16] Cf. e.g. *PTL*, 59–69.

oneself are always false. The person does not believe that there is such a norm and therefore it does not exist and the statement is false. Normative statements about other people would be on this view true if and only if they accord with those other people's beliefs about themselves. Thus it is true that a racist should behave in a racist way.

None of this is acceptable and Kelsen does not explicitly draw such conclusions. He simply avoids talking of truth as applied to moral statements though he has no alternative account consistent with the rest of his doctrine. I believe that it is possible to provide a coherent relativist account of morality and that it can serve as a basis for a cognitivist interpretation of moral statements. But this is obviously not a task for this occasion. All that one can derive from Kelsen himself is the view that normative statements should be given a cognitivist interpretation, that they state the existence of duties, rights, powers, or permissions and do not merely express the speaker's attitude. Whatever other speech acts are performed in normative discourse the one speech act common to it is that of stating what is alleged to be the case.

V

Legal statements are normative statements in the same sense and in the same way that moral statements are normative. This is as we saw the gist of Kelsen's semantic anti-reductivism. The implication of his persistent emphasis is that legal statements are 'ought' statements, not to be confused with 'is' statements. The threat that this view poses to the purity of one's theory of law is evident. If legal statements are as normative as ordinary moral ones, if they are moral statements, then the law and its existence and content, which is what legal statements state, seem to be essentially moral facts. But the study of moral facts and their identification cannot be pure of moral considerations and arguments.

Kelsen's solution is threefold. First, he points out that the existence of law can be established and its content ascertained without the use of normative statements. The law can be described in sociological terms, be described as a power structure in a society, etc. Such a description is not synonymous with a normative description of the law. If it were then it would amount to a reductive analysis of the normative description. But such a description will convey all the social facts which form the factual basis of the law, all the social practices which Hart regards as constituting the existence of law. What will be left out is the claim that these social facts are 'objectively valid': that they give rise to rights and duties and to other normative consequences. Some people have the appropriate moral beliefs and they regard the law as a normative system and describe it using legal statements. Those who do not share those moral views deny that the law is normative. But they can acknowledge its existence as a social fact.

But this first answer to the problem is not enough. It shows the possibility of a pure study of law as a complex social fact but it does not by itself establish the possibility of a pure study of law as a *normative* system. Therefore, Kelsen reinforces the first move with a second one. People have many moral beliefs. It is likely that for any individual in a society some of his moral beliefs coincide with the law and some diverge from it. But imagine a man whose moral beliefs are identical with the law. He does not add nor detract one iota from it. Furthermore assume that his moral beliefs all derive from his belief in the moral authority of the ultimate law-making processes. For him, in other words, his belief in the validity of all and only the legal norms is not a haphazard result of chance but a logical consequence of one of his beliefs. Let us call this person the legal man. Legal science, says Kelsen, studies the law as a normative system but without committing itself to its normativity. Basically the legal statements of legal science are conditional legal statements: if the legal man is right, they say, then this is what you ought to do: 'The Pure Theory', he says, 'describes the positive law as an objectively valid normative order and states that this interpretation is possible only under the condition that a basic norm is presupposed according to which the subjective meaning of the law-creating acts is also their objective meaning. The Pure Theory thereby characterizes this interpretation as possible, not necessary, and presents the objective validity of positive law only as conditional—namely conditioned by the presupposed basic norm.'[17] Therefore all the legal statements of legal science are hypothetical.[18]

My legal man is one who endorses the basic norm and all that follows from it and nothing else. Scientific legal statements, being

---

[17] *PTL*, 217–18.   [18] *PTL*, 71.

conditional statements of the form 'if the legal man is right then one ought to . . .' or 'if the basic norm is valid one ought to . . .' etc., are value-neutral. They are free of any moral presuppositions. By using them legal science can both be pure and describe the law as a normative system.

The problem with this second answer is that although it allows legal science to describe the law as a normative system it does not allow it to use categorical statements for they state that the law is a system of valid norms. It merely enables legal science to state what the law is *if it is valid*. This may be all that legal scholars need do. But it is not all that legal practitioners, barristers and solicitors, do. They do not merely talk about the law. They use it to advise clients and to present arguments before courts. Kelsen does not distinguish between the scholar and the practitioner. His analysis of legal discourse is meant to apply to both. But the practitioner does not state what the law is if it is valid. He states that it is valid. Yet if legal theory is pure such statements cannot be moral statements. They cannot be full-blooded normative statements. Kelsen requires a value-neutral interpretation of categorical legal statements. He solves this problem by making his third move. Legal scientists, he says, do not merely describe what the law is if the basic norm is valid. They do actually presuppose the basic norm themselves. They assume its validity. 'The basic norm really exists in the juristic consciousness.'[19]

Kelsen sometimes draws obscurely on a distinction between positing and presupposing the basic norm,[20] to suggest that legal scientists (by which he refers to practitioners as well) presuppose but do not posit it as do people who actually believe in the moral validity of the law. This terminological distinction is not a happy one. His idea seems to be that not all scientific legal statements are hypotheticals of the type analysed above. Some or most are categorical statements based on a presupposition of the basic norm as a fiction.[21] Categorical legal statements are therefore of two types which I have called elsewhere committed and detached.[22] Committed statements are those of ordinary people who use normative language when stating the law because they believe or purport to believe in its binding force. Detached statements are

---

[19] *GTLS*, 116.   [20] *PTL*, 204 n.

[21] Cf. 'On the Pure Theory of Law', 1 *Israel Law Rev.* 1, 6 (1966).

[22] Cf. Raz, *The Authority of Law* (Oxford, 1979), essay 8 and see, also, essay 7.

typical of legal science which assumes the point of view of the legal man without being committed to it. It describes the law in normative statements but this is a description from a point of view which is not necessarily accepted by the speaker. He talks as if he accepts the basic norm and this pretence is what Kelsen refers to as presupposing the basic norm as a fiction. Detached statements state the law as a valid normative system; they do not merely describe what would be valid if the basic norm is valid. But they do so from a point of view, that of the legal man, to which they are not committed. Therefore, legal science is pure of moral commitment despite its use of normative language.

VI

I have ascribed to Kelsen the view that there are three types of legal statements.

(1) Statements conditional on the validity of the basic norm, which are morally uncommitted since their normative force depends on the unasserted condition: if the basic norm is valid then . . .

(2) Detached statements, which are also morally uncommited since they are statements from a point of view. They state what rights and duties there are on the assumption that the basic norm is valid but without commitment to that assumption.

(3) Committed statements, which are ordinary moral statements about what ought to be done, what rights and duties people have because of the law.

Legal theory contains statements of the first two kinds only and is therefore pure.

It has to be admitted, of course, that this is more a reconstruction than a straightforward interpretation. Kelsen does not distinguish clearly between the three classes and he himself confessed to confusing the last with the other two on occasion.[23] Worse still, while I believe that he was generally aware of the distinction between the committed statements and the others, he appears completely unaware of the difference between the detached

---

[23] *PTL*, 204 n.; 218 n.

statements and those conditional on the validity of the basic norm. Here I think it is fair to accuse him of confusion and equivocation. He does shift from one position to the other without noticing the difference. I have tried to separate the strands of thought as clearly as I can. But such a reconstruction is bound to remain tentative and controversial.

Interpretation apart the question arises how illuminating are these distinctions. I ask 'how illuminating' and not 'are they true' for it is clearly a programme for an explanation rather than a full explanation that Kelsen provides. We may approach the problem by comparing Kelsen (or should I say the reconstructed Kelsen?) with Hart.

Committed statements are essentially the same as Hart's internal statements with two important differences. First, Kelsen's is a cognitivist whereas Hart's is a non-cognitivist interpretation of the normativity of a statement. For Kelsen such statements are normative because they express a belief in the validity of a norm. For Hart they are normative because they express an attitude of willingness to be guided in a certain way. Second, Kelsen tends to identify all normative attitudes and beliefs as moral ones. Hart takes pains to explain that moral reasons are only one type of reason for accepting rules and for having the kind of practical attitude manifested in internal statements.

I will disregard the first difference for the moment. The second is sometimes thought to explain why Hart need not resort to Kelsen's distinction between committed and detached statements. All that Hart has to establish to be consistent with his own doctrine of the separation of law and morals[24] is that ordinary legal discourse does not commit one to a moral approbation of the law. Ordinary legal discourse consists of internal statements and those though expressing a practical attitude of acceptance of the law as a guide for behaviour do not necessarily express acceptance on moral grounds. Even if one accepts that the interpretation of legal discourse has to be freed only of moral evaluation and not of other kinds of normative evaluation Hart's position is still difficult to maintain. The crucial point is that much legal discourse concerns the rights and duties of others. While one can accept the law as a guide for one's own behaviour for reasons of one's own personal

---

[24] Cf. Hart, *The Concept of Law*, ch. IX and 'Positivism and the Separation of Law and Morals', 71 *Harvard Law Rev.* 593 (1958).

preferences or of self-interest one cannot adduce one's preferences or one's self-interest by themselves as a justification for holding that other people must, or have a duty to, act in a certain way. To claim that another has to act in my interest is normally to make a moral claim about his moral obligations.

There are to be sure reasons on which claims about other people's duties and rights can be based which are neither moral reasons nor the speaker's self-interest or preferences. But none of them nor any combination of them is likely to explain the widespread use of normative language in legal discourse. I find it impossible to resist the conclusion that most internal or committed legal statements, at any rate those about the rights and duties of others, are moral claims.[25]

This conclusion creates a dilemma. Either most legal statements express moral endorsement of the law or not all legal statements are internal statements as understood by Hart or committed statements à la Kelsen. Hart rejects the first horn of the dilemma and he is surely right to do so. Clearly many legal statements do not express a moral position either way. This fact need not be disputed by natural lawyers and is indeed accepted by Finnis.[26] Hart is therefore bound to conclude that not all legal statements are internal. They cannot plausibly be said to be external statements since these are not normative statements but statements about other people's actions and beliefs. Hart has no alternative account. Kelsen has his doctrine of detached statements which provides the framework for a solution to the dilemma by explaining a class of statements which are normally made by the use of normative language, which are not about behaviour or beliefs but about rights and duties and which are none the less not committed and not internal statements.

VII

I have said in my introductory remarks that Kelsen's most celebrated doctrine, that of the basic norm, is a direct result of the purity of the theory of law. Let me conclude by commenting on the connection between the theses. First, the ground for the doctrine

---

[25] I am not saying that people who make such statements have the moral beliefs they express. They may be insincere.

[26] See *Natural Law and Natural Rights*, pp. 234-7.

of the basic norm is prepared by Kelsen's cognitivist interpretation of legal statements. A person who believes that one should behave in accordance with a certain social practice does not merely have an attitude which inclines him to demand conformity to and criticize deviation from the practice. He is so inclined to behave because he believes in the validity of norms requiring such behaviour.

Norms can be divided into two types. Some are dynamically derivative while others are not. A norm is dynamically derivative if its validity depends on the occurrence of an action which creates it. Actions can create norms if they are authorized to do so by some other norms. Those other norms may themselves be derivative ones. But any normative system must contain at least one non-derivative norm and all its derivative norms must be subsumed under non-derivative norms. Both these conclusions are immediate results of Kelsen's principle of the autonomy of the normative, of his insistence that 'ought' cannot be derived from 'is', values cannot be derived from facts.

Laws are, as we have emphasized before, positive norms. That is, they are all dynamically derivative norms. But this means that the legal system will not be complete unless it also contains a non-derivative, that is, a non-positive, norm which authorizes, directly or indirectly, all the positive laws of the system. That norm is the basic norm, that is, a norm authorizing the creation of the historically first constitution and thus indirectly of all the other norms of the system.[27]

I have said that the basic norm has to be non-derivative, non-positive. This calls for further explanation. Individuals who do not regard the law as normatively valid do not, of course, believe in the validity of the basic norm at all. Those who accept the validity of the law may still not believe in its basic norm. Some may, for example, believe that many but not all of its norms are intuitively self-evident. Some but not all of the others may be believed by them to have been authorized by divine command and the rest to be binding because it was their parents' will that they should obey them. Such people while accepting the validity of all the law do not attribute it to the basic norm described by the theory of law.

[27] Cf. Harris, 'Kelsen's Concept of authority', 36 *Cambridge Law J.* 353 (1977); Paulson, 'Material and Formal Authorization in Kelsen's Pure Theory', 39 *Cambridge Law J.* 172 (1980).

Others may believe in the moral validity of some but not all the laws of the system. They too do not believe in the validity of the basic norm (which authorizes all the laws). They derive the validity of those laws they believe in from some other norm(s) which do not entail the validity of the laws they do not believe to be valid.

The point is that norms relativistically understood are always to be looked at from the point of view of some person or group and that every person or group is likely to believe in more or less than the validity of all positive law. Very few people are like the legal man postulated above. But legal men are the only ones likely to accept the Kelsenian basic norm as their ultimate non-derivative norm. Despite this the basic norm is the key to the scientific understanding of the law. The reason is that legal theory to remain pure cannot study the law in so far as it is embedded in the moral beliefs of one person or another. That would violate the sources thesis by making the identification of the law dependent on a particular set of moral beliefs. To be pure, legal theory must strictly adhere to the sources thesis and identify the law by social facts only. Hence to describe it normatively it must non-committally or fictitiously accept the basic norm of the legal man, that is, the Kelsenian basic norm, for it is the only one to give validity to the *empirically established* law and to nothing else. This, then, is the sense in which the basic norm is the scientific postulate of legal thought.

This claim clarifies the dual role of law-creating facts in the law. On the one hand they establish the character of law as a social fact. All the norms created and identified in certain ways which are by and large efficacious, constitute a complex social practice by which members of the society guide and co-ordinate their actions. This is the function of law-creating facts as establishing the membership of certain norms in a system which is socially practised. On the other hand those facts transmit normative force from the authorizing norm to the authorized one. Since the authorizing norm is valid and since it endows those acts with law-creating status the norm they are meant to create is also valid. This is the role of law-creating acts as conferring validity, transmitting binding force from one norm to another.

Moreover, it is not accidental that law-creating facts fulfil both roles. Legal theory is the normative study of a social normative system. Therefore, given its purity it represents as norms only those rules which belong to the effective social order. In other words it is the character of law-creating acts as criteria for membership in a socially effective system which qualifies them to serve as facts transmitting validity from one norm to another.

Once more we can improve our understanding of Kelsen's meaning by comparing it with Hart's. Hart's focus of interest is on the character of law as complex social practice. He describes the existence conditions of social rules and then he turns to normative social systems and introduces the notion of criteria of validity as a test of membership in a social practice tying legal rules indirectly to the complex practice. He is not specifically interested in the descent of normative force from one norm to another. Validity for him indicates just membership in a system established in a certain way. It has little to do with binding normative force.

Therefore from Hart's point of view there is no difference between the role of legislative acts and the social practice which establishes the existence of a rule of recognition. Both are relevant as establishing the membership of certain rules in a legal system. Not so for Kelsen: he emphasizes the fact that a legislative act not only establishes membership, it also confers normative force on the norm created. But the social practice which ties the ultimate legal rules to social reality, while it too is relevant to establish membership of the rule in an effective legal system (and also to establish the effectiveness of the system) does not fulfil the other role of transmitting normative force. To assume otherwise is to regard law as consisting of derivative laws only, which is, for Kelsen, a logical impossibility. If the judicial practices which according to Hart establish the existence of the rule of recognition were also to endow it with normative status this could only be in virtue of yet another norm which would then become itself the ultimate rule of the system.

I believe that this argument correctly reflects our unreflective thinking about the law. Judges regard the fact that a statute was enacted by Parliament as a reason to regard it as binding and to hold the litigants to be bound by it. But they do not necessarily regard the judicial practice of enforcing Parliamentary enactments as a reason for enforcing them, that is, as a reason for accepting the rule of recognition as binding. They may accept the rule of recognition because they believe in Parliamentary democracy or in some law and order argument, etc. But those norms which make them accept the binding force of the rule of recognition are not themselves part of the law. From the point of view of the study of law the ultimate rule is the rule of recognition directing the courts to apply Parliamentary legislation. The judicial practice of following the rule identifies it as part of a system effective in that society and helps establish the social existence of the whole system. Hart is right about this and Kelsen is guilty of overlooking or oversimplifying many of the facts which establish the social character of the law. But Kelsen is right in pointing out that these judicial social practices do not confer binding force on the ultimate legal rules and are not generally believed to do so. In this they differ from other law-creating acts. From the point of view of a pure study of law the validity of ultimate legal rules is simply (non-committally) assumed.

CHAPTER 4

KELSEN'S *RECHTSSÄTZE* AS DETACHED STATEMENTS

ROBERTO J. VERNENGO

I

I SHALL discuss some of Dr Raz's theses concerning not only the semantical, but mainly the pragmatical status of some normative statements found in the *Reine Rechtslehre*.[1] I do not intend to deal with the web of sentences that constitute the theoretical discourse of Kelsen's work. This point has already been examined elsewhere.[2] I shall try to examine some kinds of normative statements that are studied by the *Reine Rechtslehre*.

It is required, according to the prevailing reading of the *Reine Rechtslehre*,[3] to draw a clear distinction between those normative statements that Kelsen calls *Normen* and those normative statements, referring to norms, that are designated as *Rechtssätze*. The difference between *Norm* and *Rechtssatz* (translated into English as *rule of law*[4]) may be envisaged as one between different levels of language. Norms are the expression—at least in the very late Kelsen[5]—of the sense (*Sinn*) of acts of will. Norms are stated usually through linguistic signs (written or verbal); but they can adopt another form of external representation, like the red or green lights in a system of traffic controls. *Rechtssätze*, on the

---

[1] Cf. *RR*², translated into Spanish by the author of this paper.
[2] Cf. Gioja, *Ideas para una filosofía del derecho* (Buenos Aires, 1973), t. 1. The essay, 'El tema de la Teoría Pura del Derecho', p. 85 ff has a foreword by Kelsen: 'I [Kelsen] assure you of my complete agreement with the views you expressed regarding the questions we discussed, especially the relationship of the pure theory of law and logic, and the object of jurisprudence.'
[3] The theme appears first in *HPS*¹; it was discussed at length by Kelsen in *Problemas escogidos de la Teoría Pura del Derecho* (Buenos Aires, 1952) and was developed further in *RR*², p. 73 ff.
[4] That is how Wedberg translates it in *GTLS*. The original German is unknown.
[5] Cf. *Recht und Logik*, (Wien, 1965); *ATN*, ch. 1, iii.

other hand, can only be linguistic expressions; they are descriptive sentences about norms.

I would agree, without much ado, that it is not clear, prima facie, that a normative statement (and *Rechtssätze* are normative sentences for Kelsen) might be understood as a pure description of a norm. To describe, in principle, is to enunciate a property, or a set of characteristics, that the object or fact described has. A description is a kind of definition or classification. Because every description depends on the set of properties that he who proposes the description wants to emphasize, there is not one exclusive description of an object, but an infinite number of possibilities.

When Kelsen suggests that the normative sentences called *Rechtssätze* are to be understood as descriptions of norms, he claims, at least, that they state: (1) that the mentioned norm exists (that is, in Kelsen's terminology, 'is valid') in a certain positive legal order; (2) that the stated norm specifies some duty or right. Or, perhaps even better, that the function accomplished by the norm in some context is clarified (norms, according to Kelsen, may order some conduct or its omission; they may also authorize some organ to create new norms or to derogate from them). Finally, (3) the *Rechtssatz* must give some hint of the categorization applied to the empirical normative material given by the law-giver.[6] In other words, *Rechtssätze* state what the law is for a certain case or for a class of cases. If there is a norm prohibiting theft and fixing a sanction for it—what continental criminal theory calls the 'precept' and the 'norm' respectively—that fact[7] may be described by a set of sentences indicating (1) that a norm (or norms) to that effect (or effects) exists (has been promulgated); (2) that it has accordingly to be taken as true that a law-creating organ has ordered the judge to send thieves to prison; and, (3) that it is possible, in

---

[6] The essay mentioned in n. 2, above, discusses how Kelsen distinguished between material and formal categories, following ideas formulated at the beginning of the century by Husserl. There are material categories of the general theory of law (*Zurechnung* is specifically mentioned as such) including 'right', 'duty', and 'judicial person'. Other concepts are part of legal science and are used to classify, order, and systematize normative material; some of these notions can be construed as *regional* categories in Husserl's sense, e.g. 'contract' or 'guilt' (*culpa*) which are neither pure categories nor empirical or descriptive concepts.

[7] For Kelsen we can say a norm is a fact in that in the test for its existence (validity) an empirical fact has to be verified, namely the fact of its creation. Furthermore, as Moore indicated long ago, the word 'fact' is so vague that it would not be a sensible objection to say that the existence of a norm is not a 'fact'.

consequence, to conceive that what is technically called a legal sanction ought to take place, with the implied theoretical corollaries.[8]

It is clear—at least in the latest form of the *Reine Rechtslehre*—that the distinction between *Norm* and *Rechtssatz* is not a purely grammatical one. The grammatical surface structure of a norm and a *Rechtssatz* may be the same. The norm condemning theft, mentioned above, can be read in the penal code of a certain country; exactly the same words can be found in a legal commentary. If they differ, there must be some contextual marker referring to different syntactical, semantical, and pragmatical structures—a deep structure—where norm and *Rechtssatz*, although literally identical, diverge.

We must find in a *Rechtssatz* some sign, or set of signs, set apart for the purpose of naming the norm that is to be described (classified, analysed, systematized, etc.). It is a well-known feature of natural languages that they may use the surface form of a sentence (in our case, of a norm) to describe the mentioned sentence (the norm described). In verbal utterances, the distinction must be given by some contextual marker; in written language, quotation marks are conventionally used to that effect. In a *Rechtssatz*, therefore, we could say that norms are mentioned, or referred to, by the same linguistic sentence that is used to apply them. Norms, we can say, appear in the *Rechtssätze* obliquely,[9] and consequently they cannot perform any of the functions considered as distinctive of norms by Kelsen.[10]

Kelsen considers that the difference is basically semantical; in a norm, performing any of the functions he considers essential, the verb *sollen* does not only the job of a general syntactical marker of

---

[8] If the fact, A, is classified as a legal sanction, that implies not only the existence of other norms that can be logically derived from it (e.g. if the sanction is a duty of an organ, then it is also an act legally permitted to it), but also implies the existence of other norms that have to be presupposed (e.g. those designating the sanctioning organ). There is no norm in isolation, as Kelsen remarks.

[9] Cf. in Frege, *Über Sinn und Bedeutung*, the discussion of embedded sentences in imperative contexts.

[10] Cf. *ATN*, ch. 25 for an analysis of the functions of norms; *Gebieten, Erlauben, Ermächtigen, Derogieren*. These functions of norms are different possible senses (*Sinne*) of acts of will. They should not be confused with the deontic modality of the norm resulting from the act of will. Thus the sense of an act of will may be ordering (*Gebieten*), but the norm resulting from that act can have whatever deontic character be wished.

a deontic modality,[11] but it expresses as well a volition. In other words, it expresses the signification of an act of will: *der Sinn eines Wollens*. In *Rechtssätze*, therefore, the verb *sollen* is not used, but mentioned. It is mentioned through the modal verb appearing in the norm embedded in the *Rechtssatz* (or is implied in the name designating the norm in the legal sentence). But, as the *Rechtssatz* also indicates what normative function the norm performs and under what normative category it has to be construed, it has to use the *Sollen* descriptively, says Kelsen.[12] The *Sollen* in the *Rechtssatz* —the 'descriptive' *Sollen* and the 'mentioned' *Sollen*—does not order, forbid, authorize, or derogate anything at all. It does not perform any normative function. The descriptive *Sollen* cannot be reduced to the normative *Sollen* nor vice versa. They are semantically different things. This is also one of the important features of what is known as the purity of the *Reine Rechtslehre*.

These theses, and the arguments following from them, are rather difficult to accept. In any case, they ratify one aspect of Raz's pronouncement concerning Kelsen's semantic anti-reductivism.

II

Kelsen believes that norms are either valid or invalid. *Rechtssätze*, on the other hand, are true or false. Truth and validity are not even analogous.[13] They are not isomorphic syntactical or semantical properties of sentences. When Raz states that 'legal statements are normative statements in the same sense and in the same way that moral statements are normative',[14] and when he adds that there is to be found 'the gist of Kelsen's anti-reductivism', one is tempted to conclude that some confusion has crept in between norms and sentences describing norms. Moral statements would be ordinarily understood as norms, and not as metaethical sentences. 'Legal statements' may refer both to norms and to sentences describing norms. Norms, evidently, are normative; whereas *Rechtssätze* are not normative in Raz's meaning. For Kelsen, they would be 'descriptively normative'.

It is true that legal norms, as has been said before, may have the

---

[11] That is the thesis in *RR*², 5.   [12] *RR*², 77.
[13] Cf. *Recht und Logik* (1965).   [14] Raz, p. 88.

same syntactical structure as other norms (moral norms, for instance) and even, of sentences describing norms. But that resemblance obtains only if we remain at the level of a syntactical (grammatical) surface analysis. Semantically and pragmatically it is not true that legal norms have the same structure as legal statements, if by legal statements one understands *Rechtssätze*. Indeed, given the characteristics regarded by Kelsen as essentially belonging to *Rechtssätze*, it is clear that they cannot have the same sense as normative or declarative statements concerning moral rules. *Rechtssätze* are not metaethical pronouncements in any sense whatsoever.

In this context, I think it would be useful to discuss Raz's interpretation of the basic norm. The notion of a basic norm (*Grundnorm*)—which, as is well known, did not originate in Kelsen's writing, but was taken from Merkl's work—has a very complicated development in the *Reine Rechtslehre*[15] and in the general theory of law. It should be clear that what the *Reine Rechtslehre* enunciates and analyses is not a basic norm of a positive law, but the general scheme of a *Grundnorm überhaupt*. The basic norm that legal scientists assume as valid when describing and systematizing a concrete positive legal order is a material presupposition of an objective knowledge of that positive law; the *Grundnorm überhaupt* and its scheme is, for Kelsen, without doubt, an epistemological category.

As a category of legal thinking it is not a psychological ingredient of that kind of intellectual activity; it is, in Kant's words, a *reine Verstandesbegriff*. As such, it is not an empirical, but a transcendental, condition of a type of *synthetische Vorstellung und ihre Gegenstände*.[16] The epistemological synthesis that objective (scientific) legal thinking brings about is called by Kelsen 'imputation' (*Zurechnung*); the object or fact thus made possible is *law*. The basic norm of a positive legal order is not a

---

[15] Cf. *La función sistemática de la norma fundamental* (University of Buenos Aires, 1960) where the several functions of the *Grundnorm* are studied and where its characterization as a sentence in the metalanguage of legal science is examined. Account must be taken in the evolution of Kelsen's thought about the basic norm and of his recanting the theory of the *Grundnorm* and the later assumption of a fictitious will.

[16] *CPuR*, A 92; B 124. If the *Grundnorm* implied some kind of moral attitude, it could not be understood, as Kelsen wished, as an epistemological (transcendental) category.

category in this sense; it is worked out by an intellectual process where the pure category is applied to empirical material.[17]

Serious difficulties are encountered in the interpretation of Kelsen's doctrine, if this distinction between the basic norm as epistemological category and the basic norm as a defining factor of a concrete legal order is not taken into account.

Kelsen assigns different functions to the *Grundnorm* in its second sense (i.e. not as a pure epistemological category). The core of these functions consists in being the ultimate theoretical criterion for conferring normative validity, in an objective manner (i.e. intersubjectively), to the normative material that the legal scientist tries to describe and to systematize. The *Grundnorm*, in that sense, is for Kelsen also a norm, not only from a syntactical but also from a semantical point of view as well. It is not a *positive* norm because it has not been willed by any law-creating organ. The basic norm has no source. It has to be envisaged as a mere presupposition of whatever type of objective legal knowledge is to be attained. Objective legal knowledge is a *possible* theoretical endeavour that sometimes, in some cultures, lawyers (legal scientists) can bring about by elaborating certain empirical data.[18] By presupposing a basic norm, as a specific criterion of validity (that is, determining the primary source of all data that will be recognized as positive norms), it becomes possible to reconstruct, at an objective theoretical level, parts of or the totality (ideally) of some determinate normative material.

Against Raz's assertion,[19] I believe that it would be nonsense for Kelsen to say that the 'study of law must be adjusted to its object . . . One can learn from the nature of an object how it should be investigated, but one cannot postulate that the object has a certain character because one wishes to study it in a certain way.' For Kelsen, as for any neo-Kantian, there could not be an object, as object of objective knowledge (science), before it is epistemologically constituted or constructed. The construction of the object—in our case, *law*—requires not only a logically well-structured language, but also a congruent set of categories. Only in that logical space would it be possible to work out a scheme

---

[17] I refer to Kant's theory of *Schematismus* as regards its significance for an interpretation of the pure theory, see my essay, 'Norma jurídica y esquema referencial' (*Boletín Mexicano de Derecho Comparado*, No. 21, Mexico, 1977).
[18] Cf. Kelsen's prologue to *RR*[1].   [19] Raz, p. 83.

through which some transcendental category would specify what is law and what is not. This function, in Kelsen's work, is fulfilled by the *Zurechnung* as category and the *Grundnorm* as its scheme. For Kelsen, there is no law in itself, with its own nature and proper characteristics, before it is constituted as such by the objective knowledge of positive jurisprudence; law, as a pre-scientific object, would be, for Kelsen, something perhaps given in another field of experience, different from the law that the legal scientist studies and the lawyer works upon.[20]

III

If what has already been said on the theme of the *Grundnorm* of a positive legal order—a sentence, or set of *Rechtssätze*, defining the criteria of validity applicable to some empirically given normative material—is correct, it seems to me that Raz's distinction between three kinds of 'normative statements' cannot be brought to bear upon the basic norm.

In the first place, what Raz calls 'morally uncommitted statements', such as: 'if the basic norm is valid, then . . .', where the legal statement formulated by the 'legal man' does not imply any moral commitment whatsoever, could not be used or predicated of basic norms of positive legal orders without falling in the trap of self-reference: the validity of a basic norm of a positive legal order would be conferred by the same basic norm, which is nonsense. The basic norm of a positive legal order does not give validity to itself. Besides, the phrase 'the basic norm is valid' cannot refer to, nor does it express, a norm (a directive expressing a will) in respect of which there is place for attitudes of moral commitment. As the *Grundnorm* is not, in Kelsen's terminology, the sense (*Sinn*) of an act of ordering, prohibiting, authorizing, or derogating, it can be construed, as an alternative, as a sentence in a metalanguage. For instance, in the language of theoretical legal discourse the phrase referring to the validity of the basic norm (of a positive legal order) says something about an element of the theoretical reconstruction of the normative material. But then, for *this* interpretation, the property of 'validity', attributed to the

---

[20] Cf. Gioja's essay mentioned in n. 2, above, as regards the problem of the pre-scientific constitution of the object 'law'. Kelsen refers to the point in the first pages of *GTLS* when he mentions the possibility of defining 'law' on the basis of ordinary language.

basic norm in the metalanguage, cannot mean the same as the property of 'validity' that, presupposing the basic norm, can be asserted or denied of positive norms.

Validity in the legal metalanguage (the discourse of positive jurisprudence, at one level, and in the discourse of a general theory of law, at a superior one) would perhaps resemble Tarski's concept of truth, that is, a semantical concept. As the sentence 'the snow is white' is true (has the semantical characteristic of being true), if the fact is that the snow is white, we would have, in the legal discourse, that the norm (normative sentence) 'thieves ought to be condemned to prison' is valid (that is, descriptively, that it ought to be followed), if there is, as a fact, the presupposition by legal science of a basic norm establishing when a norm is valid.

What is clear, so far, is that it is unthinkable that basic norms of positive legal orders (and *a fortiori*, as category of legal thinking) could be the object of moral attitudes. These are absolutely irrelevant. As moral attitudes imply reference to a moral code, or to some moral norm, we would have to face the problem of unifying or differentiating two or more normative systems, a task that would have no place within Kelsen's scheme.

It is also undoubtedly clear that in Kelsen's thought the basic norms of positive legal orders have nothing to do with a material justification of the content of positive norms—they are only one of the necessary elements for the descriptive formulation of a dynamic system of norms, as Kelsen envisages the theoretical reconstruction of normative material as objective law. Therefore, it does not add anything to our understanding of Kelsen to state that basic norms could be considered as 'morally uncommitted statements'.

But if that is true, then neither does it make sense to regard the basic norm of a positive legal order as what Raz calls a 'detached statement', or 'statements from a moral point of view.'[21] A statement can be envisaged as 'detached' only when it is susceptible of positive or negative (moral) commitments. But, to what attitude can one refer when one speaks of a detached or a committed attitude regarding what is only an epistemological presupposition? It sounds odd to speak of, or to discuss, the possibility of

---

[21] Raz, 90; *The Authority of Law* (Oxford, 1979), p. 153 ff.

'believing' a basic norm, if that expression is taken in one of Kelsen's senses.[22]

On the other hand, it must be accepted as true—more: it is true by definition inside the theory—that if, according to Kelsen's ideas, some empirically given normative material can be ordered and systematized by legal science, the system thus set up 'must contain at least one non-derivative norm', namely, the basic norm.[23] But then, some misunderstanding arises when it is stated that the system also contains the basic norm. The basic norm is part of a legal system in quite a different sense than the derivative norms, that is, the positive norms. That a legal system contains a derivative norm—in Raz's terminology—means that there is a norm authorizing an organ to create a norm and that the act of creation has taken place. That a system contains a basic norm—as it must also contain other elements necessary for the construction of a theoretical language, like some kind of logic, for instance—means that it is possible to formulate what are the sufficient criteria lawyers (legal scientists) take into account when determining whether a norm is part of the system or not; whether or not it is a valid norm.

Therefore, it is correct to say, as Raz does,[24] that 'the basic norm has to be non-derivative, non-positive'. That is true in so far as it means that the basic norm (of a positive legal order) is not a thesis attained by derivation into the system, but is, as Kelsen says, a hypothesis or presupposition of the system as a whole and of the validity of each of its derivative norms. As such, as a working hypothesis of the theoretical elaboration of normative material (expression of acts of will), it makes no sense to inquire whether or not it is susceptible of beliefs; whether or not it can be the matter of moral, political, or religious attitudes; whether or not it is the possible subject-matter of moral commitments. Pragmatically speaking, it works as an assumption, not as a belief. As an assumption, it must be valid, in order that other norms (derivative in Raz's terminology) may be valid or invalid. From a logical point of view, it resembles what is called a logical presupposition.[25]

---

[22] Raz, 94.   [23] Ibid.   [24] Ibid.

[25] Cf. Cooper, *Presupposition* (The Hague, 1974); Petöfi and Franck, eds., *Presuppositions in Philosophy and Linguistics* (Frankfurt, 1973). 'The presupposition of a sentence is standardly defined as a necessary condition of that sentence being true or false. For example "He has been a smoker" is said to be a

It can certainly be taken as a mere terminological question to consider whether or not the basic norm is part of the law, whether or not it is contained in the legal system. It depends only on what we are to understand by 'system'. But, if what we are dealing with is what Kelsen understood, then I would suggest that the basic norm of a positive legal system is not a norm, performing normative functions, contained in the system, but, on the contrary, a theoretical assumption of jurists. It is not a norm at all, but a sentence obtaining in the theoretical discourse that 'describes' norms, as Kelsen likes to characterize it. Such epistemological presuppositions need not be ideological. Nor are they, as presuppositions, unconditionally true; they may be adequate for establishing an ordered and systematized reconstruction of the law. This is important, because it must be remembered, if Kelsen is to be understood correctly, that there is no cognition of law prior to legal theory.

The point of departure is not the law, or its nature; the point of departure of the *Reine Rechtslehre* is the fact of the existence, in some cultures, of an objective knowledge of the law, the fact of the existence of legal science.

presupposition of "He has given up smoking", in the sense that one would not be inclined to assert or deny the latter unless the former were true'—Smith and Wilson, *Modern Linguistics* (London, 1979), p. 165. Or, in another interpretation, 'propositions can be regarded as functions from the set of all possible worlds to the truth-values "true" and "false". In a logic with presuppositions, one could regard these functions as being defined (having values) only for a restricted set of worlds, namely those worlds where the presuppositions of the proposition are fulfilled. This set of worlds would then be the domain of the proposition.' Allwood, Andersson, Dahl, *Logic in Linguistics* (Cambridge, 1977), pp. 149–50.

CHAPTER 5

THE FUNCTION OF A CONSTITUTION

HANS KELSEN

TRANSLATED BY IAIN STEWART

TRANSLATOR'S INTRODUCTION

'Die Funktion der Verfassung' originated as a paper written for a
law conference in Vienna in 1964—although, owing to illness,
Kelsen was unable to attend and the paper was read on his behalf
by someone else. It appears in the published proceedings of the
conference.[1] A revised version was published in the same year in a
Viennese journal.[2] The revised text is translated here. The
principal difference between the two texts is that the revised
version omits toward the end some discussion on the applicability
of logic to norms. This or similar material appears in later articles
that are already available in English.[3]

[1] *Verhandlungen des zweiten Österreichischen Juristentages Wien 1964* (Vienna,
Manz), Bd. II, Tl. 7, pp. 65–76.
[2] 11 *Forum* 583–6 (1964); reprinted, with only editorial variations, in *WRS* II,
1971–9.
[3] See the articles on law and logic in *ELMP*. I would like to express my sincere
gratitude to Dr. Bärbel Meyer for her assistance with the original version of the
translation, [1980] *Juridical Review* 214–24 and to Professor Stanley Paulson for his
assistance with this version. Notes to the original version discuss in detail the
differences between the two German texts.

THE FUNCTION OF A CONSTITUTION

The law is a system of norms, and norms are the meaning of acts of will that are directed toward the conduct of others. These acts of will are acts of will of human beings or of suprahuman beings—as with the acts of will of God or, as in the case of so-called natural law, of Nature. However, only norms that are the meaning of human acts of will are to be considered as legal norms—more exactly, as norms of a body of positive law. These have the characteristic of regulating their own creation and application.

Acts of will that are directed toward the conduct of others are, primarily, commands. But not every command is a norm, and not every norm is a command. A norm may also be an authorization to issue commands. If a robber demands that I give him my money, the meaning of his act of will, i.e. of his command, is not a norm. Nor do I violate any norm if I refuse to comply with his command. The subjective meaning of his act of will, that I *ought* to give him my money, does not become its objective meaning—that is, it is not interpreted as a binding norm, such as for example a command addressed to me by a tax official that I ought to hand over a specified sum of money. Why is the meaning of the act of will, the *ought*, in the one case also the objective meaning of the act—that is, a binding, valid norm—but in the other case not? To put it differently: what is the basis of the validity of the norm, which exists in the one case but not in the other? The answer is: because in the one case—that of the command by the tax official—the act, the meaning of which is an ought, is authorized by a valid norm, but in the other case it is not. By virtue of this norm authorizing the act, the subjective meaning of the act becomes also its objective meaning—a binding, valid norm. The authorizing, higher norm is the basis of the validity of the authorized, lower norm.

The idea that the basis of the validity of a lower norm is the validity of a higher norm appears to lead to an infinite regress. For the higher, authorizing norm is itself the subjective meaning of an act of will directed toward the conduct of others; and only if this act too is authorized by a still higher norm is its subjective meaning also its objective meaning—that is, a binding, valid norm. A simple example may clarify this point: A father addresses to his son the individual norm, 'Go to school.' The son asks his father, 'Why should I go to school?' That is, he asks why the subjective meaning of his father's act of will is its objective meaning, i.e. a norm binding for him—or, which means the same thing, what is the basis of the validity of this norm. The father responds: 'Because God has commanded that parents be obeyed—that is, He has authorized parents to issue commands to children.' The son replies: 'Why should one obey the commands of God?' What all this amounts to is: why is the subjective meaning of this act of will of God also its objective meaning—that is, a valid norm? or, which means the same thing, what is the basis of the validity of this general norm? The only possible answer to this is: because, as a believer, one presupposes that one ought to obey the commands of God. This is the statement of the validity of a norm that must be presupposed in a believer's thinking in order to ground the validity of the norms of a religious morality. This statement is the basic norm of a religious morality, the norm which grounds the validity of all the norms of that morality—a 'basic' norm, because no further question can be raised about the basis of its validity. The statement is not a positive norm—that is, not a norm posited by a real act of will—but a norm presupposed in a believer's thinking.

LAW AND MORALITY

Let us now take an example from the domain of law. The distinction between law and morality consists in the fact that the law is a coercive order—that is, that the law seeks to bring about a specific mode of human conduct by attaching to the opposite mode of conduct, as sanction, a coercive act, the forcible taking away of life, of freedom, or of economic or other value. If someone steals, he ought to be imprisoned—by force if necessary. By this norm, the law prohibits theft. Morality too seeks to bring about a specific mode of human conduct, and morality too provides for sanctions. But these sanctions are the approbation of moral conduct and the disapprobation of immoral conduct, not coercive acts—nor do these sanctions serve as the means by which moral conduct ought to be brought about.

The general legal norm, 'If someone steals, he ought to be imprisoned' is, to begin with, only the subjective meaning of an act of will of the legislator. This norm is applied through the judicial decision that Smith, who has stolen a horse from Jones, ought to be imprisoned for one year. This judicial decision is interpreted as a binding, valid, individual norm. Yet this norm too is, to begin with, only the subjective meaning of an act of will of the judge directed toward the conduct of an executive organ. If we interpret this subjective meaning also as the objective meaning—that is, as a binding norm—and hence understand a person performing that act as a 'judge'—we do so because that act is authorized by a general norm, contained in a statute: 'If someone steals, the judge competent to hear the case ought to punish him with imprisonment'. The validity of the lower, individual norm is grounded by the validity of the higher, general norm. And the judge, in fact, so grounds his judgment that it conforms to a valid general legal norm that authorizes him.

However, a general norm contained in a statute—as, indeed, the whole statute—is, to begin with, itself (as we have noted) only the subjective meaning of the act of will of a person, or of the majority of the persons forming a legislative body. The essential function of a legislator is the positing of general norms that determine the procedure of the law-applying organs, in particular the courts, and the content of the individual norms to be posited by these organs. To be sure, a 'statute' may also contain things other than such general norms. This is why one distinguishes 'statute' in the formal sense from 'statute' in the material sense—or, more precisely, 'statute-*form*' from 'statute'—that is, a specific procedure from the essential function of that procedure, the creation of general norms.

If one asks why the subjective meaning of the legislator's act is also its objective meaning, i.e. a general norm; why the person performing that act is a 'legislator'; in other words, what is the basis of the validity of the norm posited by the legislator's act; the answer is: because the act, the subjective meaning of which is the general norm, is authorized by the *constitution*. In this authorizing of specific persons to create general norms lies the essential function of a constitution. If one distinguishes various forms of state—such as monarchy, aristocracy and democracy—the decisive criterion is that the constitution authorizes in the first case a single specifically qualified individual, in the second a relatively limited group of specifically qualified individuals, and in the third the (as it is sometimes inexactly put) whole people—more correctly, a popular assembly or a popularly elected parliament—to create general norms.

True, the document that one calls 'the Constitution' usually also contains other provisions than this kind of authorization. Thus one must distinguish between constitution in the formal sense and constitution in the material sense—more correctly, between constitution-*form* and constitution. Constitution-form is a particular procedure in which a constitution created in the material sense, whatever the way in which it has come into existence, can be passed or amended. This procedure is distinct, essentially if not always by this alone, from the ordinary procedure of legislation, in that the coming into existence of a valid resolution—that is, an act of will passing or amending the constitution—is bound by constraining conditions. The aim of such constraint is to lend the greatest possible stability to the authorization to create general legal norms, i.e. to the form of the state. Occasionally a constitution—that is, the document so named—contains the provision that the norms regulating the procedure of legislation must not be altered at all, or not in such a way as to alter the form of the state.

If one asks what is the basis of the validity of a given constitution, the answer may be that that constitution came into existence through amendment of a preceding constitution, and that this amendment was made in the way that constitutional amendments on the basis of the preceding constitution have to be made. Thus one can refer back to a historically first constitution. This historically first constitution too is, to begin with, the subjective meaning of an act of will or a number of acts of will; and if one asks why the subjective meaning of the act creating the constitution is also its objective meaning—that is, a valid norm—or, in other words, what is the basis of the validity of this norm, the answer is: because one presupposes, as jurist, that one ought to conduct oneself as the historically first constitution prescribes. That is the basic norm. This basic norm authorizes the individual or the sum of individuals who laid down the historically first constitution to posit norms that represent the historically first constitution. If the historically first constitution was laid down by a resolution of an assembly, the basic norm authorizes the individuals forming that assembly; if the historically first constitution arose by way of custom, the basic norm authorizes this custom—or, more correctly, it authorizes the individuals whose conduct forms the custom giving rise to the historically first constitution.

NORM AND JUSTICE

This is the basic norm of the legal order that is founded ultimately upon the historically first constitution. It is the 'basic' norm, because no further question can be raised about the basis of its validity; for it is not a posited but a presupposed norm. It is not a positive norm, posited by a real act of will, but a norm presupposed in juristic thinking. It represents the ultimate basis of the validity of all the legal norms forming the legal order. Only a norm can be the basis of the validity of another norm.

To grasp the essence of the basic norm, one must above all keep in mind that it refers directly to a particular constitution that has in fact been laid down, whether created by custom or by formal statement. That is to say, it refers to the facts in which the norms of the constitution are posited, which norms are the subjective meaning of these facts—yet indirectly it refers to the general and individual norms of the legal order which are in fact posited in conformity with the constitution, i.e. the basic norm refers indirectly to the facts whose subjective meaning these norms are. That means that the basic norm refers only to an effective constitution—that is, to a constitution in conformity with which statutes, and judicial and administrative decisions in conformity with statute, are in fact made.

The basic norm is thus not a product of free invention. It refers to particular facts existing in natural reality, to an actually laid down and effective constitution and to the norm-creating and norm-applying facts in fact established in conformity with the constitution. Nevertheless, what content this constitution or the national legal order built on its foundation has, be that order just or unjust, does not come into question, nor whether that legal order in fact guarantees relative peace within the community constituted by it. In the presupposing of the basic norm, no value transcending positive law is affirmed.

Inasmuch as only the presupposing of the basic norm makes it possible to interpret the subjective meaning of the facts in which the constitution is laid down and of the facts established in conformity with the constitution as their objective meaning—the norms which are the subjective meaning of these facts as objectively valid legal norms—the basic norm as presented in legal science may be characterized (if a concept from the Kantian theory of knowledge may be applied here by analogy) as the transcendental-logical condition of the judgments with which legal science describes law as objectively valid order.

Just as Kant asks how it is possible to have an interpretation, free from all metaphysics, of the facts given to our senses, in terms of laws of nature formulated by natural science, so a pure theory of law has asked how it is possible to have an interpretation of the subjective meaning of certain facts as a system of objectively valid legal norms, describable in legal propositions, without recourse to metalegal authorities such as God or Nature. The epistemological answer of a pure theory of law is, on the condition that one presupposes the basic norm: one ought to conduct oneself as the constitution prescribes, that is, in conformity with the subjective meaning of the act of will creating the constitution, the commands of the creator of the constitution. The function of this basic norm is to ground the objective validity of a positive legal order, i.e. the norms, posited by human acts of will, of a by and large effective coercive order—that is, to interpret the subjective meaning of these acts as their objective meaning.

The basic norm may be termed 'constitution in the transcendental-logical sense', as distinct from the constitution in the positive-legal sense. The latter is the constitution posited by human acts of will, whose validity is grounded by the presupposed basic norm.

The basic norm may, but need not, be presupposed. What ethics and legal science say about it is: only if it is presupposed can the subjective meaning of acts of will directed toward the conduct of others be interpreted also as their objective meaning, these meaning-contents be interpreted as binding moral or legal norms. Since this interpretation is conditioned by the presupposing of the basic norm, it must be granted that ought-propositions can be interpreted as objectively valid moral or legal norms only in this conditioned sense.

To the assumption of a norm not posited by a real act of will but only presupposed in juristic thinking, one can validly object that a norm can be the meaning only of an act of will and not of an act of thinking, that there is an essential correlation between 'ought' and 'willing'. One can meet this objection only by conceding that, along with the basic norm, presupposed in thought, one must also think of an imaginary authority whose (figmentary) act of will has the basic norm as its meaning.

With this fiction, the assumption of the basic norm turns out to be contradictory to the assumption that the constitution, whose validity is grounded by the basic norm, is the meaning of an act of will of a supreme authority, over which there can be no higher authority. Thus the basic norm becomes a genuine fiction in the sense of Vaihinger's philosophy of 'as if'. A fiction in this sense is characterized by its not only contradicting reality but also containing contradiction within itself.[4] For the assumption of a basic norm—such as, for instance, the basic norm of a religious moral order, 'One ought to obey the commands of God', or the basic norm of a legal order, 'One ought to conduct oneself as the historically first constitution determines'—not only contradicts reality, since no such norm exists as the meaning of an actual act of will, but also contains contradiction within itself, since it represents the authorization of a supreme moral or legal authority, and hence it issues from an authority lying beyond that authority, even though the further authority is merely figmentary.

For Vaihinger a fiction is an aid to thinking, of which one avails oneself if the aim of one's thinking cannot be reached with the material available. The aim of one's thinking in presupposing the basic norm is: to ground the validity of the norms forming a positive moral or legal order; that is, to interpret the subjective meaning of the acts positing these norms as their objective meaning, i.e. as valid norms, and the acts in question as acts positing norms. This object can be attained only by way of a fiction. Therefore one has to keep in mind that the basic norm in the sense of Vaihinger's 'as if' philosophy is not a hypothesis—as I myself have occasionally characterized it—but a fiction, which is distinct from a hypothesis in that it is or should be accompanied by an awareness that reality does not correspond to it.

HIERARCHY OF NORMS

The relation between a higher and a lower norm lies in the validity

---

[4] This sentence summarizes Hans Vaihinger, *The Philosophy of 'As If'*, 2nd edn. (London, 1935), pp. 97–100.

of one norm grounding, in one way or another, the validity of another norm. A norm is related to another norm as higher to lower if the validity of the latter is grounded by the validity of the former. If the validity of the lower norm is grounded by the validity of the higher norm, in that the lower norm was created in the way prescribed by the higher norm, the higher norm, as it relates to the lower, has the character of a constitution; thus the essence of 'constitution' consists in the regulating of the creation of norms. Then a statute—which regulates the procedure in which the law-applying organs, in particular the courts, create individual norms —is a 'constitution' in relation to these organs' procedure, just as the 'constitution' in the more narrowly specific sense of the word is a constitution in relation to the procedure of legislation and the constitution in the transcendental-logical sense is a constitution in relation to the historically first constitution, the constitution in the positive-legal sense.

In this manner, the concept 'constitution' is relativized. Seen from the viewpoint of the basic norm, both a positive moral order and a positive legal order are a generative framework, inasmuch as the basic norm only determines by whom the norms of the moral or legal order ought to be posited—that is, only the highest norm-positing authority is determined, without determining the content of the norms that this authorized authority is to posit. The norms that are posited by the highest moral or legal authority—God, or the creator of the constitution—authorized by the basic norm can themselves authorize further authorities to posit norms and thereby determine or not determine the content of the norms to be posited. Seen from the viewpoint of the highest moral or legal authority authorized by the basic norm, the structure of the positive norms forming the moral or legal order is not necessarily merely a generative framework.

In the sphere of morality this is quite evident, since the highest moral authority never authorizes another, lower authority to posit norms with any content the latter may like. The norm proclaimed by Paul, 'One ought to obey the authorities,' certainly does not mean that one ought to obey even a command of the authorities that offends against certain norms posited directly by God, such as 'You shall have no other god but me.' In the sphere of law it is, as a rule, just the same, since the constitution usually does not confine itself to determining the procedure for creating general legal norms—legislation, as it is called—but very often also at least negatively determines the content of future statutes, by precluding certain contents—such as the limitation of freedom of expression or freedom of religion, or the taking into consideration of certain inequalities, such as that of race.

However, the general norms posited by the legislator always determine not only the procedure of the organs that are to apply these norms, but also the content of these norms, so that a positive legal order, too, at least as seen from the viewpoint of the statutes, is not merely a generative framework. A legal order of the latter character is conceivable, however: the legal order of Plato's ideal state authorized the judges, without their being bound by predetermined general norms, to decide individual cases according to their own discretion.

In any case, a positive legal order represents a system not of co-ordinate but of superordinate and subordinate norms—that is, a hierarchy of norms, whose highest tier is the constitution, which is grounded as valid by the presupposed basic norm, and whose lowest tier is the individual norms positing a particular concrete mode of conduct as obligatory. In this way the validity of the higher norm regulating the creation of the lower norm always grounds the validity of that lower norm.

The function of a constitution is the grounding of validity.

PART THREE

SOCIAL THEORY AND JURISPRUDENCE

CHAPTER 6

KELSEN AND THE EXEGETICAL TRADITION

IAIN STEWART

THROUGH what he thought of as an immanent critique of existing jurisprudence,[1] Kelsen attempted to raise jurisprudence 'to the level of a genuine science',[2] freeing it from 'ideology' in the sense of excluding evaluation from description.[3] Why he wished to do this and how far he may have succeeded, however, are obscured by uncertainty about his philosophical orientation and consequently as to the kind of theory that the 'pure theory' is supposed to be. I will try first to situate Kelsen philosophically and show what kind of theory the pure theory is—so far as is germane to my second concern, which will be to suggest that in the pure theory Kelsen not only indicates both possibilities and limits of legal positivism,[4] but also points through those limits into the possibility of constructing a different kind of theory.

METAPHYSICAL BASES OF LEGAL SCIENCE

Kelsen is clearly some kind of Kantian: the pure theory is replete with Kantian notions and expressions.[5] Equally clearly, he is not simply a Kantian: he denies the existence of practical reason,[6] and

---

[1] 'Juristischer Formalismus und reine Rechtslehre', 58 *Juristische Wochenschrift* 1723, 1724 (1929).

[2] *RR*[1], iii; *RR*[2], iii.

[3] E.g. 'The Function of the Pure Theory of Law' in Reppy ed., *Law: a Century of Progress 1835–1935* (New York, London, 1937), vol. ii, p. 231, at pp. 236–8; *RR*[2], 112–13; *PTL*, 106–7.

[4] Fechner, 'Ideologische Elemente in positivistischen Rechtsanschauungen, dargestellt an Hans Kelsens "Reiner Rechtslehre"', in Schneider ed., *Sein und Sollen im Erfahrungsbereich des Rechtes, Archiv für Rechts- und Sozialphilosophie*, Beiheft, n.F., no. 6, p. 199, at pp. 205–6 (1970); Fassò, *Histoire de la Philosophie du Droit: XIXe et XXe Siècles* (Paris, 1976), p. 225.

[5] E.g., *RR*[2], 74–5; *PTL*, 72.

[6] E.g., 'Naturrechtslehre und Rechtspositivismus' (1961), in *WRS* I, 817, 824–5; *ATN*, 6.

conceives mysteriously of a 'descriptive' ought.[7] He acknowledges debts to a number of neo-Kantian philosophers, yet his one apparent declaration of allegiance seems rather overstated.[8] Kelsen seems, even on the level of philosophy, to be a first-order neo-Kantian, going directly 'back to Kant'[9] and then drawing on whatever parts of the Kantian heritage provided grist for his jurisprudential mill,[10] particularly factors that will allow him to move, in the name of 'science', closer to philosophical positivism.[11] Nevertheless, he remains a jurisprudent first and a philosopher afterwards, reserving his position on philosophical issues so far as he sees no need to take a firm position on them.[12]

Kant's 'Copernican revolution', in its insistence on the epistemological priority of subject over object, postulates that any knowledge will be possible only under a priori forms. Considered in their apriority—that is, as yet independently of any sensuous element—these forms can be characterized as 'pure'.[13] On the level of a particular science, the most basic forms specific to that science under which the knowledge in that science is to be possible will constitute a 'pure part' of the science, distinct from the empirical part which they will make possible, and may be called collectively the 'metaphysical bases' of the science.[14]

The pure theory of law seems to be 'metaphysical bases' of legal science.[15] The pure theory provides, Kelsen claims, 'the fundamental

---

[7] *GTLS*, 45–6.   [8] To Hermann Cohen: see n. 65, below.
[9] Copleston, *A History of Philosophy* (Garden City, 1962–), vol. vii, pt. 2, p. 134.
[10] E.g., discussions in the preface of *HPS*[2].
[11] On the meanings of 'positivism' see Kelsen, 'Was ist juristischer Positivismus?', 20 *Juristenzeitung* 465 (1965); Waline, 'Positivisme Philosophique, Juridique et Sociologique', in *Mélanges Carré de Malberg* (Paris, 1933), p. 517.
[12] E.g. *PTL-IMFC*, 481.   [13] *CPuR*, A 50–1; B 74–5.
[14] Kant, *Metaphysical Foundations of Natural Science*, trans. Ellington (Indianapolis, 1970), pp. 4–6.
[15] Cp. Stewart, 'The Basic Norm as Fiction' [1980] *Juridical Review* 199; Klenner, 'Kelsen's Kant' 138 *Revue Internationale de Philosophie* 539, 540–1 (1981). See also Dagory, *Kant et Kelsen* (undated typescript; Paris, Bibliothèque Cujas de Droit et Sciences Économiques), pp. 43–6, 189; Hart, 'Kelsen Visited' (1963) in Hart, *Essays in Jurisprudence and Philosophy* (Oxford, 1983) p. 286, at pp. 289–90; van de Kerchove, *Les Deux Versions de la Théorie Kelsénienne des Conditions de Validité d'une Norme Juridique* (*licence* thesis, Université Catholique de Louvain, Faculté de Philosophie et Lettres, 1970), pp. 178, 183–4; Goyard-Fabre, 'L'Inspiration Kantienne de Hans Kelsen' 83 *Revue de Métaphysique et de Morale* 204, 211–13 (1978); Troper, 'La Pyramide est Toujours Debout!' 94 *Revue de Droit Public* 1523, 1531 (1978).

principles by means of which any legal order can be comprehended'.[16] It is a 'general jurisprudence' furnishing 'the basic conceptions that enable us to master any law' and accordingly serving as 'the theoretical basis for all other branches of jurisprudence', such as dogmatic, historical, or comparative jurisprudence,[17] and even sociology of law.[18] Kelsen seems to take Kant's advice to state the pure part quite separately from the empirical part.[19]

Now, Kant himself offers 'metaphysical bases of legal doctrine'[20] and 'metaphysical bases of natural science'.[21] But Kelsen rejects the first because he denies the existence of practical reason and yet cannot adopt the second because its principle, causality, leaves no room for the 'ought', for norms—at least, without reducing them to something else, such as feelings. Rather, it seems, he constructs the pure theory as new 'metaphysical bases of legal science', in theoretical reason, on analogy with Kant's 'metaphysical bases of natural science'. One may take Kelsen to mean this when he says that the pure theory asks how a science of law is possible in the same way as Kant asks how natural science is possible.[22] Thus it is as metaphysical bases of legal science that the pure theory is a 'general theory of law', presenting 'the essence of law', its 'typical structure',[23] 'the form of all possible law'.[24]

The vehicle for this analogy seems to be Simmel's proposal to add to the Kantian list of 'categories' a new category of 'ought' (*Sollen*)'.[25] Kelsen assumes that the essential subject-matter of

[16] 'The Pure Theory of Law and Analytical Jurisprudence' (1941), in *WIJ*, 266.
[17] 'The Function of the Pure Theory of Law' (loc. cit. n. 3), pp. 231–2; cp. 'Was ist die reine Rechtslehre?' (1953) in *WRS* I, 611.
[18] E.g., *HPS*[2], 92; 'Zur Soziologie des Rechtes', 34 *Archiv für Sozialwissenschaft und Sozialpolitik* 601 (1912); *GTLS*, 175–7.
[19] *Metaphysical Foundations of Natural Science* (loc. cit. n. 14), p. 5.
[20] *Metaphysische Anfangsgründe der Rechtslehre* (first part of *Die Metaphysik der Sitten*) in *Gesammelte Schriften* (Akademieausgabe), vol. vi. p. 203; translated as *The Philosophy of Law* (Hastie) and as *The Metaphysical Elements of Justice* (Ladd).
[21] See n. 14, above.
[22] *RR*[2], 205; *PTL*, 202; 'Die Funktion der Verfassung' in *WRS* II, 1971, 1976; 'The Function of a Constitution', 116.
[23] 'Was ist die reine Rechtslehre?' (1953), in *WRS* I, 611: cp. 'The Pure Theory of Law and Analytical Jurisprudence' (1941), in *WIJ*, 266.
[24] *ASL*, 44; cp. *HPS*[2], 92.
[25] *HPS*[2], 7, 8; *ATN*, 2 and n. 2 (221–2); referring to Simmel, *Einleitung in die Moralwissenschaft* (Berlin, 1892–3), vol. i. pp. 8, 9. The category of 'ought' is over against that of 'is' or 'being' (*Sein*). Later, in an economic context, Simmel was

legal science is legal norms. He also asserts that norms are 'intuitively' oughts.[26] A value-free description of law, hence a 'normative jurisprudence',[27] will therefore be possible only if one can know an ought without also judging what ought to be. Value-freedom seems to be vital for Kelsen both because 'is' and practical 'ought' are qualitatively different and because science must be rational. He remains unconvinced by Rickert's suggestion that reference to universal values is value-neutrality,[28] and prefers Simmel's radical proposal that, under a category of 'ought', a situation may be known as involving an ought.

The category of 'ought' is mediated with individual meanings through the 'schema', in the Kantian sense, of 'norm': 'norm' is a 'schema of meaning'.[29]

Theoretical oughts, determined under the category of 'ought' and the schema of 'norm', are for Kelsen quite different from practical oughts as such. Kelsen calls the theoretical ought in legal science the legal proposition (*Rechtssatz*) and the legal practical ought the legal norm (*Rechtsnorm*).[30] However, since the role of the proposition is to represent the norm and the norm appears in

instead to place over against the category of *Sein* a category of 'value' (*Wert*): *Philosophie des Geldes* 2nd edn. (Leipzig, 1907), p. 5; *The Philosophy of Money* (London, 1978), p. 60. But Kelsen does not use this idea.

In 1916 Kelsen praises Herbart for distinguishing between is and ought more rigorously than Kant: 'Die Rechtswissenschaft als Norm- oder als Kulturwissenschaft' (hereafter 'RNK') 40 (3) *Schmollers Jahrbuch für Gesetzgebung, Verwaltung und Volkswirtschaft im Deutschen Reiche* 95, 95 (1916); referring to Herbart, *Allgemeine Metaphysik* in *Sämmtliche Werke* (ed. Hartenstein), vols iii and iv, at vol. iii, p. 353; Wilson, above p. 52. If there is a debt to Herbart, it is complementary and not contradictory to that to Simmel. Herbart's distinction between is and practical ought, reducing the latter to aesthetics—which is consistent with Kelsen's ethical relativism. Herbart deals with knowledge of norms in psychological terms, which Kelsen was anxious to avoid and does not refer to. However, Kelsen is in sympathy with Herbart's attempt to distinguish is and ought without splitting them into separate worlds and, although in some later works he seems to insist on just that, at his most explicit he follows both Herbart and Simmel by, with Simmel, characterizing is and theoretical ought as two different modi (*RR²*, 6; *PTL*, 6) determining as their contents a 'modally indifferent substratum' (*ATN*, 46–7).

[26] RNK, 138; cp. *RR²*, 5; *PTL*, 5.
[27] *HPS²*, 4–6; *GTLS*, 162 ff.   [28] RNK.
[29] Kelsen in discussion, reported in Schmölz, ed., *Das Naturrecht in der politischen Theorie* (Vienna, 1963), p. 121; *RR²*, 3, 4; *PTL*, 3, 4. 'Norm', too, in a 'descriptive sense' (*GTLS*, 46).
[30] *RR²*, 73–7; *PTL*, 71–5. I make my own translations of *Rechtssatz* and, later, *Rechtsgesetz* since those in *GTLS* and *PTL* have caused confusion.

science only through that representation, most of the time in legal science one can speak, as it were in a shorthand sense, simply of legal 'norms'.

The relational construction of reality that follows upon the 'Copernican revolution' and that operates in natural science in terms of laws of nature (*Naturgesetze*) formulated according to the principle of causality can operate in legal science in terms of laws of law (*Rechtsgesetze*) formulated according to a principle of imputation (*Zurechnung*): as a cause is conditionally related to an effect as its consequence, so a delict can be conditionally related to a sanction as its consequence; the sanction can be 'imputed' to the delict.[31]

Kelsen distinguishes different respects, but not different senses, in which the pure theory is 'pure'. He seems to mean essentially that it is rational, conceiving 'purity' as the operation of the logical law of identity together, where appropriate, with the category of unity: 'science' is defined as 'systematic unity of cognitions'.[32] The purity of the metaphysical bases in their transcendence of empirical elements seems to be the ultimate corollary of the possibility, vital to science, that concepts may contradict 'reality'.[33] Likewise the pure theory maintains the identity of legal science in avoiding the contradiction on the plane of method which is 'methodological syncretism'[34] and that on the plane of subject matter which is to assimilate 'norm' to something other than itself[35]—these two planes being inseparable.[36]

This interpretation of the pure theory as multidimensionally pure metaphysical bases of legal science seems to account for Kelsen's insistence that it is a pure theory of law and not a theory of pure law.[37] He envisages no such chimera as a 'pure norm'.[38] It also indicates that the various charges of 'formalism'—that the pure theory is remote from life,[39] or that it is not concerned with

---

[31] *RR²*, ch. 3; *PTL*, ch. 3.
[32] RNK, 96; cp. *GTLS*, 199. Cp. *CPuR*, A 11, 80; B 106.
[33] 'Die Funktion der Verfassung', in *WRS* II, 1971, 1977; 'The Function of a Constitution', 117
[34] *RR²*, 1; *PTL*, 1.
[35] See Hart, 'Kelsen Visited' (loc. cit. n. 15), 287.
[36] RNK, 152.
[37] 'Was ist die reine Rechtslehre?' (1953), in *WRS* I, 611, 620; cp. Laski, *A Grammar of Politics* 5th edn. (London, 1948), p. vi.
[38] As contended by Harris, *Law and Legal Science* (Oxford, 1979), pp. 34–5.
[39] E.g., Laski (loc. cit. n. 37); Klenner, *Rechtsleere* (Berlin, 1972).

the content of norms[40] or with their justice[41]—are misdirected. Rather, the pure theory provides the basic forms under which meanings can be known scientifically as legal norms—which will have a content, although the particular content is empirically contingent, and which, once determined as having a particular content, can be morally evaluated. Far from being an attempt to exclude considerations of experience, content, and justice, the pure theory is intended to make attention to them more rigorously possible.[42] By the same token, the pure theory is not impure in envisaging the use of the principle of causality in the empirical part of the science, to determine through the criterion of effectiveness whether a legal order that has been determined as intellectually concrete (*ideell*) in that it is valid[43] is also actual; purity is maintained if the enquiry is into the actuality of norms, without attempting to assimilate them to something else.

That Kelsen uses the word 'metaphysical' in order to condemn[44] need not deter one from understanding him to employ the concept that Kant had in mind when using it in order to approve.[45]

THE BASIC NORM

The best known of these metaphysical bases is the presupposition 'basic norm'. If successful, this presupposition is the keystone of the pure theory; if not, it is its Achilles' heel.[46]

Kelsen seems to construct the presupposition on two levels, which envisage a third. There are the generic construct, without particular content, and the specific construct, referring to a certain type of legal order, in which a typical content is stated; and the specific construct envisages the basic norm that will be presupposed

---

[40] E.g., Hart, 'Kelsen's Doctrine of the Unity of Law' (1970) in Hart, *Essays in Jurisprudence and Philosophy* (Oxford, 1983), p. 309, at p. 313.

[41] E.g., Villey, *Philosophie du Droit* (Paris, 1975), p. 198.

[42] 'Juristischer Formalismus und reine Rechtslehre' (loc. cit. n. 1) 1723, 1726; 'Was ist juristischer Positivismus?' (loc. cit. n. 11), 468–9.

[43] E.g., Kelsen in discussion, reported in Schmölz (loc. cit. n. 29), pp. 120–4.

[44] E.g., 'Natural Law Doctrine and Legal Positivism' (1928), in *GTLS*, 389, 419 ff.; *RR*², 80, 206 n. (208), 227, 289; *PTL*, 77, 221, 286.

[45] See also Kant, *Prolegomena to Any Future Metaphysics that will be Able to Present Itself as a Science*, trans. Lucas (Manchester, 1953).

[46] Martyniak, 'Le Problème de l'Unité des Fondements de la Théorie de Droit de Kelsen, 7 *Archives de Philosophie du Droit et de Sociologie Juridique* 166, 185 (1937); cp. Klenner, *Rechtsleere* (op. cit. n. 39), p. 58.

for the empirical cognition of a certain legal system. The pure theory contains only the first two levels, which are to make the third possible. Thus Kelsen speaks in a general way of 'the basic norm', referring to the first two levels as envisaging the third.

A basic norm is to have two functions. On the assumption that legal norms occur not in isolation but in some sort of order, Kelsen constructs such order a priori in the concept 'legal order'. This concept is to consist of theoretical oughts, 'norms' in the shorthand sense: thus the concept is possible only if its validity is grounded in a basic theoretical ought, a 'basic norm'. Yet there is no indication that such a norm can be found empirically. Thus the basic norm will be only a presupposition, in transcendental logic.[47] The validity established through this presupposition will be 'objective' validity,[48] by which Kant means the validity of a form that has 'real possibility' in contrast with the merely subjective validity of a form that is only speculative.[49]

The second function of a basic norm is to make it possible to understand the 'subjective meaning' of an act of will as its 'objective meaning', which is to say, as a legal norm.[50] Kelsen seems to intend that 'objective' here shall mean the same as in speaking of objective validity. However, what kind of objectivity is supposed, what kind of 'real possibility'?

'OBJECTIVE MEANING'

For Kant, reality lies in two directions: material and ideal. Meanings can only be ideal. Kelsen believes them to be not ideal (*ideal*) but intellectually concrete (*ideell*).[51] In this case, a meaning can be 'objective' not in the strong sense of exceeding human control but only in the weak sense of being humanly shared. However, what is objective in the strong sense will also be objective in the weak sense. Since it is not in doubt that legal

---

[47] *RR*², 201–9; *PTL*, 199–205.

[48] E.g., *RR*², 10, 204–5; *PTL*, 11 (omits 'objectively'), 202 'Die Funktion der Verfassung', in *WRS* II, 1971, 1976; 'The Function of a Constitution', 116.

[49] *CPuR*, B xxvii; A 89–92; B 121–4; *Prolegomena* (loc. cit. n. 45), pp. 56–8. In 1928 Kelsen distinguishes emphatically between the 'absolute' and the 'objective', defining the latter as the '*historically* given': *Rechtsgeschichte gegen Rechtsphilosophie* (Vienna, 1928), p. 15. We shall see whether this is realized.

[50] *RR*², 205; *PTL*, 202; 'Professor Stone and the Pure Theory of Law', 17 *Stanford Law Rev.* 1128, 1143 (1965).

[51] In discussion reported in Schmölz (loc. cit. n. 29), pp. 120, 122–3.

norms are humanly shared to some extent, both cognitively and
practically, the question is whether in any way Kelsen implies that
they are also objective in the strong sense.

Kelsen identifies his principal enemy in jurisprudence as
absolutism, the attribution of legal norms to an alleged absolute
subject as their author. He contends that all forms of iusnaturalism
are absolutistic in this way: even the apparently secular forms deify
human reason.[52] His speculative formulations of the basic norm of
a natural legal order, 'One ought to obey the commands of
nature',[53] and 'One ought to obey the commands of God',[54] come
to the same, since if nature is to command it must be a subject. He
also sees earlier forms of legal positivism as absolutist, in
personifying and hypostatizing the state.[55] He understands such
absolutism as a form of objective idealism, which he criticizes for
metaphysically (in the denunciatory sense) doubling the object of
knowledge,[56] mixing description and evaluation, and parading the
chimera of practical rationality.

Now, Kelsen does not start pure. In the *Hauptprobleme* of 1911
he insists on the 'objectivity' of legal norms in what appears to be
the strong sense, grounded in hypostatization (as Kelsen would
later have identified it) of the state. The will of the state may be
reduced to merely a 'point of imputation' (*Zurechnungspunkt*),[57]
but the 'modern state' is none the less 'an entirely extra-individual
authority' which 'fulfils its obligating function independently of the
will of the individual', so that its positive law is 'objective' in
existing 'over and above human beings, independent of the
subjective feelings of the individual'. Consequently that law can be
represented in legal science only by an objectivistic method that
will present it as 'objective' and entirely 'heteronomous'. It cannot
be accurately represented by a subjectivistic method, which would
make legal norms appear, like moral norms, as 'subjective' and
'autonomous', deriving their binding character merely from the
individual's 'recognition' of them as obligating. Worse, from a

---

[52] 'Die Grundlage der Naturrechtslehre', in Schmölz (loc. cit. n. 29), p. 1; 'The
Foundation of the Theory of Natural Law', in *ELMP*, 114.

[53] *RR*², 227; *PTL*, 220.   [54] *RR*², 205; *PTL*, 202.

[55] E.g., *ASL*. 76; *GTLS*, 185, 191, 197–8, 377; 'Absolutism and Relativism in
Philosophy and Politics' (1948), in *WIJ*, 198, 203; Schreier, 'Die Wiener
rechtsphilosophische Schule', 11 *Logos* 309, 314–15 (1923).

[56] 'Natural Law Doctrine and Legal Positivism' (1928), in *GTLS*, 389, 419 ff.

[57] *HPS*², ch. 6.

subjectivistic standpoint the apparent objectivity of legal norms seems to be nothing but a product of 'projection' or 'objectivation': since it is not, the picture of law from a subjectivistic standpoint is 'fiction'.[58]

At stake here is the specificity of the legal. Kelsen directs his criticisms of subjectivism against Bierling, for whom 'law in the juristic sense' (*Recht im juristischen Sinne*) is any social norm that is socially recognized as binding.[59] So wide a view begs the question of what people mean when they call certain such norms 'legal' but not other such norms and attach important consequences to the difference, especially that the 'legal' norms are to take precedence over the others. A view such as Bierling's leads one, at the least, to having to talk about 'law' and 'legal law'.[60] Yet Kelsen does not argue in these sociological terms and one may ask why.

RISE AND DECLINE OF THE BASIC NORM

The *Hauptprobleme* predates both the presupposition 'basic norm' and the concept of the identity of law and state. The supposition of the state as the author of legal norms grounds both the unity and the objectivity of the legal order.[61] By 1914 Kelsen had introduced the presupposition 'basic norm' to take over the first function.[62] But this profoundly complicated the relation between law and state. A reviewer's remark[63] led Kelsen to the ethico-political doctrine of Hermann Cohen,[64] from where he derived the concept of the identity of law and state.[65] The objectivity of legal norms

[58] *HPS*[2], chs. 1 and 2, *passim*.

[59] Bierling, *Juristische Prinzipienlehre* (Freiburg and Tübingen, 1894–1917), vol. i. p. 19.

[60] As MacIver does: *The Web of Government* (New York, 1947) pp. 61–6. (This sense of 'legal law' has nothing to do with its use in *PTL*, 79.) Kelsen's attempt to establish the specificity of law by reference to coercion (e.g., *GTLS*, 15–29, esp. (criticizing Ehrlich) 24–8) is vulnerable to Hart's critique of confusion between having an obligation and being obliged, in the 'gunman situation' (*The Concept of Law*, Oxford, 1961), pp. 6, 7), a problem that Kelsen deals with as that of understanding an apparent subjective meaning as an objective meaning.

[61] *RR*[2], 209; *PTL*, 205.

[62] 'Reichsgesetz und Landesgesetz nach Österreichische Verfassung', 32 *Archiv des öffentlichen Rechts* 202–45 and 390–438, at 216–17 (1914); preface to *HPS*[2], XV.

[63] Ewald, 'Die Deutsche Philosophie im Jahre 1911', 17 *Kant-Studien* 382, 397–8 (1912); Métall, *Hans Kelsen: Leben und Werk* (Vienna, 1969), pp. 7, 8, 15.

[64] Cohen, *Ethik des reinen Willens* (Berlin, 1904).

[65] Preface to *HPS*[2], XVII, XX. There are traces of Cohen's epistemology in Kelsen's writings of the 1920s, particularly the presentation of the *Grundnorm* as

could no longer be grounded in that of the state; the presupposition 'basic norm' was made to take on this function as well.

A basic norm is presupposed as valid, and 'it is valid because it is presupposed to be valid; and it is presupposed to be valid because without this presupposition no human act could be interpreted as a legal, especially as a norm-creating, act';[66] moreover, it is the 'basic' norm 'because no further question can be raised about the basis of its validity'.[67] Unpacking this: the presupposed basic norm is the nodal point at which the pure part of legal science passes over into the empirical part; on the pure side, the basic norm stands in a relation of validity to the specific and generic formulations of the presupposition 'basic norm' and through them to the pure theory as a whole, while on the empirical side it stands in a relation of validity to the remainder of the legal order; its validity on the pure side cannot be questioned from the empirical side, since it is the condition of possibility, furnished by the pure side, for the empirical side.

In 1964 Kelsen came to the view that, at the level of the generic formulation, the presupposition 'basic norm' was self-contradictory, because it involved an infinite regress. A basic norm is not posited (*gesetzt*), through an act of will, but presupposed (*vorausgesetzt*), through an act of thought. Nevertheless, the presupposition is of a norm and a norm can only be the meaning of an act of will. But then it can be asked, what authorizes that act of will? This can only be a higher norm, which itself can only be the meaning of a higher act of will—and so on.[68]

This argument is presented together with, and one may suggest confused with, another, which must be discussed in order to

---

an *Ursprungsnorm*, which echoes Cohen's doctrine of thinking by reference to origins. But the argument of Treves and Donati that Kelsen generally adheres to Cohen's philosophy is not convincing: Treves, 'Il Fondamento Filosofico della Dottrina Pura del Diritto di Hans Kelsen', 69 *Atti della Reale Accadémia delle Scienze di Torino* (Classe di Scienze Morale, Storiche e Filologiche) 52, 70–7 (1934); Donati, *Note sul Normativismo* (Milan, n.d.). Nor did Kelsen by any means wholly subscribe to Cohen's theory of the state (*HPS*[2], XX); Cohen may have tended to identify state and law, but he still tended to absolutize both: see Winter, *Ethik und Rechtswissenschaft* (Berlin, 1980), pp. 349–86.

[66] *GTLS*, 116.
[67] 'Die Funktion der Verfassung', in *WRS* II, 1971, 1972; 'The Function of a Constitution', 112, 115.
[68] 'Die Funktion der Verfassung', in *WRS* II, 1971, 1977–8; 'The Function of a Constitution', 116–17.

distinguish it. In 1962 Kelsen had arrived at the view that, because the presupposing of a basic norm envisaged a norm that did not exist, the presupposition was 'fictional' (*fiktive*).[69] Now, this was to accept an argument that a legal historian had raised in 1928[70] and to which Kelsen had then replied that no question of truth or falsity arose, since the jurist was not to postulate a basic norm as a real norm but to presuppose it in 'legal logic' or, to use Kelsen's more exact Kantian expression, transcendental logic.[71]

In 1964 Kelsen adds the argument about self-contradiction to the 1962 argument and finds their sum to accord with Vaihinger's concept of a 'fiction' as something that is 'characterized by its not only contradicting reality but also containing contradiction within itself',[72] Now, both Vaihinger and Kelsen are I think mistaken here, since, at least in Kantian terms, what is self-contradictory is a nothing and therefore no question of truth or falsity can arise.

The crucial point is whether the presupposition 'basic norm' is valid in its generic formulation and Kelsen's argument that it is not evaporates it. This is so, whether the question is of a transcendental-logical presupposition or of a concept. With the presupposition 'basic norm' goes the concept, grounded in it and involving it, 'legal order', and thus the core of the pure theory. Provided, that is, that these elements are still reckoned to be *in* the pure theory—to which I will come in a moment.

The regress was already evident in Kelsen's specific formulations of the typical basic norm of an independent positive legal order, which involve a reference to a 'constitution'.[73] If a basic norm is a necessary condition for knowing a meaning as a legal norm, it cannot refer a priori to any legal norm. Kelsen had acknowledged this in the 1950s as a 'petitio principii', though in an oblique way. Why is it, he asked, that the act by which a constitution is established comes afterwards to appear as authorized by the legal order based on that constitution? He offers the answer that the act establishes only a 'potential' legal order, which becomes an

---

[69] In discussion reported in Schmölz (loc. cit. n. 29), pp. 119–20.

[70] Schwind, *Grundlagen und Grundfragen des Rechts* (Munich, 1928), *passim*.

[71] *Rechtsgeschichte gegen Rechtsphilosophie*, (loc. cit. n. 49), ch. 6. This seems here to be at least the principal meaning of 'legal logic'.

[72] 'Die Funktion der Verfassung', in *WRS* II, 1971, 1977; 'The Function of a Constitution', 117. And see Vaihinger, *The Philosophy of 'As If'* 2nd edn. (London, 1935), pp. 97–100.

[73] E.g., RR^1. 65–6; RR^2, 203–4, 212, 214, 219; *PTL*, 200–1, 208, 210, 212.

'actual' legal order after the people concerned presuppose, themselves, a basic norm that they ought to behave in the way prescribed by that constitution. Legal science neither posits nor presupposes the basic norm, but only brings it 'to consciousness'[74] (just as hitherto it had stated what most jurists do, at least unconsciously, when they are neither absolutists nor behaviourists[75]). Yet, so long as the formulation of the basic norm is circular, the contradiction is merely displaced from the plane of the jurist's self to that of the other and the jurist then has the task of constructing a new concept under which to understand other people as contradicting themselves in this way.

Kelsen wavers. In 1960 the basic norm is back in legal science: he is confident that the problem is solved by the distinction between positing and presupposing[76]—which it is not, because either way there is a contradiction in the formulation. In 1966 the basic norm is back in other people's thought, but, following the 1964 acknowledgement of the regress on the plane of the jurist's self and the then characterization of the basic norm as a 'fiction' in Vaihinger's sense, the presupposed basic norm now appears as a 'fiction' in other people's 'juristic thinking'.[77]

Yet this is not to displace legal science entirely to the plane of the other, which would be to destroy it. The fact that other people think this way is an object of enquiry for legal science.[78] Thus the presupposition 'basic norm' and consequently the concept 'legal order' are no longer elements of the pure theory.

This shift subjects the pure theory to a double development. Deprived of the factors that made it a theory of law, it widens, as one can see in Kelsen's last works, into a general theory of norms. At the same time, the argument that the presupposition 'basic norm' resides on the plane of the other is already the implicit development, within this general theory of norms, of an element in terms of which the presupposition 'basic norm' and the concept 'legal order' are hypothesized as social phenomena.

This new element, however, is established only in principle, as

[74] 'Was ist ein Rechtsakt?' 4 *Österreichische Zeitschrift für öffentliches Recht* (n. F.) 263, 271 (1951–2).
[75] RR^2, 209; *PTL*, 204–5.
[76] RR^2, 208 n.; *PTL*, 204 n.
[77] 'On the Pure Theory of Law', 1 *Israel Law Review* 1, 6 (1966).
[78] Ibid.

the mere notion of the presence of 'basic norm' and consequently 'legal order' on the plane of the other. It needs elaboration.[79]

TRANSFORMATIONS OF THE BASIC NORM

Kelsen discusses the displacement of the presupposition 'basic norm' to the plane of the other only as to the specific formulation given it formerly for use in the pure theory—that is, as the typical basic norm of an independent positive legal order. But the displacement, to be complete, must be effected at the level of the generic formulation; or, at least, this is required by one's knowledge that norms have very often been socially understood as positive within a natural legal order.[80]

If the fate of the presupposition 'basic norm' is the failure of an attempt to rescue legal positivism from absolutism, its specific formulation in legal positivism must be of the kind 'One ought to obey the commands of the state (or sovereign, or equivalent)', in which the state or whatever is absolutely personified. Kelsen's speculative formulation of the basic norm of a natural legal order was 'One ought to obey the commands of nature (or God)'. These formulations can be generalized as a generic formulation with definite content: 'One ought to obey the commands of the absolute subject.' From this general hypothesis one can then develop particular hypotheses of the formulation of the typical basic norm of a type of legal order and of the formulation of an actually presupposed basic norm.

[79] The following development will employ a distinction between a plane of the self and a plane of the other as self-oriented and other-oriented planes of cognition. Cp. Bohannan's distinction between 'analytical' and 'folk' concepts: *Justice and Judgment among the Tiv* (London, 1957), pp. 4–6; 'Ethnography and Comparison in Legal Anthropology', in Nader ed., *Law in Culture and Society* (Chicago, 1970), p. 401; see also Marvin Harris, *The Rise of Anthropological Theory* (London, 1969), ch. 20. The plane of the other is still the enquirer's construct: Ayoub, 'Review: the Judicial Process in Two African Tribes' in Janowitz ed., *Community Political Systems* (New York, 1961), p. 237, at p. 241. Language on each plane will have the status respectively of 'use' and 'mention': Searle, *Speech Acts* (Cambridge, 1969), pp. 73–6. In the argument that follows, the word 'legal' is shifted from use to mention and then into a new use in which the previous use, now displaced to the plane of the other, is mentioned.

[80] See 'Naturrecht und positives Recht', 2 *Revue Internationale de la Théorie du Droit* 71 (1927–8); 'Die Idee des Naturrechts' (1928) in *Aufsätze zur Ideologiekritik* (Neuwied, 1964), p. 73; 'The Idea of Natural Law', in *ELMP*, 27; Kuttner, 'Sur les Origines du Terme "Droit Positif"', 15 *Revue Historique de Droit Français et Étranger* (4e sér.), 728 (1936).

This last would have the form 'One ought to obey the commands of nature (or God or the state or the sovereign, and so on).' This is an unbeliever's hypothesis of a believer's statement. But from the standpoint of a believer the statement is otiose. For the believer in an absolute subject, the absoluteness excludes the possibility of a norm contrary to a norm created by that subject. Disobedience to that subject's norm could be justified only by reference to such a renegade norm. Justifiable disobedience of the absolute subject is thus unthinkable. By the same token, obedience to the absolute subject does not have to be justified: the determination of conduct as obedience is sufficient. To put this another way: once conduct is determined as conformity to a norm that is attributed to the absolute subject as its author, the notion of a norm that that norm ought to be conformed to is otiose.

The unbelieving jurist wishing to determine a norm as legal therefore needs only to hypothesize that the believer in an absolute subject attributes the norm to that subject as its author. From the unbeliever's standpoint, that subject does not exist: the believer is considered merely to allege it. Thus the unbelieving jurist needs to hypothesize that the believer accepts, at least tacitly, the proposition: 'A norm is a legal norm if it is the meaning of an act of the will of the absolute subject' (named 'nature' or whatever).[81] This hypothesis can be generalized as the definition of a legal norm: a norm is a legal norm if it is understood as the meaning of an act of the will of an alleged absolute subject. This norm will be 'binding' in the way just discussed and it will be 'objective' because absoluteness involves objectivity.[82]

The unbelieving jurist presumes that a norm is the subjective meaning of an act of will. It is then necessary to account for why that meaning appears to other people to be objective. To do so, the jurist can hypothesize that those people attribute the norm to an alleged absolute subject as its author. In the hypothesis, that subject and therefore that attribution are assumed to be fallacious. Accordingly, if the hypothesis is true, the apparent objectivity will also be fallacious.

[81] On this plane, 'the' absolute subject, since a believer posits an absolute as unique.

[82] So long as objectivity involves (final) bindingness, the author must be absolute. An author that is objective but relative, such as a deity in a pantheon, can issue objective norms but they will not be (finally) binding: one may get a thunderbolt on one's head, but that is still a 'gunman situation' (n. 60).

Thus from the standpoint of the unbeliever a norm is legal when, as a real subjective meaning, it is clothed in the fallacious form of an objective meaning. This fallacious form is real as a belief. The legal norm is therefore the unity of two real elements: a subjective meaning and a fallaciously believed objective meaning.

What is the relation between the real subjective meaning and its fallacious form of appearance as objective? Kelsen offers a possible concept at the level of philosophy,[83] although he declines to apply it at the level of legal theory: 'projection' or 'objectivation'.

A norm is defined as the meaning of an act of will, which can only be the will of a subject. 'Norm' thus implies the analytical set: subject—act of will—meaning—norm. This set, then, is objectivated.[84] To the believer it appears simply as objective. To the unbeliever, studying the believer's statements, it appears as the unity of a real subjective set with a real fallacious belief in an objective set.

TRANSFORMATIONS OF THE LEGAL PROPOSITION

Kelsen identifies 'juristic thinking' on the plane of the other, but without asking whether this 'juristic thinking' is of the same kind as that on the plane of the self in what is left of, or can be made of, the pure theory. In view of one of the contributions of the 'Copernican revolution', that appearances are to be considered to be not given but constructed, which raises the possibility of differing constructions, this is a notable omission—particularly since the presupposition 'basic norm' was to be the principal juristic instrument of construction.[85]

Such a non-realization of apparent potential has also been noted on the level of the legal proposition, which a presupposed basic norm was to validate.[86] Kelsen rightly underlines the importance of the difference between the legal norm and the legal proposition,[87] but it is far from clear what makes this difference.

---

[83] 'Natural Law Doctrine and Legal Positivism' (1928), in *GTLS*, 389.

[84] The word 'projection' can be dropped, especially because of its psychological association.

[85] Cp. 'Natural Law Doctrine and Legal Positivism' (1928), in *GTLS*, 389, 434–5; *RR²*, 74–5; *PTL*, 72.

[86] Lenoble and Ost, *Droit, Mythe et Raison* (Brussels, 1980), pp. 467–546; see also Amselek, *Méthode Phénoménologique et Théorie du Droit* (Paris, 1964), pp. 45–62, saluting Kelsen as a 'precursor' of transcendental phenomenology of law.   [87] *RR²*, 83 n., cp. 74 n.

The legal norm is prescriptive while the legal proposition is descriptive.[88] The one is the meaning of an act of will while the other is the meaning of an act of thinking. The meaning of an act of will may be subjective or objective; only in the latter case is it a legal norm. Kelsen also implies that the meaning of an act of thinking may be subjective or objective; it will be the latter if it is an element, the cognition of the legal norm authorizing the knower to create a further norm, in an 'authentic' interpretation of law.[89] In either situation the criterion of objectivity is legal authorization. What Kelsen means by a legal proposition, then, is the subjective meaning of an act of thinking.

What's new? If this is all that Kelsen is doing, he is merely making a little more explicit, mainly through a verbal differentiation, what has always been the basis of legal studies. However, there are signs that he is also doing something more radical.

In 1911 Kelsen considers the standpoints of judge and 'theoretical jurist' with respect to statutes to be the same. They have in common that their concern is to understand not human behaviour as such but systematic connections between norms.[90] By the 1940s, at least, the distinction between legal norm and legal proposition is established—in concept, if not in mode of expression.[91] In 1960 its mode of expression is clarified,[92] and judicial interpretation is distinguished as 'authentic' from juristic interpretation as 'non-authentic'.[93] In between, however, the interpretation of positive law given by a 'scientific jurist' is equated with that which a 'theologian' gives of a biblical passage.[94]

In view of what has happened to the presupposition 'basic norm', these discussions might be understood in terms of the following model. The alleged absolute subject creates norms authorizing certain human beings to create further norms. It will be the author of these norms both in the sense of being the ground of their validity and in the historical sense that, in the last analysis, those human beings are its own refractions. The creation of these further, positive norms will involve interpretation, which will have a cognitive element. This cognition will be exegetical: it will

---

[88] *RR*², 75, 77; *PTL*, 73, 75.   [89] *RR*², 74, 349–52; *PTL*, 72, 351–5.
[90] *HPS*², 42.   [91] *GTLS*, 45.
[92] *RR*², 73–7; *PTL*, 71–5; that is, at least, in *RR*².
[93] *RR*², 346, 351–2; *PTL*, 354–5.
[94] 'Was ist die reine Rechtslehre?' (1953), in *WRS* I, 611, 619.

examine both the authorizing norms and human behaviour in order to discover through them objective ideals, in the supposed mind of the alleged absolute subject, that they are assumed to refract and that are assumed to combine existence and norm in mutual perfection. On the side of existence, unauthorized cognition cannot present the positive norms as legal without attributing them to the alleged absolute subject as their author, which commits that cognition ontologically to objective idealism and epistemologically to exegesis; on the side of norm, the unauthorized knower cannot but accept the authority of the authorized, agreeing with their authorized statements (and disagreeing with their statements only by saying that they were not the statements they were authorized to make) and generally aiding and abetting them. And this is not a matter of choice: from belief in the alleged absolute subject, it follows that the authorized and the unauthorized alike are 'always already'[95] refractions of the objective ideals, as to both existence and norm.[96]

The legal proposition may thus be understood as an unauthorized —that is, neither with nor contrary to authority—exegetical proposition. And Kelsen also holds exclusively to its counterpart on the side of duty, the conception of the relation between the practice of legal theory and the practice which is lawmaking, as that of the jurist as worthy underlabourer.[97]

It can equally be suggested that a legal proposition is something different. There is, at least, a grey area. He says that law-applying organs have to know 'as it were from the inside' what law they are to apply, while afterwards legal science describes law 'as it were from the outside'.[98] This bleeds over, however, into the explicit development of legal science on analogy with natural science, until Kelsen can say that theory of positive law 'is parallel to the empirical science of nature'.[99] This is at the least a different conception of legal science. But Kelsen's philosophical positivism is strong, and it leads him into a confusion that may be accounted

---

[95] Althusser, 'Ideology and Ideological State Apparatuses', in *Lenin and Philosophy and Other Essays* (London, 1971), p. 121 at p. 161.

[96] Cp. Berman, 'The Origins of Western Legal Science', 90 *Harvard Law Review* 894, 899, 908, 933 (1977). And see generally Kafka, *The Trial* (Harmondsworth, 1953), ch. 9; Huizinga, *The Waning of the Middle Ages* (Harmondsworth, 1955), chs. 15–17.

[97] *The Law of the United Nations* (London, 1950), p. xiii.

[98] *RR*[2], 74; *PTL*, 72.   [99] *GTLS*, 163.

for as a conflict between the two ideas of science that struggle for supremacy in his work.

In his philosophical positivism he strives on one hand to express law in terms of laws of law, while on the other denying the existence of practical rationality. Now, if there is no practical rationality, the structure that laws of norms are to express cannot be found in norms themselves but must be sought on a further plane, such as is offered by psychology. This achieves objectivity, but at the cost of the norm. Nor, for the same reason, could Kelsen have adopted the attitude of *Verstehen* (at least, as science) or later have become a structuralist. Both presuppose rationality of the meanings they examine. Not surprisingly, the concept of a law of law is hardly realized: it does little if anything but draw attention to the joint operation of norms saying what ought to be done and norms providing for sanctions. It does not really go beyond the general idea of a legal proposition as juristic representation of a legal norm. This idea, from a philosophical-positivist standpoint such as Kelsen's, is fine so far as norms are spoken of singly but, as soon as one envisages gathering legal propositions into 'legal orders', with no suggestion of an ordering principle other than a norm, the idea falls into the contradiction that the disorderly is to be presented directly as orderly.

This contradiction, it can be suggested, arises because of a deeper contradiction, that underneath this idea of the legal proposition lies the first one, in which divine practical rationality is assumed.

If this is right, how did Kelsen get to such a pass? Here I have to draw upon some reflections on ideology that have been sketched elsewhere.[1] Let us call an 'ideology' any body of ideas that is grounded in an attempt to absolutize. An ideology will therefore always be objectivistic. The forms of absolute idealism in question here present Kelsen with the issue whether the appearance of legal norms as objective can or should be maintained without the objectivism of such ideologies. The answer, as he seems painfully to have found, is that, because norms are meanings, there is no other way to maintain it. In the meantime he thought it could be sustained through the alternative objectivism furnished by philo-

---

[1] 'Sociology in Jurisprudence: the Problem of "Law" as Object of Knowledge', in Fryer *et al.* eds., *Law, State and Society* (London, 1981), p. 107, at pp. 108–9.

sophical positivism as he understood it, which epistemologically was scientism, with its ontological corollary, reification.

I have suggested that reification is a major component of an 'evolutionist' ideology[2]—other major elements of which, such as instrumentalization, are also emphasized by Kelsen. Kelsen seems to exemplify the possibility that, although in their absolutism two ideologies will be totally opposed, they may plausibly be confused because of the very feature that most divides them and which at the same time is the only thing that they have in common, that they are ideologies. Being ideologies, they will be objectivistic and their respective realities, although entirely different, will share the status of apparent objectivity and thus the one may be glossed onto the other. Kelsen seems to gloss an analogy of reification onto an objective-idealist reality. The fate of the presupposition 'basic norm' may be understood as the realization, from the standpoint of the former, that the basis of the gloss had to be the rejected foundation of the idealist objectivity, absolute authorship.

Kelsen's relativism seems less to be a positive standpoint than to be a prospect squeezed out from between the millstones of the two ideologies. Sometimes it appears as philosophical protest.[3] On the juristic level, he insists that 'legal positivism goes hand in hand with *relativism*', holding that justice 'is essentially an *absolute value*, and the absolute in general and absolute values in particular lie beyond rational-scientific cognition'.[4] But this relativism is realized only with respect to moral values as such. Kelsen tends to leave open the question of their status as contents of legal norms, which, so far as the gloss operates, appear as almost subjectless moments of normativity in reified experience.

These conflicts can perhaps be seen most clearly in Kelsen's critique of 'hypostatization' of the legal person and the state. Each, he says, is a metaphorical personification—in the one case of a bundle of duties and rights, in the other of a national legal order—which gets 'hypostatized' as a real subject. They are to find their true representation in legal propositions in which the hypostatization has been removed. The human beings who are the

---

[2] Ibid., pp. 120–3.
[3] E.g., 'Absolutism and Relativism in Philosophy and Politics', where 'political absolutism' is linked with 'philosophical absolutism' and the latter is characterized as 'epistemological totalitarianism', *WIJ*, 202.
[4] 'Was ist die reine Rechtslehre?' (1953), in *WRS* I, 611, 621.

bearers of these metaphorical personalities can also be represented in causal terms—that is, biologically and psychologically—but this is relevant to legal science only as determining one kind of content of legal norms.[5] However, Kelsen's reduction of the norm-creating and responsible human wills to 'points of imputation', while detaching the norm from absolute authorship yet preserving it from reduction to causal terms, begs the question of conceiving relativistically the human subjectivity that is now acknowledged as the bearer and cement of the legal person and the state.[6] Maybe it is in partial recognition of this gap in the pure theory that, in one presentation of it, a 'moral personality' appears rather as an afterthought.[7]

A site of these conflicts that involves more explicitly the issue of the status of the legal proposition is the question of the generality or universality (the *Allgemeinheit*) of the pure theory, especially in relation to public international law. What is meant by representation of 'the form of all possible law'?

In 1911 Kelsen explains that his approach is 'formal', but not in the 'scholastic' sense. The aim, as in geometry, is to construct a form under which a content may be determined; but legal theory will not create that content, any more than geometry creates the physical content of its determinations. The aim in legal theory is to construct, as it were, 'a geometry of the total appearance of law (*Rechtserscheinung*)'.[8] As in geometry, the form which is the general theory of law will be universal not in a 'material' sense, in being the form of an actual universal legal order, but in a 'formal' sense, that under it any number of entities may be determined separately.[9] The unity of the pure theory as a general theory of law is to be 'only epistemological, not organisational'.[10] It is in this sense that, as the task of natural science is to describe physical reality 'in one system of laws of nature, so it is the task of jurisprudence to comprehend all human law in one system of rules

[5] *GTLS*, 93–6, 108–9, 191, 197–8; *RR*[2], 172 ff., 288 ff.; *PTL*, 168 ff., 285 ff.

[6] Cp. Campagnolo, 'La Notion de "Personne Juridique" dans la Doctrine Pure du Droit', 11 *Revue Internationale de la Théorie du Droit* 215, 218–19, 222–3 (1937).

[7] *GTLS*, 377.

[8] *HPS*[2], 92–4.

[9] Cp. Fraenkel, 'L'Universalisme et la Théorie Pure du Droit', 11 *Revue Internationale de la Théorie du Droit*, 295 (1937).

[10] *RR*[1], 153.

of law'[11]—that is, of legal propositions. Even if the public international legal order subsumes all national legal orders, so that they compose 'one uniform universal legal system',[12] the legal propositions describing this system will not have material universality in the sense above, since 'all possible law' comprises law not only of the present but also of the past and possible in the future. This being so, the concept 'legal proposition', like the presupposition 'basic norm', must be formulated on a number of levels of generality.

Now, Kelsen considers that some national legal orders have been presented as absolute by those who have created them and he denounces this as grievously wrong.[13] Yet, to identify absolutism as error or deception is not enough. It has to be understood as a form of appearance of the order that it clothes. The pure theory therefore needs to contain, in its formal universality, a kind of legal proposition with which one could paint it, if necessary, as clothed in a fallacious form.

Such a type of proposition was proposed at the end of the previous section. There is space here to develop it in only one respect.

In regulating, norms also in a sense constitute.[14] Behaviour that follows the norms of football or contract law is constituted by those norms as the 'institutional fact' that is a football game or a contract.[15] A proposition of the kind proposed can represent a contract, or a state, as on one side a real norm-constituted event and on the other a real belief in an objectively ideal entity.[16]

---

[11] 'The Pure Theory of Law and Analytical Jurisprudence' (1941), in *WIJ* 266, 287.

[12] Ibid.

[13] 'Absolutism and Relativism in Philosophy and Politics' (1948), in *WIJ* 198, 202–3; cp. *GTLS*, 386–7.

[14] Haesaert, 'Notion du Droit Positif', 2 *Archives de Philosophie de Droit et de Sociologie Juridique* 447, 459 ff. (1932). Cp. Kelsen, 'Science and Politics' (1951), in *WIJ*, 350, 369.

[15] Searle, *Speech Acts* (loc. cit. n. 79), pp. 50–3; MacCormick, 'Law as Institutional Fact', 90 *Law Quarterly Review* 102 (1974); Rottleuthner, 'Marxistische und analytische Rechtstheorie', in Rottleuthner ed., *Probleme der marxistische Rechtstheorie* (Frankfurt am Main, 1975), p. 159, at p. 182; Weinberger, 'Tatsachen und Tatsachenbeschreibungen', in Salamun ed., *Sozialphilosophie als Aufklärung* (Tübingen, 1979), p. 173; 'Zur Idee eines institutionalistischen Rechtspositivismus', 138 *Revue Internationale de Philosophie* 487 (1981); 'Jenseits von Positivismus und Naturrecht', *Archiv für Rechts- und Sozialphilosophie*, Supplementa, vol. i, pt. 1, p. 43 (1981).

[16] The concept of the fallacious form might be developed through transformation of

This too is prefigured in Simmel's 'ought' and in Kelsen's intention that the initial object of enquiry should be behaviour[17]— the enquiry apparently is to be non-exegetical.

BEYOND THE EXEGETICAL TRADITION

The pure theory is anchored in the philosophy of its time and accordingly realizes the possibilities and the limits of those foundations. Kelsen tries to make jurisprudence a *Geisteswissenschaft*,[18] yet one capable of formal universality. Beyond this seems to lie an ultimately ethical and political championing of rationality against its self-denial in behaviourism on one side and romanticism on the other.[19] His attempt to endow jurisprudence with the rationality of natural science through an analogy led him to a confrontation between two modes of objectivation, one of which tacitly presupposed the other while explicitly removing its basis and both of which militated against the relativism necessary to overcoming their opposition, an opposition however the very pressure of which tended to relativize the opponents and thus commence their supersession.

If Kelsen could have found the required relativism in Marxism, which may through an 'anti-Copernican revolution'[20] have overcome objectivation by realizing the standpoint of the unity of subject and object,[21] enabling it effectively to theorize their apparent separation, it has also to be noted that through most of Kelsen's life Marxism appeared primarily in distinctly non-relativistic clothing. And, though he was wrong to say that Marxism denies the ought,[22] this criticism is accurate in so far as it points out that Marxists have yet to confront the question of knowing an ought without judging what ought to be. Nevertheless, it seemed worth

the doctrines of Hauriou and his followers: see Broderick ed., *The French Institutionalists* (Cambridge, Mass., 1970).

[17] *RR*², 1–3; *PTL*, 2, 3.
[18] *RR*¹, iii; *RR*², iii.
[19] Cp. Musil, *The Man Without Qualities* (London, 1979); Hughes, *Consciousness and Society* (Brighton, 1979).
[20] Rancière, *Lire le Capital*, vol. iii (Paris, 1973), p. 51.
[21] Schmidt, *The Concept of Nature in Marx* (London, 1971).
[22] 'Allgemeine Rechtslehre im Lichte materialistischer Geschichtsauffassung', 66 *Archiv für Sozialwissenschaft und Sozialpolitik* 449 (1931); *The Communist Theory of Law* (London, 1955); cp. *RR*², 107–13; *PTL*, 101–7.

seeing what the Feuerbachian line in transformative criticism[23] could do to take the pure theory beyond the parlous circumstance in which Kelsen left it.

The difficulties of the pure theory link with Kelsen's contention that all iusnaturalism supposes an absolute subject as author of legal norms, to suggest a historical reflection on the identity of 'legal positivism'.

Kelsen wished to rescue legal positivism from belief in an absolute subject as author of positive legal norms and his rescue attempt failed. Essentially, he knew it would be a mistake to try to employ the Christian concept 'positive law'[24] without providing a substitute basis for the objectivity of positive law[25] and he tried to counter the state-absolutist substitute by constructing a basis, through an analogy, in a natural-scientific kind of objectivism. But, since the two objectivities resided in different ideologies, the one could not ground the other. Neither, however, could the one ideology theorize the other adequately.

Kelsen conceives 'legal positivism' as the theory that the only law is positive law.[26] He tells us from the beginning that legal positivism requires an objectivistic viewpoint. The difficulties of the pure theory also suggest other important things about legal positivism. One is that philosophical positivism cannot be reconciled with it. Another is that legal positivism, in resting on the assumption of absolute subjectivity, differs from iusnaturalism not in kind but only in degree. They form a single tradition which for convenience may be characterized according to its essential method, as the 'exegetical' tradition. This emphasis on method also serves to indicate the influence (if that is not too weak a word) of this tradition in the study of specific sectors of particular legal systems, where there is specialized exegesis of texts.[27]

This character of legal positivism as one of the frayed ends of

---

[23] See e.g., McLellan, *The Young Hegelians and Karl Marx* (London, 1969), pp. 85–116.

[24] Kuttner, 'Sur les Origines du Terme "Droit Positif"' (loc. cit. n. 80).

[25] Cp. Carroll, 'What the Tortoise Said to Achilles' (1894) in Carroll, *Complete Works* (London, 1939), p. 1104.

[26] 'Was ist juristischer Positivismus?' (loc. cit. n. 11[1]), 465.

[27] Cp. Twining, 'Treatises and Textbooks', 12 *Journal of the Society of Public Teachers of Law* (n. s.) 267 (1973); 'Some Jobs for Jurisprudence', 1 *British Journal of Law and Society* 149 (1974).

iusnaturalism[28] has already been explored elsewhere in an examination of the sociological tendencies within jurisprudence, which led to the same hypotheses as have been developed here through transformation of the pure theory.[29] In both cases the outcome has been grounded in a particular concept of ideology. But it may be suggested that that concept and its outcome on the level of jurisprudence find support in the extent to which Kelsen may have been moving in a similar direction and confirmation in the extent to which the pure theory as transformed may be true of the pure theory as Kelsen formulated it.

These conclusions on the identity of legal positivism both locate it in an exegetical tradition and segregate it from theories of law that have their main philosophical basis (it is necessary to be ideal-typical here) in philosophical positivism or in relativism. Since these theories will belong to a different kind of ideology or to an unideological perspective, their method and their concept of law may be comparable with those in legal positivism, if at all, only through analogy. At the same time, there may be plausible confusion, because of common ideological character or because relativism has yet to find its own feet.

Of philosophical-positivist legal theory, no more need be said here. The most relativistic legal theories would seem to be those that are grounded philosophically in Marxism, transcendental phenomenology and perhaps linguistic studies. These theories can be developed both through philosophical refinement and through critique of exegetical jurisprudence. The critique of exegetical jurisprudence, however, will be as subject-matter. That is: the primary object of enquiry for relativist theory must be the whole ideologies within which legal norms are created—the ideologies themselves will impose this through their exclusivity—and exegetical jurisprudence will be a secondary object of enquiry, as a component of each such ideology.

For this purpose, at least, the most interesting exegetical jurisprudence will be that which agonizes on the frontier of its ideology, such as some of the sociological tendencies or the pure theory.

Where then is Kelsen's lurking deity? Whether Kant's was the

---

[28] Cp. Amselek, 'Kelsen et les Contradictions du Positivisme Juridique', 138 *Revue Internationale de Philosophie* 460 (1981).

[29] Stewart, 'Sociology in Jurisprudence' (loc. cit. n. 1).

Christian God or a deification of human reason, it might be thought to lie, probably in the latter form, behind Kelsen's categories and metaphysical bases as the ground of their universality. It might also be said to lie, in its practical reasoning, behind the 'constitution' that is always already one and, at least once, behind a validity of legal norms that pre-exists the presupposing of a basic norm.[30] Its presence can also be identified negatively, if one finds it absurd for Kelsen to envisage an almost carbon-copy representation, in terms of highly rational sets of legal propositions, of legal norms that are assumed to be irrational. And is it too much, to find in Kelsen a desire to achieve a coincidence of formal and material universality in a supreme public international legal order that to all intents and purposes is coeval with law itself, that would evade the problem of achieving material universality without iusnaturalism by abolishing the distinction between natural and positive law, and that would appear to heal the pure theory's philosophical conflicts by confining them almost impenetrably to the concept of the customary?[31]

Yet Kelsen could also declare that behind 'positive law' lies neither absolute truth nor absolute justice but 'the Gorgon-head of power'.[32] Is he, then, in saying that the presupposition 'basic norm' is a transcendental-logical 'minimum' of natural law and 'means the transformation of power into law',[33] admitting that he is in the business of illusionism? But a trick with the workings on view can produce no illusion.

Maybe, on his objective-idealist side, Kelsen does fall into a liberal 'ideological wish-dream of objectivity', producing an *Antimachtideologie*,[34] while the work of construction is visible mainly on the side of his scientism. Nevertheless, in affirming the transcendental moment in cognition at all, Kelsen naturalizes in legal science a principle that may falsify not only the obviousness of reificatory reality but also an idealist 'transparency'[35] of legal meaning.

---

[30] 'Why Should the Law be Obeyed?' (1957), in *WIJ*, 257.

[31] On the customary, see Stewart, *Law and Custom* (Ph.D. thesis, University College London, 1981).

[32] Quoted, Métall, *Hans Kelsen* (loc. cit. n. 63), p. 30.

[33] 'Natural Law Doctrine and Legal Positivism' (1928), in *GTLS*, 389, 437.

[34] Fechner, 'Ideologische Elemente . . .' (loc. cit. n. 4), 210, 212.

[35] Miaille, *Une Introduction Critique au Droit* (Paris, 1976), pp. 37–68.

CHAPTER 7

THE KELSENIAN ENTERPRISE

RICHARD TUR

IN responding to the final version of Stewart's paper I am conscious not only of the very real difficulties which his critique raises for the pure theory but also of the great tribute paid to Kelsen both by Stewart's extensive and meticulous scholarship and by his attempt to supersede rather than dismiss a theory which he regards as fatally flawed. As I understand Stewart, to supersede means to incorporate and go beyond on the model of Feuerbachian transformative criticism.[1] This is an extremely ambitious project and lesser spirits than Stewart might have rested content with exposing a major defect in Kelsen's theory. The ambitious nature of his project required Stewart to cover a great deal in limited compass and this has contributed to a highly allusive style and following up all the reading prescribed in Stewart's notes is, I admit, easier to contemplate than to complete. Consequently there may well be points at which I have failed wholly or in part to understand important elements in Stewart's argument.

A further and related difficulty flows from Stewart's use of undefined labels; for example, Kelsen is frequently referred to as a 'philosophical positivist' without further qualification or explanation and yet it is evident that Kelsen could not subscribe to the major tenets of logical positivism because of its denial and his affirmation of the significance of the 'ought' nor could positivism in social science be attributed to Kelsen however 'transformative' the criticism because it affirms and he denies that the methods of natural science are or ought to be duplicated in social science.[2] Again, the 'objective idealism' which according to Stewart continues, albeit vestigially, to infect Kelsen's theory and which, in Stewart's judgement, ultimately destroys it is illustrated by its

---

[1] Tucker, ed., *The Marx-Engels Reader* (New York, 1972), pp. xviii–xix; and Tucker, *The Marxian Revolutionary Idea* (London, 1969), p. 57.

[2] Giddens, ed., *Positivism and Sociology* (London, 1974), pp. ix; 1–3.

Richard Tur

paradigm, Christianity, rather than defined and yet Kelsen repeatedly denies the propriety of founding the validity of law upon the will of God or of founding the objectivity of knowledge on a deity. As to Kelsen's 'relativism', Stewart writes of it as being 'squeezed out . . . between the millstones of . . . ideologies'[3] without it being made clear whether epistemological or ethical relativism (or both) is in issue. Such use of labels contributes to my unease in assessing the significance of Stewart's criticisms of Kelsen because at important points in the argument I find myself uncertain as to the precise point which is being made.

Yet another concern is methodological. For the most part, Stewart does analyse what Kelsen has written, assesses his reasons and rejects his conclusions where they are, in Stewart's judgment, unsupported, incoherent, or unsatisfactory. Of course reasonable men might differ as to what Kelsen meant or as to how the various elements of his theory fit together and philosophical debate might be joined. But Stewart also devotes considerable energy and ingenuity to explaining what caused Kelsen to hold such views as he espoused and even what caused him to hold views, unwillingly or unwittingly, which he did not espouse and, indeed, emphatically rejected. Thus Kelsen's alleged 'objective idealism' is born of a 'liberal "ideological wish-dream of objectivity"',[4] and Kelsen allegedly retained a vestigial place for an absolute subject because of his scientism or 'philosophical positivism' which forced him to seek inept analogies in natural science objectivism. This, I think, distorts what Kelsen meant by 'analogy' just as 'philosophical positivism' misrepresents Kelsen's account of social science and his view of not only the common features of natural and normative science but also the specific differences.

Stewart's analysis of Kelsen's theory is historicist. Kelsen did not start pure, but, as it were, had purity thrust upon him in his attempts to raise jurisprudence to the level of a genuine science. Try as he might, Kelsen could not entirely rid himself of the objectivism with which, according to Stewart, he commenced because it remained immanent in the objectivism of the natural science that Kelsen took as his analogy. Consequently, the various influences upon Kelsen such as Kant, Simmel, and Vaihinger are paraded not as intellectual fellow-travellers in a common, though

---

[3] Stewart, above, p. 141.   [4] Stewart, above, p. 147.

not joint, philosophical adventure to whom Kelsen might legitimately turn in his repeated attempts to refine his theory but as
crutches to which Kelsen eclectically turned in his necessarily vain
attempts to avoid an historically inevitable destiny. Stewart thus
reduces Kelsen to total bondage, imprisoned in the inevitable
trend which moves from a Christian natural law openly espousing
God as absolute subject, through state-positivism which regards
the real personification of the state as absolute subject to legal
positivism which though it purports to deny any reliance upon the
absolute subject still logically entails it. It follows that the
difference between natural law and positivism is, for Stewart, only
a matter of degree because both schools found the specificity of the
legal in the will of the absolute subject; one consciously and
openly, the other tactitly and covertly.

Positive law is thus interpreted as 'one of the frayed ends of
iusnaturalism'.[5] This, perhaps, is not as surprising as might first
appear in that positivism consciously reacted to natural law
thinking and by constantly referring to *positive* law it suggested
that there is indeed some other kind of law. A thoroughgoing
positivist should regard the expression 'positive law' as pleonastic.
I agree with Stewart that trace-elements of natural law may well be
retained in some positive law theories. What is less clear to me is
that Kelsen's positivism necessarily retains the vestigial elements
of natural law perceived by Stewart who regards it as rooted in its
time as the apogee of the exegetical tradition. This 'tradition',
though it embraces dogmatic or expository jurisprudence, goes
beyond it in that everything is susceptible of explanation through
the interpretation of the will of the absolute subject. As absolute,
the will of this subject coincides with its reason and exegesis of its
essence reveals not only what is but also what ought to be. Stewart
regards the exegetical method, that is the interpretation of the
objective ideals located in the mind of the presupposed absolute
subject as the dominant method in jurisprudence, be it 'analytical',
'historical', or 'sociological'.[6] The exegesis of legal texts he takes
as supportive evidence for the proposition that jurisprudence, in
whatever form it may present itself is, ultimately, theological in
method and assumptions.[7] Such doctrines are, of course, in direct

---

[5] Stewart, above, pp. 145–6.
[6] Stewart, 'The Basic Norm as Fiction' [1980] *Juridical Review*, 199–224, p. 211.
[7] Stewart, above, p. 145 ff.

contradiction to Kelsen's repeated denials of the existence of practical reason as a source of norms, to his repeated insistence that cognition cannot be a source of norms and to his 'steps and stairs' theory of the concretization of legal norms which necessarily calls into play more than exegesis because 'every law-applying act is only partly determined by law'.[8] That the law-applying organ cannot proceed solely by way of exegesis is a cornerstone of Kelsen's theory. The exegetical role of the legal scientist as underlabourer is essentially modest and limited in sharp contrast to the monolithic and all-embracing exegesis of Christianity which Stewart takes as paradigmatic of systems of thought founding upon an absolute subject. Thus there is nowhere in Kelsen's works the suggestion that there is but 'one right answer', an assumption which might be expected of one actually participating in the monolithic and all-embracing exegetical tradition depicted by Stewart.

Stewart's historicism leads him to suppose that the difference between classical natural law and Kelsen's pure theory is but a matter of degree; that the pure theory in particular and positivism in general is merely natural law in distintegration and that the disintegration appears to be ultimately a matter of fate rather than of philosophical defect. The historical moment for the total disintegration of the entire exegetical tradition occurs sometime in the early 1960s, specifically when Kelsen rejects his earlier attempts to characterize the basic norm as 'hypothesis' and redefines it as 'fiction' in the sense of Vaihinger's philosophy. What others may see as a minor though necessary adjustment in the presentation by Kelsen of his theory of law takes on epoch-making significance in Stewart's historicist interpretation of the pure theory of law. Doubtless 'hypothesis' did suggest something about how things really are whereas Kelsen almost certainly used the word 'hypothesis' in its ideal sense, following Cohen, of 'invented basis'.[9] This is consistent with Kelsen's insistence that the basic norm is not, however, a product of 'free invention'.[10] Kelsen clearly was concerned to blunt criticism born of misunderstanding and adopted the 'fiction' account to emphasize that the basic norm was to be presupposed, if at all, in full consciousness that its presupposition does not entail a belief in the existence of God, or a

---

[8] *PTL*, 349.　　　[9] Ebenstein, 92.　　　[10] *PTL*, 201.

norm-creating Nature, or a real, personified State. There is, therefore, no epistemological pay-off in the nature of the imaginary will the meaning of which is the basic norm and consequently there can be no ontological commitment either.

The basic norm is wholly formal and therefore empty of content. Exegesis of the consciousness of the absolute subject can produce nothing when, by definition, that consciousness is wholly exhausted by the thought that something ought to be; *ex nihilo nihil fit*. The content of the normative order flows not from the imaginary will of the imaginary absolute subject but from the acts of actual human beings. Custom is a solution for Kelsen and not a problem as it is for others. The concretization of norms is ultimately found in and exhausted by actual human conduct, which conduct is necessarily wholly concrete in a way in which no description of or prescription for such conduct in words can ever be. The fullest and most detailed description imaginable of a sunset is not a sunset and the fullest and most detailed prescription imaginable for an act is not the act itself. Consequently norms created by custom do not differ radically from norms created by acts of will. All such norms, in contradistinction to the basic norm are created by acts of actual human beings. Thus the basic norm provides only the formal category under which actual human conduct may be interpreted as norm-creating or norm-applying. Of course actual human conduct is also susceptible of interpretation under the category of causality as either cause or effect. Without recourse to an a priori category we have but a 'modally indifferent substratum'.[11] 'At the end—or in the beginning, according to the point of view, is the word or the deed.'[12] The 'word', or basic norm is pure, unconditioned by anything empirical, and undetermined by any other, higher norm. Exegesis of this is empty. The 'deed', or actual human conduct is, absent the basic norm, simply what is and exegesis of it is mere behaviourism, a purely empirical theory which 'like the wooden head in Phaedrus' fable, is very beautiful, but, alas, it has no brain!'[13] It seems to follow from this analysis of norm and conduct that far from history determining the nature of law or legal theory, history may be understood as ossified law. Consequently, Stewart's location of Kelsen in the exegetical tradition, especially as that tradition is defined by Stewart, strikes me as highly implausible.

[11] *ATN*, ch. 16.   [12] *ASL*, 250.   [13] *MEJ*, 34.

Doubtless, the above rehearsal and reaffirmation of Kelsenism will strike some, Stewart included, as unsatisfactory but it is at least consistent with Kelsen's substitution of function for substance, consciously following in the footsteps of Cassirer.[14] Just as the state is not an entity different from the law but is to be explained, indeed explained away, as the unification of the normative functions of the law, the basic norm is not something actually willed by any real or imaginary being or superbeing but merely the function of making possible a normative interpretation of a 'modally indifferent substratum'. Given the actual existence of such interpretations within historically existing cultures,[15] it follows that such interpretation is possible and the basic norm is Kelsen's answer to the Kantian question, What makes such an interpretation possible? The basic norm is the minimum necessary presupposition entailed by such interpretations. This suggests that much of Stewart's criticism of Kelsen puts the cart before the horse by understanding the objectivity of legal knowledge as warranted by the basic norm whereas the opposite is more nearly true. Just as Kant did not invent a novel method to acquire knowledge but explained how pre-existing knowledge of nature, for example Newtonian physics, was possible so Kelsen does not invent a new method of acquiring knowledge of the legal order but offers a new theory of what it is which legitimates such knowledge claims; he is concerned, therefore, 'not so much with . . . [law] as with our way of knowing . . . [law], insofar as this is a priori possible'.[16]

---

[14] *Der soziologische und der juristische Staatsbegriff* (Tübingen, 1928), p. 212.

[15] E.g. Pollock, *Essays in Jurisprudence and Ethics* (London, 1882), p. 26: 'we deny that the jurist requires, as Professor Lorimer assumes him to require, "an absolute basis for his science". Why should he not, like other people, be content with a basis of acknowledged fact? Positive law exists. In other words, there are certain social institutions which are protected, and certain rules of conduct which are in various ways and degrees enforced, by the courts of justice of all civilized countries. The fact is notorious and intelligible to all men of all ways of thinking, whether they account for it by deduction from the law of nature or otherwise. If the jurist accepts it as for his purposes ultimate, he does only what all other students of special sciences do . . . Where would geometry be if the geometer were expected at the outset of his work to grapple with the metaphysical difficulties that beset our notion of space?' See, too, Bosanquet, *The Philosophical Theory of the State* (London, 4th edn. 1923), p. 32: 'For here, as the plainest and most unmistakable data of experience, we are confronted with *ideal facts*. The vast mass of documents which form the basis of the Science of Right—a more complete and comprehensive set of records, perhaps, than any other branch of social science can boast—bears witness in every case to one social phenomenon at least, to a formal act of mind and will. . .'   [16] *CPuR*, A 11–12; B 25.

Objectivity within the Kantian tradition flows from the synthesis of concept and intuition; of a priori category and empirical data and not from any Cartesian *deus ex machina*. Consequently the relationship of the basic norm and objectivity is not analogous to the relationship of objectivity and the absolute subject within what Stewart calls the exegetical tradition.

To go beyond the minimum function of the basic norm to the substance of an absolute subject, or a deity, is to indulge in an extravagant presupposition going beyond what is logically entailed. Philosophically, the existence of God is not less nor more plausible than his non-existence. Since we cannot explain how things came into being by the principle of causality alone we might be tempted to presuppose some thing or being which created them but it is an enormous and unwarranted step from presupposing a formal, empty 'first cause' as an alternative to an infinite regress to go beyond that minimum some thing or being to a god created in the image of man but benevolent, omniscient, just, and omnipotent. That there is something may well be a logical entailment of the causal mode of explanation; that that something is a conscious agent, all-knowing and good, is an additional and logically unwarranted step. The historicism which Stewart brings to bear upon Kelsen and the pure theory contributes to my reservations as to my capacity fully to appreciate the nuances of his argument. Each reading of his paper leaves me with an impression of a futile attempt to fit Kelsen into Stewart's historicist framework rather as one might 'madly squeeze a right-hand foot into a left-hand shoe'.[17] It is also my impression that in order so to fit Kelsen into the historicist account, Stewart is constrained to massage even Kelsen's clearest statements by means of an *ad hoc* error theory which suggests that such of Kelsen's pronouncements as do not fit the historicist model reveal Kelsen's inability to appreciate the implications of his own theory. That Stewart attempts to fit Kelsen into his historicism irrespective of Kelsen's own pronouncements is revealed most clearly by his asking just where and what is Kelsen's 'lurking deity', and answering that it is most probably to be found in Kant's deification of human reason.[18]

The remainder of my response to Stewart proceeds in two main parts; first, an account of my interpretation of the Kelsenian

---

[17] Carroll, *Through the Looking-Glass*, ch. 7.
[18] Stewart, above, pp. 146–7.

enterprise and, secondly, some comments on major issues canvassed by Stewart, namely (*a*) natural law and positive law; (*b*) the basic norm as a fiction; (*c*) jurisprudence and sociology.

The Kelsenian enterprise is, indeed, the raising of jurisprudence 'to the level of a genuine science'.[19] It is primarily an epistemological project. Clearly a great deal of philosophical spadework has to be done before one can tackle the special epistemological problems of the normative. Kelsen avails himself of two short-cuts. First he relies heavily upon the Kantian tradition in epistemology as mediated and refined by neo-Kantianism; 'The decisive epistemological viewpoint for the correct construction of the concept of law and the state I acquired by means of Cohen's interpretation of Kant.'[20] Secondly, and consequently, Kelsen takes the epistemological validity of natural science for granted and seeks to establish the possibility of normative science by constructing it on analogous lines. This is not mere scientism; Kelsen does not advocate that the methods of natural science be taken over wholesale by the social scientist. The 'analogy' which Kelsen draws between natural science and social science is to be understood as intimating simultaneously common membership of the *genus*, knowledge, and mutually specific differences. Accordingly, Kelsen seeks to show how legal science parallels natural science without being identical to it. Thus it would follow that if natural science is epistemologically valid so, too, is normative science. The disintegration of the pure theory which Stewart perceives and argues for cannot be brought about by a frontal attack on the basic norm; one would need to demonstrate either that the analogy Kelsen seeks to draw is imperfect or that the Kantian account of the epistemological validity of natural science is itself untenable, following, perhaps the conventionalism of Kuhn[21] or the scepticism of Feyerabend.[22]

Hume criticized the rationalist metaphysics of his day as follows: 'If we take in our hand any volume; of divinity or school metaphysics for instance; let us ask, *Does it contain any abstract reasoning concerning quality or number? No. Does it contain any experimental reasoning concerning matters of fact and existence?*

---

[19] *RR*[1], iii.   [20] *HPS*[2], XVII.
[21] *The Structure of Scientific Revolutions*, 2nd edn. (Chicago, 1970).
[22] *Against Method: An Outline of An Anarchist Theory of Knowledge* (London, 1978).

No. Commit it then to the flames: for it can contain nothing but sophistry and illusion.'[23] Thus only mathematical statements and statements of fact are epistemologically valid. Similarly, logical positivism proclaimed that only such statements as are logically warranted or empirically verifiable are meaningful; all else is nonsense. Armed with such principles what havoc must we make of our law libraries? With what confidence now do we take in our hand any legal treatise or textbook? What epistemological validity can such works claim? Normative statements and propositions of law are neither analytic nor synthetic; 'if we regard empirical verifiability as a necessary feature of any knowledge claim, then at least two areas of discourse, ethics and theology, start to look silly'.[24] Jurisprudence, too, looks silly, given the normativity which it shares with ethics and theology. Indeed, 'the *ought* expresses a kind of necessity . . . which we do not find elsewhere in the whole of nature . . . if we look only at the course of nature, the ought has no meaning whatever'.[25]

It is clearly a possible philosophical move at this point to take normativity seriously and to reject logical positivism and Humean empiricism. One would then require a theory of knowledge which does not rule out jurisprudence, ethics, and theology *ab initio*. Such would be an urgent question for jurisprudence had the ground not been covered already by Kelsen. The pure theory is a thoroughgoing attempt to develop an epistemology for jurisprudence. It is a recipe for legal knowledge. Thus Weyr characterizes the pure theory not as a systematic discipline which classifies the content of law, that is, dogmatic jurisprudence, but as *methodology*.[26] Consequently it is one-sided to stress the under-labourer conception of legal science. Granted there are passages emphasizing this conception; 'the aim . . . is to enable the jurist, the lawyer, the judge, the legislator, or the law-teacher to understand and describe as exactly as possible his own legal system'.[27] But even here there is as much emphasis upon

---

[23] Hume, *An Enquiry Concerning Human Understanding*, Section XII, Part III, Selby-Bigge, edn., p. 165.

[24] Wilkerson, *Kant's Critique of Pure Reason* (Oxford, 1978), p. 153.

[25] *CPuR*, A 547; B 575.

[26] Weyr, 'Rechtsphilosophie und Rechtswissenschaft' in *Gesellschaft, Staat und Recht: Festschrift gewidmet Hans Kelsen zumm 50*, ed. Verdross (Vienna, 1931), p. 375.

[27] *GTLS*, xiii.

understanding as upon exposition. Further, Kelsen sharply contrasts
the party interest viewpoint of the jurisconsults whose advisory
role was received through Roman Law with the objectivist and
universalist aspirations of pure theory.[28]

The theory of knowledge inherited by Kelsen from Kant as
mediated by neo-Kantianism is extraordinarily difficult to sum-
marize. Kant did not start as a critical philosopher but as a
rationalist. Rationalism in this sense seems identical to what
Stewart calls the exegetical tradition. The only knowledge worth
having is necessary knowledge. Such knowledge is obtained by
pure reason intuiting essences and deriving conclusions by purely
deductive reasoning. The edifice is indeed frequently supported by
an absolute subject as, notoriously, in the rationalism of Descartes
who, uniquely among major philosophers, did not develop a
parallel ethics. Considering only ideal types, the dialectical
contrary of rationalism is empiricism, the crux of which is that all
ideas in the mind entered by way of sense-impressions. Rationalists
regard empiricists as concerned only with the appearances of
things and as out of touch with the real essences of being. Further,
appearances are mutually contradictory; the straw in the glass of
water appearing visually bent but tactually straight. For their part,
empiricists regarded rationalists as hopelessly deluded illusionists
building their metaphysical edifices on no foundation other than
their own subjective reason. These epistemological extremes have
jurisprudential isomorphs. *Begriffsjurisprudenz* and classical natural
law are wholly rationalist. Benthamite positivism and the various
forms of legal realism on both sides of the Atlantic are profoundly
empiricist.

Kant, however, ultimately rejected rationalism, two reasons
being widely canvassed. First, his discovery of the antinomies of
reason, for example the possibility of proving rationally that the
world must have had a beginning in time and that it could not have
had a beginning; that individuals units, or atoms, are necessary
and that they are impossible; that freedom is necessary and
determinism inescapable, etc. This, Kant thought, was 'a scandal
of pure reason' and this scandal 'first aroused him from his
dogmatic slumbers'.[29] Secondly, Kant was awakened from his

---

[28] *PTL-IMFC*, 497–8; *PTL*, 89, 'cognition of the law must not be confounded
with legal advice'.
[29] Kant, *Philosophical Correspondence: 1759–1799* (Chicago, 1967), in a letter

dogmatic slumbers by Hume's radical scepticism.[30] Kant, in any event was entertaining doubts about the validity of rationalism and had asked, 'What reason do we have for thinking that intellectual representations, the basic concepts of our understanding, have any necessary relationship to the world?'[31] One such basic concept is causality. It bespeaks a necessary relation of events. Hume remarked that we never observed the necessity in the connection; '. . . all events seem loose and separate'.[32] Hume explained the necessity by way of a habit of thought. If one experiences A after B often enough one is, as it were, caused always to expect A after B. But this solution fails splendidly, invoking causality to explain causality. Kant saw at once, however, that the necessity of causality posed as great a problem for his rationalism as it did for Hume's empiricism.

Kant's solution was bold and inventive. What rationalism and empiricism had in common for all their opposition was the exclusivity of the analytic/synthetic distinction. All statements concerned the relation of ideas or matters of fact. Kant conceived of the possibility of the a priori synthetic proposition. Such a notion seems about as plausible as a round square yet Kant advanced argument upon argument to demonstrate the possibility and the epistemological role of such propositions. Thus, as the rationalists maintained, reason indeed has a role in the acquisition of knowledge. None the less, the creative power of reason is restricted because without the data of experience the forms of the mind have nothing to systematize, order, understand, or know. Hence the famous aphorism; 'Thoughts without intuitions [that is, perceptions] are empty; intuitions without concepts are blind.'[33] Thus Kant synthesized the opposition of empiricism and rationalism into a new *critical* philosophy, critical because it was borne of criticism of the rationalist tradition. He offers a middle way between extravagant metaphysics and radical scepticism. His *Prolegomena to Any Future Metaphysics* is an account of worthwhile as against worthless metaphysics.

---

to Christian Garve, 1798; cited in Zweig, *The Essential Kant* (New York, 1970), p. 15.

[30] *Prolegomena to Any Future Metaphysics*, ed. Beck (Indianapolis, 1950), p. 8.

[31] Kant, *Philosophical Correspondence: 1759–1799*, in a letter to Marcuse Hertz, 1792, cited Zweig, *The Essential Kant*, pp. 20–1.

[32] Hume, *Enquiry*, Section VII, Part II. [33] *CPuR*, A 51; B 75.

Now, just as empiricism and rationalism have jurisprudential isomorphs, so, too, has Kant's critical philosophy, namely the pure theory of law. Pure reason is the faculty of knowledge a priori. The critical philosophy reveals that knowledge is necessarily a synthesis of a priori form and a posteriori data. Consequently *The Pure Theory of Law* is not a book of knowledge but a book about knowledge. As a prolegomenon to all future jurisprudence which aspires to be scientific it must necessarily relate to the forms of knowledge and not provide legal knowledge itself. The a priori element of law is its form, not its content. Kelsen is frequently criticized for his empty formalism.[34] To his credit, Stewart does not take such points and the matter need not be further discussed here except to note that Kelsen justifiably regarded such criticisms to reveal a lamentable misunderstanding of the nature of science.

Kant, however, overstated his case in that he regarded certain modes of thought, not least of all causal explanation, as necessary rather than as merely possible. He failed to steer sufficiently away from rationalism in that he regarded his categories of the mind as in some sense static, immutable, and innate. If, then, societies have existed which knew nothing of causality such societies must be dismissed as non-human or it must be allowed that causality is merely a possible not a necessary mode of human thought and explanation. Such societies have existed and it would strain credulity to believe that Greek society, pre-dating Ionian philosophy and the insights of Heraclitus of Ephesus, was non-human.[35] In societies where animism dominates, the basis of explanation is social and normative rather than natural and causal. Kelsen himself discusses his circumstances in detail, tracing the emergence of the category of causality in the history of ideas, seeing it as emerging by a slow series of modifications out of the norm of retribution. Historically, imputation pre-dated causality as a mode of thought and explanation.[36] This places Kelsen squarely in the

[34] E.g. Stone, *Legal System and Lawyers' Reasonings* (1964), p. 109: 'The pure theory of law is formal and empty and inapplicable to any legal problems'; Laski, *A Grammar of Politics*, 5th edn. (1948), p. vi; see above 18 ff.

[35] Frankfort, *et al.*, *Before Philosophy* (Baltimore, 1949), especially ch. 1 and ch. 8.

[36] *ELMP*, Ch. VIII, 'The Emergence of the Causal Law from the Principle of Retribution'; *Society and Nature: A Sociological Enquiry* (London, 1946). See, too, Cassirer, *Die Begriffsform im mythischen Denken* (1922), p. 31, '[The causal law] . . . is no self-evident possession of the mind, but one of its latest methodological achievements'.

neo-Kantian tradition as a contributor not as a mere borrower. It explains why he seeks to distance himself from Kant's philosophy by praying such as Cohen and Cassirer in aid. Indeed, if, as Kant proposed, natural science was a necessary product of the human mind, the wonder is why the world had to wait for Newton; 'if the fact of our attainment of *episteme* can be explained at all by the fact that our intellect legislates for and imposes its own laws upon nature, then the first of these two facts cannot be contingent any more than the second.'[37] Conversely, if the acquisition of knowledge is contingent and possible, then the intellectual equipment which it requires is also contingent and possible. Consequently one may regard Kant, for all his critical philosophy, as remaining within what Stewart calls the exegetical tradition but the decisiveness of the neo-Kantian break from the absolutist tendencies remaining in Kant's conception of the categories should immunize neo-Kantians from the charge of conniving at the existence of an absolute subject.

The suspicion that Kant remained within the exegetical tradition becomes a certainty when we turn from his epistemology to his ethics;

Kant abides by his critical standpoint only in his treatment of nature; in the ethics he offers us not epistemology but a practical theory of morals. It is worthy of note that in his treatment of law he makes legal theory a part of his *Metaphysics of Morals*. He does indeed ask what law is, not merely what it ought to be, but just as in the ethics he fails to distinguish form and content sharply and so produces not an epistemology of law but a legal axiology.[38]

Kelsen was wholly aware of the schizophrenia which rent Kant's philosophy; 'the pure theory of law rests not on Kant's philosophy of law but on his theory of knowledge'.[39] A recent commentator 'would not consider it an exaggeration to say that much of his [Kant's] epistemology . . . is right and important but that most of his ethical views are disastrously wrong.'[40]

Kelsen is distinguishable from Kant in two important and related ways. First, he denies the existence of practical reason as a source of norms. As a non-cognitivist in ethics he holds that

---

[37] Popper, *Conjectures and Refutations* (London, 1963), p. 95.
[38] Ebenstein, 26–7.   [39] *GTLS*, 444; Ebenstein, 88, n. 41.
[40] Wilkerson, *Kant's Critique of Pure Reason*, p. 3.

ultimate moral values cannot be rationally known. If ultimate
values are susceptible of rational cognition the whole Kelsenian
enterprise is seriously threatened. Secondly, he developed a
wholly formal category of 'ought' in contradistinction to Kant's
material 'ought'. Kant referred to the causality possessed by our
reason which 'is clear from the imperatives which, in all practical
matters, we impose as rules upon our executive powers. . .'

This 'ought' expresses a possible action, the ground of which cannot be
anything but a mere concept, while in every merely natural action the
ground must always be a phenomenon [that is, be causally determined]
. . . it is true that the action to which the 'ought' applies must be possible
under natural conditions [that is, ought implies can], but these natural
conditions do not affect the determination of the will itself . . . there may
be ever so many natural grounds which impel me to will and ever so many
sensuous temptations, but they can never produce an ought, but only a
willing which is always conditioned but by no means necessary . . . reason
does not yield to the impulse that is given empirically . . . but frames for
itself . . . a new order . . . to which it adapts the empirical conditions and
according to which it declares actions to be necessary, even though they
have not taken place and, maybe, never will take place . . . if we compare
action with reason . . . we find a rule and order totally different from the
order of nature . . . from this point of view everything, it may be, ought
not to happen which according to the course of nature has happened.[41]

Kant goes on to argue that the causality of reason is complete in
itself and not a concurrent cause in the world of phenomena; that
permits him to 'impute' action to a man's intelligible character.
Here, then, are the bare bones of Kelsen's normative epistemology.
For Kant's 'causality of reason' or 'causality of freedom' Kelsen
substitutes 'imputation' and for the 'spontaneous order created by
reason' Kelsen substitutes the 'normative order'. Freedom for
Kant and Kelsen alike is constituted by treating human beings as
'end point[s] of imputation',[42] even though from the point of view
of natural science their conduct is necessarily part of the chain of
cause and effect and therefore causally determined.

These substitutions are merely terminological but the final
substitution by Kelsen of 'will' for Kant's 'reason' is of the first
importance and is wholly in accordance with the critical philosophy
which Kant introduced. Just as pure reason is empty without
empirical data, so, Kelsen argues, pure reason is also empty in the

[41] *CPuR*, A 544–8; B 572–6.   [42] *PTL*, 98.

normative sphere without the empirical data which flows from human acts of will and from human acts. Reason can tell us only that it is possible that something ought to be. What ought to be is thus contingent matter flowing from the willing and acting of human beings. Just as positive law can have any content, any content can be normative. This radically distinguishes Kelsen from ethical naturalists who hold that the word 'ought' carries a material implication of human welfare, just as it distinguishes him from all forms of ethical rationalism which find in pure reason alone the source of the content of norms.

Kelsen frequently stresses the difference between his ought and Kant's;

> It is necessary to remember of course, that when the principle of imputation is applied, and when it is stated that under the condition of certain behaviour, other behaviour *ought* to take place, the term 'ought' has not its usual moral, but a purely logical meaning. It designates, like causality, a category in the sense of Kant's transcendental logic.[43]

Clearly there is a powerful need for Kelsen to distance himself from Kant on this point so much else being common property and this explains, perhaps, why he prays in aid oath-helpers so obscure as Herbart and Lotze or so unlikely as Simmel.[44] If, as Stewart hints but neither explains nor demonstrates, Simmel's 'ought' embraces both the practical and the theoretical 'ought', we have to understand Kelsen as adopting only the theoretical 'ought'. Consequently, even if Simmel is a significant influence, it does not follow that Kelsen swallowed him whole. Kelsen makes a formal logical distinction between is and ought; an insoluble opposition which has radical consequences for science, founding an unavoidable division of the sciences; 'According as the object of research is the Is of actual events—that is, *reality*—or an ethical, legal, aesthetic, or other Ought—that is, an *ideality*—so our knowledge divides itself into two fundamentally distinct groups . . . [and] sciences are in turn divided into *causal* sciences and *normative* sciences.'[45] Nature for Kelsen, in wholly Kantian fashion, is a

---

[43] 'Science and Politics', in *WIJ*, 363.
[44] Herbart, an early nineteenth-century philosopher, is mentioned by Ebenstein, 6; Wilson, above, p. 52 and Stewart, n. 25; Lotze, a nineteenth-century logician, was recommended to Hart by Kelsen, see, 'Kelsen Visited' 10 *UCLA Law Rev.* 709–28, 715 (1963); Simmel is discussed by Stewart, especially at n. 25.
[45] Ebenstein, 6.

system of elements related by the principle of causality as cause and effect; society is a system of elements linked by the principle of imputation as condition and consequence. It follows from Kelsen's definition of the ought that normative science, if we had it, could not tell us how we ought to behave in a practical sense; it could tell us only how we ought to behave according to the norms of our society. Thus normative science is utterly conventional, historical, and sociological; it describes positive law, positive morality, and positive relgion.[46] It is not a critical endeavour going beyond current standards and proposing reform. Kelsen's normative science describes the ought-to-be-that-is; of the ought-to-be-that-ought-to-be it says, and by definition can say, nothing. But it would be wrong to regard this as a defect; indeed, for Kelsen, it is a virtue because it is a fundamental aspect of science that it does not and cannot, as science, prescribe how human beings ought to behave; as Merkl observes, 'It can never be regarded as unscientific when a science stops short at the boundaries of its subject.'[47]

Stewart proposes that, from the point of view of the exegetical tradition, natural law and positivism may be assimilated. Startling as the proposition is, it is not wholly false. In so far as it is true, however, it is true for reasons other than those advanced by Stewart for whom the common element is the absolute subject. Kelsen certainly admits that a metalegal norm validates positive norms. This looks very similar to Kant's proposition that behind positive law there must be a natural law.[48] But similar as these propositions appear they are radically different because of the radical difference between the material 'ought' presupposed by Kant and the formal 'ought' presupposed by Kelsen. Thus an absolute subject may, perhaps, be found in Kant's but not in Kelsen's basic norm. There is another sense in which Kelsen's pure theory approaches natural law thinking. To explain how this is so I shall adopt a device much favoured by Kelsen though nowhere explicitly presented, 'dialectically contrary ideal types'.[49] An ideal

---

[46] Avineri, *Hegel's Theory of the Modern State* (Cambridge, 1972), ch. 2.

[47] Merkl, *Das Recht im Lichte Anwendung*, p. 17; cited in Ebenstein, 205.

[48] *MEJ*, 26; see Steiner, above, p. 75.

[49] *GTLS*, 441–4. This is not the occasion for a discussion of the methodology of ideal types nor for a detailed account of the device I have called 'dialectically contrary ideal types'. It is employed here simply to outline the way in which some versions of natural law and some versions of positivism merge, without any claims

type, unlike a moral ideal, is not a model for action but a guide to thought. But it is ideal in a different sense in that as a caricature, it exaggerates salient features beyond the possibility of empirical instantiation. Such ideal types hunt in pairs of dialectical contraries and may thus be regarded as the end points of a continuum. Judicial process may be taken as an example of the device in operation. At one extreme we might imagine a system of absolute discretion such as envisaged in Plato's *Republic*; at the other, a system of rigid logical deduction such as envisaged in Plato's *Laws*. No actual legal system conforms, or could conform, to such extremes. Actual legal systems and departments of law within them may however be situated at various points along the continuum according to one's perception of the mix of logic and discretion exhibited. Again, theories of judicial process can be similarly located; 'free law' tending to one extreme, *Begriffsjuris-prudenz*, to the other. Moving in from one end we may locate versions of positivism which stress strong discretion; moving in from the other, such theories as propose 'one right answer'. Kelsen uses the ideal types 'static' and 'dynamic' legal systems in this way, natural law being ideally static and positivism being ideally dynamic; actual legal systems being mixed.[50]

One might treat positivism and natural law in similar fashion as endpoints on a continuum. The characterization of each end point will be the simplistic exaggeration of a figure 'cut in cartoon'. The natural law extreme may be characterized by such terms as reason, justice, legitimacy, and a material and practical ought. Further it will be static in Kelsen's sense whereby all the dependent norms are contained tacitly within its basic norm and may be discovered by the purely intellectual process of subsuming the particular under the general. At the positivist extreme, characterization proceeds in terms of will, power, and instrumentalism; ideally such extreme positivism will be fact-based rather than normative, dynamic in Kelsen's sense, involving command and arbitrary decision-making. It is notoriously difficult to trap and exhibit in

as to historical accuracy. When I apply the device to a tentative classification of jurisprudential theories, I do so speculatively without seeking to claim that serious jurisprudents can be so simply understood.

[50] Compare Raz, *The Concept of a Legal System* (Oxford, 1970 and 1980), p. 135; 'For some undisclosed reasons Kelsen adopts the odd view that there are only two types of normative systems: Dynamic . . . and Static. . .' Perhaps the view is less 'odd' given Kelsen's use of what I call dialectically contrary ideal types.

captivity jurisprudents who fit such extreme paradigms but classical natural law and, perhaps Kant, himself might be placed at the natural law extreme and Frank, if interpreted as an extreme particularist, and the early Ross,[51] adjacent to the positivist extreme. Bentham, for whom everything must pay up in the hard currency of fact, and Austin occupy a position fairly adjacent to the positivist extreme but, in comparison to Frank, the commitment to some degree of legal system would justify a slightly more central position. Hart's theory would be even more centrally located, not so much because of the minimum core of empirical good sense which he perceives in the terminology of natural law but because his positivism purports to be normative rather than fact-based. Given, however, the facticity of the rule of recognition, Hart might properly remain nearer the positivist end of the continuum. Aquinas, as interpreted by Finnis, clearly cannot go too far out from the centre towards the natural law end partly because, apparently, he allows that an unjust law is still a law but primarily because he apparently rejects the rationalist stance that all decisions flow from logical deductions, allowing for 'determinations' in his system.[52] A determination involves an irreducibly dispositive element flowing from the will of the law-applying organ and not from logical deduction. Aquinas's theory is thus revealed as a synthesis of the dynamic element of positivism and the static element of natural law.

Where might one properly locate Kelsen on such a continuum? Clearly, given a stronger normativity than Hart's, he must be placed nearer to natural law than Hart's theory. But that must put him rather closer to Aquinas than might otherwise be anticipated. Kelsen and Aquinas both presuppose that something ought to be and although Kelsen denies and Aquinas affirms some content to the ought, both admit of subsumption and delegation, of deduction and determination as alternative modes of 'deriving' dependent norms and decisions. But if Kelsen and Aquinas might justly be placed more or less side by side on the continuum, Stewart's

---

[51] Ross, 45 *California Law Rev.* 568 (1957): 'the idea of "validity" or "binding force" of law has no place in empirical science'. Such classification of authors is always tentative not only because their views develop over time but also because the richness and extent of a jurisprudent's thoughts can hardly be adequately captured in so schematic and simplified fashion.

[52] Finnis, *Natural Law and Natural Rights* (Oxford, 1980), pp. 351–66, as to unjust laws; pp. 284–9, as to determinations.

assimilation of natural law and positivism is no longer surprising. Indeed, Kelsen acknowledges that 'very little objection can be raised . . . [to regarding the basic norm] . . . as an element of a natural law doctrine . . . [but it is] . . . the minimum . . . of natural law' without which a cognition of laws is impossible.[53] And one can go even further. Considering the limits of positivism, Kelsen observes that the static principle cannot be wholly eradicated from positive law because the basic norm of a particular system can be presupposed only on the basis of some content, meaning thereby the content of the empirical data which its presupposition unifies as a legal system; 'the validity of the basic norm of a given positive legal order does not rest on the dynamic principle . . . The basic norm is not valid because it has been created in a certain way, but its validity is assumed by virtue of its content'.[54] Ross criticizes Kelsen as follows: 'From Natural law—and common legal-moral consciousness saturating also legal 'positivism'—Kelsen has taken over a belief in a 'validity' as a quality inherent in a legal order.'[55] From their respective positions on the continuum this observation is also unsurprising, if, indeed, the presentation of even the most vacuous ought constitutes natural law thinking. Kelsen could only reassert the formal logical nature of his ought or, perhaps, retreat to pragmatism, defending the basic norm as a useful idea for the systematizing of legally relevant data.

The focal point in Stewart's attack is Kelsen's substitution of 'fiction' for 'hypothesis' as the appropriate characterization of the basic norm. Stewart refers to this redefinition of the basic norm as the pure theory's 'swan song'.[56] According to Stewart, the fiction account of the basic norm is tantamount to an admission that Kelsen was in the end unable to dispense with the assumption of an absolute subject. This argument has already been criticized and found wanting. Here I seek to question Stewart's assessment of Vaihinger and to develop a Kantian account of the basic norm as a regulative idea of reason.[57] The redefinition of the basic norm is

---

[53] *GTLS*, 437. [54] *GTLS*, 401.

[55] Ross, op. cit. note 51 above, p. 568.

[56] Stewart [1980] *Juridical Review*, 199.

[57] There was a suggestion at the conference that Kelsen had repudiated this interpretation in one of his many articles. Unfortunately no citation was forthcoming and therefore the text is unavailable to me. See, however, Ebenstein, 30, commenting on Cassirer's transformation of the atom from 'a firm substantial

mentioned by Kelsen in several different articles.[58] In all but one,[59] he makes no real attempt to specify precisely in which sense the basic norm is a fiction. Stewart distinguishes two senses of fiction as used by Vaihinger, the 'semi-fiction', which does not conform to reality, and the 'full-fiction', which not only does not conform to reality but also contains contradiction within itself. What Kelsen writes about an awareness that the basic norm does not correspond to reality[60] is at least as suggestive of the 'half-fiction' as the 'full-fiction'. That the redefinition of the basic norm constitutes the swan song of the pure theory is, however, highly suggestive of the 'full-fiction' of self-contradiction. However, Kelsen cannot plausibly be rescued from the 'full-fiction' characterization of the basic norm because in a crucial passage he observes that it 'not only contradicts reality, since no such norm exists as the meaning of an actual act of will, but also contains contradiction within itself since it represents the authorization of a supreme moral or legal authority, and hence it issues from an authority lying beyond that authority, even though the further authority is merely figmentary'.[61] Thus Stewart is entitled to conclude, as he does, that Kelsen adopted the 'full-fiction'

core' to a 'virtual point'. This Ebenstein remarks is to treat the atom as an 'idea' in the strict Kantian sense. Such ideas 'have one admirable and indispensable function . . . they direct the understanding to a definite end, direct all its laws to a single point, which, though but an idea, a *focus imaginarius*, a point completely beyond the limits of possible experience, yet serves to provide the greatest measure of unity'; A 644; B 672 and see, generally, *CPuR*, A 669–704; B 697–732. I take further reassurance from *TPD*, 271 n–272 n. Also, Bjarup, 288–9. Finally, in correspondence with the author, 13 February, 1984, Vernengo confirmed that this interpretation was popular with Argentinian legal philosophers in the 1940s, specifically mentioning Cossio. Vernengo also drew my attention to Gioja, 'La arquitestenica del conecimente juridice' (1945) and 'El tema de la teoría pura del derecho' (1949) which interprets some of Kelsen's categories as Husserlian ideas and remarked on Kelsen's preface assuring Gioja of his 'complete agreement with the views . . . expressed'. According to Vernengo, Gioja did not pursue these insights, following other philosophical influences such as Wittgenstein.

[58] (1) 'Die Funktion der Verfassung' (1964) 11 *Forum* 583–6, reprinted in *Die Wiener rechtstheoretische Schule* (Vienna, 1968), p. 1971–9, translated by Stewart as 'The Constitutional Function' in [1980] *Juridical Review*, 214–24; revised translation by Stewart as 'the Function of a Constitution', for this volume; (2) *Osterreichische Zeitschrift fur Offentliches Recht*, 119–20 (1963); See Ross, *Directives and Norms* (London, 1968), p. 158. (3) 'On the Pure Theory of Law', 1 *Israel Law Rev*. 1, 6 (1966), (4) *PTL*, 9–10.

[59] 'Die Funktion der Verfassung', translated as 'The Function of a Constitution' in this volume.

[60] 'The Function of a Constitution', 117.   [61] Ibid.

characterization of the basic norm. If so, it appears to follow, and Stewart concludes, that, as a theory based upon a manifest self-contradiction, the pure theory has no further claim to be taken seriously.

Prior to the redefinition, Kelsen appeared to be presupposing an unwilled act of will and that is obviously self-contradictory even without Kelsen's claim, 'no norm without an act of will'.[62] Therefore the redefinition of the basic norm was an attempt to avoid criticism based on internal self-contradiction of the type now brought by Stewart against the basic norm as fiction. Having redefined the basic norm, Kelsen is no longer committed to presupposing, absurdly, an unwilled act of will. Now, Kelsen is committed to the proposition that a norm, being the meaning of an act of will, cannot be presupposed without presupposing also a will which correlates to it, in the full awareness that no such will exists in empirical reality. Consequently, he who presupposes the basic norm presupposes an imaginary will of which it is the meaning. That might stretch credulity but it is not logically unthinkable. This deprives Stewart of the argument that the pure theory is based upon a logical contradiction in anything like the vicious sense necessary to destroy it. Here, as ever, Kelsen presents his theory as analogous to natural science. Causality is, it might be admitted, a useful category of thought, guiding research into and judgments about nature. Yet causality would, on Stewart's analysis, be illegitimate in that either it presents us directly with the metaphysics of infinity or a 'first cause' must be presupposed in order that the series be complete. But a 'first cause' is inconsistent with the principle of causality which holds that every event, without exception, necessarily has a cause. However, we may assume a first cause as a limiting idea, knowing that no such entity exists or even could exist.

Such a conclusion as Stewart draws would be profoundly embarrassing not only for the normative knowledge which the pure theory seeks to legitimate but for all knowledge. Such radical scepticism and the solipsism which it entails suggests that a 'full-fiction' cannot be interpreted simply as a self-contradictory 'nothing'.[63] Vaihinger distinguished fictions and hypotheses.[64]

---

[62] *ELMP*, 240.

[63] Stewart [1980] *Juridical Review* 208; Stewart, above, p. 133.

[64] See Handy, 'Hans Vaihinger', in *The Encyclopaedia of Philosophy* (New York, 1972), pp. 221–4.

Hypotheses are directed towards reality and are susceptible of verification or refutation. Fictions are not susceptible to verification or refutation because they are known to be false, though, going beyond Vaihinger, one might prefer to say that fictions are incapable of bearing truth-values. None the less, 'an idea whose theoretical untruth or incorrectness, and therefore its falsity, is admitted is not for that reason practically valueless and useless; for such an idea, in spite of its theoretical nullity may have great practical importance'.[65] A Vaihingerian fiction exhibits the following characteristics: first, it either deviates from reality or is self-contradictory; secondly, a fiction is used provisionally, hypothetically rather than categorically; thirdly, he who uses a fiction is aware that it has no claim to truth although the first users of a fiction may well erroneously take a fiction for an hypothesis; fourthly, a fiction is a means to an end and not a mere subjective fancy.

Vaihinger illustrates his idea of a fiction with many examples, including the atom. His view is that both the defenders of its reality and the positivists who would have nothing to do with it because it was internally inconsistent were mistaken; it is a contradictory concept which is, none the less, useful in order to deal with empirical reality, even though, as Kant realized, indivisible units or atoms though necessary are impossible. Consequently many of the theoretical concepts of science and not only Kelsen's basic norm would be illegitimated if self-contradictoriness alone disqualified from use. Further, it is not so much the nature of the contradiction, that is, whether it merely contradicts nature or is also self-contradictory which is definitive and decisive; rather, what marks a fiction off from other propositions is that it is explicitly false, that is to say, it wears its falsehood on its face. Thus the basic norm is a fiction in the sense of Vaihinger's philosophy in that it presents itself, as redefined, not as a guess or hypothesis about the reality behind the law but explicitly as a methodological maxim, a norm of method which is ontologically neutral. Far from being the swan song of the pure theory, Kelsen's redefinition, utterly consistent as it is with Vaihinger's philosophy, simply makes evident the limits of human knowledge generally and the limits of positive, normative legal knowledge in particular.

---

[65] Vaihinger, *The Philosophy of 'As If'* (New York, 1924), p. viii.

Stewart canvasses a second argument to the effect that Vaihinger's fictions, at least in the sense of full-fictions, are meaningless, because self-contradictory and therefore 'nothing', within the framework of Kantianism. This, like the alleged self-destruction of the pure theory, emphasizes more the vicious self-contradictoriness and less the openness of fictions. But Vaihinger thought of himself as influenced by Kant; he is an acknowledged Kant scholar; he founded the journal, *Kant Studien*; he asserted his indebtedness to Kant and tried to demonstrate that Kant's transcendental dialectic prefigured his own philosophy, though he sought to modify Kant in a more material and empirical direction styling himself an 'idealist positivist' or a 'positivist idealist'. There is considerable support for this view in Kant's own observations; 'You should philosophise about nature *as if* there were, for everything which belongs to existence a single necessary ground, for the sole purpose of giving your knowledge a systematic unity.'[66] Again, considering psychology, Kant observes that it may be useful 'to connect all appearances, actions and the receptivity of our mind . . . *as if* it were a simple substance which is endowed with personal identity (at least during life), permanently existing, while its states, to which those of a body belong only as external conditions, continuously change'.[67] Consequently, Vaihinger's fictions appear to bear a strong family resemblance to Kantian ideas of reason, and Kelsen's adoption of the fiction characterization, following Vaihinger, is altogether consistent with his general neo-Kantian position.

Kant's philosophizing proceeds through a series of levels. First, the transcendental aesthetic concerns intuitions, that is, perceptions. However in the world of sense we can have nothing before us but phenomena. Secondly, concepts are obtained by transcendental logic. The logic itself does not constitute knowledge; it provides the form but not the content of knowledge and as a criterion of truth it is useless for discovery. A concept requires not only the logical form of a concept but also the possibility of an object to which it refers. Hence the basic norm is no concept. This leads on to the categories; one proceeds sequentially: what makes Z

---

[66] *CPuR*, A 672–3; B 700–1.
[67] *CPuR*, A 672; B 700; contrast Stewart [1980] *Juridical Review* 222, n. 92, '. . . Vaihinger's 'as if' is not the same as Kant's . . .'; but see too, Körner, *Kant* (Harmondsworth, 1955), p. 125.

possible? Y. So what makes Y possible? X; and so on. But here we face potentially infinite regress. The fundamental principle of pure reason demands a last term in order that the series be complete. This leads to the transcendental dialectic which produces ideas which correspond to the categories. Unlike categories, which apply to sensibility generally, that is, what Kelsen refers to as a 'modally indifferent substratum', the ideas do not apply to facts and if there is an attempt to make them complete in experience one crosses Kant's boundary between legitimate and illegitimate metaphysics. Since ideas cannot be the content of any possible experience transcendental deduction is not possible. Thus freedom, immortality, and the existence of God as ideas of reason are a priori notions which are neither applicable to nor abstracted from experience. Thus, these ideas are not theoretical dogmata but maxims which have necessarily only heuristic import. Consequently they do not 'extend speculative knowledge beyond the objects of possible experience but extend only the empirical unity of such experience'.[68]

Kant's transcendental dialectic purports not only to show that such ideas are immanent in our thinking about matters of fact but also to give an exhaustive list of such ideas. Such ideas are concerned not with perceptions under the categories of the understanding but with judgments. These ideas give systematic unity to a series of judgments by arranging them syllogistically. Thus if one seeks systematic unity one should proceed towards the ultimate condition which, being unconditioned, closes the circle of a complete science. And so we proceed along a syllogistic chain of reasoning until we reach 'a presupposition which itself presupposes nothing else'.[69] Kant believed himself to have produced an exhaustive list of transcendental ideas. This is altogether implausible. It is evident just how closely Kelsen's mature writings on the basic norm parallel this account of an idea of reason.[70] Thus the Kantian account of such ideas, of their role in our theoretical inquiries and of the limits to which such ideas can be taken, beyond which we cannot legitimately go without straying into worthless metaphysics sheds considerable light upon the basic norm, while Kelsen's basic norm, as a Kantian idea, reveals Kant to have been optimistic in his claim to have produced an exhaustive list.

[68] *CPuR*, A 674; B 702.   [69] *CPuR*, B 379–80.
[70] See *TPD*, 271 n.–272 n.

The ideas can readily be misused in that we can seek, illogically, objects of experience to which they apply. Thus speculation on the nature of the will which is fictitiously correlated to the basic norm is sophistry and illusion. 'It is', Kant wrote,

> a great and necessary proof of wisdom and sagacity to know what questions may reasonably be asked. For if a question is absurd in itself and calls for an answer where there is no answer it does not only throw disgrace upon the questioner, but often tempts an incautious listener into an absurd answer, thus presenting as the ancients said, the spectacle of one person milking a he-goat and another holding the sieve![71]

As against which the ideas have 'in the field of theoretical thinking an excellent and unavoidably necessary regulative use, namely to direct the understanding to a certain goal . . . which serves the purpose of giving the greatest unity and the greatest breadth at the same time'.[72] The *genesis* of such ideas is not in issue;

> The physical sciences, with all the means at their disposal—their concepts of space and time and causality—can say nothing as to the genesis of nature or being, but must simply accept that nature as a hypothesis [fiction], conditioning all further knowledge. Their knowledge stops short of the realization of being; it concerns itself with processes *within* being, i.e., nature. The same is true of a normative science which is conscious of its limits. It can say nothing about the real creation of the [basic] norm.[73]

Kelsen had originally denied that his theory had anything to say about the genesis of law but realizing the inconsistency of this with his proposition that law is unique among normative orders in that it regulates its own creation he refined his position: 'the basic norm, although it functions as the chief principle of genesis determining the unity of the entire system of legal norms is itself presupposed and not enacted; its own genesis, therefore, stands outside the legal system.'[74] Thus, 'nature and norm as cognitive objects have in common "being" in the sense of "being given" as hypothesis for the cognitive subject.'[75]

We have seen that Kant candidly adopts an 'as if' formulation

---

[71] *CPuR*, A 58; B 82–3.   [72] *CPuR*, A 428; B 672.

[73] Ebenstein, 32.

[74] *HPS*[2], XIV. Cassirer, *Substance and Function and Einstein's Theory of Relativity* (London, 1923), p. 128: 'The "being" of the idea, however, consists in this function and needs no other support and no other proof.'

[75] Weyr, 'Natur und Norm', 6 *Revue Internationale de la Théorie du Droit*, 12–22, 17 (1932).

when considering the philosophy of nature and psychology. This 'as if' aspect of the ideas of pure reason may be taken from the transcendental philosophy and regarded as a methodological maxim, that is as a norm of method. This cuts off even the possibility of improperly moving beyond acceptable metaphysics to illusory speculation about the nature of the will which logically correlates to the basic norm. Such pragmatism is wholly consistent with Kant. Peirce, the American pragmatist, was reputed to have spent two hours a day over three years reading the *Critique of Pure Reason* until he almost knew it by heart and Vaihinger, as we have seen, justifiably claimed Kantian parentage.

A methodological pragmatist would treat the basic norm *as if* willed by an imaginary will, but conscious that no such will exists in reality. This would satisfy the fundamental principle of reason that the series be finite so that law would be an autonomous science, separate and complete of itself. Is that not exactly what Kelsen is doing? And is that not wholly acceptable? There are more possibilities in Kant's philosophy than dreamed of by many of his inheritors. If one emphasizes the dialectic one is a pragmatist; the logic, an empiricist or positivist. It is possible to turn the dialectic into an ontological gateway to Hegelian metaphysics. It is even possible so to interpret Kelsen; 'I was impressed' wrote Laski to Holmes, 'by a clever German book . . . *Allgemeine Staatslehre* which puts the Hegelian case with . . . great ability, even though its ability does not seem to me less disastrous'.[76] Laski wrote later of the same work, '. . . like most Hegelian structure, it seems to me entirely false to life'.[77] With that use of the dialectic and given the dramatic similarity of Kelsen's *Pure Theory of Law* to both Hegel's *Philosophy of Right* and Bosanquet's *The Philosophical Theory of the State*, Kelsen's Hegelianism might be just as readily proved as his Kantianism.

However, I now firmly believe that such a metaphysical adventure goes beyond Kelsenism into illusory metaphysics and consequently I conclude that Stewart's reliance upon the absolute subject immanent in Kelsen's philosophy of law is misconceived. Thus one can retain Kelsen's account of natural law as the jurisprudential isomorph of epistemological absolutism, whereas Kelsen's critical, normative positivism is the jurisprudential

---

[76] *Holmes-Laski Letters* (London, 1953), vol. ii, p. 830 (132/2/26).
[77] Ibid., vol. ii, p. 851 (19/4/26).

isomorph of epistemological relativism. Any attempt to go beyond the formal, empty presupposition of the basic norm necessarily involves an attempt to substitute a categorical basis for the hypothetical basis of pure theory; it reverts to natural law thinking and invokes speculative and illusory metaphysics. In Kantian terms, if we do not restrict the ideas of reason to a regulative role, reason is inevitably led astray into the murky nether-world of high metaphysics. The idea, for example, that nature has a purpose goes far beyond observation. It is therefore invalid as an alleged truth about the universe. However, as a regulative principle of reason, a merely methodological maxim, it can be extraordinarily fruitful. Presumably, methodologically astute Marxist sociologists already know that.

In this defence of Kelsen I am conscious of elements in and nuances of Stewart's critique to which I have not attended. Chief among these are, first, 'relativism', and, secondly, the issue caught in the cluster of terms such as 'objectification', 'reification', 'projection', and 'alienation'. As to relativism, my argument is that Kelsen out-relativizes the epistemological relativism even of Kant. Consequently, I see no need to supersede Kelsen with any 'transcendental relativist science', such as Stewart appears to require. If such a science requires that the concept of law adopted by a scientific jurisprudence must be as 'unbelieving' as the concept of religion in atheistic sociology of religion,[78] then the pure theory of law, properly understood and not misused as an ideology itself, rather than as a science of ideologies, already provides it. Otherwise a comparative science of law would be impossible. Kelsen's critics are frequently more at ease with destructive criticism than with constructive suggestion. We have already noted Ross's criticism of the ideological, natural law element in Kelsen's basic norm. He also wrote: 'A behaviouristic interpretation . . . achieves nothing. The changing behaviour of the judges can only be comprehended and predicted through ideological interpretation.'[79] But ideologies are descriptively normative; therefore one must presuppose and understand norma-

---

[78] See Stewart, 'Sociology in Jurisprudence', in Fryer *et al.* eds., *Law, State and Society* (London, 1981), p. 125.

[79] *On Law and Justice* (London, 1958), p. 37; see, too, Mannheim, *Ideology and Utopia* (London, 1972), p. 39, 'There can no longer be any doubt that no real penetration into social reality is possible through this approach [that is, 'Behaviourism'].'

tivity, if one is to describe ideologies from the inside rather than explain them, behaviouristically, from the outside. Thus Ross is shown to be methodologically syncretist, espousing simultaneously a predictive, and therefore causal enterprise, wholly consistent with his general empiricist stance, and a normative enterprise, the interpretation of ideologies. Stewart seems to me to have much in common with Ross.

As to reification[80] and the like, I have difficulty in understanding precisely what point is being made and how it impinges upon Kelsen's jurisprudence. Even Kant, who is altogether more plausibly seen as a participant in the exegetical tradition, denied the propriety of reifying the ideas of reason and speculating metaphysically upon what is or exists beyond the limits of knowledge. Kelsen, as I have noted, was impressed with the substitution of function for substance which he found in Cassirer's works. That seems to me wholly opposed to the reificatory tendencies detected by Stewart. If by 'alienation' one is to understand falsely conceiving, as 'objective', that which can only be understood as a product of *human* consciousness, and therefore 'subjective' then law, like religion, may be falsely projected into some suprahuman 'objective' realm and thus 'alienated' from humanity. If that is the charge, I pronounce Kelsen innocent.

Kelsen performs for law the task performed for religion by Feuerbach, while preserving that which distinguishes law from nature, namely the normativity of law. For Kelsen law is an artifact, just as religion is for Feuerbach. Just as Kelsen locates law in human society and in human consciousness, so Feuerbach located religion. Unlike Marx, Feuerbach did not appear to believe that this transformation of religion necessarily destroyed it. Rather, by explaining God away, Feuerbach rendered religion problematic. One solution is to regard religion as performing a like social function to myth. A myth is not merely a perverted consciousness of the universe but also a prescription for human action. The necessary social function of determining how individuals ought to behave in order that social life be possible at all was performed in primitive societies by myths.[81] Kelsen is a non-cognitivist. He therefore believes that how individuals ought to behave cannot be determined by reason alone. Consequently the

---

[80] Stewart, above, p. 141.
[81] Frankfort *et al.*, *Before Philosophy*, Ch. 1.

content of social norms is always problematical, requiring to be decided rather than discovered and in different societies the content of social norms may be decided upon differently. Law, in common with religion and myth, not only performs the essential social function of determining what ought to be but also, again in common with religion and myth, is readily surrounded with metaphysical justification. In criticizing the unwarranted metaphysical justification which attaches to law, the law itself may be demythologized away. However, Kelsen, for all his radical criticism of the ideologies in which law may clothe itself,[82] retained the element of 'pure' normativity, without which society is reduced to nature, whereby only causal, behaviouristic explanation is possible. Consequently, to see law as an inter-subjectively valid normative order is to see it as it is, demythologized, warts and all. Behind positive law there is 'neither the absolute truth of metaphysics nor the absolute justice of natural law. He who lifts the veil, if he close not his eyes, will find himself confronted by the Gorgon's head of power.'[83] Stewart expresses puzzlement with this; how can Kelsen sustain the illusion with its workings on view?[84] But only by seeing Kelsen as a participant in the exegetical tradition, conniving at the existence of an absolute subject, can he be thought of as an 'illusionist'. If normativity is alienated false consciousness what, it may be asked, constitutes true consciousness? To regard even the minimum of natural law, the 'pure ought', as false consciousness seems to me to denature man-in-society and that in turn seems far more alienating than anything within the pure theory of law.

Finally Stewart's paper raises the issue of the relationship of jurisprudence to sociology and social theory.[85] It is remarkable that a defence of Kelsen's normative science in general rather than

---

[82] See Ross, *On Law and Justice* (London, 1958), p. 317–18: 'In the field of constitutional law, Hans Kelsen has been indefatigable in showing how large parts of it have been written in a procuratorial manner to defend the interests of an existing régime. In a masterly way he has laid bare the trickery and fraud whereby political attitudes, consciously or unconsciously, get themselves camouflaged as science, thus deceitfully trying to arrogate to themselves the authority which the name of science bestows.'

[83] Cited Ebenstein, 110.   [84] Stewart, above, p. 147.

[85] In responding to Stewart, I adopt his broad use of the word 'sociology' to embrace 'any social scientist', without tracing the distinctions properly to be drawn among 'sociology of law', 'legal sociology', 'sociology' and 'social theory'; see, Stewart, 'Sociology in Jurisprudence', loc. cit., p. 126, n. 2.

his science of law in particular is both easier and more plausible.[86] The basic norm as a generic idea of theoretical reason founding the distinctiveness of normative science in general over against causal science is more plausible, theoretically, than the specific basic norm of a particular system is as the criterion of identity. Thus the specificity of the legal over and against the normative in general remains problematic and cannot, I think, be dealt with solely by presupposing a particular basic norm. Coercion as a criterion of the specificity of the legal has struck many commentators as inadequate, especially as Kelsen regards all normative orders as coercive, at least in a psychological sense.[87] More persuasive is the fertile notion that a distinctively legal order regulates its own creation. None the less it remains difficult to separate out the legal from the total normative order which constitutes society.

It seems that Kelsen provides a fruitful framework for the scientific study of society which is sharply distinguishable both from the positivism of Comte or Marx in some moods[88] and from the *Verstehende* sociology associated with Weber. As to this last a distinction might be drawn between an individualist and a collectivist *Verstehende*, an opposition, as it were, of Dilthey and Rickert. Since *Verstehende* suggests some kind of empathy and understanding of minds and since minds are empirically individual the presupposition of a collective consciousness such as would warrant collective *Verstehende* can be saved from criticism only by treating it as a regulative idea. Simmel clearly held the view that a sociological study of society went beyond methodological individualism.[89] Kelsen's pure theory offers a methodological basis for the interpretation and description not of subjective and individualistic meanings and understandings alone, but of the objective, or rather inter-subjective, system of meaning with which individual meanings may but need not correspond. The pure theory of law is therefore a model for a collectivist *Verstehende* sociology.

---

[86] That *ATN*, Kelsen's most recent major work, is devoted to a general theory of norms is, as Stewart observes, of significance.　　　　　[87] *PTL*, 24 and 27.

[88] Marx, *Economic and Philosophical Manuscripts* (1844), cited in Bottomore and Rubel eds., *Karl Marx, Selected Writings in Sociology and Social Philosophy*, 2nd edn. (Harmondsworth, 1961), p. 85; 'Natural science will one day incorporate the science of man, just as the science of man will incorporate natural science; there will be a *single* science' (emphasis in original).

[89] *The Sociology of Georg Simmel*, tr. and ed. Wolff (1950), pp. 4–6.

This in turn leads on to a theory of ideology. Kelsen cheerfully admits that his pure theory of law shows how law is to be understood as an ideology but, as with Kant's discussion of metaphysics, 'ideology' has both a pejorative and a non-pejorative sense in Kelsen's theorizing:

> if 'ideology' is understood as a contrast to the reality of facts—that is, if ideology is understood as everything that is not causally determined reality or a description of this reality—then the law as a norm . . . is an ideology . . . [and] the subject of the science of law . . . is an ideology. Then the Pure Theory of Law has opened the way to that viewpoint from which the law may be understood as an 'ideology' . . . a system of connections different from that of nature.[90]

As against which 'the Pure Theory has an outspoken anti-ideological tendency'.[91] It seeks the law that is, not the law that ought to be, and so it is a 'radical realistic' theory of law;[92] it does not seek the 'ideal' or the 'right' law; it refuses to serve 'any political interests'.[93] Thus pure theory is very different from that traditional jurisprudence which prostituted itself to apologize for and defend power and patronage. Although positivist theories can be ideological, Kelsen directed his sharpest invective to criticizing natural law and rationalist and pseudo-scientific theories of justice.[94] He sees similar ideological elements at work in the 'misrepresentation of the anthropomorphic metaphor "juristic person" . . . as a kind of superman or organism . . . [an] impermissible hypostatization of a thinking aid or auxiliary concept'.[95] Whither now Stewart's attribution to a belief in or a logical entailment of an absolute subject in Kelsenism? Pure theory 'is a truly organic legal theory . . . [but] it does not mean by this some supra-empirical metaphysical entity . . . but . . . [that] . . . the law is an order'.[96]

Scientifically unacceptable ideology for Kelsen is rooted in will and politics and it corresponds with no actual society. Scientifically acceptable ideology conforms with empirical reality as interpreted normatively. Consequently the descriptive account of the legal order which is advocated by pure theory is simultaneously a description of the socially dominant ideology, that is, the system of

[90] *PTL*, 104–5.   [91] *PTL*, 106.   [92] Ibid.
[93] Ibid.
[94] See, e.g., 'What is Justice?' in *ELMP*, 1–26; *GTLS*, pp. 407–17.
[95] *PTL*, 177–8.   [96] *PTL*, 192.

ideas and meanings according to which social conduct is normatively determined in inter-subjective validity independently of the will, desires, interests, or personal ideals of individuals. Thus pure theory provides not only a sophisticated epistemology, but points the way to a scientific study of ideologies. Stewart expresses concern about 'socially prevalent illusions',[97] seeing in them fallacy and error but where an ideology is by and large socially effective the 'delusion' is scientifically cognoscible even if it is neither philosophically defensible nor politically appealing.

Feuerbach is more closely aligned with this Kelsenian doctrine than is Marx. Hegel, perhaps, saw society and history as God's march through the world and Marx saw himself as turning Hegel 'right way up',[98] characterizing religion as an ideology, an 'inverted world-consciousness . . . the opium of the people' and an 'illusion'.[99] The withering away of law is a wholly consistent notion. Feuerbach, however, adopted a middle way between Hegel's assertion and Marx's denial of religion. Assume that the Enlightenment had disproved the existence of God, as Feuerbach believed it had. How then is religion to be explained? One solution is that religion operates as a socially effective ideology which normatively determines the conduct of members of society in inter-subjective validity independently of their subjective desires and interests. Therefore positive religion has a necessary social function and the disproof of God's existence, even if valid, does not simultaneously defuse positive religion. Kelsen's 'positivizing' of law is structurally similar to this secularizing of religion.

The normative order may be understood as the socially prevalent 'ought-to-be-that-is'. The content of such an order may flow from law, morals, religion, or social custom and practice. In different societies or even within the same society at different times the contribution of these different subsystems of norms may vary considerably. Thus positive religion may have been the dominant source when Feuerbach wrote. Today it is arguable that law is perceived as the dominant source of the content of the normative order in many societies. None the less, morality, as mediated by the Supreme Court, remains significant in America

---

[97] Stewart, 'Sociology in Jurisprudence', loc. cit., p. 125.
[98] See Tucker, *The Marx-Engels Reader*, p. xix.
[99] Marx, 'Zur Kritik der Hegelschen Rechtsphilosophie', *Karl Marx—Friedrich Engels Historisch-kritische Gesamtausgabe* (Frankfurt, 1927), pp. 607, 608, 573–4.

and religion dominates in Iran. Crudely positivist theories, with their emphasis on the exclusivity of sources, reinforce but do not prove the role of law as the dominant source of the content of the normative order. Even so, such domination is frequently illusory since it is domination by incorporation rather than by exclusion. Thus positive law may authorize the norms of other subsystems, not only religion and morality but also custom and practice.[1] Such incorporation poses problems for rigid conceptions of legal positivism, espousing exhaustive and exclusive sources theses. Kelsen's pure theory of law as a theory of the specifically legal encounters the converse difficulty; in its attempt to be universal and comprehensive, pursuing 'breadth and unity' as the Kantian regulative idea or methodological maximum prescribes, it is forced outwards in ever-increasing circles of incorporation including, for example, the rules of private clubs, in an attempt to be all-embracing. In this sense there are no gaps in the law; all human conduct, being permitted or prohibited, is either in accordance with or contrary to the normative order in its exclusive universality for which Kelsen appropriates the title 'law'. If the problem for empiricist positivism such as Hart's *Concept of Law* is the step-motherly limitation of authorized and accepted sources, the problem for pure theory is the open-endedness which ultimately equates the specificity of the legal and the generality of the normative. This is most clearly illustrated by Kelsen's methodological commitment to monism and his arguably ideological commitment to the primacy of international law. The erosion of the specificity of the legal involves the merging of jurisprudence and sociology, albeit a specific and clearly defined variety of sociology, namely collective *Verstehende* sociology. Consequently, if a little jurisprudence leads away from sociology, more leads

---

[1] As to positive religion, the courts of the Church of Scotland provide an example; '. . . within their spiritual province the church courts are as supreme as we are within the civil', *Wight* v. *Presbytery of Dunkeld* (1870) 8 M 921, 925, per Lord Justice-Clerk Moncrieff. As to positive morality, *R* v. *Tan* [1983] All ER 12 and *R* v. *Feely* [1973] QB 530, reaffirmed in *R* v. *Ghosh* [1983] QB 1053 and establishing, as the criterion of 'dishonesty', the current standards of ordinary decent people. As to custom etc., see *Lister* v. *Romford Ice and Cold Storage Co. Ltd.* [1957] AC 555, a decision of the House of Lords overtaken by a 'gentleman's agreement' among members of the British Insurance Association; but contrast *McKendrick* v. *Sinclair* (1972) SLT (HL) 110, 116–17, per Lord Simon, 'a rule of English common law, once clearly established, does not become extinct merely by disuse'.

back to it.[2] Gurvitch remarks on the 'impossibility of detaching the reality of law from the whole of social reality, seen as an indestructible totality'.[3] Where is the difference between the respective regulative ideas of Gurvitch and Kelsen?

At the beginning of this paper, I congratulated Stewart for the compliment which his scholarship and the attempted supersession of pure theory pays to Kelsen. It will now be clear that I regard the supersession as unnecessary in that all the criteria of an acceptable social theory which treats law as atheist sociology treats religion are already consciously met in Kelsen's pure theory. What more can the sociologist reasonably ask of the jurisprudent? We have here a profoundly relativist theory of knowledge which out-relativizes even Kantian epistemological relativism; a theory, moreover, which defines its 'ought' in such a way as to exclude any practical inference or conclusion from it; which refuses to serve political interests of any colour; which acknowledges that law is but a socially prevalent ideology that legal science in particular and normative science in general are sciences of ideologies and that normativity implies no immutability of values, no Holmesian 'brooding omnipresence in the sky'; rather societal oughts or ideologies can have any content whatsoever. Stewart rightly praises a theory such as Kelsen's which agonizes on its own frontiers. What may be generally missed is that out of that *Angst* comes the only jurisprudence ever to take sociology seriously; not the causal, behaviourist, 'positivist' social atomism of a Comte, but sociology as a science of the mind and of meaning and of values as instantiated in actual human societies.[4] Kelsen has the intellectual honesty and rigour to present and defend his basic norm. As Kant well knew, every science presupposes an idea of reason as a maxim of method in order that the series be complete and the science be independent and autonomous; what, one may

---

[2] Compare Hauriou, cited by Gurvitch, *Sociology of Law* (1947, 1953), p. 2: 'a little sociology leads away from the law but much sociology leads back to it'. Gurvitch, 'for the sake of precision' adds, '. . . little law leads away from sociology but much law leads back to it'.

[3] Gurvitch, *Sociology of Law*, p. 1.

[4] See Sawer, *Law in Society* (Oxford, 1965), p. 5: 'From this point of view, even Hans Kelsen was engaging in sociology when writing his *Pure Theory*, notwithstanding his indignant denials . . .'; see, too, Balog, 'Kelsen's Kritik an der Soziologie', LXIX *Archiv für Rechts- und Sozialphilosophie*, 515–27 (1983).

ask, is the basic norm of sociology if it is not that something ought to be? And what more 'thoroughly relativized jurisprudence'[5] is possible?

[5] Stewart, 'Sociology in Jurisprudence', loc. cit., p. 126.

PART FOUR

LOGIC AND LAW

CHAPTER 8

LOGIC AND THE PURE THEORY
OF LAW

OTA WEINBERGER

TRANSLATED BY ALFRED SCHRAMM

I   THE CLASSICAL CONCEPTION OF THE
PURE THEORY OF LAW

THE Pure Theory of Law is one among the most important schools
of analytical jurisprudence. It originated within the Austro–
Hungarian Empire at the beginning of our century and is
represented mainly by two schools: the Vienna School and the
Brno School.[1] The acknowledged leading figure for the Viennese
School is Hans Kelsen, as is his friend František (Franz) Weyr for
the Brno School. Both schools descend from an identical intellectual
climate: they both developed under the influence of Kantian
Critical Idealism; both stress the distinction between 'is' and
'ought', between declarative and normative sentences, between
knowledge and will, as well as between considerations *de lege lata*
and considerations *de lege ferenda*.

Both Kelsen and Weyr have faith in the idea of the constitutional
state and they both fight strongly for the general legality of all
activities of the state, especially of administration. They are both
ardent supporters of the ideals of democracy. They both subscribe
to the doctrine of legal positivism.[2] Their relativistic conception of
value theory leads to their postulate of tolerance in political and
general philosophical outlook.

The essential difference in opinion between Kelsen and Weyr

---

[1]   Further information and a bibliography on the Brno School of the Pure Theory
of Law can be found in Kubeš and Weinberger, eds., *Die Brünner rechtstheoretische Schule (Normative Theorie)* (Vienna, 1980) which also contains essays by the
main representatives of that school.

[2]   In both schools there are also some authors with tendencies towards a natural
law conception: Verdross and Marcic in the Vienna School, and Kallab and Kubeš
in the Brno School.

lies in the fact that Kelsen holds a sanction theory of legal norms and, accordingly, takes anything for legally irrelevant which is not stated by a sanction norm, while Weyr rejects the sanction theory and defines the notion of a legal norm as any norm which is accounted to the state as its generating subject.

The Pure Theory of Law, that is, the classical schools as well as later doctrines held by Kelsen, tries to develop a formal theory of the structure of law and of all legal processes. It intends to 'analyse the very essence of law, its typical structure, independently of varying contents which it may have assumed at different times or different places'.[3]

The Pure Theory's orientation towards a structural analysis of law has led some critics to object that this approach leads to a one-sided interest in the *form* of law while taking its *content* for secondary. This objection is totally unjustified: the analysis of the form establishes merely a formal framework for the cognition of the content of law, but it does not intend to replace the knowledge of normative content by an analysis of the form of law. Indeed, the formal analysis of law is based on the distinction between form and content.

The general structure of law, as described in the classical Pure Theory of Law, is basically different from the views expressed by Kelsen in his last book *Allgemeine Theorie de Normen* [General Theory of Norms].[4] The classical view understands all the problems concerning the generality of legal notions, the structure of the legal rule, the theory of legal dynamics,[5] and the hierarchy of legal norms including the theory of the basic norm as objects of logical analysis. 'As a theory about the specific method of the cognition of law [the Pure Theory of Law] is concerned with problems of logic.'[6] Accordingly, the distinction between 'is' and 'ought' is conceived of as purely logical. 'The logical distinction between "Is" and "Ought" and the impossibility of reaching from one domain to the other by purely logical reasoning is one of the main tenets of the Pure Theory of Law.'[7] In my opinion, it would be more appropriate to distinguish the semantic categories of

---

[3] Kelsen, 'Was ist die Reine Rechtslehre?' in *Demokratie und Rechtsstaat. Festschrift für Zaccharia Giacometti* (Zurich, 1953), pp. 143–61. Quotations are translated from a reprint in *WRS* I, 611–29.

[4] Cf. Weinberger, *Normentheorie als Grundlage der Jurisprudenz und Ethik* (Berlin, 1981).

[5] Cp. *RR*^{2}, 169 f., 363 f.   [6] *WRS* I, 611.   [7] *WRS* I, 614.

declarative and normative sentences, because their logical difference originates from a difference in meaning.[8]

That the main intention of the classical Pure Theory of Law is to provide a logical analysis of law based on a specific logic of norm-sentences is proved by Kelsen's own words:

In the course of its logical investigations, the Pure Theory of Law has been the first to stress that the logical law of non-contradiction must be applied to the ought sentences of jurisprudence just as it is to be applied to the declarative sentences of natural science. Among the logical problems the Pure Theory has to deal with, there is the question of what constitutes unity within a plurality of legal norms, i.e. what constitutes the unity called 'legal system' or 'legal order'. As an answer to this question, the Pure Theory arrives at the idea of the *basic norm* as a hypothetical presupposition of all cognition of law. The basic norm provides the ultimate reason for the validity of all norms belonging to one legal order. From the basic norm we can deduce only the validity of legal norms but not their content as has sometimes been erroneously assumed. Only by presupposing the basic norm, can certain human acts be interpreted as legal acts, i.e. acts which create legal norms, and only because of this presupposition can we justify the assertion that legal norms are the meanings of these acts. The Pure Theory of Law investigates . . . the logical structure of given legal orders and thus arrives at the cognition of the hierarchic structure of the legal order—an insight which is of fundamental importance for the cognition of the essence of law. Finally, the Pure Theory of Law investigates the logical relations which may hold between different legal orders, viz. between legal orders of particular states as well as between the latter and the order of international law. Thus, the Pure Theory arrives at the methodological postulate of the *unity of the legal view of the world* [*Einheit des rechtlichen Weltbildes*]. This unity is a logical-systematic one and its criterion is consistency. This unity is not given as such in legal reality; rather, it is to be established by the cognition of law. It may be the case that positive law—some particular law or international contract—may contain mutually inconsistent norms; or some law may be in contradiction with the constitution or with international law. But the cognition of law has to do away with these inconsistencies by way of interpretation and that is, indeed, what it generally does in one way or another. Just like nature, law becomes a meaningful, that is, a consistent whole through scientific investigation. And just as the scientific view of the physical world differs from a naive

---

[8] Cp. Ch. Weinberger and O. Weinberger, *Logik, Semantik und Hermeneutik* (Munich, 1979).

everyday view, the view of jurisprudence differs from the picture which the layman may hold of the immediately given positive law.

Problems like these have usually been subsumed under the heading of 'legal logic'. But the insights gained in this respect by the Pure Theory of Law do not only refer to legal norms but also to norms of different kinds as, for instance, moral norms. The kind of logic used in jurisprudence is not a specific 'legal' one. Such a logic does not exist, and least of all is there one in that field where lawyers usually talk about 'legal logic', namely in the field of interpretation of positive legal norms. What one finds under that heading are usually fallacies and logical deceptions, like the *argumentum a contrario*, or the deduction of norms from a preconceived concept—the pseudo-logic of the *Begriffsjurisprudenz*—or the derivation of norms from the 'nature of the cause' (*Natur der Sache*)—the self-deception of the natural law doctrine. The kind of logic which, so to say, the Pure Theory of Law has discovered is a *general logic of norms*, that is, a logic of 'ought' or of 'ought-sentences', a logic directed towards the cognition of norms, not of physical reality. If it is at all meaningful to speak about legal logic or legal reasoning, it is so only in the sense that we mean by this the principles of a general logic of norms which find their application in the field of the cognition of law.

This leads me on to deal with the misunderstanding that the Pure Theory of Law is merely logic, or legal logic. Logic is the theory of thought while the Pure Theory of Law is a theory of law and not—at least not foremost—a theory of thought. The Pure Theory deals with problems of logic only as far as this is necessary for the cognition of law, the determination of the concept of law, and the definition of the fundamental concepts of all cognition of law. These definitions themselves are no more functions of logic than would be definitions of the circle or the square. Quite in the same sense as these latter definitions are functions of geometry—and geometry is not logic—so are the definitions of legal concepts functions of a general theory of law—which again is not logic. Beside that, the kind of logic developed by the Pure Theory of Law is, as I said, no specific legal logic but a logic of norms which must be presupposed for any correct theory of law, just as general logical considerations must be presupposed for doing theoretical physics without the allegation that therefore theoretical physics is pure logic.[9]

In my opinion, the problem of the unity of the legal order is more complex than Kelsen's treatment of this topic would suggest. If we conceive the legal order in accordance with the dynamic theory of law, that is, as generated on the basis of empowering norms, then it is primarily this principle of generation which constitutes the

[9] *WRS* I, 616–18.

legal system. This construction, by itself, does not exclude conflicts within the normative system because it may be the case that two norms simultaneously satisfy all the conditions for the creation of norms. Consistency of the content of a legal system is a logical postulate. In order to be meaningful, every normative system should be consistent. In my opinion—and following Kelsen's purely cognitive conception of juristic interpretation—legal science cannot establish a consistent system of norms if, in fact, the respective legal order is inconsistent. Only if the interpretation arrives at two alternatives one of which is inconsistent with the remaining system, but not the other, can interpretation help to establish consistency.

II THE PURE THEORY OF LAW AND THE LOGIC OF NORMS

Given the characteristics of the Pure Theory of Law described so far, that is, the distinction between 'is' and 'ought' and the thesis of non-entailment between them, and further, the intention to pursue a structural analysis of law, one is inevitably led on to the problem of a *logic of norms*. Incidentally, this interest of the Pure Theory for logical analysis of normative sentences coincided historically with similar interests within the field of metaethics and logic.

Since the 1930s various proposals have been put forward for dealing with logical relations and operations in the field of normative sentences. So far, none of the proposed systems is generally accepted and there are still many unsolved problems.[10]

As early as 1937, Jørgensen tried to prove that inference among normative sentences (imperatives) is conceptually impossible. Nevertheless, he himself was convinced that the actual practice of reasoning acknowledges inference within normative contexts as evident.[11] The Czech economist Karel Engliš has

[10] See the bibliography on Logic of Norms (Deontic Logic) by Berkemann and Strasser in Lenk, ed., *Normenlogik* (Pullach, near Munich, 1974); further, compare Ch. Weinberger and O. Weinberger, *Logik, Semantik und Hermeneutik*.

[11] Jørgensen, 'Imperatives and Logic', in 7 *Erkenntnis* 288–96 (1937/8); see also Weinberger, *Die Sollsatzproblematik in der modernen Logik* [The Problems of Ought-Sentences in Modern Logic], reprinted in Weinberger, *Studien zur Normenlogik und Rechtsinformatik* [Studies in the Logic of Norms and Legal Informatics] (Berlin, 1974), pp. 59–186. In this monograph, I propose another solution to Jørgensen's Dilemma.

also tried to prove that a logic of norms cannot be established.[12]

Engliš's conviction, in turn, influenced the views held by Kelsen in *Allgemeine Theorie der Normen*.[13] Nevertheless, this line of reasoning had already been foreshadowed by earlier ideas of Kelsen.

Even by the time of the second edition of the *Reine Rechtslehre* (1960) there are two points which indicate Kelsen's renunciation of the logicism of the classical Pure Theory of Law: (i) On the one hand he holds that 'The sentences "A ought to be" and "A must not be" are mutually incompatible; only one of the norms described by them can be valid.' On the other hand, Kelsen doesn't conceive of the circumstance that a certain behaviour is obligatory and forbidden at the same time within the same legal order as a *logical* incompatibility.[14] This is a consequence of his holding a sanction theory of legal norms: the sanction-sentences which correspond to the conflicting norms are not incompatible. If we consider a conflict between obligation and prohibition of the very same behaviour merely as a teleological incompatibility as Kelsen does, and not as a logical one, then we are already half-way towards an irrational conception of norms. (ii) Kelsen stresses the difference between legal norms and legal sentences. Legal norms are created by organs of the state; they must be applied by them and be observed by the subjects of legal duties. Only legal norms

---

[12] Engliš, *Malá logika. Věda myšlenkovém řádu* [Short Logic. The Science of the Order of Thought] (Prague, 1947) and Engliš, 'Die Norm ist Kein Urteil' [The Norm is no Judgment], 50 *ARSP* 305–16 (1964). Engliš tries to prove that norms (normative sentences) are not judgments, presupposing at the same time that only judgments can be the objects of deductive reasoning. He offers the following arguments. (i) A judgment is a piece of knowledge; a norm is not an expression of knowledge. (ii) A judgment is an answer to a question. A norm is not an answer to a question. (iii) Any judgment is either correct or incorrect. Furthermore, an empirical judgment is true or false. Norms are neither correct or incorrect nor true or false. (iv) A judgment can be negated. A norm cannot be negated. (v) Judgments can be elements (premisses or conclusions) of deductive operations. Norms are not elements of deductive operations. Thesis (v) is equivalent to the *probandum* and—in my opinion—is not evident at all. I do not believe that these arguments justify Engliš's view that there is no deductive reasoning in prescriptive language; Cp. Weinberger, 'Die Sollatzproblematik in der modernen Logik', loc. cit. note 11 above.

[13] Kelsen was informed about Engliš's conception and he knew of Jørgensen's paper. He quoted from my 'Sollatzproblematik' in 'Law and Logic Again' (English version of 'Nochmals: Recht und Logik' 14 Neues Forum 39–40 (1967)) in *ELMP* 256. However, as my essay was mainly written for logicians, he may not have studied it in detail.

[14] Cp. RR^2, 26 f.

are normative entities proper. But legal sentences are hypothetical judgments asserting that according to a particular legal order certain normative consequences impend under certain conditions. There is no doubt that we must make a distinction between the creation of law and the cognition of law. Nevertheless, I think that the way Kelsen introduces this distinction leads to grave difficulties.[15]

It is important to distinguish between the meaning of a sentence and the pragmatic function which it fulfils in a given situation. If a law-creating organ utters a norm-sentence, this use of the sentence *may* fulfil the pragmatic function of legislation. The sentence itself bears a message which is to be grasped by the receiver (an addressee of the norm or any other person). The meaning of the sentence should be identical for the sender and the receiver of the message. The set of consequence clauses of the message should also be identical on both sides of the communication.[16] The pair of notions 'legal norm' and 'legal sentence' is based on a misconception of the character of communication and led—together with other questionable arguments—to Kelsen's erroneous rejection of normative entailment.

In the second edition of *Reine Rechtslehre* (1960) Kelsen still holds the view that it does make sense to speak of logical contradiction between norms.[17] However, his attempt to define contradiction between norms indirectly is evidently false: he presupposes that the descriptive sentences 'In the legal order L there is a valid norm that A ought to be' and 'In the legal order L there is a valid norm that not-A ought to be' are in contradiction with one another, so that we can hold that the corresponding norm-sentences 'A ought to be' and 'not-A ought to be' are indirectly proved to be in contradiction as well. However, the descriptive sentences just mentioned are in no way contradictory. If L really contains the norms 'A ought to be' and 'not-A ought to be', then both declarative sentences are true, but the legal order L is inconsistent. And this fact evokes the impression that the corresponding assertions about the legal order are in contradiction among each other.

---

[15] Cp. Weinberger, 'Intersubjektive Kommunikation, Normenlogik und Normendynamik' [Intersubjective Communication, Logic of Norms and Dynamics of Norms] in 8 *Rechtstheorie* 19–40 (1977), where I criticize this pair of notions.
[16] Ibid.   [17] RR^2, 210.

In his essay 'Law and Logic' (1965)[18] Kelsen argues against the possibility of deducing individual norms from a general norm as follows:

The individual norm 'Smith the thief should be sent to prison' could be implicit in the general norm 'All thieves should be sent to prison' only if the act of will whose meaning is the individual norm were implicit in the act of will whose meaning is the general norm. But the legislator who wills that all thieves should be sent to prison cannot already will that Smith, who has stolen a horse from the farmer, should be sent to prison, since he cannot know that a person called Smith will exist and steal the farmer's horse. For one cannot will that of which one knows nothing, and the will whose meaning is the norm 'Smith should be sent to prison' is the condition for the validity of this norm as a positive norm.[19]

Evidently, this kind of reasoning follows a psychologistic line. But logical relations must not be understood as relations between mental acts, as has been pointed out so convincingly by Edmund Husserl.

III KELSEN'S LATER IRRATIONALISM CONCERNING NORMS

Kelsen's irrationalism in respect to norms originates mainly from the following elements

(i) The general situation in the research on prescriptive language and its logic, with the unsettled fundamental problems of the logic of norms.

(ii) Following an idea of Walter Dubislav,[20] Kelsen is convinced of the thesis that 'there is no imperative without imperator', and he takes this thesis in a very strict sense. The creating act of will is not only a necessary condition for the creation of a norm but rather the existence of a norm N is possible only where a real act of will takes place whose meaning is exactly N.

(iii) The supposition of a strict act-relativity of the norm leads to Kelsen's definition of the norm: a norm is the sense (*der Sinn*) of an act of will whose meaning is the norm.

---

[18] Kelsen, 'Recht und Logik', 142 *Forum* 1965, 421–5 (1965), and 143 *Forum* 495–500 (1965); quoted from the translation, 'Law and Logic' in *ELMP*, 228–53.
[19] 'Law and Logic', in *ELMP*, 242.
[20] Dubislav, 'Zur Unbegründbarkeit von Forderungssätze', 3 *Theoria* 330–42 (1937).

This stipulative definition is the basis for Kelsen's argument that there cannot exist any deductive inference with norms as premisses and/or conclusions.

Yet if we conceive—as I think we should—a norm as an ideal entity which—though produced by an act of will—has its own ideal being such that the consequences of a valid norm must also be valid, Kelsen's objection against the possibility of normative inference loses its force.

(iv) In *Allgemeine Theorie der Normen* (1979) Kelsen denies the possibility of contradiction between normative sentences. There is no doubt that the notion of contradiction, defined as a relation between declarative sentences, does not apply to normative sentences. Contradiction in this sense is defined by truth-functional criteria, and thus it is inapplicable to normative sentences which cannot be characterized as true or false.

Kelsen introduces the notion of 'conflict of norms' as a relation which holds for instance between the sentences 'A should be' and 'A must not be'. Now, the essential question is, whether the coexistence of conflicting norms within one system of norms (e.g., in a legal order) is to be considered as a *logical* defect or merely as a teleological or pragmatic failure of the system. Evidently, both normative sentences cannot be satisfied at the same time. Our knowledge that the joint satisfaction of both norms is not possible is *logical knowledge*, given by the structure of the sentences under consideration (and perhaps by the meaning of their terms). It is not a matter of experience, like knowing that the norm 'You shall run 100 metres within 3 seconds' cannot be satisfied. The incompatibility (that is, the logically excluded joint satisfaction) is to be acknowledged as a logical relation between normative sentences. It is of no importance, whether we call this relation 'norm-conflict' or 'incompatibility' or 'inconsistency' or 'contradiction of norms'.

(v) Though Kelsen is very well aware of the non-psychological character of deductive reasoning, and though he explicitly refers to Husserl in this respect, he believes that the objective relation of inference applies only to declarative sentences, but not to normative ones. He seems to believe that in the field of declarative sentences the objective connection between the objects mentioned in the premisses and conclusions does offer a basis for deductive operations such that the latter remain completely independent of any mental acts. However, in the normative realm he takes the existence of any norm as dependent on the existence of a corresponding act of will, and an act of will corresponding to a conclusion is not an effect of the act of will corresponding to its premiss or premisses. 'The truth "Socrates is mortal" is implied by the truth "All men are mortal", because between the sense of the general statement and the sense of the singular statement there need not intervene any act of thought whose sense consists in the singular statement.'[21]

As between the validity of the general norm and the validity of the according individual norm there must intervene an act of will whose sense is the individual norm, the validity of the individual norm cannot follow logically (that is, by way of an operation of thought) from the general norm as the truth of a singular statement follows from the truth of the general statement to which the singular statement corresponds.[22]

Even in descriptive language, logical relations or deductive operations are not based on relations between real objects. Rather, logical operations are based on structural relations between sentences or, perhaps, on relations between the meanings of the terms involved. Deductive operations apply also to suppositions, hypotheses, false premisses, counterfactual sentences, or statements about possible worlds, and of course, in all these cases there does not exist any basis in a constellation of real objects. Kelsen's argument against the possibility of deductive reasoning in the realm of norms is valid if and only if we accept his strictly act-relative definition of the notion of a norm.

But I think we should introduce an apparatus of concepts into the field of prescriptive language which is constructed parallel to descriptive language and which allows for the introduction of deductive reasoning into the field of prescriptive language in an analogous way to descriptive language. From this point of view, Kelsen's argumentation and presupposed definition of a norm are void and lack conviction. Besides, what could general quantification (the words 'all', 'every') mean in a normative context, if individual norm-sentences were not consequences of general norm-sentences? In descriptive language, general quantification is defined by the rule *de omni et nullo*: $\wedge xFx > Fx_1$ ('For every x: x is F' entails 'x_1 is F'), where 'x_1' designates a member of the universe of quantification.

---

[21] *ATN*, 184.   [22] *ATN*, 186 f.

An analogous rule should define general quantification for prescriptive language.[23] It is of some interest that Kelsen believes that there is a kind of valid inference from a more general to a less general norm, but not from a general to an individual norm. From 'Nobody ought to harm anybody' follows 'Nobody ought to defame anybody'.[24] However, inference of this type is, as such, manifestly invalid, if we don't presuppose the truth of the further premiss 'Any case of defaming a person is a case of harming this very person', which is not a logical truth but a—contingently true—piece of information about the relation between defaming and harming.[25]

In my opinion, the following three features in Kelsen's teaching are in conflict with his irrationalism in respect of norms.

(*a*) Only a qualified act of will yields a valid legal norm. The act of will is qualified, if it is an authorized act. The authorization must be stated by a norm. Only by subsuming this act under the criteria of the authorizing norm can we qualify this act as a creative act for a valid legal norm. Thus, the theory of creation of valid law is manifestly dependent on the logical operation of subsumption under a norm which, however, Kelsen does not accept.[26]

(*b*) Kelsen holds that the secondary rule stating the forbidden behaviour is superfluous, as it follows from the primary rule.

It is, indeed, *superfluous*, explicitly to formulate a norm forbidding theft or commanding to repay loans, that is, a norm commanding behaviour which avoids the respective sanction, because such a norm is—as indicated above—already *implied* by the sanction stating norm itself. Thus, the norm stating an act of coercion as sanction emerges as primary, while the implied norm, which is not—and need not be—explicitly formulated, is secondary.[27]

(*c*) Though Kelsen rejects deductive reasoning in the realm of norms, he introduces the notion of 'correspondence' (*Entsprechung*) between individual and general norms.[28] I doubt that this

---

[23] Cp. Ch. Weinberger and O. Weinberger, *Logik, Semantik und Hermeneutik* (Munich, 1979), pp. 124–5. Note that the meaning of 'For every x: x should F' in a universe of discourse $x_1, x_2, \ldots x_n$ is defined as ' "x_1 should F", "x_2 should F", . . . "x_n should F" '.

[24] *ATN*, 201.

[25] Walter, 'Das Problem des Verhältnisses von Recht und Logik in der Reine Rechtslehre' [The Problem of the Relation between Law and Logic in the Pure Theory of Law], 11 *Rechtstheorie* 299–314 (1980).

[26] Cp. RR^2, 196 f.   [27] *ATN*, 115.   [28] Cp. *ATN*, 208 f.

'correspondence' can be other than the logical deducibility of an individual norm from a general one.

IV CONSEQUENCES OF KELSEN'S LATE CONCEPTION FOR THE THEORY OF LAW

Kelsen's conception of the norm, conceiving the validity of a norm as strictly linked to the creating act, leads to a specific conception of legal positivism which I propose to call 'act-relative positivism'.[29] For any norm which may be considered as valid law there must exist a real act of will of a person (or persons) the sense of which coincides exactly with the norm. Thus, it does not follow from the fact that a general norm is valid law, that the corresponding individual norms are valid law as well. Only if the individual norm is accepted (*anerkannt*) by the judge does it become valid law. In this way, Kelsen is led to a theory of legal validity which had previously been emphatically rejected by the classical Pure Theory of Law, namely a theory of acceptance (*Anerkennungstheorie*). This conception that individual legal duties are not constituted by general rules but only by the corresponding individual act of the judge is[30]—in my opinion—an absurd theory. The act of the judge leads to a transformation of the legal situation, but it is not a creation of legal duties, independent of the previous state of duties of the persons concerned.

The validity of customary law is conceived by Kelsen as produced by a collective act of will. However, the class of those acts which constitute jointly the collective act of will have—so I believe—rather individual content as they refer to individual legal relations. But if my opinion is correct then, in the process of creating general rules of customary law, there does not exist an act of will whose sense is this *general* rule. In consequence of Kelsen's late teaching, legal dynamics is no longer based on logical relations, as had been held by the classical Pure Theory of Law. Instead, it consists of a system of creating acts which may correspond to authorizations by other norms.

The irrationalist conception of the relations between norms

---

[29] Cp. Weinberger, 'Die Idee eines institutionalistischen Rechtspositivismus' [The Idea of an Institutionalist Legal Positivism] in 138 *Revue Internationale de Philosophie*, 487–507 (1981).
[30] *ATN*, 191.

leads to the destruction of the ingenious dynamic and hierarchic theory of law. The relevance of a norm-type is defined by its derogatory force, and derogation is conceptually dependent on the notion of incompatibility between norms.[31] By rejecting the notion of incompatibility between norms we annihilate the basic tenet of the theory of hierarchic structure of the legal system.

According to Kelsen's late teaching, the basic norm is a fictitious entity.[32] There is no act of will, the sense of which would be the basic norm. Thus, even the normative character of the basic norm becomes fictitious, if we accept Kelsen's act-relative definition of the norm, that is, if the norm is defined as the sense of a real act of will. If there is no real act but only a fictitious one, this act can be individualized only by its sense which must be given as an ideal entity, as a piece of meaning in language, not as the meaning of a reality, that is, a real act. A fictitious real act is a *contradictio in adjecto*.

CONCLUSION

Kelsen's conviction that the structure theory of law is concerned with general formal relations in the legal system and in legal processes is as justified as is his recognition that the logical rules of descriptive language do not apply to norms. Yet his contention that there cannot exist a logic of norms is unacceptable and has detrimental consequences for jurisprudence.

The development of a well founded analytical jurisprudence requires the creation of a genuine logic of norm-sentences. By a genuine logic of norm-sentences I understand a logic of prescriptive sentences (and descriptive sentences), not a logic of deontic sentences (which are defined as declarative sentences about the content of a normative system).[33]

---

[31] Cp. Merkl, *Die Lehre von der Rechtskraft* [The Doctrine of Definite Legal Validity] (Leipzig and Vienna, 1923).

[32] *ATN*, 206 f.

[33] Weinberger 'Versuch einer neuen Grundlegung der normenlogischen Folgerungstheorie' [New Foundations for a Theory of Normative Entailment], in *Argumentation und Hermeneutik in der Jurisprudenz, Rechtstheorie, Beiheft 1*, 301–24 (1979).

CHAPTER 9

KELSEN AND NORMATIVE CONSISTENCY

J. W. HARRIS

I INTRODUCTION

IT is a mark of a great thinker that he is prepared to change his mind. If a theorist returns again and again to the same issues over a period of sixty years, it would be astonishing if his last thoughts diverged not a whit from his first. In the voluminous writings of Hans Kelsen, there are many shifts of view. Whatever may be true of norms, no one surely would claim that the principle of non-contradiction should be applied to Kelsen himself. In this paper, I am concerned with those alterations in his theory of law arising out of changes made in his analysis of norms after the publication of the second edition of his *Reine Rechtslehre* in 1960. Two of the things which, in this work and in previous writings, Kelsen claimed to be true of normative systems like the law were, first, that conflicting norms could not be simultaneously valid, and, second, that it was possible (indirectly) to deduce one norm from another. After 1960, Kelsen reversed both these claims: conflicting norms could coexist, and normative inference was impossible. I shall consider these changes in his normative theory only in so far as they have implications for his theory of law; and it is the first of them, the problem of normative consistency, to which I shall give most attention. It will be suggested that Kelsen's earlier view is to be preferred to the later one. What he said in 1960 and before about the necessity of normative consistency has sound implications for a theory of law, with the exception of the connection he made between the consistency of different levels of norms and his doctrine of alternative authorization. The implications for a theory of law of his post 1960 writings on normative consistency and normative inference are unacceptable and, in some respects, bizarre. I shall argue that the principal reason for these unfortunate changes of view was Kelsen's increasing preoccupation with the reification of norms.

The criticisms offered here are made in terms of Kelsen's own theoretical perspective. A theory of law is supposed to explicate the concept of law *we have*. That, of course, raises many problems, because there are so many different moral, political, sociological, and pragmatic contexts in which we refer to 'the law'. Kelsen believed that we should investigate the concept by reference, primarily, to assertions which purport to convey information about the content of positive law. The difference between mere commands and legal norms 'appears only when the objective meaning of the command is described'.[1] Enduring effectiveness is, in the end, the sole criterion by reference to which revolutionaries' decrees are described as 'state laws'; therefore effectiveness, not justice, must be built into our concept of law.[2] Everyday descriptions of the law are the justification for claiming that the concept of law is essentially normative:

If all meaning is denied to the norm (looked upon as objectively valid) which constitutes the connection called 'imputation'—if all meaning is denied to the 'ought'—then it would be senseless to say: 'this is legally permitted, that is forbidden'; 'this belongs to me, that to you'; 'X is entitled and Y is obligated.' The thousands of statements in which the law is expressed daily would be senseless. In contrast to this, the fact is undeniable that everybody understands readily that it is one thing to say: 'A is legally obligated to pay $1.000 to B,' and quite another: 'there is a certain chance that A will pay $1.000 to B.' Everybody understands that it is one thing to say: 'This behavior is a delict according to the law and ought to be punished according to the law'; and quite a different thing to say: 'He who has done this will probably be punished.'[3]

Kelsen's most famous doctrine of the basic norm is also justified by reference to commonplace descriptions of the law. We need the basic norm to answer the question: how are 'all these juristic statements concerning legal norms, legal duties, legal rights, and so on, possible?'[4]

I shall not consider whether some other theoretical perspective is to be preferred—for example, building the concept of law by reference to judgments about the law in difficult cases, or by reference to claims about the values or functions of the law. But it

---

[1] *PTL*, 45.   [2] *PTL*, 49–50.
[3] *PTL*, 104.   [4] *GTLS*, 117.

must be stressed that Kelsen's own perspective should not be too narrowly construed. His theory seeks to elucidate the subject-matter of *all* descriptions of the law, so long as they are genuine descriptions rather than concealed evaluations or sociological comments. Some commentators have attributed to him a concern limited to legal expositions engaged in by a narrow class of specialists. This mistake is partly due to the ambiguous use he makes of the expression 'legal science'—and of similar (seemingly interchangeable) expressions like 'normative science of law', 'legal cognition', 'legal thinking', 'juristic thinking', 'normative juris-prudence', 'dogmatic jurisprudence', and 'jurisprudence'.

Citations may be drawn from Kelsen to support three different concepts of 'legal science'. In the broad sense, it refers to the activity of setting out the law, whether undertaken by textwriters, practising lawyers, informed citizens, or anyone else. An assertion of legal science, in the broad sense, conveys information about the specific provisions of some particular system of positive law; it affirms the validity of some norm or norms.[5] It is this sense which Kelsen employs when he tells us that 'the science of law has been in existence for millennia', and that it 'serves the intellectual needs of those who deal with the law'.[6] Anyone who finds it useful to measure conduct by reference to a provision of positive law is engaging in legal science, if he formulates the provision as an 'ought' standard. Throughout his writings Kelsen criticizes traditional legal science, because so often it has failed to purge its terminology of non-descriptive elements. But none the less, everyday descriptions of the law are the constant touchstone for his theoretical claims.

In the narrow sense, Kelsen uses 'legal science' to refer to the sort of activity in which he himself is engaged, namely, the 'scientific' (that is, value-free and empirical) exposition of the concepts and structures employed by 'legal science' in the broad sense—as well as by dependent disciplines such as legislation and adjudication. This narrow sense is being used when Kelsen says that the pure theory of law is itself a 'science of law'.[7] Legal science in the narrow sense is the province of specialist scholars. It provides abstracted generalizations. It does not give information

[5] See, for example, *GTLS*, 162–5; *PTL*, 58, 71–8, 87–9; Kelsen, 'Professor Stone and the Pure Theory of Law', 17 *Stanford L. Rev.* 1128, 1132–8 (1965).
[6] *PTL*, 105.   [7] *PTL*, 1, 106–7.

about the particular provisions of any system of positive law. It describes the describers' describings.

That little attention has been drawn to the distinction between these two senses in which Kelsen employs the expression 'legal science' may be due to the fact that, in many contexts where he uses it in a patently ambiguous fashion, the ambiguity is unimportant. For example, when he tells us that only legal norms are the objects of legal science,[8] the claim would be true (for him) in whichever sense the expression is interpreted. Those giving pure legal information about particular provisions do only describe legal norms. A scientific legal theory has no other concern than the general operation of legal norms. Similarly, when he condemns 'traditional science of law' for its infusion of 'alien elements'.[9] his criticism would apply equally to lawyers who introduce their personal evaluations into descriptions of the law as to theorists who have, unscientifically, imported ideological commitments into their expositions of legal concepts.

The distinction between the broad and narrow senses does, however, help to explain some apparently quirkish inconstencies. Kelsen often indicates that legal science, with its descriptive ought-sentences, presupposes a basic norm.[10] Yet in an article written in 1966 he says it does not.[11] His claim is simply that scholars and practitioners who give particular information about the law in normative terms (legal scientists in the broad sense) presuppose the basic norm; but, of course, a theorist like Kelsen himself (legal scientist in the narrow sense) does not. He records the fact that the others presuppose it. 'To make manifest this presupposition is an essential function of legal science'[12] (narrow sense).

There is a third sense of 'legal science' which some have attributed to Kelsen. This might be called the 'Never-never Land' conception of legal science. Kelsen says: 'It is the task of the science of law to represent the law of a community, i.e. the material produced by the legal authority in the law-making procedure, in the form of statements to the effect that "if such and such conditions are fulfilled, then such and such a sanction shall

---

[8] See, for example, *PTL*, 4, 53, 68, 70, 75, 76, 86, 101–5.
[9] See, for example, *PTL*, 1, 51, 53, 106.
[10] See, for example, *GTLS*, 116, 395; *WIJ*, 221; *PTL*, 8, 23, 53, 104, 204.
[11] 'On the Pure Theory of Law', 1 *Israel L. Rev.* 1, 6 (1966).
[12] *PTL*, 46.

follow"".[13] Some commentators have taken assertions such as this to mean that 'the law' explicated in Kelsen's pure theory is one which would be described only by a specialist set of scholars who had succeeded in reformulating all the details of the law in just this way.[14] No one has ever achieved such a total reformulation and, given the fantastic complexity of stipulations which set out all the constitutional, substantive, and procedural requirements which have a possible bearing on the lawful administration of sanctions, it never will be done. Consequently, if 'legal science' has this meaning, then it is a never-never discipline and the conception of law which it would presuppose is a never-never law. We must reject this third interpretation, simply because Kelsen speaks of legal science as something which exists and has for long existed; and because the law he explicates corresponds, he says, with ordinary uses of the word 'law'.[15] When Kelsen himself gives examples of legal-science statements and norms in the canonical sanction-stipulating form, they are usually simple, not complex. The lawyer (legal scientist in the broad sense) is being descriptive so long as he can, on demand, relate the bits of information he conveys to the sanction-stipulating schema. 'All legally relevant material contained in a legal order fits in this scheme of the rule of law formulated by legal science';[16] but it does not follow that all legally relevant material must be set out in every statement describing the law.

'Legal science' will hereafter in this paper be used in Kelsen's broad sense. All who describe the law are legal scientists. If Kelsen's theory, at any stage of its development, does not accurately reflect the conception of law to which we commit ourselves when we, any of us, give information about legal provisions, the theory is, in its own terms, faulty.

II   REINE RECHTSLEHRE AND AFTER

The point of departure, then, for Kelsen's theory of law is legal description. Other legal philosophers have different central concerns. The late Lon L. Fuller was primarily interested in what

---

[13] *GTLS*, 45.
[14] For a recent example, see Moore, *Legal Norms and Legal Science* (Honolulu, 1978).
[15] *GTLS*, 4; *PTL*, 30–1.   [16] *PTL*, 58.

the law could achieve as 'an enterprise of subjecting human conduct to the governance of rules'. He invented an incompetent king who repeatedly failed in this endeavour because he neglected methodological principles necessary to the success of the enterprise.[17] I suggest we borrow from this story, shifting the focus from successful control of conduct to successful description of the law. We will imagine a student named Jones reading essays to his tutor.

Day One

JONES. English land law used to recognize the concept of freehold. But, since 1973, freeholds have been abolished and the law now recognizes only long leases.

TUTOR. What! Where on earth do you get that from?

JONES. In 1973, the Campaign for Nationalising Land published a paper showing that freeholds are unnecessary and undesirable and that long leases are all we need.[18]

TUTOR. But the views of a political pressure group are not a source of law.

JONES. Not necessarily, I know. But I am going on to demonstrate that their views are objectively just, so that they do represent the law.

TUTOR. Jones, you haven't understood what describing the law is. That pressure group, and you too, are entitled to offer political criticism of the law—though I doubt whether there is any such thing as objective justice. But you must first set out what the law is; and in every jurisdiction that means that you are limited to certain legislative sources, all others being excluded. In the United Kingdom, the only sources are statutes and cases. Go away and try again.

Day Two

JONES. Title to land may be registered or unregistered. In no case does the law make registration of title compulsory.

TUTOR. What do you mean? Orders in Council have made registration of title compulsory in more than half the country.

JONES. But you said yesterday that the only sources of our law are

---

[17] Fuller, *The Morality of Law*, revised edn. (New Haven, 1969).
[18] Brocklebank *et al.*, *The Case for Nationalising Land*, Campaign for Nationalising Land, 1973.

statute and cases, so of course I ignored Orders in Council.

TUTOR. I should have made myself clearer. Sources of law include delegated legislation. Section 120 of *The Land Registration Act*, 1925, confers power to make orders declaring that registration is to be compulsory in areas defined in the order. So long as any such order is *intra vires*, it creates law. When you describe the law you must take into account, not merely the ultimate legislative sources in any jurisdiction, but also rules emanating from inferior sources, so long as the rules they produce are subsumable under rules emanating from the ultimate sources.

Day three

JONES. A person acquires a good possessory title to land if he occupies it for twelve years, provided that his occupation amounts to 'adverse possession'. Occupation does not amount to 'adverse possession' where it is by express or implied permission of the person entitled to the land.

TUTOR. Good.

JONES. By implication of law, occupation is by permission of the person entitled to the land if it is not inconsistent with the latter's present or future enjoyment of the land.

TUTOR. No, Jones, Section 4 of the *Limitation Amendment Act, 1980*, provides just the opposite. It states: 'For the purpose of determining whether a person occupying any land is in adverse possession of the land it shall not be assumed by implication of law that his occupation is by permission of the person entitled to the land merely by virtue of the fact that his occupation is not inconsistent with the latter's present or future enjoyment of the land.'

JONES. Yes, I have noted that. But there is no mention in the Act of repealing the rule laid down by the Court of Appeal in *Wallis's Cayton Bay Holiday Camp Ltd.* v. *Shell-Mex B.P. Ltd.*[19] In that case, the court held that where a strip of land belonging to a garage was occupied by someone else for twelve years, that was not adverse possession because the garage owners had in mind to develop the strip in the future when a new road should be built. I take that decision to

---

[19] [1975] Q.B. 94.

amount to a ruling that user which is not inconsistent with an owner's present or future enjoyment amounts, in law, to user by implied permission. Are you saying that I have misinterpreted the ruling of the case, or that whatever ruling the court made it has been silently repealed by the 1980 Act?

TUTOR. I am saying neither. We don't make speculations about silent repeals. We must now read the Cayton Bay case in the light of the Section. In so far as there is any conflict, the ruling has been derogated from by the Act. That is because, in stating the law, all lawyers assume a ranking amongst different sources, and rules originating in sources lower in the ranking are invalidated to the extent that they conflict with rules originating in higher sources. In our jurisdiction, statutes prevail over case law rules, later statutes over earlier statutes, and so on. If the Cayton Bay case ruling can only be read your way, it is no longer valid. If it can be read as standing for some other ruling—say, that on the particular facts there was an implied permission—then it still stands.

Day Four

JONES. If a person creates two mortgages in respect of his land, neither of which is protected by the deposit of title documents, and the first mortgagee registers his mortgage as a land charge at the Land Charges Registry after the creation of the second mortgage but before the second mortgagee registers his mortgage, then the legal position is as follows: the first mortgagee has priority over the second mortgagee, and the first mortgagee does not have priority over the second mortgagee. Section 97 of the *Law of Property Act, 1925*, provides: 'Every mortgage affecting a legal estate in land . . . (not being a mortgage protected by the deposit of documents relating to the legal estate affected) shall rank according to its date of registration as a land charge pursuant to the *Land Charges Act, 1925*.' But Section 13 (2) of the *Land Charges Act, 1925*, provides: 'A land charge . . . shall . . . be void as against a purchaser of the land charged therewith . . . unless the land charge is registered in the appropriate register before the completion of the purchase.'[20]

---

[20] Re-enacted in s. 4 (5) of the Land Charges Act, 1972.

In the definition section of the latter act (Section 20), 'purchaser' is defined as including a mortgagee. Therefore, by Section 97, the first mortgagee has priority over the second because he registered first; whereas by Section 13 (2), the second has priority over the first because, being unregistered at the time of the completion of the second mortgage, the first mortgage is void as against the second mortgagee.

TUTOR. But you can't just leave it there. The law, as you describe it, contains a direct contradiction.

JONES. What's wrong with that? I noted what you said about rules from higher sources derogating rules from lower ones; but these provisions were both enacted by Parliament at the same time: they both came into force on January 1st, 1926.

TUTOR. Even where conflicting rules cannot be reconciled by virtue of derogation, we still have to interpret them, when we are describing the law, in such a way as to eliminate contradictions. You might, for example, suggest that the express reference in Section 97 to the *Land Charges Act* indicates that the first-to-register rule does not apply where the first mortgage is void as against the second mortgagee by virtue of Section 13 (2). That is not the only possible interpretation, so you are entitled to say that, because of the seemingly inconsistent provisions, the law on the point is uncertain. But you cannot say baldly that the law is clear and that it is contradictory. What do you suppose would be the position of a trustee in bankruptcy appointed to administer the assets of a mortgagor in these circumstances?

JONES. The legal position would be quite clear. It would be the case both that the trustee had a duty to pay the first mortgagee before the second, and also that he did not have such a duty. Whatever he did, he would be acting illegally.

TUTOR. No, Jones. That is not the conception of legality we presuppose when we describe the law. We assume that we cannot say: it is the case that the law requires x, and it is not the case that the law requires x. That is why we apply a principle of non-contradiction in our descriptions of the law.

Day Five

JONES [*entering somewhat flustered*]. I say, a traffic warden has just given me a parking ticket for parking on a double yellow line.

TUTOR. I'm sorry to hear that, but . . .

JONES. I wasn't breaking the law. I've looked up the regulations. They state that it is an offence for any person to park a motor vehicle on double yellow lines, but they say nothing at all about 'Jones'.

TUTOR. If the regulations say 'any person', we can infer that they include 'Jones'.

....

Kelsen once believed that the tutor was right, and Jones wrong, every time. But in works written during the last decade of his life, he took the view that the score was three to two in Jones' favour. On days three, four, and five, it was the tutor who was in error.

In *Reine Rechtslehre* (2nd edn.), Kelsen provides grounds for saying that, on all five occasions, Jones was making a mistake in his description of the law. I have labelled the principles illustrated by the first four interviews, principles of 'exclusion', 'subsumption', 'derogation', and 'non-contradiction', respectively. I contend that they are all rules-systematizing principles presupposed in the logic of descriptive legal science. The fifth interview pictures Jones as failing to observe a principle of 'practical deduction', by virtue of which legal rules are applied to particular facts.[21]

Kelsen's book contains the basis of all these principles. The basis for the principle of exclusion is his doctrine of the basic norm. The basic norm is presupposed by legal science in so far as it describes the law by reference to norms posited by norm-authorities only, and not by reference to extraneous political or moral factors.[22] The basis for the principle of subsumption is his doctrine of the hierarchical structure of the legal order, in which the reason for the validity of any norm below the basic norm is always some immediately superior norm.[23] As to derogation, Kelsen writes:

If we have a conflict between general norms, created by the same organ at different times, then the validity of the later norm supersedes the validity of the earlier, contradictory, one according to the principle *lex posterior derogat priori*. Since the norm-creating organ—the king or the parliament —is normally authorized to prescribe changeable and therefore abolishable

---

[21] Harris, *Law and Legal Science* (Oxford, 1979), ss. 1 and 2.
[22] *PTL*, s. 34.   [23] *PTL*, s. 35.

norms, the principle *lex posterior derogat priori* may be presumed to be included in the authorization. The principle also applies if the conflicting norms are prescribed by two different organs; for example, if the constitution authorizes the king and the parliament to regulate the same subject by general norms, or if legislature and custom are both established as law-creating facts.[24]

Note that Kelsen says that the *lex posterior* principle 'may be presumed to be included' in the authorization conferred upon norm-creating organs. Similarly, in an earlier work he had written that the *lex posterior* principle 'is taken for granted wherever a constitution provides for the possibility of legislative change. . . . Insofar as such a principle has not been expressly stated it can only be established by way of interpretation.'[25] Derogation is an a priori matter. There is no question of a general derogating rule being a positive norm established by legislation or custom.

However, we are told, this derogating principle is not applicable where conflicting norms have been prescribed simultaneously. The contradiction must then be eliminated by some interpretation or other.[26] Both the principles of derogation and of non-contradiction are based, according to Kelsen, on the same a priori demand that legal science should interpret its subject-matter as a unity.

But since the cognition of law, like any cognition, seeks to understand its subject as a meaningful whole and to describe it in noncontradictory statements, it starts from the assumption that conflicts of norms within the normative order . . . can and must be solved by interpretation.[27]

Although (as Kelsen sees it) norms cannot themselves be in logical conflict, the statements of legal science can; so that, indirectly, logical principles are applicable to norms. The legal scientist denies simultaneous validity to conflicting norms. In the same way, although legal science cannot itself issue norms, it can produce particular norms indirectly by applying general norms deductively to particular facts: 'one legal norm may be deduced from another if the rules of law that describe them can form a logical syllogism'.[28]

After 1960 comes the great change of mind. A presupposed basic norm continues to exclude from descriptions of the law all besides

[24] *PTL*, 206.   [25] *GTLS*, 402.   [26] *PTL*, 205–8.
[27] *PTL*, 206.   [28] *PTL*, 74.

norms issued by authorized acts of will.[29] Norms emanating from inferior organs continue to be regarded as parts of the legal order by virtue of the principle of subsumption for, in so far as the state of affairs established *in concreto* by a particular norm can be subsumed under the state of affairs defined *in abstracto* in a general norm 'a logical relation exists'.[30] However, in his essay on 'Derogation', first published in 1962, Kelsen tells us that, when the legislator issues conflicting norms, legal science is powerless to resolve the conflict by appeal to an a priori principle of derogation or to any other a priori conflict-dispelling principle:

principles of derogation are not logical principles . . . conflicts between norms remain unsolved unless derogating norms are expressly stipulated or silently presupposed, and . . . the science of law is just as incompetent to solve by interpretation existing conflicts between norms, or better, to repeal the validity of positive norms, as it is incompetent to issue legal norms.[31]

The view now is that derogation must be treated positivistically, not a priori. Kelsen might have argued that derogation takes place only if custom has established a general norm to the effect that all later norms derogate from earlier norms emanating from the same organ, a sort of flying buttress dependent norm. His positivistic treatment of derogation is quite different. He insists that, in the absence of express repeal, an earlier norm loses validity as the result of a later inconsistent norm only if, in addition to the later norm itself, the legislator can be taken to have 'silently enacted' a specific derogating norm directed towards the earlier norm. Such a silently enacted norm would be 'dependent', because it relates directly, not to human behaviour, but to the validity of a norm. But it would be a 'positive' norm, since it correlates with a (silent) act of will.[32]

Kelsen's views on derogation, before he changed his mind, were far from satisfactory. As regards provisions issued at different times, legal science looks for a ranking among sources as the basis

---

[29] Kelsen, 'Professor Stone and the Pure Theory of Law', 17 *Stanford L. Rev.* 1128 (1965); 'On the Pure Theory of Law', 1 *Israel L. Rev.* 1. Kelsen's reference to the presupposition of the basic norm as a 'typical case of a fiction in the sense of Vaihinger's *Philosophie des Als-Ob*' (at p. 6) represents no substantial change in his position; cf. Harris, *Law and Legal Science*, pp. 78–9.

[30] *ELMP*, 246.

[31] *ELMP*, 274.   [32] *ELMP*, 216, 234, 237, 255, 271–4.

of conflict-elimination. It need not assume that later rules always derogate from earlier ones. Even with statutes emanating from the same legislature it may happen, though it is unusual, that the practices of a particular system prefer the earlier to the later. Every system has its own source-ranking, and that is, usually, a matter established by custom. All that is presupposed 'a priori'—that is, as part of the enterprise of law-description in a modern state—is that there will be a ranking upon which the principle of derogation can operate. That, as I shall argue, is an eminently more plausible position that the contention that law-description must be understood as attributing to legislators silent enactment of quite specific provisions.

In subsequent essays, Kelsen asserted that legal science is not only incapable of resolving conflicts between norms, it is also disabled from drawing deductions from the law. An act is only legally obligatory if prescribed by a norm. Therefore, a concrete act cannot be described as legal or illegal by reference to a general norm until some competent authority has issued a corresponding concrete norm—even though, once issued, the validity of the concrete norm would be founded on the validity of the general norm by virtue of the principle of subsumption.[33]

Now it is undoubtedly possible for the general norm 'All thieves should be punished, i.e., sent to prison' to be valid, since created by way of legislation, and for the statement 'Smith is a thief' to be true, and even to be asserted by the competent court, while the individual norm 'Smith should be sent to prison' is nevertheless not valid, because the competent court has for some reason failed to posit this individual norm. . .[34]

In the light of this denial of the possibility of normative inference, the tutor was wrong, and Jones was right, in the fifth interview. The implausibility of this position has been argued for elsewhere;[35] but not enough has been said about the explanation for Kelsen's adopting it. As I contend in the final section of this paper, the principal reason for Kelsen changing his views on derogation, non-contradiction and deduction concerns the reification of norms. His earlier views are preferable, except for one

---

[33] *ELMP*, chs, 10–12.   [34] *ELMP*, 240–1.
[35] Harris, 'Kelsen's Concept of Authority', 36 *CLJ* 353 (1977); Harris, *Law and Legal Science* (Oxford, 1979); Raz, 'Kelsen's General Theory of Norms', 6 *Philosophia* 595 (1976); MacCormick, *Legal Reasoning and Legal Theory* (Oxford, 1978), ch. 2.

important implication which he drew from the principle of non-contradiction, namely, his conception of alternative authorization.

III   NORMATIVE CONSISTENCY AND ALTERNATIVE AUTHORIZATION

In the section of *Reine Rechtslehre* devoted to the general topic 'Conflict of Norms', Kelsen tells us that 'the problem of norm conflicts within the same legal order presents itself in two forms, depending on whether the conflict is between two norms of the same level or between a higher and a lower norm.'[36] He then deals with the first form of conflict in terms of derogation and interpretative ruling-out of conflicts, and finishes by promising to deal with the second form in the context of his discussion of the hierarchial structure of the legal order.[37] He discharges this promise in s. 35 (j) entitled 'Conflict between Norms of Different Levels'. He begins this subsection by saying that certain expressions usual in traditional science of law, such as 'unlawful judicial decisions' and 'unconstitutional statutes', if taken literally, 'give the impression that such a thing as "a norm contrary to a norm" in general and a "legal norm contrary to a legal norm" in particular, were possible'.[38] He then goes on to explain how 'unlawful judicial decisions' (at least of the highest appellate court) must be regarded as authorized by the statute which the judge purports to apply, as an alternative to decisions whose content is determined by the statute; and that 'unconstitutional statutes' must similarly be regarded as authorized by the constitution as an alternative to statutes whose content is determined by the constitution. Given this alternative-authorization analysis, one can see that there really never is any conflict between lower and higher norms. The subsection concludes:

> It follows from this analysis that no conflict is possible between statute and judicial decision, constitution and statute, constitution and ordinance, statute and ordinance, or, formulated generally: no conflict is possible between a higher and lower norm of a legal order, which would destroy the unity of this system of norms by making it impossible to describe it in noncontradictory rules of law.[39]

---

[36] *PTL*, 206.   [37] *PTL*, 208.   [38] *PTL*, 267.
[39] *PTL*, 276; the discussion at *GTLS*, 153–62 terminates with the same conclusion.

When Kelsen came to believe that there could be conflicting valid norms, the conception of alternative authorization was retained but in a different form. Supreme courts are still authorized to hand down unlawful decisions as well as lawful ones, and legislatures are still authorized to pass either constitutional or unconstitutional statutes. The authority to make the alternative (wrong) choice, however, need not come from the same norm which confers the authority to make the lawful or constitutional choice.

In *Reine Rechtslehre*, Kelsen's view on 'unlawful judicial decisions was as follows:

That the legal order confers the force of a final judgment to a decision of a court of last instance means that not only is a general norm valid that predetermines the content of the judicial decision, but also a general norm according to which the court may itself determine the content of the individual norm to be created by the court. The two norms form a unit: the court of last instance is authorized to create either an individual legal norm whose content is predetermined by the general norm, *or* an individual norm whose content is not so predetermined, but is to be determined by the court of last instance itself. . . . If the content of these individual legal norms is determined by the pre-existing general legal norm, it is so in the sense of the alternative mentioned here.[40]

In his 1965 essay on 'Law and Logic', however, the basis for the authority of the 'unlawful judicial decision' is changed. Kelsen still believes in subsumption, still believes that the legal system is to be seen as a hierarchy of authorized acts of will, and consequently there must be a norm which confers validity on any judicial pronouncement which acquires the force of law. But now the judicial decision may be seen as conflicting with the general norm (the statute) which is supposed to determine its content. Instead of having to read one general norm as forming a unity with two alternatives (which would avoid any conflict), the individual norm created by the court's decision may now be seen as conflicting with the general statutory norm, its validity being justified simply by the general norm regarding the legal force of judicial decisions.[41]

Similarly, 'unconstitutional statutes' are catered for in *Reine Rechtslehre* in a way which avoids any conflict between them and the constitution.

---

[40] *PTL*, 269.   [41] *ELMP*, 244.

The meaning of the constitution regulating legislation is not that valid statutes may come into being only in the way directly stipulated by the constitution, but also in a way determined by the legislative organ itself. The provisions of the constitution which regulate legislation have an alternative character. The constitution includes a direct and an indirect regulation of legislation; and the legislative organ has to choose between them.[42]

Whereas in his later essay on 'Derogation', Kelsen says that a statute may or may not conflict with the constitution. If it does not, despite the fact that its contents overstep constitutional limits, this is because of the alternative-authorization analysis presented in *Reine Rechtslehre*. But if it does conflict, it may be denied validity by virtue of a special norm directed to invalidating unconstitutional statutes.

The constitution of a state can provide that all men regardless of their race shall be treated equally; later the legislator can pass a statute which grants certain rights or which imposes certain obligations only on persons of a certain race . . . a norm can, but need not be valid, which stipulates that the latter of the two conflicting norms loses its validity. It should, however, be remembered that of the two conflicting norms . . . the so-called 'unconstitutional' statute may, according to positive law, be valid, but its validity may be repealed in a special procedure provided for in the constitution . . . Then no conflict of norms exists. . .[43]

Professor Stanley Paulson has argued that Kelsen did not really intend, by his conception of alternative authorization, to indicate that judges and legislators have a free choice. He suggests that we can interpret what Kelsen says as drawing a distinction between 'material' and 'formal' authorization. He believes that Kelsen's view was in effect the same as that of Adolf Merkl: 'It should never even occur to the judge' that he can if he wishes adopt a ruling which contravenes the substantive law.[44] Such psychological speculation is, however, alien to the purity of Kelsen's theory. He insists that the concept of law must be expounded by reference only to the content of positive norms. If legal norms give judges a choice—as Kelsen claims that they do—the fact that they do not feel free is, from his perspective legally irrelevant.

---

[42] *PTL*, 273.   [43] *ELMP*, 272.

[44] Paulson, 'Material and Formal Authorisation in Kelsen's Pure Theory', 39 *CLJ* 172, 192 (1980). For further discussion of this question, see Maher, 'Custom and Constitutions' 1 *Oxford Journal of Legal Studies* 167 (1981).

Kelsen's writings provide no direct support for Paulson's distinction between material and formal authorization. They do, however, indicate that the authors of higher norms may demonstrate legally relevant preferences for lower norms which do not contradict the substantive content of the higher norms. Although the constitution must be interpreted as conferring a 'choice between two paths' on the legislative organ, there may be one or other of two kinds of provision showing that the authors of the constitution have a preference for legislation which does not go beyond constitutional limits to legislation which does. Either the constitution confers upon an organ different from the legislative organ the power to examine the constitutionality of statutes and authorizes it to repeal a statute considered unconstitutional; or it provides that those participating in the passing or promulgation of 'unconstitutional statutes' shall be punished for so doing.[45]

It should be noted that, in Kelsen's theory, the choice of the lower organ is inevitable, whereas the expressed preference for the substantially correct alternative on the part of the higher organ is contingent. Given the fact that improperly created norms may become by and large effective and so must be regarded as valid law, and given Kelsen's dogmatic assumption that all valid legal norms (except the basic norm) must have been authorized by a pre-existing norm, it follows that the law always, by virtue of alternative authorization, confers on norm-authorities the choice to follow the substantive content of higher norms or to ignore it. Whether ignoring it will lead to punishment or annulment varies from system to system. Methodological purity requires us to attribute preferences when, and only when, they are evidenced on the face of the law. In the context of 'unlawful judicial decisions' by a 'final' court there could, by definition, be no judicial organ with power to annul; we could only attribute a preference for 'lawful decisions' to the legislators if they had included some provision for punishing judges who hand down logically unsupportable interpretations. The authors of the constitution can be regarded as exhibiting a preference for constitutional as against unconstitutional statutes only if the constitution provides either for punishment of the legislators or for the constitutionality of the statute to be settled by a special organ. On this basis, it may be

---

[45] *PTL*, 273-4.

that even the authors of the United States constitution cannot be regarded as expressing a preference for constitutional legislation. No provision of the United States constitution lays down that voting for an unconstitutional enactment is a ground on which a congressman is liable to criminal sanction; and the constititution itself did not confer on any organ the power to declare statutes unconstitutional—that power was assumed by the courts fourteen years after the constitution was ratified.[46] However, Kelsen does indicate that a written constitution may be modified by custom.[47] If we can add together as 'authors of the constititution' those who promulgated the written document and those whose acquiescence led to the customary change, then we can say that, in the United States at least, the authors of the constitution have (in Kelsenian terms) given evidence of a preference for one of the two paths open to the legislature—that of enacting statutes which do not infringe constitutional limits. But the evidence of the preference does not negate the existence of a Kelsenian choice. Until a statute is declared unconstitutional, it must be regarded as authorized if it is by and large effectively applied.

I am going to argue that Kelsen's views, set out in *Reine Rechtslehre* and earlier writings, on the incompatibility of conflicting valid norms of the same level are substantially correct. The conception of law presupposed in descriptive legal science does require normative consistency in this sense. But the same is not true of his views about the absence of conflict between higher and lower norms. If a final court of appeal pronounces a questionable interpretation of a statute, or if a legislature enacts a statute whose constitutionality is disputed (in a jurisdiction where there is no judicial power to declare statutes invalid), what does the legal commentator do if he believes that the court or the legislature was in error? There are two possibilities, two senses in which he can maintain that the decision (or the enactment) is 'wrong but binding'. He may claim that the statute or the constitution was unclear, so that it authorized two interpretations, the one adopted by the court or the legislature, and another one which he (the commentator) believes to be the preferable one. He may argue that his interpretation is preferable on various grounds: that it gives effect to the true intention of the makers of the statute or of

[46] *Marbury* v. *Madison* 5 U.S. (1 Cranch) 137 (1803).
[47] *PTL*, 224–9.

the constitution; that it represents a more natural reading of the text; that it captures best the principles embodied in the historic doctrine of the jurisdiction; or that it will have better consequences than the interpretation actually adopted. Yet, the less desirable interpretation was a possible interpretation and so the commentator is not claiming that there is now a logical conflict between the statute and the court's ruling or between the constitution and the legislation. With this first sense of 'wrong but binding' Kelsen has no concern. For him, only the norm-creating organ's opinions about conflict would, in this context, be legally significant. The second possibility is that the legal commentator asserts that no possible reading of the statute or the constitution can support the final court's ruling or the legislature's enactment. There is a logical contradiction. Such situations are not common, but it appears to be just such contexts to which Kelsen refers when he speaks of 'unlawful judicial decisions' and 'unconstitutional statutes'. Here, he claims, because the judicial ruling or the statute acquires the force of law, the legal scientist must view the situation as one of authorized 'choice'. In *Reine Rechtslehre* he says that the statute itself or the constitution itself authorizes the courts or the legislature to enact either norms within the logical scope of the law, or any other norms they choose. Given the open choice, there can be no conflict. In his later writings, the statute or constitution itself only authorizes rulings or enactments within its logical scope; but, assuming again that unlawful judicial decisions and unconstitutional statutes do acquire the force of law, there must be separate norms of positive law authorizing the final court to make any ruling it chooses, and authorizing the legislature to pass any statute it chooses.

The mistake here, as I have argued elsewhere,[48] is the assumption that all authority is rule-defined. If the legal commentator really does find himself forced into the second possible view of the questionable decision or statute, he is not compelled, by his admission that the wrong ruling or statute has acquired the force of law, into acknowledging that the legal system authorized in advance the court or the legislature to do anything they please. When he claims that the decision or the statute was 'wrong but binding' in the second sense, he asserts that it was not legally

---

[48] Harris, 'Kelsen's Concept of Authority', 36 *CLJ* 353 (1977).

authorized at all, that the court or the legislature assumed an authority which (as a matter of pre-existing law) they did not have; but that, owing to the institutional deference prevalent in the jurisdiction, the decision or the enactment will be enforced as law, so that it has brought about, by unlawful or unconstitutional means, a change in the law.

Kelsen's contention that the law authorizes judges and legislators either to apply higher legal norms or totally to disregard them is at odds not only with the conception of law presupposed by legal commentators, but also with that presupposed by judges and legislators themselves (when they inform themselves about 'the law' before going on to pass judgment or to legislate). 'Alternative authorization', then, is an erroneous notion given Kelsen's own theoretical perspective, that of expounding the concept of law by reference to legal description. (It might have some merit from a different (legal realist) perspective, which analyses the concept of law in terms of 'realistic' predictions of what officials will do.) Furthermore, the view that officials have a choice gives rise to an internal inconsistency within the pure theory. Kelsen constantly stresses that legal orders must be by and large effective; and he says that judges usually apply the law as described by legal science. 'As long as the legal order is on the whole efficacious there is the greatest probability that the courts will actually decide as—in the view of normative jurisprudence—they should decide'.[49]

But how are we supposed to measure a norm's effectiveness, or to notice whether or not courts behave as normative jurisprudence says they should, if legislative and constitutional norms direct them either to apply the law or not to apply it, at their option?

IV NON-CONTRADICTION

Both the size and the nature of the problem of normative consistency are elusive. How likely is it that a copper-bottomed instance of irresolvable conflict in the law will actually arise, and what precisely would be meant by claiming that the conflict 'exists'? In his later writings, Kelsen tells us that a conflict between two norms 'occurs quite often',[50] although he is only able to furnish imaginary examples rather than instances drawn from any

---

[49] *WIJ*, 270–1.   [50] *ELMP*, 271.

system of positive law. Given his own views on the nature of normative conflict, one would have thought that actualizations of it would be rare indeed. As he had come to reject normative inference, there could be a clash (for him) if general norms are on their face contradictory; it would not be enough to show that, in a hypothetical situation, a deduction drawn from one general norm would conflict with a deduction drawn from another. Even before his change of mind about practical deduction, the occasions of genuine norm-conflict were narrowly circumscribed. The fact that two legal norms impose 'duties' to perform and to refrain from a particular line of conduct was not evidence of a contradiction—given his own definition of 'duty' (or 'objectively commanded behaviour') as conduct the opposite of which is the condition of a sanction.[51] He said that it was a possible, though politically undesirable, situation for one norm to authorize a sanction as a consequence of behaviour and for another norm to authorize a sanction as a consequence of the opposite behaviour.[52] For him, there is normative conflict in the law only when independent legal norms stipulate contradictory coercive measures, or stipulate that coercive measures ought and ought not to be executed, under the same conditions.[53] The mortgage example given above[54] is the nearest real example of such a conflict I have been able to find; and it requires the provisions of the two statutes to be interpreted as independent norms addressed to the mortgagor's trustee in bankruptcy. As has often been noted, to produce contradictions rather than mere contraries, Kelsen should strictly have used language equivalent to 'not ought' rather than 'ought not'.[55]

The version of the principle of non-contradiction which I wish to defend is as follows: one would be asserting a contradiction if one maintained that, according to law, there exists a duty, and also there exists no duty, to perform a certain act on a certain occasion.[56]

---

[51] *PTL*, 50-4.   [52] *PTL*, 25-6.
[53] *PTL*, 205-8; *ELMP*, 270-1.   [54] In the fourth Jones interview.
[55] Cf. Hart, 'Kelsen's Doctrine of the Unity of Law', in Kiefer and Munitz, eds., *Ethics and Social Justice* (New York, 1970).
[56] Harris, *Law and Legal Science*, pp. 11, 32-3, 41-2, 81-4, 95-6, 115-22, 128-9. *Pace* Raz who appears to think that such an assertion would not involve a contradiction, since he charges me with confusing conflict and contradiction—Raz, *The Concept of a Legal System;* 2nd edn. (Oxford, 1980), p. 225. For further discussion see Paulson, 'Subsumption, Derogation and Non-contradiction in "Legal Science"', 48 *Chicago L. Rev.* 802 (1981).

In a lengthy article supporting the view that valid rules or norms may conflict, Stephen Munzer concedes that constructing an example of such conflict is far from easy.[57] He builds upon an imaginary example invented by Alf Ross.[58] The devotees of a cult procure legislation making it an offence to pass their prophet's statue without raising one's hat. Their opponents procure legislation making it an offence to raise one's hat when passing the statue. Munzer stresses that, in order to be sure that one has a genuine legal conflict, it is necessary to stipulate that the imaginary legal system has rules expressly excluding all the means which actual legal systems employ for resolving conflicts—for example, prohibiting courts from looking behind the words of statutes for a rational legislative intention.

There is no doubt that legislative provisions and court rulings may, on some readings, conflict. And it is also clear that lawyers in general, and courts in particular, commonly apply a variety of devices for 'reconciling' apparently contradictory provisions—*lex posterior derogat priori*; 'the more specific ousts the less specific'; 'the legislature must be taken to have had all the rest of the law in mind'; and so on. I take the question of normative consistency—the question of whether or not there can be 'conflicting valid norms'—to be this: when we are engaged in stating the law on any topic, is a predisposition to reconcile seemingly contradictory provisions part of the conception of 'law' with which we operate? I contend that the answer is 'yes'. The elimination of contradiction takes place at what might be called a 'precognition stage'. We do not search out separate norms and then ask whether they conflict. Before we arrive at the point where we know what the law is, we have already reworked legislative materials into a unified field of meaning. Kelsen also took this view when he wrote *Reine Rechtslehre*, which is why he spoke of legal science as 'constitutive' of its object, and noted the analogy with Kantian epistemology.[59]

My claim about the precognitive elimination of contradiction is a jurisprudential claim, not one about the inevitable dictates of 'logic'. It is not as closely tied to 'law' as the elimination of contradictions among descriptive propositions is tied to 'communication'. It may be that factual information-giving which persistently ignored principles of logical consistency is inconceivable, not

---

[57] Munzer, 'Validity and Legal Conflicts', 82 *Yale L. J.* 1140, 1169–74 (1973).
[58] Ross, *Directives and Norms* (1968), pp. 172–3. [59] *PTL*, 72.

merely pointless or something different from what our current practices demand. Law-stating which ignored consistency is conceivable. All legal discourse could be related to single laws. Clients and their advisers could discuss, not 'what the law requires' on any matter, but whether there are 'any laws' in point; and all legal information could come in discrete packets labelled by reference to isolated provisions. This, however, is not the conception of law we have. We employ concepts such as 'legal', 'illegal', 'lawful', 'unlawful', which involve relating conduct to the law as a whole. These concepts, employed by lawyers and non-lawyers alike, have a political basis in the values of legality and constitutionality which are part of official life. We ascribe to officials the duty of 'upholding the law', not the duty of enforcing isolated commands. Carving the law into slices—'rules', 'principles', 'definitions', 'maxims', 'sections', 'court-rulings', 'articles', 'laws' —is something we do in many contexts, political and institutional. Nothing in our linguistic practices commits us to holding that, whatever the context, the law comes ready sliced in a fashion which some sufficiently subtle metaphysic of 'individuation' might reveal. In particular, nothing in our discourse supports the view that the law comes to us in irreconcilably conflicting units.

I have done my best in the fourth Jones interview to provide an example that comes as near as possible to an instance of real conflict in the law. However, as indicated, reconciliatory inter-pretations are available in that situation. Of course, there could be a 'legal' system (like that envisaged by Munzer) in which all means of avoiding conflict were positively excluded. Instead of operating with concepts like 'legal' and 'illegal' (which presuppose measuring conduct by the law as a whole), we could operate exclusively with concepts like 'prohibited by a particular provision'. Then, the elimination of conflicts would be a mere policy option, not something presupposed in our conception of law.

We could go further and imagine a 'legal' system which eliminated, by specific provision, all the five principles illustrated in the Jones interviews. A fundamental law of Jones Land might provide:

It shall be no objection to any assertion about the content of 'the law' that no source can be cited in its support or that it is based merely on arguments from moral truth. No argument based on a 'source' shall be regarded as strengthened by the fact that authority was conferred upon that source by a provision emanating from another source. No source for a proposition of law shall be regarded as in any way subordinate to any other source. It shall be no objection to a statement of law that it presents the law in contradictory terms. No inference shall be drawn from one statement of law to another.

In Jones Land, assertions about the law would sometimes reflect the content of a pronouncement issued by someone other than the asserter, and sometimes would consist of direct appeals to moral truth. What would be 'outlawed' would be any process of systematizing among propositions of law—no exclusion, subsumption, derogation, elimination of contradiction, or deduction. If we moved over to a Jones Land Society, our current practices of legislation, law-administration, and legal science would have to go, together with our current conception of 'law'.

V   A NORM IS A NORM IS A NORM?

Part of the explanation for Kelsen's change of mind about the compatibility of competing valid norms was his determination to keep legal science pure. Throughout his career, he had attacked impure elements in traditional legal science, instances in which those purporting to describe the law actually smuggle in ideological commitments. In *Reine Rechtslehre*, he characterized many of the traditional doctrines of legal science—such as arguments from analogy or speculations about the legislature's true intentions—as examples of 'legal politics' masquerading in the guise of law-description.[60] Then, in his essay on 'derogation', he claimed that legal science was also 'incompetent to solve by interpretation existing conflicts between norms'.[61]

The search for yet greater purity is not, however, the whole explanation of Kelsen's change. After all, his later view begs the question of what lawyers are to do when confronted with two legislative provisions, or two court rulings, which, on some interpretations, conflict, but, on other interpretations, do not. To insist that the law consists of separable entities called 'norms' (which may very likely be in conflict) is just as much a theoretical dogma imposed upon legal practice as is the (now rejected) view that legal science, 'like any cognition', 'starts from the assumption

[60] *PTL*, s. 47.   [61] *ELMP*, 274.

that conflicts of norms . . . can and must be solved by interpretation'.[62]

It may be urged against the argument I presented in the last
section that I have misunderstood the problem of normative
consistency. Even if it is true that legal practice always does
eliminate conflicts through a variety of reconciling devices, still
(some would claim) that does not prove that valid norms do not
conflict. To suggest that it does is to misunderstand the nature of
norms. Whatever lawyers do, even if no instances of irreconcilable
conflict actually occur in our legal-institutional experiences,
norms are norms and, by their nature, they can collide. Norms or
rules are like things, not like propositions. Dr Raz, for example,
has compared rules to stones.[63]

What is the justification for this reification of norms? It is
apparently this. We have the word 'norm', and its employment in
our discourse shows that it stands for a thing-like concept. That
being so, all we need to do is to develop a theory of norms which
will make clear just what sort of an abstract thing it is. The only
discourse, however, which regularly employs 'norm' is that of
moral, political, and legal philosophy—at least so far as English
usage is concerned. Unless some counterpart for 'norm' can be
found in extra-philosophical discourse, especially in the language
of the law, the concept of norm reveals itself as one which is the
result merely of philosophical in-breeding, and we cannot assume
that it sheds any light on the social and political institutions of the
law. Some philosophers are aware that, since 'norm' is a
philosophical term of art, we must take care not to take its
reification too literally.[64]

The obvious candidate for the counterpart in legal discourse for
the philosophers' conceptions of 'norm' is the word 'rule'.
Speakers of English regularly employ this term in relation to the
law. Their use of it, however, in varying contexts—legislation,
exposition, or criticism of the law, legal argument, legal sociology
and anthropology—cannot easily be squared with the assumption
of a unique concept of rule. I have argued elsewhere that we need
to distinguish between what I called 'pure-norm rules', 'rule ideas',

---

[62] *PTL*, 206.
[63] Raz, *The Authority of Law* (Oxford, 1979), p. 148.
[64] Cf. Ullmann-Margalit, *The Emergence of Norms* (Oxford, 1977), p. 19.

and 'rule situations'. It is the first of these, pure-norm rules, to which the 'logical' operations of legal science apply.[65]

In particular, discourse about the law reveals two kinds of attributes of legal rules, propositional and imperatival. On the one hand, lawyers speak of rules as 'having ranges of application', 'being consistent', 'generalizable', 'inferrable', 'reconcilable', 'subject to exceptions', and so on. On the other hand, rules can be 'issued', 'promulgated', 'obeyed', 'violated'. I suggest the term of art 'pure-norm rule', or 'normative proposition', to stand for entities which have these dual qualities.

Kelsen, seeking to lay bare the logic of purely descriptive legal science, noted that there were concepts employed by legal practice—such as 'duty', 'right', 'delict', 'legal' and 'illegal' acts—on the one hand, and there were raw legislative materials, on the other. Not all that passed, in traditional practice, for descriptions of the law could be admitted into a value-free reconstruction of legal science. Not all products of the legislative process could be admitted either, because statutes might contain purely speculative or ideological matter which was 'legally irrelevant material'.[66] Therefore, one had to interpose between the language of practitioners and the language of legislative source-materials some entity in terms of which the purely descriptive law-systematizing processes of legal science would make sense. So far so good. The trouble is that Kelsen interposed two entities: 'rules of law in a descriptive sense', and 'independent legal norms'. This duality was a source of puzzlement to his critics.[67] He defended it in *Reine Rechtslehre* by stressing that one kind of ought-stipulation was a statement in legal science whereas the other was the correlate of a legislative will.[68]

In his *General Theory of Law and State*, he had defined 'norm' simply as 'the expression of the idea . . . that an individual ought to behave in a certain way';[69] and he had denied that legal norms were necessarily created by acts of will.[70] But unless norms could be tied to something which would give them their own thing-like distinctness, how were they to be understood as something other

---

[65] Harris, *Law and Legal Science*, s. 2 and *passim*.

[66] *GTLS*, 123; *PTL*, 52–3.

[67] Cf. Hart, 'Kelsen Visited', 16 *UCLA Law Rev.* 709 (1963). Reprinted in Hart, *Essays in Jurisprudence and Philosophy* (Oxford, 1983), ch. 14.

[68] *PTL*, 71–5. Cf. Kelsen, 'Professor Stone and the Pure Theory of Law', 17 *Stanford Law Rev.* 1128, 1132–8 (1965).

[69] *GTLS*, 36.   [70] *GTLS*, 33–5; *WIJ*, 273.

than the legal-science propositions which were supposed to describe them—given that both were reconstructions of raw legislation, both were 'ought' expressions, and both were conditional directions to officials to apply sanctions? The answer was a revamped will theory. Each independent legal norm had to be correlated with a legislative act of will. Even customary norms had to be seen as products of a will,[71] and the basic norm itself became the correlate of an 'imaginary' will.[72]

The reification of norms was pressed further in Kelsen's later writings. Norms continue to be ideal entities whose 'validity' means their 'existence'; but now they are analogous, not so much to objects, as to 'forces',[73] beamed into the normative universe by individuated acts of will. Since they are the correlates of acts of will, it is impossible for one norm to be inferred from another. Mere thought-processes will not produce an act of will.[74] For the same reason, logical principles of derogation and non-contradiction cannot be applied, even indirectly, to norms. Volitional labour, not cognitive reflection, is needed to destroy the things that acts of will have produced.[75] Only desuetude or derogating norms can invalidate norms. Mere thinking will not kill a cat.

Kelsen's obsession with the reification of norms led him astray. If we look at real statutes and court decisions, we do not find fully-armed sanction-stipulating provisions (with all the conditions for the application of the sanctions) springing from legislative acts of will. Kelsen sought to deal with this difficulty in *Reine Rechtslehre* by developing the concept of 'dependent norms'.[76] Dependent norms were products of legislative acts which specified some of the conditions to be met before, according to law, sanctions should be applied. They are tied to independent legal norms. The problem is to see how this tying process is to be understood in terms of a correlate between each independent norm and a specific legislative act of will. Kelsen's examples in *Reine Rechtslehre* concern instances in which the dependent and independent provisions are contained in the same statute. But what if legislation is passed inserting a phrase in a former statute, or changing the conditions under which sanctions are to be applied across a wide spectrum of the law?

---

[71] *PTL*, 9, 266.   [72] *PTL*, 9–10.   [73] *ELMP*, 235, 271.
[74] *ELMP*, 228–31, 237–47, 257–60.   [75] *ELMP*, 228–37, 261–75.
[76] *PTL*, 54–8.

In *General Theory of Law and State*, before Kelsen had come to insist that each norm must correlate with one act of will, he had said that different parts of a legal norm might be contained in different statutes.[77] In his 'Derogation' article, however, he indicates that this is impossible. He criticizes the traditional notion that norms may be partly altered by legislation. If, for example, the legislature changes the age for capacity to enter into contracts, it is really repealing all those norms which make the existence of a valid contract a condition for the application of civil execution, and replacing them with fresh norms (which have the same content except for the changed age requirement). Its acts of will—both those creating the derogating norms which effect the repeal, and those which create the newly promulgated independent norms— are, of course, 'silent' acts of will. It would be, Kelsen says, better legislative technique if the legislature were to repeal and replace the entire code expressly.[78] One can see that it would be better for Kelsen's theorizing if legislators always repealed and replaced, because then there would be better evidence of those silent acts of will in which his norm-reification requires him to believe. It seems that, to preserve the thing-like integrity of norms, we must have one act of will for each independent norm; and this in turn means that we must interpret amending legislation as re-enacting, albeit in an unsatisfactory way, all the norms whose conditions of application are changed. Presumably, we must attribute even more subtle convulsions to the legislative wills of judges, whenever they follow previous decisions but restate their *rationes decidendi* in modified forms.

Kelsen's contention that legal science reconstructs the legislative material presented to it (in order to produce descriptions of the law) is well founded.[79] But his dogmatic assumption that norms are some kind of ideal thing came to distort more and more his understanding of the logic of descriptive legal science. We should keep our theorizing about philosophically created concepts on a short rein, if our object is to understand real social institutions like the law. We should not accept without challenge the assumption that 'a norm is a norm is a norm'.

---

[77] *GTLS*, 45.
[78] *ELMP*, 266–9.
[79] Cf. Golding, 'Kelsen and the Concept of "Legal System"', in Summers, ed., *More Essays in Legal Philosophy* (Oxford, 1971).

CHAPTER 10

ON THE STATUS OF THE *LEX POSTERIOR* DEROGATING RULE*

STANLEY L. PAULSON

INTRODUCTION

IT is a commonplace that the rule *lex posterior derogat legi priori* serves as a means of resolving conflicts between legal norms issued at different times. The norm issued earlier yields to the norm issued later. Other derogating rules—for example, the rule *lex superior derogat legi inferiori*—speak to other types of conflicts between legal norms. Beyond this elementary point, however, little is clear on the status of derogating rules in the legal system. A number of theorists have argued that derogating rules are rules of logic or are at any rate akin to rules of logic.[1] On this view, derogating rules are a priori or non-contingent in nature.[2] Others have argued that derogating rules are rules of the positive law,

Reprinted, with changes, from the *Liverpool Law Review* with the kind permission of Professor B. S. Jackson, editor.

* This paper reflects research that I undertook at the Free University of Berlin as a Fellow of the Alexander von Humboldt Foundation (Bonn-Bad Godesberg), and I remain grateful to the Foundation for its support and to my *Betreuer* in Berlin, Hubert Rottleuthner, for many kindnesses. I should like to thank B. S. Jackson for his hospitality during my visit to Liverpool in June of 1982 and for welcome encouragement in writing the paper. Also, I am grateful to J. W. Harris for many questions at the Kelsen Conference in Edinburgh in April of 1981, questions that led me to think about how and why Kelsen changed his mind on the *lex posterior* rule. Finally, I wish to thank Roberto J. Vernengo for valuable criticism in correspondence.

[1] See, e.g., Kelsen, 'Reichsgesetz und Landesgesetz nach österreichischer Verfassung', 32 *Archiv des öffentlichen Rechts* (1914), 202–45, 390–438, at 206–15; Julius Moór, 'Das Logische im Recht', 2 *Internationale Zeitschrift für Theorie des Rechts* (1927–8), 158–203, at 165, cited in *ATN*, 227, 266; Eduart Bötticher, *Kritische Beiträge zur Lehre von der materiellen Rechtskraft im Zivilprozess* (Berlin, 1930; reprinted: Aalen, 1970), pp. 54–5.

[2] Following the standard Kantian reading, to say that something is a priori or non-contingent is to say that it is known apart from experience. (I use 'non-contingent' and 'contingent' in the paper rather than the more familiar *a priori* and *a posteriori* to avoid confusion between *a posteriori* and *lex posterior*.)

enacted by the legislature or, more commonly, the result of evolution through customary practice.[3] Following this view, derogating rules are a posteriori or contingent.

What sorts of arguments support these positions? And what is at stake? In an effort to throw light on these questions, I examine Hans Kelsen's arguments on the status of the *lex posterior* rule. One might well think that the selection of Kelsen as the focal point of such an inquiry is one-sided, excessively 'positivistic'. But this is not so. Kelsen, over the sixty-year period in which he wrote, held no fewer than three different views on the status of the *lex posterior* rule, only one of which is obviously positivistic. These three views turn up in the course of four different phases of Kelsen's development on the status of the *lex posterior* rule.[4] In the first phase (lasting until roughly 1918)[5] he defends the *lex posterior* rule as a 'juridical-logical principle'. In the second phase (1918 to the mid-twenties)[6] he adopts the radically positivistic view of his gifted and highly original colleague in the Vienna School, Adolf Merkl.[7] During a long third phase (from the mid-twenties to the appearance of the Second Edition of the *Reine Rechtslehre* in 1960),[8] Kelsen's treatment of the *lex posterior* rule reflects neo-

---

[3] See, above all, Merkl, 'Die Rechtseinheit des österreichischen Staates', 37 *Archiv des öffentlichen Rechts* (1918), 56–121, at 75–88, reprinted in *WRS* I, 1115–65, at 1130–39; Merkl, *Die Lehre von der Rechtskraft* (Leipzig & Vienna, 1923), pp. 228–44; Merkl, *Allgemeine Verwaltungsrecht* (Vienna & Berlin, 1927; reprinted: Darmstadt, 1969), pp. 209–11. See also Walter, *Der Aufbau der Rechtsordnung* (Vienna, 2nd edn. 1974), pp. 53–68. A highly suggestive study of derogation generally, which came to my attention too late for use in the paper, is C. E. Alchourrón & E. Bulygin, 'The Expressive Conception of Norms', in *New Studies in Deontic Logic*, ed. Hilpinen (Dordrecht & Boston, 1981), pp. 95–124.

[4] These phases reflect Kelsen's development on the *lex posterior* rule and may serve as rough guides to some other aspects of his work too, but I do not offer them as rubrics for tracing the development of his thought generally. On some issues, e.g. that of norm collisions in both public law and public international law, Kelsen's development is in marked contrast to the pattern reflected in his treatment of the *lex posterior* rule. I have considered other aspects of Kelsen's development, with special attention to the significance of his late work for the Pure Theory of Law generally, in my paper 'Stellt die "Allgemeine Theorie der Normen" einen Bruch in Kelsens Lehre dar?' in *Die Reine Rechtslehre in wissenschaftlicher Diskussion*, 'Schriftenreihe des Hans Kelsen-Instituts', vol. vii (Vienna, 1982), pp. 122–41.

[5] See, in particular, Kelsen, 'Reichsgesetz und Landesgesetz', note 1 above; Kelsen, *Das Problem der Souveränität* (Tübingen, 1920), pp. 114–15. (On the details of Kelsen's treatment of the *lex posterior* rule in this latter work, see text at notes 23–7 below.)

[6] See references at notes 25–9 below.

[7] See references at note 3 above.

[8] See references at notes 31–51 below.

Kantian precepts. And in a final phase (after 1960)[9] Kelsen returns to the radically positivistic Merklian view that he had adopted in the second phase.

Turning to what is at stake, I have already hinted at the question of how closely the *lex posterior* rule resembles a principle of logic. More specifically, the question might be put as follows: Does the *lex posterior* rule function in the law in a manner analogous to the principle of non-contradiction in discourse? Just as the principle of non-contradiction applies to contradictory statements quite apart from whether or not it is expressly invoked by a speaker, so likewise, it might be argued, the rule *lex posterior* applies quite apart from invocation by legal officials. It does so—and this is the rub—because it is a prerequisite of normative regulation generally, just as the principle of non-contradiction applies because it is a prerequisite of coherent discourse. Or so proponents of a quasi-logical interpretation of the *lex posterior* rule would have us believe.

Still, having looked at Kelsen's arguments in his first and third phases, arguments (particularly in the first phase) lending support to the notion that there is indeed a close analogy between the *lex posterior* rule and the principle of non-contradiction, I remain unconvinced. My scepticism stems less from a conviction that the radically positivistic or contingent *lex posterior* rule of the second and fourth phases is on the mark than from a suspicion that the categories at work here—non-contingent versus contingent, a priori versus a posteriori—are inappropriate. I return briefly to this large issue in my closing section.

I   FIRST PHASE

Kelsen's initial conception of the *lex posterior* rule appears in a major paper of 1914.[10] In the course of an inquiry into the relation between federal and state law,[11] he examines 'the nature of the rule of interpretation *lex posterior derogat legi priori*'. Specifically:

---

[9] See references at note 54 below.

[10] 'Reichsgesetz und Landesgesetz', note 1 above.

[11] In fact Kelsen's inquiry, in 1914, is into the relation between the law of the Austrian Reich, itself a member state of the Austro-Hungarian Empire, and the law of the various kingdoms and *Länder* represented in the Austrian *Reichsrat* or Parliament.

That a later norm invalidates an earlier norm when the content of the one contradicts that of the other and furthermore, that the later norm in place of the earlier one lays down a particular course of conduct as obligatory—this of course counts as a *juridical-logical principle* only within a unified normative system. Within the same normative system, the basic tenet that a later norm invalidates an earlier norm when the content of the one contradicts that of the other represents the regulator by means of which the normative system *qua* logically closed system—this basic postulate of all cognition of norms [*dieses Grundpostulat aller Normerkenntnis*]—is continuously sustained. Within the same normative system, two norms, the one with content A and the other with content non-A, cannot be valid alongside one another *if the system is to be reasonable* and if the individual subject to the norms is to be able to comply in turn with each of them without thereby violating some other norm of the same system. The general logical tenet that judgment A is incompatible with judgment non-A is different from the logical principle peculiar to the cognition of norms. According to the latter, it is not the case that *either* norm A *or* norm non-A can be *valid*, as is the case with judgments, where *either* judgment A *or* judgment non-A is *true*. Rather, what distinguishes the specific logical principle of the cognition of norms is that only the later norm can be valid, given that the norms in question belong to the same system. The requirement that the later norm take precedence over the earlier norm and not the other way around is a purely *logical* consequence that follows from the nature of the norm and from the essence of unity [*Einheit*] in the normative system.[12]

The *lex posterior* rule is non-contingent, a juridical-logical principle—'juridical' because it is operative only within a legal system, 'logical' because the status of the *lex posterior* rule vis-à-vis the norms of a legal system is comparable to the status of a 'general logical tenet', the principle of non-contradiction, vis-à-vis the sentences of a natural language.

So far, so good, but there are a number of things to talk about. What would Kelsen have us understand by a logically closed normative system? What are we to make of 'reasonableness' as a purported rationale for the *lex posterior* rule? Finally, how can the *lex posterior* rule be, as Kelsen puts it, a 'purely *logical* consequence' of the unity of the normative system? With an eye to the underlying issue of the status of the *lex posterior* rule, I want to consider each of these questions in turn.

[12] 'Reichsgesetz und Landesgesetz', note 1 above, at 206–7 (italics in original). (Translations from the German, here and below, are my own.) See also Walter, *Der Aufbau der Rechtsordnung*, note 3 above, p. 57, n. 104.

By a logically closed normative system Kelsen has in mind a system that is normatively consistent. The notion of normative consistency is, however, problematic.[13] Traditional accounts have it that a system is normatively consistent only if its norms apply without conflict in all circumstances, a view familiar in moral philosophy from Kant.

A conflict of duties (*collisio officiorum s. obligationum*) would be that relationship between duties by virtue of which one would (wholly or partially) cancel the other. Because, however, duty and obligation are in general concepts that express the objective practical necessity of certain actions and because two mutually opposing rules cannot be necessary at the same time, then, if it is a duty to act according to one of them, it is not only not a duty but contrary to duty to act according to the other. It follows, therefore, that a conflict of duties and obligations is inconceivable (*obligationes non colliduntur*).[14]

We might term such an account strong normative consistency.

The problem with strong normative consistency is that it is too strong. Even if the overriding legal norms were elaborated and qualified repeatedly in order to take account of ostensibly conflicting norms, there would be, as Ruth Barcan Marcus argues, no good reason to believe that one could arrive at a single set of norms that would 'unequivocally mandate a single course of action' for every circumstance.[15]

There is, however, an alternative. Weak normative consistency may offer an entirely adequate account. On this view, norms of the legal system are consistent just in case they can be given a consistent reading in some circumstance or other, never mind that in other circumstances they are inconsistent. Ruth Barcan Marcus illustrates weak normative consistency by appeal to a two-person card game:

The deck is shuffled and divided equally, face down between two players. Players turn up top cards on each play until the cards are played out. Two rules are in force: black cards trump red cards, and high cards (ace high) trump lower-valued cards without attention to colour. Where no rule applies, e.g., two red deuces, there is indifference and the players proceed. We could define the winner as the player with the largest number

---

[13] I am indebted to Marcus, 'Moral Dilemmas and Consistency', 77 *Journal of Philosophy* (1980), 121–36, on normative consistency generally.

[14] *MEJ*, 25.

[15] Marcus, 'Moral Dilemmas and Consistency', note 13 above, p. 124.

of tricks when the cards are played out. There is an inclination to call such a set of rules inconsistent. For suppose the pair turned up is a red ace and a black deuce; who trumps? This is not a case of rule indifference as in a pair of red deuces. Rather, two rules apply, and both cannot be satisfied. But, on the definition here proposed, the rules are consistent in that there are possible circumstances where, in the course of playing the game, the dilemma would not arise and the game would proceed to a conclusion.[16]

In short, where two norms apply to a situation and they cannot both be followed, strong normative consistency has it that the norms conflict and are, therefore, inconsistent. According to weak normative consistency, on the other hand, it is enough for normative consistency that both of the norms in question can be followed in some circumstance or other. On this view the presence of a norm conflict may, then, not be telling on the question of consistency. (There may appear to be two variables here, varying circumstances and interpretation, but in fact the former alone serves to distinguish weak from strong normative consistency. Weak normative consistency requires only that there be some possible circumstance in which the norms can be applied without conflict, while strong normative consistency requires that they be applicable without conflict in all circumstances. Both accounts assume an interpretation of the legal norms, without which there is no basis for claiming a conflict in the first place.)

I assume in what follows that Kelsen's logically closed normative system is to be understood in terms of weak normative consistency, not because Kelsen himself is clear on the distinction between weak and strong consistency, opting for the former, but because the weak account is, I think, clearly the more plausible.

In the second of the questions posed above I ask what we are to make of Kelsen's suggestion, at one point in the quoted text, that the rationale for the *lex posterior* rule is 'reasonableness'. Coming, from the leading proponent of a 'pure' theory of law, a theory 'uncontaminated' by the extraneous elements of, *inter alia*, value theory, such a suggestion is surprising. Furthermore, Kelsen appears later in the same text to offer an altogether different ground for the *lex posterior* rule, namely that it is a 'purely *logical* consequence' of the unity (*Einheit*) of the normative system.[17]

None the less, taking seriously for now Kelsen's suggestion of

---

[16] Ibid. at 128–9.   [17] See text quoted at note 12 above.

'reasonableness' as a rationale for the *lex posterior* rule, what could he mean? He does not offer the immediately following line in the quoted text, regarding one's ability to comply with one norm without thereby violating another,[18] in apposition to 'reasonableness'. Rather, this line is simply a statement of what may be understood, in practical terms, by a logically closed normative system. If the line were interpreted as a gloss on 'reasonableness', and 'reasonableness' in turn were offered as a rationale for the logically closed normative system, the result would be a *circulus vitiosus*.

Still, Kelsen's use of 'reasonableness' is not in and of itself controversial. That there be an interpretation of the norms applying to a situation such that an individual can comply with one norm without thereby violating another, and so on, is indeed reasonable. And part of what Kelsen may mean here is that this modest constraint, coupled with others, assures that the system will be 'meaningful' (*sinnvoll*), a notion that he expressly develops in what I term his third or neo-Kantian phase, where he argues that a 'meaningful' normative system is a requirement of the cognition of norms. Since the German for 'reasonable' (*vernünftig*) is close to a figurative use of the German for 'meaningful' (*sinnvoll*) and, more importantly, since Kelsen in the quoted text speaks of the logically closed normative system as 'a basic postulate of all cognition of norms, it may well be that Kelsen's early rationale for a non-contingent *lex posterior* rule in terms of reasonableness is not far removed from the themes of his third, neo-Kantian phase.

This possibility aside, Kelsen's talk of 'reasonableness' appears gratuitous. For, as noted above, he goes on to speak of the *lex posterior* rule as a 'purely *logical* consequence' of the logically closed normative system, and this account of the notion is, if correct, sufficient by itself.

Exactly how the *lex posterior* rule can be a 'purely *logical* consequence' of the normative system is the third and last of the questions I posed above. If it can be answered at all, then perhaps in terms of weak normative consistency. To reiterate the doctrine: it will be enough, for weak normative consistency, to be able to show that in some circumstance or other the norms in question can

---

[18] Ibid.

be given a consistent reading. Kelsen assumes that if weak normative consistency is the case, then a *lex posterior* rule is operative. Without it, there will be no way of assuring that the required consistent reading will be forthcoming.

What about this? Kelsen's assumption is not, I think, correct. It is not obvious that the *lex posterior* rule is required to preserve weak normative consistency (as the principle of non-contradiction is required to preserve coherent discourse). That is, while the *lex posterior* rule is clearly sufficient as a means of handling certain norm conflicts, it is not necessary. The argument for weak normative consistency by itself provides no basis for choosing the rule *lex posterior derogat legi priori* over, say, the rule *lex prior derogat legi posteriori*. The former but not the latter presumably eliminates a barrier to legal change (a matter to which I return below), but this point cannot be drawn from the precept of weak normative consistency alone. The notion that the *lex posterior* rule follows logically from the nature of a logically closed normative system, in other words, from weak normative consistency, is simply a *non sequitur*.

II SECOND PHASE

Kelsen's rejection of his own early interpretation of the *lex posterior* rule was prompted by arguments of Vienna School theorist Adolf Merkl. In a major paper of 1918, Merkl defends for certain purposes the view that in a conflict between norms issued at different times, the norm issued earlier carries the day.[19] Why so? He begins with the idea that an aggregate of norms is not in and of itself capable of the sort of change that we know from abrogation—from, in Hartian parlance, secondary rules of change[20] —and that such change occurs only if express conditions for abrogation have been introduced. And, Merkl continues, in the absence of express conditions for abrogation, the conflicting norm issued earlier has priority over the one issued later, not because duration is a virtue, but because the earlier norm, already in place, pre-empts the field.[21] With, *ex hypothesi*, no basis for institution-

---

[19] Merkl, 'Rechtseinheit', note 3 above.
[20] Hart, *The Concept of Law* (Oxford, 1961), pp. 93–4.
[21] On the notion of legal validity at work here, see Harris, *Law and Legal Science* (Oxford, 1979), pp. 107–31 (in particular, Harris's 'valid/2').

alized change in the aggregate of norms making up the legal system, the later norm is an imposter.

As a rejoinder to Merkl, suppose we introduce conditions for legal change—for, *inter alia*, the abrogation of norms. Does not the *lex posterior* rule then turn up as non-contingent? In other words, granted that the introduction of secondary rules is a contingent matter, could it not be argued that a necessary condition of their operation, once introduced, is a *lex posterior* rule? Merkl would answer in the negative. The introduction of express conditions for legal change is not dispositive on the question of the status of the *lex posterior* rule. For example, the conditions for legal change might include a provision to the effect that the legislators must expressly abrogate conflicting legislation enacted earlier, on pain of recognizing *sub silentio* its continuing validity at the expense of legislation enacted later. Similarly, when problems of interpretation arise, judges and administrative officers might apply to the legislature for abrogation of legislation enacted earlier; indeed, they must do so lest the legislation enacted earlier enjoy priority over that enacted later. In short, a rule *lex prior* (that is, *lex prior derogat legi posteriori*), would not stand in the way of changes in the law; it would simply make them more difficult.

Merkl's argument here is, however, less a matter of making out a formidable case for deference to the norm issued earlier than it is a matter of raising doubts about the case for deference to the norm issued later. His more general point is that the *lex posterior* rule, rather than making change possible in the legal system, presupposes the possibility of change—presupposes secondary rules of change. He writes:

It is not correct to say that the principle *lex posterior derogat legi priori* makes it possible to change the law. Rather, it is just the reverse: it is the possiblity of change (from within the legal system) that allows one to give expression to the *lex posterior* principle in the first place.[22]

How did Kelsen respond to Merkl? In his second major work, *Das Problem der Souveränität* (1920),[23] he hints at doubts about his

---

[22] Merkl, 'Rechtseinheit', note 3 above, p. 83, reprinted in *WRS* I, 1136. (For the sake of uniformity in the material I am translating, I use the longer formulation of the *lex posterior* rule throughout, namely '*lex posterior derogat legi priori*', and not the shorter formulation, which omits '*legi*'.)

[23] See note 5 above.

early view of the *lex posterior* rule as non-contingent. He leaves the matter hanging though, at least in the text of *Das Problem der Souveränität*, when he speaks of the normative system as a 'logically closed' complex of norms, a complex that one might picture as the product of a single will, never mind that the notion is 'fictitious, anthropomorphic'.[24]

In a long footnote following this text, however, Kelsen takes the plunge, endorsing Merkl's position.[25] (The odd discrepancy between text and footnote can be explained by the fact that the text was completed in 1916, while the footnote was written several years later, after Kelsen had read Merkl's paper.)[26] A *lex posterior* rule is valid only if the system is capable of change, and whether a system is capable of change is a question of positive law, not one of logic. Even in the long footnote, however, Kelsen's position is coloured by a certain ambivalence on the status of the *lex posterior* rule. For he goes on to say that the real question is the possibility of change in the legal system, not the *lex posterior* rule. In this light, 'the question of whether the *lex posterior* principle is a juridical-logical principle or one of positive law loses its significance'.[27]

The radically positivistic Merklian view is clearly evident in Kelsen's *Allgemeine Staatslehre* (1925)[28] and without any hint of doubts about the status of the *lex posterior* rule. Kelsen writes that the *lex posterior* rule is 'only one of the possible means of solving' norm conflicts and that its validity in the legal system can be accounted for only on positive-law grounds. The rule has no status as a general principle. What is more, the requirements of the 'logically undeniable unity [*Einheit*]' of the normative system are satisfied 'as long as the function of conflicting legal organs can in the end be traced back to the unity of the basic norm'.[29] This is a far cry from Kelsen's earlier view that the *lex posterior* rule is a 'purely *logical* consequence' of the unity of the normative system.[30]

---

[24] Ibid. at 114. See also von Wright, *Norm and Action* (London, 1963), pp. 147–52, 203–7; Harris, *Law and Legal Science*, note 21 above, p. 33.

[25] See Kelsen, *Das Problem der Souveränität*, note 5 above, p. 115, n. 1.

[26] See ibid. at viii, n. 1.

[27] Ibid. at 115, n. 1. See the direct reply in Merkl, *Die Lehre von der Rechtskraft*, note 3 above, pp. 240–2.

[28] *ASL, passim.*   [29] *ASL*, 308.

[30] See text quoted at note 12 above.

III THIRD PHASE

In an important paper of 1928,[31] Kelsen takes a step back from Merkl's radically positivistic view. He writes:

The principles of interpretation . . . [namely] the rule *lex posterior derogat legi priori*, [also] the principle that the lower norm must give way to the higher [*lex superior derogat legi inferiori*], the reinterpretation of constitutional clauses concerning the enactment of statutes, the rule concerning two contradictory clauses in one and the same statute, the declaration that part of the content of a statute may be legally irrelevant, etc.—all of these have no other purpose than to lend a meaningful interpretation to the material of the positive law. They all do this by applying the principle of non-contradiction in the normative sphere. For the mòst part, they are not positive-law norms, not enacted rules, but *presuppositions* of legal cognition [*Voraussetzungen der Rechtserkenntnis*]. This means that they are part of the sense of the basic norm, which thus guarantees the unity [*Einheit*] of the norms of the positive law as the unity of a system which, if it is not necessarily *just*, is at least *meaningful* [*sinnvoll*].[32]

The neo-Kantian dimension in Kelsen's thought is in full bloom here.[33] The general thrust of this major development in his work turns on the idea that the knowing subject 'creates' the object of cognition, and that this object—the legal norm—is known only as created,[34] as, *inter alia*, manifesting a particular pattern. Norms, and relations between norms too, exhibit characteristic patterns: the legal norm itself is *hypothetical* in form,[35] a higher-order norm *authorizes* a lower-order norm, an individual norm is a *concretization* of a general norm,[36] and so on. Where details of one or another of

---

[31] Kelsen, 'Natural Law Doctrine and Legal Positivism', *GTLS*, 389–446. The original, German-language version appeared in the series 'Philosophical Lectures published by the Kant Society' (Charlottenburg, 1928).

[32] Kelsen, 'Natural Law Doctrine and Legal Positivism', note 31 above, at 406–7 (italics and minor changes stem from the German-language original).

[33] Compare Kelsen, 'Les rapports de système entre le droit interne et le droit international public', 14 *Recueil des Cours* (1926), 227–331, at 267–74, 314–17; Kelsen, 'Aussprache', 4 *Veröffentlichungen der Vereinigung der Deutschen Staatsrechtslehre* (1928), 168–80, at 173–6. Kelsen's first fairly full statement of neo-Kantian precepts is to be found in his paper 'Rechtswissenschaft und Recht', 3 *Zeitschrift für öffentliches Recht* (1922), 103–235, at 104, 127–235, which he wrote in reply to Fritz Sander's scathing 'realist' attack, 'Rechtsdogmatik oder Theorie der Rechtserfahrung? Kritische Studie zur Rechtslehre Hans Kelsens', 2 *Zeitschrift für öffentliches Recht* (1921), 511–670.   [34] See *RR*[1], 21–4; *RR*[2], ss. 14–18.

[35] Kelsen, 'The Idea of Natural Law', *ELMP*, 27–60, at 32–3.

[36] See ibid. at 41–3.

these patterns are not clear, the result is a puzzle about the import of the legal norm or about how, say, a pair of legal norms is to be understood (a question that arises in a particularly acute form in the conflict situation). These puzzles require for their solution principles of interpretation, among which Kelsen lists the rule *lex posterior derogat legi priori*. Such principles, never mind how they may have evolved in actual practice, are understood as presuppositions of what Kelsen calls legal cognition (*Rechtserkenntnis*).

The notion of presupposition at work here is taken from the Kantian transcendental argument. In formulating a transcendental argument one adduces the presuppositions of 'systematic' or 'scientific' experience—*wissenschaftliche Erfahrung*, in Hermann Cohen's words.[37] Following for the sake of simplicity the analytic or regressive method of Kant's *Prolegomena*,[38] the form of a transcendental argument might be outlined as follows. One starts with (i) some aspect of systematic experience that is beyond question and then moves to (ii) a tenet without which the experience at (i) would not be possible. Since the experience at (i) is in fact the case, the tenet at (ii) must be the case. The tenet at (ii) is, in other words, presupposed. One of Kelsen's uses of the transcendental argument is in connection with the problem of normativity. I want to look briefly at Kelsen's argument here, for his pioneering work on normativity underscores the force of transcendental arguments in the Pure Theory of Law generally.

From the very beginning Kelsen rejects reductionistic legal positivism in its different forms. For example, in the *Hauptprobleme der Staatsrechtslehre* (1911), he considers at some length Ernst Rudolf Bierling's celebrated psychological recognition theory, arguing that because the theory is reductionistic, it cannot take account of commonplace normative matters.[39] Having rejected reductionism, Kelsen must come up with a defensible alternative. He cannot appeal to the natural law theory (where normativity is understood); to avoid reductionism in this way would be to

---

[37] See Cohen, *Logik der reinen Erkenntnis* (Berlin, 2nd edn. 1914; reprinted with an introduction by Holzhey: Hildesheim, 1977), pp. 257–8, 275, 320.

[38] See Kant, *Prolegomena*, transl. Lucas (Manchester, 1953), pp. 13, 29, 31 n.

[39] *HPS²*, 355–61. To be sure, Kelsen's powerful critique of reductionistic legal positivism comes much earlier than his own development of a non-reductionistic, normative position. See generally Paulson, 'Zu Hermann Hellers Kritik an der Reinen Rechtslehre', in *Der soziale Rechtsstaat. Gedächtnisschrift für Hermann Heller, 1891–1933*, ed. Müller & Staff (Baden-Baden, 1984), pp. 679–92.

abandon the separability of the law and morality, the one tenet of traditional legal positivism that he champions. Is there a third possibility, something other than reductionistic legal positivism or natural law theory? Kelsen thinks so, and his case rests on what I shall call a *basic norm argument*, that is, a transcendental argument in the normative sphere. He begins with (i) an aspect of systematic experience that, he contends, is beyond question—the fact that we distinguish between lawful and unlawful directives, that we interpret interpersonal relations normatively, as, *inter alia*, legal relations, that is to say, as legal rights, obligations, and powers.[40] In short, we distinguish normative relations from relations between mere matters of fact. Kelsen then moves from (i) to its presupposition, namely (ii) the intellectual category of imputation (*Zurechnung*).[41] Imputation supplants, in normative contexts, the more familiar Kantian intellectual category of causality. Without imputation, so-called normative relations in the law would be nothing more than power relations, governed by causal laws—in short, reductionism all over again. Since we do, however, interpret interpersonal relations normatively, it must be the case that the category of imputation is presupposed.

Kelsen's use of a transcendental or basic norm argument to spell out the role of imputation as the fundamental intellectual category in the normative sphere is, I think, the most suggestive application of a transcendental argument in the Pure Theory, certainly the most fundamental. My direct concern, however, is with a different transcendental argument, that adumbrated in the quotation at the beginning of the section. Here Kelsen suggests that the *lex posterior* rule, a means of applying the principle of non-contradiction in the normative sphere, is itself a presupposition of legal cognition. The argument he hints at is parallel to the argument, considered above, that he addresses to the problem of normativity. He begins, again, with (i) an aspect of systematic experience that, he contends, is beyond question—the fact that in their relations to

[40] See Kelsen, 'On the Basis of Legal Validity' (first published in 1960), transl. Paulson, 26 *American Journal of Jurisprudence* (1981), 178–89, at 185–6; *RR*[1], 63–7; *RR*[2], ss. 4, 17, 26, *et passim*.

[41] In a full reconstruction of Kelsen's transcendental argument, imputation (*Zurechnung*) would supplant the basic norm *qua* presupposed concept altogether. The brief statement in the text of Kelsen's transcendental argument on normativity reflects this displacement of the basic norm by imputation; my statement of the transcendental argument addressed to the *lex posterior* rule, text at note 42 below, does not.

one another the norms of the legal system are meaningful
(*sinnvoll*). Norms understood as meaningful in this sense presuppose, as Kelsen puts it, (ii) a basic norm that comprises such
principles of interpretation as *lex posterior derogat legi priori* as
'part of [its] sense'.[42] Without such principles of interpretation,
conflicts between norms in the legal system could not be resolved
and norms in their relations to one another would lack a
determinate sense. Since the norms of the legal system in their
relations to one another do have a determinate sense, it must be
the case that the *lex posterior* rule and other principles of
interpretation are presupposed.

Even if a version of this argument is sound when addressed to
the principles of interpretation generally, it is not at all clear that
such an argument is defensible when addressed to the *lex posterior*
rule alone. For the key to a transcendental argument is the notion
that the phenomenon described at (i) would not be *possible* but for
the presupposed tenet at (ii), and Kelsen offers no argument to the
effect that the norms of the legal system could not be meaningful
without the *lex posterior* rule. Another collection of principles of
interpretation, one in which *lex posterior derogat legi priori* did not
figure at all, could also 'lend a meaningful interpretation to the
material of the positive law'.[43] As I have noted elsewhere,[44] the use
of a different rule in place of the *lex posterior* rule may indeed
make some matters (e.g., changes in the law) more difficult, but
such a substitution cannot be ruled out.

IV   FOURTH PHASE

In 1958, only two years before the publication of the Second
Edition of the *Reine Rechtslehre*, Kelsen still appears comfortable
with the neo-Kantian view he adopted on the *lex posterior* rule in
the late 1920s. In an article on 'The Concept of the Legal Order',[45]
he grants that the acts of legal officials may 'in fact conflict with
one another', but adds, significantly, that where norms do conflict,
where 'one norm prescribes A as obligatory and a second

---

[42] See text quoted at note 32 above.
[43] Ibid.
[44] See text at notes 21–22 above.
[45] Kelsen, 'The Concept of the Legal Order' (first published in 1958), transl.
Paulson, 27 *American Journal of Jurisprudence* (1982), 64–84.

prescribes non-A, these norms cannot be regarded as simultaneously valid'. Norm conflicts arising between general norms 'enacted by the legislature at different times' are resolved by the rule *lex posterior derogat legi priori*. And if

the acts through which the norms in question are posited take place at the same time—if, for example, one and the same statute contains mutually exclusive prescriptions—then we have no meaningful act whatever, we have no act whose subjective meaning can also be interpreted as its objective meaning, and we therefore have no objectively valid norm either.[46]

Whether Kelsen, in the Second Edition of the *Reine Rechtslehre* (1960), is taking a first, tentative step away from the neo-Kantian view is less than clear. There he writes:

Since the organ issuing legal norms—the king, say, or the parliament—is normally authorized to issue norms that may be changed and therefore repealed, the maxim *lex posterior derogat legi priori* can be assumed [*angenommen*] to be included in the authorization.[47]

If, with Merkl, one argues that the introduction of conditions for change in the law is itself a positive-law development and further that the *lex posterior* rule is but one means, not a necessary one, of facilitating change, then Kelsen's statement that the rule is 'assumed' in a system providing for legal change is best interpreted contingently. That is, the rule is in fact 'assumed'—on grounds, say, of convenience—but it need not be. Merkl's argument is, however, hardly a safe guide as to what Kelsen has in mind here. For the Second Edition of the *Reine Rechtslehre* comes at the end of Kelsen's long neo-Kantian phase with respect to the *lex posterior* rule, a phase that represents, after all, his rejection of the radically positivistic Merklian view.

On first glance it appears that a purely textual argument can be made for an interpretation of the *lex posterior* rule in the *Reine Rechtslehre* as a priori or non-contingent. Suppose we distinguish synchronic from asynchronic norm conflicts—that is, conflicts between simultaneously issued norms and conflicts between norms issued at different times.[48] In the lines quoted above from 'The Concept of the Legal Order', and at greater length in the *Reine*

---

[46] Ibid. at 70. [47] *RR*[2], s. 34 (e).
[48] See generally Paulson, 'Stellt die "Allgemeine Theorie der Normen" einen Bruch . . . dar?', note 4 above.

Rechtslehre itself, Kelsen considers synchronic norm conflicts and argues that one or the other of the conflicting norms is invalid on a priori grounds, owing to a *per analogiam* application of the principle of non-contradiction.[49] There are good reasons for interpreting synchronic and asynchronic norm conflicts as species of the same genus, such that if one class of cases is handled by appeal to a principle that is non-contingent in nature, say, the principle of non-contradiction, so likewise for the other class. Both classes of cases, then, are subject to the principle of non-contradiction, with the *lex posterior* rule understood as an extension of the principle, specifying which of the norms of an asynchronic norm conflict is valid.[50]

An argument along these lines might indeed suggest that in the Second Edition of the *Reine Rechtslehre* Kelsen sees the *lex posterior* rule as non-contingent in nature. It might, that is, if Kelsen were consistent in that work in his treatment of synchronic norm conflicts. He is not. At two points he treats the resolution of synchronic norm conflicts as non-contingent in nature,[51] but at a third point he anticipates, in a striking way, his own later view, claiming that both norms are valid and thereby rejecting any non-contingent resolution of the conflict.[52] That incompatible positions on synchronic norm conflicts appear in the *Reine Rechtslehre*, along with the fact that no very helpful treatment of the *lex posterior* rule itself is offered in that work, deflates the so-called textual argument for an a priori or non-contingent interpretation.

Nevertheless, the *Reine Rechtslehre* does for the most part reflect Kelsen's long neo-Kantian phase, on norm conflicts and on a number of other issues too.[53] The real break comes immediately thereafter. As Kelsen puts it in the article 'Derogation' (1962) and again in the posthumously published *Allgemeine Theorie der Normen* (1979): 'A conflict [between two norms] can but need not be resolved by derogation, and derogation will take place only if a

---

[49] RR^2, ss. 16, 34 (e).

[50] One problem with an a priori approach to the resolution of synchronic norm conflicts is that there is no way to determine *which* of the conflicting norms is valid, a problem that does not arise in the case of the asynchronic norm conflict. Kelsen hints at this problem in *ATN*, 168.

[51] RR^2, ss. 16, 34 (e).

[52] RR^2, s. 5 (a).

[53] See RR^2, ss. 4 (a), 6 (c), 16–18, 26, 34 (c) (d) (h), *et passim*.

legislative authority has provided for it.'[54] Here Kelsen looks to the more general phenomenon of abrogation as a point of reference for his position on the status of the *lex posterior* rule itself. He argues that just as abrogation, understood apart from conflict situations, is left to the discretion of legal officials, so likewise is the application of the *lex posterior* rule. Derogation is a 'specific function' of a third norm, not of one or the other of the conflicting norms, and therefore the application of a so-called derogating norm to one of the conflicting norms (say, to the norm issued earlier) is in principle the same as the more general phenomenon of abrogation or repeal independent of any conflict.

Kelsen, without compromising his position here, might have acknowledged that some of the details of the status of the *lex posterior* rule have no parallel in the case of abrogation *per se*. The status of the *lex posterior* rule depends largely on the nature of the conditions surrounding its adoption. Once adopted, the application of the rule to at least some cases of conflict may be fully automatic. There is, however, no question of automatic application in the case of abrogation or repeal considered apart from conflict situations. Here abrogation, simply a convenient means of eliminating unwanted legislation, is by definition *ad hoc*. Kelsen's argument, then, turns on a comparison between the adoption of one rule (a derogating rule) and the application of another (an abrogating rule).

This detail of the argument aside, Kelsen's point is clear. The *lex posterior* rule is contingent through and through, a matter left to the positive law. And this last phase in Kelsen's development with respect to the *lex posterior* rule represents a return to Merkl's extreme positivistic position, the position Kelsen had defended much earlier, in his second phase.

V 'NON-CONTINGENT' AND 'CONTINGENT' AS CATEGORIES

As I suggested at the outset, none of the positions on the status of the *lex posterior* rule represented by Kelsen's four phases is

---

[54] Kelsen, 'Derogation', in *Essays in Jurisprudence in Honor of Roscoe Pound*, ed. Newman (Indianapolis & New York, 1962), pp. 339–55, at p. 351; reprinted *ELMP*, 261–75, at 271; *ATN*, 101. See also Guest, 'Two Problems in Kelsen's Theory of Validity', 2 *Liverpool Law Review* (1980), 101–8, at 105–7.

entirely convincing. The problem, I think, is owing at least in part to the categories of analysis he uses. 'Non-contingent vs. contingent (or positivistic)' puts an inappropriate question. One cannot, using either category, come very close to an adequate characterization of the place and function of the *lex posterior* rule in the modern municipal legal system. Indeed, Kelsen comes perilously close to confronting a dilemma. The non-contingent view, in the hardheaded no-nonsense version of Kelsen's first phase, an example of his early flirtation with *Begriffsjurisprudenz*,[55] is unconvincing. In particular, the argument he makes by analogy to the principle of non-contradiction, essential as support for the non-contingent view, is singularly unpersuasive. The second version of the non-contingent view, that of Kelsen's third, neo-Kantian phase, is less implausible on its face, but it fails too. Kelsen does not show what he would have to show, namely, that the very possibility of a meaningful or coherent system of legal norms turns on the existence of a *lex posterior* rule.

The situation is not much better with regard to the radically positivistic Merklian view of the *lex posterior* rule, adopted by Kelsen in his second and fourth phases. The problem does not lie with Kelsen's argument, but rather with the inability, from the Merklian standpoint, to distinguish the intractability of the *lex posterior* rule in the modern municipal legal system from the relative instability of many ordinary legal rules. It is here, I think, that the traditional categories of analysis betray their inadequacy. The first category, 'non-contingent', has no application at all, and the second, 'contingent' or 'positivistic', while applicable, is trivial, failing to distinguish the intractable *lex posterior* rule from less stable, ordinary rules of law.

My own view is that the quasi-logical categories of non-contingent and contingent might well be replaced by something taken from the model of Duhemian holism.[56] Suppose we conceive

---

[55] As is well known, Kelsen reacts sharply in much of his work to *Begriffsjuris-prudenz* or legal conceptualism; see, e.g., the paper 'Juristischer Formalismus und reine Rechtslehre', 58 *Juristische Wochenschrift* (1929), 1723–26, where Kelsen, protesting 'the deduction of legal norms from legal concepts', dismisses it as 'naked natural law' (ibid. at 1724).

[56] See Duhem, *The Aim and Structure of Physical Theory*, transl. Wiener (Princeton, 1954); Quine, 'Two Dogmas of Empiricism', in Quine, *From a Logical Point of View* (Cambridge, Mass., 1953), pp. 20–46, at 41 *et passim*; Quine, 'On Empirically Equivalent Systems of the World', 9 *Erkenntnis* (1975), 313–28, at 313–15.

of the law as a sphere, with well-entrenched norms such as the *lex posterior* rule toward the centre and norms subject to alteration out toward the periphery. Revisions—amendment, abrogation, and the like—of material near the centre of the sphere would call for major changes in the character of the system as a whole, while revisions toward the periphery would leave the system as a whole largely unchanged. This view is, to be sure, highly metaphorical, and many details would have to be worked out. Still, as a model for handling our problem, the status of the *lex posterior* rule in the legal system, I find it more suggestive than anything that has been said within the framework of the traditional categories.

IDEALISM AND REALISM IN KELSEN'S TREATMENT OF NORM CONFLICTS

INÉS WEYLAND (FORMERLY ORTIZ)

I. INTRODUCTION

ONE of the main concerns of Kelsen's theory is to resolve the theoretical difficulties arising from the existence of conflicts between norms at the same or at different levels of the legal system. However, his proposals for their solution have created problems of no less a complexity for his commentators than the ones he confronted.[1] Their task is further complicated by the fact that his ideas kept developing and changing over the years and that his most recent writings, in particular, mark a radical departure from earlier assertions.

Some writers who have dealt with this area of his theory have sought to resolve what they consider to be only apparent contradictions.[2] My own view is that though it sometimes proves fruitful to attempt to reconcile conflicting passages in his writings, in this particular instance it is more valuable to accept the contradictions and to seek to understand their underlying causes. One of them, I will argue, is that Kelsen often pursued irreconcilable aims. This is particularly true of his treatment of conflicts of norms at different levels of the legal hierarchy, which constitutes one of the most puzzling and controversial aspects of his theory. The inconsistencies in this case arise from the incompatibility between his desire to construct a logically coherent model of legal systems and his attempt to fit into it certain anomalous aspects of legal reality.

[1] Harris, above, p. 201; 'Whatever may be true of norms, no one surely would claim that the principle of non-contradiction should be applied to Kelsen himself.'
[2] See Paulson, 'Material and Formal Authorisation in Kelsen's Pure Theory', 39 *CLJ* 172 (1980); 'Zum Problem der Normenkonflikte', LXVI/4 *ARSP* 487 (1980); Review—Moench, *Verfassungswidriges Gesetz und Normenkontrolle*, 20 *Columbia Journal of Transnational Law* 391, (1981).

Kelsen's conception of the legal system as a hierarchy of norms deriving their validity from higher norms and ultimately from a basic norm which is presupposed to be valid, constitutes a formal ideal which shares important structural features with the substantive ideal postulated by natural law theories.[3] According to Kelsen, in both types of systems norms derive their validity from a basic norm and validity, which is equated to binding force, is given an objective character by whoever presupposes the basic norm of the system. Moreover the fact that on each level validity is made dependent on conformity with norms of higher levels, rules out the possibility of conflicts between norms of different levels. The main difference between the two kinds of systems derives from the dynamic character of the legal order, which ensures a link with social reality. This is due to the fact that norms are created by human acts and that the requirement of conformity between those acts and the norms that authorize them guarantees the efficacy of the system.

Norms are characterized by Kelsen in his later writings as the objective meaning of acts of will. These acts and their meaning are not however the objective of the Pure Theory, which is a characterization on a more abstract and general level of the description of positive law made by legal science. As such it makes explicit the logical presuppositions on which the latter is based. Kelsen's conception of legal science has its origins in Kantian thought. Kant's belief that knowledge is conditioned by the specific structure of the human mind, which by means of certain a priori concepts and categories imposes a particular order on the manifold of sense perception, is applied by Kelsen to legal cognition and leads him to assert that legal science, like the empirical sciences, creates its object of cognition.[4] It is however possible to detach Kelsen's model of the legal system from its Kantian foundation and view it not as a necessary structure determined by categories of thought but as a conception based on a particular ideology shared by jurists and legal officials.[5] The

---

[3] See Amselek, 'Kelsen et les Contradictions du Positivisme Juridique', 138 *Revue Internationale de Philosophie*, 460 (1981).

[4] *GTLS*, 391 ff., 'Natural Law Doctrine and Legal Positivism'. However, in his more recent writings (*ELMP* and *ATN*), by rejecting his earlier idea that the principle of non-contradiction should be applied to the description of positive law, Kelsen has abandoned the view that law must be interpreted as a meaningful order.

[5] See Harris, *Law and Legal Science* (Oxford, 1979), ch. I, where the official ideology is characterized in terms of legality and constitutionality.

function of such an ideology is both to describe and to shape reality. The belief in the binding force of laws and the internal coherence of the system ensures that, to a great extent, such characteristics are possessed by actual legal systems. On the one hand, in countries where officials are committed to the values of legality and constitutionality their behaviour tends to conform to legal norms. On the other hand, it is the task of jurists to identify the material validly created and to systematize and organize it in accordance with certain principles of logical reconstruction.[6]

So far as the role of legal science is concerned, it is very important to stress that Kelsen firmly believes that it is possible to identify the content of any legal system by objectively ascertaining the fulfilment of the conditions of validity of norms.[7] This belief is reflected in the conceptions of objective validity, the objective meaning of acts of will, and the objective character of judgments of legality.

Thus Kelsen's theory faces the problem stemming from the possible discrepancy between an objective assessment of the correspondence between lower and higher norms of the legal hierarchy and statements of validity explicitly or implicitly made by legal organs. In addressing this problem he proposes three different solutions, none of which—I will argue—proves satisfactory. I shall therefore suggest a further possibility based on the application of Kelsen's views on interpretation to the area of conflicts, which considerably diminishes their practical relevance. Given however the theoretical difficulties to which the possibility of conflicts give rise I will, after having discussed the view of two other writers, consider whether they are capable of resolution within the confines of Kelsen's concept of the legal system.

---

[6] See Harris, ibid., ch. III, where, on the basis of Kelsen's earlier writings, Harris identifies exclusion, subsumption, derogation, and non-contradiction as principles of legal science.

[7] These conditions are as follows: (1) a norm to be valid must have been created in accordance with the prescriptions of an effective constitution, which is presupposed to be valid. This presupposition entails that all norms derive their validity from a basic norm. Conformity between norms at different levels must exist in respect of three aspects: organ, procedure, and contents; (2) the norm must not have been repealed through any of the methods established in that constitution; (3) the system as a whole must be by and large efficacious. Kelsen believes that the fulfilment of these conditions can be objectively ascertained; see *GTLS*, 49: 'There is, however, only one positive law. Or—if we wish to account for the existence of various national legal orders—there is for each territory only one positive law. Its contents can be uniquely ascertained by an objective method.'

II KELSEN'S FIRST SOLUTION

Kelsen was well aware of the fact that the lack of conformity between an act purporting to create a norm and one or more norms authorizing its creation normally only has legal effect after the declaration of a competent organ and that the opinion of any other individual has no legal relevance.[8] This made him conclude that such declarations have constitutive character and that no norms are void *ab initio*.

According to his reasoning, the crucial issue is not the existence of correspondence between, say, a judicial decision and relevant statutory provisions but the views that the judge of first instance or an appellate court express in respect of the validity of the norm created by the judgment. From the fact that only authoritative pronouncements have legal consequences Kelsen concludes that any other judgments are irrelevant to the issue of validity.[9] This entails that a prescription which does not fulfil Kelsen's conditions of validity must be deemed a valid norm if it has been incorrectly declared valid by its organ of creation or an organ of revision. There is, then, only a high degree of probability but no certainty in systems where the rule of law prevails, that statements which are officially declared to be norms fit Kelsen's definition.

Validity, however, cannot depend both on objective criteria and on subjective judgments of officials. Therefore when coincidence between both is lacking, a confusion between two different meanings of the term norm arises. A clear illustration of these two different senses is provided precisely by those cases where a competent organ declares the invalidity of a norm because of its lack of conformity with a higher norm. The organ declares the norm to be invalid and yet recognizes that before his pronouncement, it enjoyed some form of precarious existence. If he were to

---

[8] *GTLS*, 154; 'The lower norm belongs together with the higher norm to the same legal order only in so far as the former corresponds to the latter. But, who shall decide that the lower norm corresponds to the higher, whether the individual norm of the judicial decision corresponds to the general norms of statutory and customary law? Only an organ that has to apply the higher norm can form such a decision . . . The opinion of any other individual is legally irrelevant.' See, too, *PTL*, 267–70.

[9] Notice the contrast between such a conclusion and: 'What significance, what value, what validity their acts shall have, i.e. their value as official acts, as functions of a system . . . is a matter for cognition' (my translation); 'Rechtswissenschaft und Recht', 3 *Zeitschrift für öffentliches Recht*, 151 (1922).

describe that existence in terms of validity he would be making conflicting statements. On the other hand, legal writers and other external observers express opinions about the validity of norms based on their own assessment of their relationship with higher norms. If they decided that a norm declared valid by a judge is invalid, they would not use the term valid but a different one to describe it.

Furthermore if valid is equated to 'declared by a competent organ to be valid' the term not only acquires a different meaning from that originally accorded to it by Kelsen but also becomes meaningless. This is so because the notion competent organ itself is dependent on objective validity, since an individual only acts as a legal organ when he follows the prescriptions of valid norms.[10] Valid in this new conception means, then, declared to be valid by someone who appears to be acting in the capacity of a legal organ, though this may not be the case.

Even though in the *General Theory of Law and State* Kelsen prefaces his discussion of conflicts with a rejection of the decisionist emphasis of 'American Realists' such as Gray it is apparent from the above formulation that his first solution brings him uncomfortably close to their position.[11]

III   KELSEN'S SECOND SOLUTION

Kelsen himself must have been dissatisfied with a line of reasoning which involved a shift from an objective to a subjective notion of validity and from a permanent to a shifting one. This is shown by the fact that when dealing with unconstitutional statutes he puts forward a different answer to the problem of reconciling the fallibility of subjective statements of validity with the requirement for objective conformity. The answer is provided by his assumption

---

[10] *GTLS*, 99; 'An individual is, as was said before, acting as an organ of the community only when this act is determined by that order in a specific way.' See, too, *PTL*, 150–8.

[11] It is therefore understandable that M. Troper reaches the conclusion that the meaning of an act of will is determined by a court of last resort and that legal systems consist not of one hierarchy of norms but 'd'autant de pyramides qu'il y a d'ordres de juridictions, le sommet de chacune de ces pyramides étant constitué des normes que la cour suprême de cet ordre de juridictions énonce par la voie de l'interprétation' and that Kelsen's basic norm is dispensable: 'Kelsen, la Théorie de l'Interprétation et la Structure de l'Ordre Juridique', 138 *Revue Internationale de Philosophie*, 518, at 528–9 (1981).

about the alternative character of the stipulations of a constitution. Thus he says: 'If a statute enacted by the legislative organ is considered to be valid although it has been created in another way or has another content than prescribed by the constitution, we must assume that the prescriptions concerning legislation have an alternative character.'[12] He draws this conclusion from the fact that constitutional norms do not normally stipulate that disregard of their provisions results in the automatic invalidity of statutes.[13] Constitutions either require the pronouncement of an organ competent to declare the unconstitutionality of statutes or fail to institute such organs. In either situation, says Kelsen, it must be inferred that the constitution has conferred validity on the norms whose creation it determines by authorizing their organs of creation either to follow its explicit prescriptions or not. Hence, apart from its explicit provisions, a constitutional norm is assumed to have an implicit part, which in effect authorizes the organ below to follow any procedures whatsoever and gives it complete discretion to decide on the contents of the statute. If the norm commands the organ of application to do A, reading an alternative clause into it implies that its real meaning is that the organ is permitted to do either A or not A. Through this conception of normative alternatives, the possibility of conflict between higher and lower norms is eliminated since an organ's behaviour will always conform to one or the other term of the alternative. However, this solution entails also the removal of the distinction between validity and invalidity. Kelsen asserts: 'The usual saying that an "unconstitutional statute" is invalid (void) is a meaningless statement, since an invalid statute is no statute at all. A non-valid norm is a non-existing norm, is legally a nonentity.'[14] What he does not seem to realize is that as a result of his theory of normative alternatives the term 'valid statute' becomes meaningless too.[15]

Kelsen introduces one qualification to his assertion about the alternative character of norms. If an organ of revision of the

---

[12] *GTLS*, 156; see, too, *PTL*, 271–6.

[13] On the development of the doctrine of *ipso jure* nullity see Paulson's review of C. Moench cited at n. 2, above.

[14] *GTLS*, 157.

[15] Maher reaches similar conclusions on the incompatibility of Kelsen's doctrine of normative alternatives and the basic tenets of his theory: 'Customs and Constitutions', 1 *Oxford Journal of Legal Studies*, 172–5 (1981).

constitutionality of statutes, or more generally of the validity of norms in the system, has been established, the two terms of the alternative have different weight. The explicit prescriptions are given preference over the implicit ones since the organ of review is commanded to declare the invalidity of norms that conflict with the former. But this preference must also be deemed to be expressed in the form of an alternative. For if the organ fails to declare the invalidity of the norm in question his decision will not be invalid unless and until a further organ declares it to be so. This implies that the organ of review is authorized either to declare invalid or not to declare invalid a norm which conflicts with higher norms of the system.[16] As Kelsen says: 'There can, therefore, never exist any absolute guarantee that the lower norm corresponds to the higher norm.'[17]

I have concluded that by putting forward the theory of normative alternatives Kelsen has removed the distinction between norm and no-norm, between validity and invalidity, and one is only left with the conception of a prescription declared to be valid or invalid. Is it possible however to argue that, since Kelsen primarily discusses the alternative character of norms that determine the procedure of creation and contents of lower norms, validity still implies conformity in respect of the organ of creation? The answer to this question must be negative. First because, as already stated, it is not possible to separate the notion of legal organ from the provisions that regulate its behaviour. Secondly, because Kelsen's reasoning about the alternative character of norms is equally applicable to this situation. Just as it is possible for an official to contravene procedural and substantive norms, it is feasible—though perhaps less likely—for someone who has not been duly appointed to purport to act in an official capacity. In such a case the system may require an authoritative declaration of the nullity of his act, failing which, its product will be a valid norm, according to Kelsen. When he examines the topic of nullity and annullability he considers the possibility that the 'sham norm has not been issued by the competent organ or has been issued by an individual who has no competence whatsoever to issue legal norms or has no quality of organ at all' and states:

---

[16] Kelsen appears to be unaware of this further implication of his theory of normative alternatives.

[17] *GTLS*, 155.

If the legal order should determine such conditions on which something which presents itself as a norm is null *ab initio* so that it need not be annulled in a legal procedure, the legal order would still have to determine a procedure the purpose of which is to ascertain whether or not these conditions are fulfilled in a given case, whether or not the norm in question has been issued by an incompetent organ or by an individual not competent to issue legal norms, etc. The decision made by the competent authority that something that presents itself as a norm is null *ab initio* becaue it fulfils the conditions of nullity determined by the legal order, is a constitutive act; it has a definite legal effect; without and prior to this act the phenomenon in question cannot be considered to be 'null'.[18]

It is clear, then, that both solutions make the validity of norms dependent on the declaration of officials. Yet the reasons provided in each case differ: according to the first one, an official statement of validity is correct because it is either final or the only authoritative pronouncement for the time being; according to the second one, an official cannot err because the norms that regulate his behaviour have given him absolute discretion.

It is obvious that Kelsen prefers the second solution because it enables him to assert that 'the alternative character of the higher norm determining the lower norm precludes any real contradiction between the higher and the lower norm'.[19] This is essential within his theory as 'there cannot occur any contradiction between two norms from different levels of the legal order. The unity of the legal order can never be endangered by any contradiction between a higher and a lower norm in the hierarchy of law.'[20]

Yet Kelsen fails to realize that the whole conception of validity is turned upside down through the theory of the alternative character of norms: because certain prescriptions are deemed to be valid it is inferred that they conform to higher norms, rather than—as he initially postulated—they are valid if and only if they conform to them.[21] Furthermore if no contradiction between norms of different levels can occur, the idea of conformity becomes totally meaningless and Kelsen's concepts of validity and of the legal system break down.

[18] *GTLS*, 161.
[19] *GTLS*, 161.
[20] *GTLS*, 162.
[21] The following remark illustrates this point clearly: 'For if the statute in question is valid it must be considered to be constitutional', 'Derogation' in *Essays in Honor of Roscoe Pound* (1962), p. 352.

IV   KELSEN'S THIRD SOLUTION

In the course of the discussion of a further example of this type of conflict, Kelsen introduces an alternative explanation, without seemingly being aware of its inconsistency with the previous two or of the fact that he is proposing a novel answer. Let us assume, he says, that a usurper, instead of the constitutionally authorized legislature, enacts a statute and that statute becomes effective because the decision of the organ of review that it should not be published is disregarded. His conclusion is that in such a situation 'we are faced by a revolutionary change of the constitution and therefore by a constitutional statute because it conforms to a new constitution'.[22]

This example is somewhat different from the ordinary conflict of norms in that not just a norm but also the decision of a competent organ have been disregarded. There is no reason, however, why from a logical point of view the solution should be different in this case. The net result in both cases is that a norm which conflicts with a higher norm, remains in force.

This reasoning, like the previous two, can be applied to norms of all levels of the hierarchy. Every act of law creation must be authorized by the constitution and if a norm is created otherwise than in accordance with its prescriptions and remains in force it could be inferred that an unconstitutionally created constitutional norm has authorized it. This view evidently conflicts with the idea that constitutional provisions have an alternative character, according to which there cannot be usurpers but only constitutionally authorized organs.

More crucially, we are led to conclude that any conflict between a lower and a higher norm results in the invalidity of the latter, of the constitutional norm that has authorized it and ultimately of the basic norm. This solution, too, must be rejected. It is as contrary to common assumptions to assert that every violation of a norm by a legal authority entails a change of the whole legal system as to say that one act of non-conformity leads to the invalidity of the higher norm. As Kelsen clearly states, validity cannot be equated to efficacy and only permanent lack of efficacy, that is, *desuetude*, results in loss of validity.[23]

[22] *PTL*, 275.
[23] *GTLS*, 119.

V   KELSEN'S IMPLIED FOURTH SOLUTION

As suggested at the beginning of this article, a more satisfactory solution to the problem posed by conflicts of norms is to be found in Kelsen's assertions concerning interpretation, even though he himself did not seem to realize their implications for this issue. In one of the most relevant passages he states:

If 'interpretation' is understood as cognitive ascertainment of the meaning of the object that is to be interpreted, then the result of a legal interpretation can only be the ascertainment of the frame which the law that is to be interpreted represents and thereby the cognition of several possibilities within the frame. The interpretation of a statute, therefore, need not necessarily lead to a single decision as the only correct one, but possibly to several, which are all of equal value, though only one of them in the action of the law-applying organ (especially the court) becomes positive law.[24]

According to the above view, organs operating on all levels of the hierarchy are authorized to choose among a number of alternative meanings and whatever their choice, their actions will conform to the relevant norms.[25] Hence from every norm, not one but a number of norms may be derived. It is only when legal organs go beyond the boundaries set by norms that their acts will not result—from an objective point of view—in the creation of valid norms.

Kelsen assumes that it is possible to ascertain objectively the frame of a norm and contrasts its determination as an act of cognition to the act of volition consisting of the choice made by a legal organ.[26] Thus the distinction between objectivity and subjectivity, between cognition and volition, so crucial to Kelsen's methodology and which becomes blurred in the first two solutions, is retained.

It is, however, questionable whether total objectivity can be achieved even in determining the boundaries of meaning of legal

---

[24] *PTL*, 351, where Kelsen also writes, 'The fact that a judicial decision is based on a statute actually means only that it keeps inside the frame represented by the statute; it does not mean that it is the individual norm, but only that it is *one* of those individual norms which may be created within the frame of the general norm.'

[25] The further down the rungs of the hierarchy one moves, the more concrete norms become and the more limited, therefore, the choices available to the organ of application; see *PTL*, 353.

[26] *PTL*, 354.

norms. As Kelsen points out, legal science can rely on a number of methods of interpretation which will often justify conflicting conclusions and perhaps all one can say, is that any meaning which is extracted from the norm according to some acknowledged method of interpretation must be included within its frame. No interpreter could possibly foresee the full range of meanings that may legitimately be given to legal norms by organs of application. Hence the task attributed to him by Kelsen, though feasible in theory, will seldom be accomplished in practice. Legal organs, on the other hand, will rarely fail to find some justification for the meaning they have chosen, in the wording of the statute, the presumed intention of the legislator, considerations of policies or principles, various rules of interpretation and presumptions, the purpose of the statute, and so on.[27]

Just as there is no method for determining the correct interpretation of a norm, there is no recognized procedure for establishing the limits of permissible interpretations. Hence the boundaries are fluid rather than fixed. This fact reduces considerably the possibility of conflicts but also shows that it is not always possible to determine with total objectivity whether two norms conflict.

Kelsen's doctrine of interpretation has also implications for his no-gaps theory, which places him into the same kind of quandary as his notion of normative alternatives.

Very briefly, his denial of the existence of gaps in the law derives from his assertion that every form of behaviour is either forbidden or permitted by the legal system. The widely held belief that there are gaps in the law is a fiction which enables legal organs, and in particular judges, to create norms in situations where the solution dictated by the system appears to them unjust or unsatisfactory. This fiction also has the function of restricting the activity of the judge in two ways. First, the judge is only allowed to create a norm in the case of permissions, that is, when there is no norm forbidding the behaviour in question. Secondly, the belief that he

---

[27] Kelsen even envisages a situation where an interpretation derived from the intention of the legislature cannot be fitted into any of the meanings warranted by the language used; see *Teoría Pura del Derecho*, 1st edn. (1960), p. 168. Bearing in mind Kelsen's views on interpretation, it could be argued that in Paulson's example of a conflict of norms at different levels, namely, *Korematsu* v. *United States* (1944) 323 U.S. 214, the Supreme Court chose one of the many permissible interpretations of the norm in question; see Paulson, op. cit., 39 *CLJ* 180–3 (1980).

can only create norms when there is a gap in the law will inhibit him psychologically, as he will only change the law when he is convinced that the lack of a sanctioning norm is due to an oversight of the legislator. Finally, when a judge falsely believes in the existence of a gap, he is authorized to create whatever norm appears desirable to him.[28]

Kelsen's analysis, though accurate in important respects, exhibits two failings: on the one hand, he disregards the fact that the crucial problem that normally confronts the judge is one of interpretation, that is, of determining whether the behaviour in question is forbidden or permitted. On the other hand, he fails to realize that the assertion that the judge is both bound not to apply a sanction when the behaviour is permitted and authorized to create a sanctioning norm for that situation, implies the existence of two conflicting norms. Thus both in the context of his discussion of gaps in the law and of normative alternatives he is led to the conclusion that the legal system contains norms which forbid and permit the same course of action.[29]

Fortunately this type of problem does not often arise in practice either. Judges usually only create norms when higher ones offer them a range of choices, that is, when they are required to fill genuine gaps in the law.

Finally, Kelsen's ideas on interpretation have implications for his definition of the legal norm as the objective meaning of an act of will, for the latter must be understood to cover not just one but a range of meanings.

M. Troper claims in a recent article that the meaning of a norm stands for the meaning of the text produced by the act of will of a legal organ. He then argues that the meaning of the latter is always

---

[28] *GTLS*, 146–9.

[29] It is perhaps significant that in the 2nd edition of *RR* Kelsen places the chapter on interpretation at the end of the book, whereas in the previous edition its position integrates it into the rest of his theory. In particular it is interesting to note that in the first edition it lies between the sections on conflicts and on gaps in the law. Does this indicate that Kelsen sensed—even though he did not explicitly state the connection—its relevance to these two other topics? Indeed in the first edition he links at one point his ideas on interpretation and on gaps by stating that it is possible to distinguish a situation where the judge applies a norm by remaining within its frame from a situation where a judge replaces it by another norm which he believes to be more just and better; see *Teoría Pura del Derecho*, 1st edn. (1960), p. 140. It is, however, very difficult to draw this distinction in practice, particularly if one bears in mind that in both cases the judge may reach the result he finds desirable by imputing a particular intention to the legislator.

established through an act of interpretation by the organ of application. Therefore, he concludes, it is the judge, and in particular a court of last resort, that creates the norm, not the organ that issued it originally, that is, the creator of the text.[30] This is to associate Kelsen with the extreme decisionist emphasis of such writers as Gray, which Kelsen clearly rejected.[31]

It is puzzling that Troper should have reached such a conclusion after reviewing Kelsen's doctrine of interpretation. If a norm consists of a range of meanings, its creator establishes the frame and the organ of application remains within it by choosing one of those meanings. At most, if the judge has the authority to establish a binding precedent, he will have modified the frame by possibly narrowing down the number of choices. He will then have acted in the capacity of a legislator.

VI KELSEN'S POSITION IN RECENT WRITINGS

In his later writings, Kelsen adopts a new position and maintains the possibility of the existence of conflicts between norms of the same or of different levels of the legal hierarchy.[32] Such conflicts cannot be resolved through the application of a priori logical principles and must, therefore, await resolutions by legal organs in accordance with positive principles of interpretation, like *lex superior* and *lex posterior*.[33] These principles then will only be binding upon legal organs if they have been validly created, if, for instance, they derive from judicial custom or have been enacted in a statute.

---

[30] M. Troper. loc. cit. note 11 above, pp. 518–29 concludes, 'Mais si la signification de cet acte, par exemple la signification de l'acte du législateur, est déterminée par l'organe d'application, il en résulte immanquablement qu'une loi valide est la signification objective d'un acte humain, telle qu'elle est déterminée par le juge. L'existence juridique d'une norme législative ne résulte pas de sa conformité à la Constitution, mais de l'interprétation par le juge. *La validité ne provient pas de la norme supérieure, mais du processus de production de normes inférieures*' (p. 526); and 'Si l'expression "norme valide" désigne la signification objective de norme d'un acte humain, alors la validité d'une norme ne découle pas de sa conformité à une norme supérieure, mais seulement de l'activité d'interprétation à laquelle s'est livrée une autorité dotée d'une existence de fait' (p. 528).

[31] Gray, *The Nature and Sources of the Law*, 2nd edn. (1947), p. 125: 'It has sometimes been said that the Law is composed of two parts—legislative law and judge-made law, but, in truth, all the Law is judge-made Law.' See *GTLS*, 150–3 and Ebenstein, 132–4.

[32] See *ELMP*, 233, 252, 272 and *ATN*, 168–73.   [33] *ELMP*, 273–4.

In the case of conflicts between norms of different levels, the lower norm conflicting with a higher one will only be invalid if the higher one states so explicitly.[34] This would be the case if, say, a constitution established the automatic invalidity of unconstitutional statutes. Since this possibility rarely arises in practice, in the majority of cases such statutes remain 'valid' until invalidated by an organ of revision. Kelsen is thus faced, once more, with the problem of justifying the validity of lower norms conflicting with higher ones. To say that they are both valid and yet conflict is in contradiction with his basic tenet that norms are only valid if their creation has been authorized by higher norms.[35] He is therefore driven again to resort to the theory of the alternative—originally formulated to deny the existence of conflicts—which leads him here, too, to conclude that there cannot be a conflict between a constitutional and a statutory norm.[36] Having started by asserting the possibility of conflict between norms of different levels and having stated that their resolution can only take place through the application of positive principles of interpretation, he inadvertently reverts to an a priori position by assuming the absence of conflict. In the case of unconstitutional statutes it cannot be held that a principle of positive law determines their validity on account of the existence of alternative norms in the constitution. This is obviously a reconstruction of the constitutional norms made by Kelsen

---

[34] *ELMP*, 272.

[35] In *ELMP*, Kelsen reiterates views he expressed in earlier writings: 'The subjective meaning of every act of command is an "ought", even the act whereby the highway robber commands somebody to hand over his money to him. But the subjective meaning of an act of command is only its objective meaning as well, and thus a binding norm, if the act is authorised by a norm presupposed to be valid' (244). And: 'What the general norm is aiming at is the validity of an individual norm in accordance with the general norm . . . The problem is the nature of the relation between the validity of two *norms*, one general and the other individual. What is essential is that the individual norm posited by the judge should accord with the general norm posited by the legislator. It is this, indeed, that constitutes the "founding" of the validity of the former by the latter' (259–60).

[36] *ELMP*, 272; 'It should, however, be remembered that of two conflicting norms in the second case, that is, the case of an unconstitutional statute, the so-called "unconstitutional statute" may, according to positive law, be valid, but its validity may be repealed in a special procedure provided for in the constitution, for instance, by the decision of a special court. Then no conflict of norms exists, for if the statute in question is valid, it must be considered to be constitutional, that is to say, the legislator must be considered to be authorised by the constitution to pass such a law.'

himself in order to justify the validity of unconstitutional statutes, where no other justification is available.

His rationalization of the validity of judicial decisions which conflict with general norms differs somewhat from earlier statements. In the *General Theory of Law and State* and the *Pure Theory of Law* such decisions are deemed valid because only the subjective judgment of the organ of creation of the norm has legal relevance. The theory of the alternative, of course, also has bearing on judicial decisions because, as stated earlier, the same reasoning is applicable on all levels of the hierarchy. Elsewhere, however, he affirms that if the validity of the individual norm cannot be derived from the general norm that determines its contents, it must stem from another general norm that establishes 'the legal force of judicial decisions'.[37] Kelsen, however, fails to confront the difficulties to which the assumption of the existence of such a norm gives rise. Is it a customary norm and if so, what are its contents? In particular, how does it define a judicial decision? Kelsen's own definition is based on accordance with the norm or norms that authorize its creation and is obviously inapplicable to a case where the decision is given legal effect in spite of lack of conformity.

A further problem derives from the fact that it is self-contradictory to assert, as one must, that the decision is invalid because it conflicts with the norm that determines its creation and yet valid because it conforms to another general norm of the system. As Kelsen himself says in the *Essays*: 'Such statements [referring to statements about norms] are subject, not only to rules of inference but also to the law of contradiction. The two statements "In legal order L the norm 'Adultery is to be punished' is valid" and "In legal order L the norm 'adultery is to be punished' is not valid" are logically contradictory; only one or the other can be true. It is self-evident that the two logical principles are applicable to statements about norms, since logic is applicable to all statements.'[38]

Kelsen's recognition of the existence of conflicts of norms constitutes a positive development towards a more realistic perception of legal phenomena but has inevitably faced him with problems that are incapable of resolution within the conceptual framework of his theory.

[37] *ELMP*, 244.   [38] *ELMP*, 245.

VII SOLUTIONS PROPOSED BY OTHER WRITERS

Paulson discriminates between formal and material authorization on the basis of Kelsen's distinction between the formal and material aspects of the determination of lower by higher norms.[39] Both types of authorization are required for the creation of valid norms but if due to 'legal errata' material authorization is lacking, then, according to Paulson, formal authorization will suffice. As stated above, such a conclusion is unacceptable because if material authorization is to be meaningful at all, non-compliance must lead to invalidity and if validity is then based on formal authorization, conflicting statements of validity result. Paulson is aware of this difficulty and in an effort to overcome it, he relies on Kelsen's concept of normative alternatives. As seen earlier, that concept enables Kelsen to assert that whatever its contents, a norm is always materially authorized. Paulson, however, rejects the conclusion that legal organs are thereby given a choice to either follow the explicit stipulations of higher norms or not on the basis that the institution of official review establishes a preference for those stipulations. I have already discussed this argument—which is also Kelsen's—but I wish to add here that the line of reasoning pursued manifests a confusion between two different issues.

The first one relates to the perception that a judge, for instance, has of the meaning of the norm addressed to him and the psychological constraints it imposes in terms of possible legal and non-legal sanctions and the likelihood of reversal by appellate courts. In this respect, it is undeniable that the two terms of the alternative carry different weights and consequences.

The second one deals with the implications that non-compliance with the explicit term of the alternative has for the validity of the norm created by the judge. The only reason why Kelsen introduces the notion of an alternative is, as Paulson points out, to justify validity in cases involving errata and from the point of view of validity it makes no difference whether one or the other term of the alternative is followed by the judge. In that sense and no other is he given total discretion. It is true that if he does not follow the explicit term of the alternative and if an organ of review is instituted, the norm is more likely to be declared invalid than if he had followed it, but Kelsen's concept of validity is not a matter of

---

[39] Paulson, op. cit. 39 *CLJ* 172–93 (1980).

prediction of what the courts will do. According to Kelsen, if an organ of review declares the norm invalid, invalidity stems from that act and not from the fact that the implicit part of the alternative was followed. That act itself, whether it conforms to the explicit stipulations of the higher norm or not, will create a valid norm until a further organ, if instituted, declares it invalid. So at every stage of the process of norm creation and revision, validity, according to the conception of the alternative, will be unaffected by material authorization. Only the likelihood of declarations of validity will be so affected.

A second objection to both Kelsen's and Paulson's reasoning is that formal authorization raises exactly the same problems as material authorization. The stipulations in respect of the organ of creation and the procedure it ought to follow, may in practice be disregarded and yet the prescription created may not be automatically invalid. As in the case of conflicts concerning the contents of the norm, the system will usually require an authoritative pronouncement of invalidity. That is why Kelsen applies the theory of normative alternatives to both types of authorization. The fact that in practice claims of invalidity are more frequently made in respect of material than formal authorization does not affect the theoretical issue.

A third objection is that, as Paulson's imaginary realist perceives,[40] Kelsen's concept of legal organ inextricably links formal and material authorization. This is reflected in the complete formulation that every norm is given by him in a static presentation of the legal system. From a static point of view all norms contain a sanction and all the conditions for its application. These conditions not only include the act that constitutes the delict, that is, material authorization, but also conditions relating to the appointment of the individual authorized to apply the sanction and the procedures he ought to follow, in short, all the requirements covered by formal authorization.[41] As stated earlier, an individual only acts in the capacity of a legal organ if he

[40] Ibid. Paulson creates a dialogue between Kelsen and a realist, in which the latter puts forward very cogent objections against the former's views (pp. 183–7).

[41] *PTL*, 231; 'This formulation of the rule of law, then, shows—and therein lies the essential function of the rule of law describing the law—the systematic connection between the so-called formal and the so-called material law (that is, between the determination of the delict and the sanction on the one hand and the determination of the law-applying organ and his procedure on the other).'

complies with all the stipulations of the norms addressed to him.

Harris draws similar conclusions to Paulson's though via a different route.[42] He discriminates between two situations: (1) a person is authorized or has authority to create a norm if another norm in the system makes it binding upon certain individuals; (2) a person is authorized or has authority to create a norm if its contents conform to the higher norm that determines its creation. The fact that he refers to norms created in situation (1) which do not also fall under the scope of (2) as wrong but binding, indicates that he also differentiates between validity and binding force.

Harris' second concept of authority is very close to Paulson's formal authorization and to Kelsen's latest rationalization of the validity of judicial decisions. He does, however, reject Kelsen's theory of the alternative character of norms and formulates his position on the status of norms created in contravention to the stipulations of higher norms in the following terms:

Where a prescription is subsumable under a general rule of a normative system by virtue of the fact that the general rule makes the existence of duties conditional on the prescription being issued, we may speak of the prescriber being authorized; but this is not inconsistent with saying that the normative system in question prohibits the act of prescription. This situation is not well described by Kelsen's doctrine of alternative authorization.[43]

It is not clear whether Harris believes that such general rules conferring binding force on prescriptions which cannot be subsumed under the rules that determine their creation need to be explicitly established or whether they are to be implied from the need for official declarations of nullity. Either way, such rules would have to specify the conditions under which the prescriptions in question are binding. It cannot be maintained that any decision emanating from a judge, for instance, is binding, regardless of whether it is clearly outside his jurisdiction or whether its contents are totally against the stipulations of the system. To take an extreme and highly improbable example, if an English judge were to sentence someone to death for smoking in public, no one would take his judgment seriously. Such conditions, however, are by their very

---

[42] Harris, 'Kelsen's Concept of Authority', 36 *CLJ* 353 (1977).
[43] Ibid., p. 363.

nature, incapable of precise determination. It is possible to define the limits of a legitimate exercise of authority but not the point at which those limits have been so obviously overstepped that a declaration of nullity becomes unnecessary. This is the kind of issue that is normally decided on an *ad hoc* basis if and when it arises. This brings us back to the question of whether it is possible to define the concept of legal authority otherwise than in terms of the rules that regulate the behaviour of the person empowered to exercise it.

VIII CONCLUSION

Given the shortcomings of most of the solutions to the problem of conflicts of norms discussed so far, it remains necessary to clarify the theoretical issues raised by Kelsen's analysis. The basic point of departure must be, in my view, the acceptance of the ideal nature of Kelsen's model of the legal system, which entails that not all prescriptions which share functional characteristics with norms can be fitted into it. A formally coherent picture of the law can never totally correspond to reality because of the fact that norms are not derived from other norms through a purely intellectual process but are created by human beings, who are capable of fallibility, ignorance, dishonesty, and self-deception. Moreover, as Kelsen himself points out, no system can establish foolproof safeguards against disregard of its stipulations. The above considerations should have led him to the recognition that law is not only composed of valid norms but also of 'ought' statements that function as such but which, from an objective point of view, do not fulfil the requirements for legal validity. It is puzzling that he was unable to take this step. Was he trying to reach an impossible compromise between theory and facts or did he dogmatically view his theory as the only correct description of normative reality?[44]

However, the step must be taken and Kelsen's own premises must be developed to their logical conclusion to avoid the inconsistencies deriving from his views on conflicts.

---

[44] See *GTLS*, 430–3 where, in a discussion of various philosophical and psychological types, in the context of metaphysical dualism, so much is revealed about his own theory by his analysis of the compromise type though he is referring to other schools of thought.

Once we admit that Kelsen's concept of the legal system cannot incorporate everything that has the appearance of being valid, prescriptive statements which do not satisfy Kelsen's conditions of validity and yet have legal effects, must be deemed to be part of a wider notion of positive law and a different term must be used to describe them. I propose to call them 'norms in force' and define them as prescriptive statements which are deemed to be binding by legal officials because they have been issued by individuals who appear to be acting in the capacity of legal organs even though they have not complied with one or more norms that regulate their behaviour.[45] Norms in force are more likely to be declared invalid or to fall into *desuetude* than valid norms. If notwithstanding their invalidity they eventually become efficacious and the *opinione necessitatis* required by Kelsen for the formation of customary law is present,[46] they then become part of the legal system on the grounds that custom is a valid method of law creation. If, for instance, a general norm derived from a judgment made *per incuriam* is consistently followed by other judges, a judicial custom will develop which accords validity to that norm and renders invalid the norm with which it conflicts. The doctrine of precedent cannot be relied on for its validity because to constitute a binding precedent a norm must lie within the boundaries of the general norm that determines the creation of the relevant individual norm.[47]

A related problem, neglected by Kelsen and highlighted by

---

[45] Amselek points out that Kelsen confuses the notions 'norme valable' and 'norme en vigueur' in 'Réflexions Critiques autour de la Conception Kelsénienne de l'Ordre Juridique', 94 *Rev. Dr. Publ.* 5, 15 (1978). See, too, op. cit. 138 *Revue Internationale de Philosophie* 473 (1981).

[46] *GTLS*, 34.

[47] See *GTLS*, 149 where Kelsen seems to take a different view: 'A judicial decision may have the character of a precedent, i.e. of a decision binding upon the future decision of all similar cases. It can, however, have the character of a precedent only if it is not the application of a pre-existing general norm of substantive law, if the court acted as a legislator.' Such a conception of precedent leads to the type of inconsistencies that I have discussed in this article. I therefore believe that the only view on precedent that is compatible with Kelsen's concept of objective validity is one which holds that the judge creates valid precedents when he chooses one of the interpretations within the frame of the norm which is binding on him. I do agree, however, with Kelsen's claim that judges are then acting as legislators. See further, Tur, 'Positivism, Principles and Rules', in Attwooll ed., *Perspectives in Jurisprudence* (Glasgow, 1977), pp. 42–78 and Tur, 'Varieties of Overruling and Judicial Law-Making; Prospective Overruling in a Comparative Perspective', [1978] *Juridical Review* 33–64.

Fuller's conception of the inner morality of law,[48] concerns the determination of the degree of real—as opposed to ostensible— conformity between norms of different levels required for the existence of a legal system. Kelsen makes validity dependent on the efficacy of the whole system and this condition entails a high degree of correspondence between lower and higher norms. In order to determine the efficacy of the system this correspondence must be assessed objectively. Otherwise one would be driven to the conclusion that false assertions made by officials about the legality of their actions would have to be taken at face value by legal scientists describing the orders in question. When there is a high degree of discrepancy between official action and validly enacted norms, the inference to be drawn from Kelsen's theory is that the system has lost its validity and that a set of customary rules has replaced the 'rules on paper', that is, the originally valid norms. As a result, a picture of law emerges which embraces the decisionist emphasis of American Realism as well as Kelsen's conception of a hierarchy of valid norms. In fact, there is still a hierarchy, but it becomes very much simplified. With a basic norm that confers validity on custom and any norms derived from it, it bears greater similarity to the orders of primitive societies and to international law than to the developed legal systems of con- temporary democratic societies. What Kelsen's theory fails to take account of, is the fact that official ideology and verbal behaviour may pay lip service to the constitutionally enacted norms in an attempt to deceive the population into believing that the rule of law is adhered to. Statements of validity made by officials, legal writers, and citizens may not, therefore, reflect the underlying legal reality. Kelsen's model, which presupposes a correspondence between efficacy and statements of validity, is not applicable to this kind of situation.

However, the weaknesses in Kelsen's treatment of conflicts of norms do not detract from the internal coherence and value of the rest of his theory. He has provided us with a formal model of the legal system which by its very nature cannot encompass all legal phenomena but which constitutes a very good approximation to legal orders in societies where officials are committed to the value of legality and constitutionality.

---

[48] Fuller, *The Morality of Law* (New Haven, rev. edn. 1969), ch. II.

PART FIVE

JUSTICE

CHAPTER 12

KELSEN'S THEORY OF LAW AND PHILOSOPHY OF JUSTICE

JES BJARUP

KELSEN'S pure theory of law 'does not deny—as it is sometimes misunderstood—the existence of justice; it only—as a science—refuses to recognise an *absolute* justice which is supposed to exist only according to a religious belief in the justice of God; the pure theory of law considers justice as a *relative* value, different according to different value systems'.[1] Thus, Kelsen's thesis, put forward in his philosophy of justice, is the claim that 'justice is a relative value'. How is this thesis to be interpreted? I should like to suggest that Kelsen's thesis is to be interpreted as a normative claim, which means that Kelsen's philosophy of justice is a version of what is called normative ethical relativism.[2] This position is opposed to normative ethical absolutism. The difference between these two positions is that the ethical absolutist affirms, and the ethical relativist denies that 'a judgement about what is just or unjust can be as objective as a judgement about what is true or false. Value judgements can claim to be valid for everybody, always and everywhere, and not only in relation to the judging subject.'[3] Kelsen rejects normative ethical absolutism, since a judgment about what is just or unjust is only valid in relation to the judging subject. Thus Kelsen's conclusion is that he 'can only say what justice is for me' (i.e. Kelsen).[4] Justice for Kelsen is tolerance, which again means freedom, which in turn implies a democratic form of government. This form of government is better than anti-democratic forms of government, that is, autocracy. I should like to suggest that Kelsen is not a consistent ethical relativist, since he regards what is just for him to be just for all

[1] 'On the Pure Theory of Law', 1 *Israel Law Rev.* 1, 3–4 (1966).
[2] For the terminology see Taylor, *Problems of Moral Philosophy* (Belmont, 1967), p. 47 f.
[3] *WIJ*, 199. [4] *ELMP*, 24; *WIJ*, 24.

rational thinking people. I shall try to substantiate my thesis that Kelsen is an ethical absolutist in disguise by giving an account of the basis of Kelsen's position.

I THE BACKGROUND. LAW AS NORM

It was Kelsen's lifelong effort to try to solve theoretical problems of politics, morality, and the law by insisting on a sharp distinction between the law as a social and legal phenomenon on the one hand, and the various disciplines dealing with these phenomena on the other hand. The law is a social phenomenon, manifested in the actual behaviour of the individuals who are subject to the legal system of a definite society. In this sense, there is no difference between legal phenomena and natural phenomena, since it is possible to describe and explain these phenomena by the principle of causality. The law, however, is also a legal phenomenon, a specific reality, which does not manifest itself in the actual behaviour of individuals, but rather manifests itself as a normative order, which determines how the conduct of individuals in a society ought to be. In this sense, there is a vital difference between legal phenomena and natural phenomena, which is tantamount to the difference between the realm of ought and the realm of is. How the conduct of individuals in a society ought to be is a matter of morality and politics. What is common to morality and politics is an activity directed at values, that is to say determining norms according to which an individual's behaviour is judged to be right or wrong, and what duties, obligations, and rights individuals have in various circumstances of life in society. The law, Kelsen says, is norm, which is used as a specific social technique[5] by politicians to determine how individuals in society ought to behave in relation to each other in order to promote peace and order in society.

The specific technique consists in the acts of will of individuals, who are, by law, authorized to create norms, which make the behaviour of individuals legal (lawful, right) or illegal (unlawful, wrong) by providing the execution of sanctions in case the individual does not comply with the norms. The law is a coercive order, it is a system of norms backed up by sanctions, which 'pacifies the community' by threats of force.[6] As a coercive order,

---

[5] *GTLS*, 15 ff.; *WIJ*, 231 ff., *RR*², 31 ff.; *PTL*, 30 ff.
[6] *GTLS*, 21.

a legal order can be distinguished from a moral order. If the individual, by a legal norm, is commanded to behave in a specific way under threat of a coercive act, that is, an evil, then what is the difference between this command and the command of a robber? The robber, too, commands an individual to behave in a certain way, for example to surrender his money, under a threat of an evil, such as the threat of death. Is there, then, any difference between the subjective act of a tax-collector and the subjective act of a robber? And if so, what is the difference? The tax-collector as well as the robber demands money, and their acts of will, Kelsen says, 'both have the subjective meaning of an "ought"'.[7] The subjective meaning of 'ought' is 'directed at the behaviour of another',[8] which is verbally expressed in an 'ought-sentence'.[9] What this sentence expresses is 'Thou shalt' [which] is the meaning of an "I will"'.[10] Thus it seems that there is no difference between the two acts of will, since anyone who commands or prescribes something wills that something should happen, in this case the delivery of money.

Kelsen, however, insists that there must be a difference, since the tax-collector's conduct is legal, the robber's conduct illegal. How is it possible to explain this difference? Why does the tax-collector's subjective act of will establish an 'objectively valid norm, stipulating a coercive act as sanction',[11] which is valid for everyone regardless of any feelings or volitions? Kelsen's problem, then, can be formulated as follows. How is it possible that an act of will, which has a subjective meaning only, also has an objective meaning? The subjective meaning of an act of will is expressed in a subjective ought-sentence, which is valid only for the individual who pronounces the sentence. The objective meaning of an act of will is expressed in an objective ought-sentence, that is, a norm, which claims to be valid not only for the individual who pronounces the sentence but for all individuals in a society.

The decisive question, then, is, how is it possible to move from the subjective ought to an objective ought? Or, to put the same

---

[7] *PTL*, 45; *RR*², 46.   [8] *PTL*, 7; *RR*², 7.

[9] *ELMP*, 217. In the German edition of this essay, *WRS* II, 1457, Kelsen writes 'Sollsatz', which is translated as 'ought-statement', but perhaps it might be better rendered 'ought-sentence', since Kelsen's opinion is that 'ought' as an act of will cannot be a statement, which is an act of thought; compare *ELMP*, 114; *WRS* I, 869 f.

[10] *ELMP*, 217.   [11] *PTL*, 45; *RR*², 46.

point differently, how to distinguish between a subjective or personal command on the one hand and an objective or 'impersonal and anonymous command'[12] on the other? Kelsen's answer to this question is that the objective meaning of ought can be established by 'an analysis of what those who are concerned with law—legislators, judges, lawyers, parties in lawsuits, and theoretical jurists—actually mean when making such judgements',[13] i.e., 'judgements that interpret the act as legal (that is, as acts whose objective meaning is norms)'.[14] The result of this analysis is, Kelsen claims, that the objective meaning is established because, what Kelsen terms a basic norm 'is presupposed in our juristic thinking'.[15] The basic norm, then, provides that a sentence expressed by a subjective act of will has an objective meaning. The basic norm functions as a criterion of meaning, which must be presupposed if one wants to interpret the subjective meaning of ought as having an objective meaning of ought, that is to say as 'objectively valid legal norms'.[16]

Considering norms, it is vital to distinguish, Kelsen says, between the act of will on the one hand, and what is expressed by this act, that is its meaning, on the other hand.[17] The act of will, as an individual and mental phenomenon, belongs to the realm of is, whereas what is expressed, as a norm, belongs to the realm of ought. The realm of is and the realm of ought are different and separate realms. The realm of is can be described and explained by the principle of causality, which says that if A is the case, then B is the case. This principle is used to connect successive events, for instance the relation between metals and heating, under the assumption of sequences between the heating of metals that are regular because determined by a law of nature. The realm of ought must be described and explained by a different principle, which Kelsen calls the principle of imputation.[18] This principle is expressed in the formula 'if A is, B is (or ought) to be, even though

---

[12] *GTLS*, 36. [13] *WIJ*, 210.

[14] *PTL*, 45; *RR*², 46. [15] 1 *Israel Law Rev*. 1, 6 (1966).

[16] *PTL*, 201; *RR*², 205. For a discussion of the basic norm in this respect see Raz, *The Authority of Law* (Oxford, 1979), pp. 122 ff. and Harris, *Law and Legal Science* (Oxford, 1979), pp. 78, 108, 125.

[17] *PTL*, 5; *RR*², 5.

[18] *GTLS*, 91. In German, '*Zurechnung*'; *RR*², 79 ff., *PTL*, 76 ff. This principle is also referred to by Kelsen as the principle of normativity (*GTLS*, 46; *WIJ*, 139), or the principle of accounting (*ELMP*, 155 ff., *WRS* I, 664 ff).

B perhaps is not, in fact'. Thus, if an individual does not pay his taxes, a distraint ought to be inflicted upon him. Or, if a norm is to be created, then the constitution ought to be obeyed. Consequently Kelsen's analysis of the meaning of legal norms is a version of a non-naturalistic theory of the meaning of ethical terms.[19] The important thing to notice is that if Kelsen's analysis is correct, then legal science—like ethics—will be an autonomous science with an irreducible peculiar subject-matter, that is, 'the specific reality' or 'the legal reality', the specific existence of the law, (which) manifests itself in a phenomenon which is mostly designated as the positiveness of law'.[20] The positiveness of law is something given in experience, manifested by acts of will of human beings, for example the tax-collector's act of will. In order to grasp the meaning of this act, we need to presuppose the basic norm. The basic norm has then a similar function to the Kantian ideas of space and time as forms of intuitions, or ways in which what is given in sensation appears to the human mind.[21]

Further, the basic norm must be supplemented by the principle of imputation, which is imposed upon a piece of behaviour, which an individual wants to bring about or not by threats of sanctions. The principle is neutral, it has to do with the form of willing rather than with its matter, that is, what in fact is commanded, permitted, or authorized. Thus an examination of judging a behaviour to be legal or illegal, or an act of will to express an objective ought (i.e. legal norm) or a subjective ought, reveals that this involves the basic norm and the application of the principle of imputation. These are the common structural elements of legal reality, and by means of them legal norms can be accounted for as parts of an objective legal order, which is then regardless of our particular feelings, volitions, and individual experiences. Since the basic norm and the principle of imputation are neutral, it depends very much on human beings what kind of behaviour it is desirable to bring about or not. This matter, that is, the contents of legal norms, is for the legal authority to decide. In this respect, Kelsen says, 'any kind of content might be law. There is no human

---

[19] Cf. Broad's *Critical Essays in Moral Philosophy* (ed. David Cheney) London 1971, p. 226 f.

[20] *GTLS*, xiv.

[21] Cf. *PTL*, 201, *RR*[2], 204 f.: 'The Basic Norm as a Transcendental-logical Presupposition', cf. Kant, *CPuR*. I draw on Walsh, *Kant's Criticism of Metaphysics* (Edinburgh 1975) for the exposition of Kant's views.

behaviour which as such is excluded from being the content of a legal norm.'[22] A legal norm, then, is valid not because of its contents, but rather because of its form.

II   VALUES OF LAW AND VALUES OF JUSTICE

What is given in experience is, then, that it can be observed that individuals by and large behave in accordance with the norms issued by legal authorities. General obedience to the constitution, and to the legal norms established in conformity with the constitution, promotes the values of law, or legality, that is to say peace and order in society among individuals, and observance by the legal authorities of the requirements for creating legal norms laid down in the constitution. The product of this procedure, that is, the law, can be characterized in two different ways. In one way, 'the law constitutes a value precisely by the fact that it is a norm; it constitutes the legal value which, at the same time, is a (relative) moral value, which merely means that the law is norm'.[23]

In another way, the legal norm can be characterized as a just or an unjust legal norm, which implies the value of justice. In Kelsen's opinion, values of law and values of justice are different values, or in other words, legality and justice are different concepts. The value of legality relates to the legal authority, and his capacity to affect the behaviour of members of society by means of norms, in order to promote peace and order in society. Now, to have the authority to enact legal norms is equivalent to having 'the right to mold the whole group's way of life'.[24] Clearly it is an important question to consider whether this right is used in a lawful manner or not, and to ask whether judgments to that effect are meaningful and capable of being true or false. It is clearly also important to consider whether the order of norms established by legal authorities is a just or unjust legal order, or whether legal norms can be characterized as just or unjust in a meaningful way. That is a legitimate question. It is, however, not a question admissible within legal science. Within legal science the legitimate question is, 'Is a norm a valid legal norm?', which can be answered and 'tested objectively by the help of facts'.[25] Questions of the

---

[22] *PTL*, 198, *RR*² , 201; cf below p. 287.
[23] *PTL*, 65, *RR*², 67; cf. *PTL*, 36, *RR*², 37, below p. 290.
[24] Baier, *The Moral Point of View* (London, 1958) p. 137.   [25] *GTLS*, 49.

justice or injustice of legal norms belong to the different discipline of philosophy of justice. In Kelsen's own words,

Like the question of the origin of the law, the question of whether a given legal order is just or unjust cannot be answered within the framework and by the specific methods of a science directed at a structural analysis of positive law. This does not necessarily imply that the question of what is justice cannot be answered in a scientific, and that is to say in an objective, way at all. But even if it were possible to decide objectively what is just and what unjust, as it is possible to determine what is an acid and what a base, justice and law must be considered as two different concepts. If the idea of justice has any function at all, it is to be a model for making good law and a criterion for distinguishing good from bad law.[26]

Is it possible that the questions of what is law and what is justice can be answered in a scientific, that is to say in an objective, way?

III   KELSEN'S CONCEPTION OF KNOWLEDGE

Knowledge is expressed in propositions. Knowledge involves the possibility of making judgments about objects, and these judgments must be objectively true. Or, as Kelsen puts it, propositions (or statements or judgments—as far as I can see, Kelsen uses these as equivalent terms[27]) are acts of thought, in contrast to norms, which are acts of will. This is a basic distinction for Kelsen. 'A norm is not a statement, nor [is] a prescription a description.'[28] A proposition (statement, judgment) is a 'description, i.e. a statement whose import is—or more properly, which is the meaning (of the statement)—that something exists, i.e. is present or somehow created, and in particular that things, living creatures or men do actually behave under certain circumstances in a certain way'.[29]

---

[26] *WIJ*, 295.

[27] *ELMP*, 242. *WRS* II, 1486: 'Since the term "statement" [*Aussage*] designates not only the meaning of an act of thought [*Sinn eines Denkaktes*], but also the act of thinking and speaking itself, it would be preferable to speak of the application of logical principles, not to statements [*Aussagen*], but to propositions [*Sinngehalte*] that are true or false. The act of statement [*Aussageakt*] is neither true nor false; only the proposition [*Sinngehalt*] it expresses can be this'. However, Kelsen also writes of 'the truth of a statement [*Aussage*], so far as it is the meaning of an act of thought [*Sinn eines Denkaktes*]' (*ELMP*, 233, *WRS* II, 1475). Further, 'truth and falsity are properties of a statement [*Aussage*]' (*ELMP*, 239, *WRS*, II, 1483), and, elsewhere, he writes of 'the law of non-contradiction, which applies to two statements [*Aussagen*]' (*ELMP*, 115, *WRS* I, 870).

[28] *ELMP*, 115, *WRS* I, 870. 'Eine Norm ist keine Aussage, eine Vorschreibung ist keine Beschreibung.'   [29] Ibid.

Statements directed at reality can be true or false, and 'they are true when they correspond to it [the real]. Their truth does not depend on our will. If true at all, they are objectively true. The statement that if a metallic body is heated, it expands, is true whether anyone wills it or not, and is true for all thinking beings.'[30] This is important, because Kelsen wants to contrast judgments about empirical objects, which claim to be true for 'all thinking beings', with judgments about what is just or unjust, which make the similar claim, but, in Kelsen's opinion, are true 'only in relation to the judging subject'. In Kelsen's view, then, knowing is to be thought of as a mental act or activity, which we can perform. It is something which we do, aiming at 'knowing nature or reality' with the purpose in mind 'rationally to explain reality'.[31] This is expressed in statements, which proceed, as Kelsen puts it, 'from the thinking or knowing of one to the thinking or knowing of another. Hence a statement is true or false.'[32]

How is it possible, then, to identify true statements from false statements? Kelsen's answer is true judgments are judgments about reality. Reality or 'nature is a system of facts connected by the principle of causality'.[33] One can only know the empirical world by means of transcendental-logical principles.[34] The ideas of space and time provide the form of all experience, sensation provides the content of experience. What is given in this way must be subsumed under concepts in statements if knowledge or rational cognition is to result, that is to say the contents of reality 'can be uniquely ascertained by an objective method'.[35] Thus for knowledge to be possible it must be concerned with what is real as opposed to what is ideal. Knowledge must be restricted to statements, which are necessarily true, that is, to statements which in no circumstances could be false. Kelsen puts it,

a statement does not begin or cease to be true. If it is true, it always has been and always will be. It cannot lose its truth. Even a statement about something limited in time, e.g. the statement that the earth at a certain time is at a certain distance from the sun, is no less true before this time

---

[30] *ELMP*, 116, *WRS* I, 871.　　　[31] *GTLS*, 420.

[32] *ELMP*, 115, *WRS* I, 870, 'Die Aussage [geht] von dem Denken (Wissen) des einen zu dem Denken (Wissen) des anderen. Daher ist eine Aussage wahr oder unwahr.'

[33] *ELMP*, 258, cf. *GTLS*, 436, '. . . a complex of empirical facts'.

[34] *GTLS*, 436.　　　[35] *GTLS*, 49.

than after it. Newton's statements about gravitation, if they were true, were true long before Newton made them, and will be true long after his making them. A statement is the meaning of an act of thought, and its truth is independent of this act, i.e. of the fact that it has been made, i.e. thought and uttered.[36]

The criterion of the truth of a statement is the correspondence between the statement and what is real. The truth of statements about reality is grasped by simple inspection of the statement alone, using the law of non-contradiction,[37] establishing scientific knowledge as a system of consistent statements, which describe its objects as an objectively determined order.[38] Cognition for Kelsen 'must assume an active, productive role in relation to its objects. Cognition itself creats its objects, out of materials provided by the senses and in accordance with its immanent laws'.[39] If cognition is viewed as a creative activity, then the question arises how to account for the success or failure of that activity. Further, the object of cognition becomes 'relative to the knowing subject'[40] and his system or way of ordering what is given to his mind. This implies that Kelsen notices that '[the truth], which is affirmed within the system is never more than a relative truth' or that 'a cognition which produces its own objects can only claim subjective validity for its judgements'.[41] Clearly, if this is the case, then there can be no contrast between empirical judgments and value-judgments. They are—so to speak—in the same boat. As far as value-judgments are concerned, Kelsen says that he 'can only say what justice is for me'.[42] Exactly the same thing can be said in the case of an empirical matter, where Kelsen only can say that iron is heavy is true for him. But then, to say 'As far as I [i.e. Kelsen] am concerned it is true' is highly misleading, since it is not clear, whether Kelsen says that it is true that iron is heavy, or whether he believes that iron is heavy.

Kelsen explicitly endorses the view of philosophical relativism, which 'recognizes only relative truth and relative values'.[43] But he is also aware of the danger of the notion of relative truth, which

[36] *ELMP*, 230, *WRS* II, 1472–3; 'statement' is a translation of *Aussage*.
[37] *ELMP*, 252, *WRS* II, 1470, n. 3.   [38] *GTLS*, 374, 441.
[39] *GTLS*, 434.   [40] *WIJ*, 198.   [41] *GTLS*, 434.
[42] *ELMP*, 24.
[43] *WIJ*, 199, cf. *ELMP*, 38, 'Positivism and (epistemological) relativism belong together, just as natural law theory and (metaphysical) absolutism do.' See, too, *GTLS*, 396. Cf. below p. 300.

implies the abandonment of any difference between belief and knowledge, which Kelsen wants to stress. He writes

the statement that the sun revolves around the earth was not true although men believed in it; men believed in it because they erroneously thought it was true. If a statement were true because men believe in it, then two contradictory statements were true at the same time if there were people who believed in the one and also people who believed in the other. This would imply the abandonment of logic.[44]

Kelsen avoids this by insisting that his version of philosophical relativism is based upon 'the objective conditions under which the process of cognition occurs'.[45] It is a 'true relativism taking into consideration the mutual relation among the various subjects of knowledge'.[46] Kelsen's 'true relativism' is based on the assumption that 'individuals, as subjects of cognition, are equal', which implies that 'the various processes of rational cognition in the minds of the subjects are—in contradistinction to their emotional reactions— equal, and thus the further assumption becomes possible that the objects of cognition, as the results of these individual processes, are in conformity with one another, an assumption confirmed by the external behaviour of the individuals.'[47] I do not think that Kelsen succeeds in establishing his 'true relativism'. If Kelsen's assumptions are empirical assumptions, then these assumptions turn out to be false. It is not the case that all individuals—as subjects of cognition—are equal. One need only to point to new-born babies and individuals who are severely mentally retarded, to refute Kelsen's assumption.

Kelsen believes that his assumptions are confirmed by the conformity of 'the external behaviour of individuals'. However, this conformity of the external behaviour of individuals, that is, the fact that individuals render identical empirical judgments, by no means establishes that the judgments are true or false. This is to confuse 'the objectivity of a judgment with the frequency of the act of judgment' as Kelsen himself remarks in another context.[48] But this is precisely the error committed by Kelsen's version of 'true relativism'. According to this 'true relativism' no distinction can be made between what is true and what is thought to be true. The true relativist must deny that there is any difference between

---

44 *WIJ*, 391; cf. *ELMP*, 230.   45 *GTLS*, 435.
46 *WIJ*, 201.   47 Ibid.   48 *WIJ*, 391.

knowledge and belief. Kelsen wishes to uphold this distinction, and believes that his 'true relativism' makes room for that distinction. In this Kelsen fails because he then must presuppose a distinction between reality and what we say about this reality. The view that there is a reality independent of human cognition is central, according to Kelsen, to philosophical absolutism. Thus, Kelsen's 'true relativism' is just another version of philosophical absolutism. Kelsen's success in creating a common world of facts by cognitive acts depends in the last analysis upon his claim to be in possession of a method, which in principle can only be successful. The method is that of rational insight into 'the real and possible',[49] in contrast to, I suppose, the unreal and the impossible. The meaning and truth of statements must be traced back to its origin in infallible acts of thought.[50]

When Kelsen makes the assumption that 'the various processes of rational cognition are equal' it may be the case that this is not an empirical assumption but rather an epistemological assumption concerned with the very possibility of objective experience of reality. If this is so, then individuals as subjects of cognition are equal in the sense, as Kant puts it, that 'it must be possible for the "I think" to accompany all my representations'.[51] Thus the subject of thinking must be one and the same in all its intellectual operations, if it is to be a subject at all. What Kelsen refers to is not any actual individual but rather he refers to—to use an expression by Walsh—'an ideal subject self which is the same in all of us or would be, if we were wholly rational'.[52] As Walsh notices this is the impersonal self which operates and expresses itself through the activity of judgments. But perhaps the flaw in Kelsen's argument is that he passes from an empirical self to an impersonal self. The difference between an objective judgment and a subjective judgment lies in the following features. First, an

---

[49] *GTLS*, 13.
[50] It may be objected that my act of thought cannot be identical with, say, Kelsen's act of thought. What I—and Kelsen—think, however, may be shared. This is perhaps what Kelsen had in mind too. The truth or falsity of what we think does depend upon the theory by which we describe the world. The theory, however, does depend upon its origin or foundation in an act of thought, and this infinite regress can only be stopped by basic commitments, e.g. a commitment to be rational or not. Cf. MacCormick, *Legal Reasoning and Legal Theory* (Oxford, 1978). Ch. X, esp. p. 269.
[51] *CPuR*, B 131.
[52] Walsh, *Kant's Criticism of Metaphysics*, p. 50; cp. *RR*[2], 7.

objective judgment refers to facts existing in time and space and not merely as the subjective judgment, to a subjective impression or a subjective feeling. Secondly, an objective statement is, if true, true for everybody in contrast to a subjective judgment, which is only true for the judging individual.

I do not intend to argue for or against this Kantian epistemology. What I want to point out is that Kelsen thinks that the Kantian view implies epistemological relativism.[53] Epistemological relativism is the doctrine that the individual's beliefs and statements are relative to his freely chosen perspective or conceptual framework. When Kelsen only recognizes 'relative truth' he must then recognize that the truth of the statement that the earth revolves around the sun is relative to a heliocentric theory. But equally the statement that the sun moves around the earth is true according to a geocentric theory. Thus the two statements, (*a*) 'the earth moves around the sun', and (*b*) 'the sun moves around the earth', are not contradictory statements. But Kelsen explicitly claims that the statements are contradictory, and by rules of logic the statements (*a*) and (*b*) cannot both be true. It is statement (*a*) which is true, and statement (*b*) which is false.

Thus Kelsen in effect rejects epistemological relativism and claims that the statement (*a*) is not just relatively true in relation to the judging subject and his perspective but absolutely true to everybody, always and everywhere, because all individuals inhabit a common world and share the same perspective. Kelsen is forced to adopt this position, I believe, because otherwise there can be no contrast between statements about reality, which are objective, and value-judgments, which are subjective and hence relative to the individual. But if Kelsen is consistent, there can be no such contrast since statements about reality also are relative to a scientific system. Consequently Kelsen must recognize that he cannot speak of statements about reality but must instead speak of statements about realities.[54] This implies further that Kelsen's theory has no answer to the question, which of the different realities is the true reality. The choice between competing theories is similar to the choice involved in conflicts of moral ideals. In a

---

[53] Cf. *GTLS*, 444.

[54] Cp. *WIJ*, 200, 'If . . . the existence of many egos must be admitted, the consequence seems to be inevitable that there are as many worlds as there are knowing subjects'. This 'pluralism' is rejected by Kelsen.

case of conflicts of values, for example, whether one has an obligation to sacrifice his own life, and to kill others in war or not, Kelsen claims that 'it is absolutely impossible to decide in any rational or scientific way between the two value-judgements underlying these conflicting views. It is, when all is said, our feelings, our will, not our understanding, the emotional rather than the rational element of our consciousness, which resolves the conflict.'[55] In the case of conflict between competing theories the situation is exactly the same. If judgments are true only in relation to a theory, then it is absolutely impossible to decide in any rational way between the competing theories. In effect, there can be no contrast between value-judgments and judgments of facts, as Kelsen contends. In both cases we are left with the free and equal individuals and their choices.

IV.   KELSEN'S CONCEPTION OF LEGAL KNOWLEDGE

Since knowledge must be expressed in propositions or judgments, legal knowledge must be expressed in legal statements or legal judgments. How is this possible? Kelsen's pure theory tries to answer this question, and like Kant, Kelsen endeavours to establish that the study of the phenomenon of law enters on the secure path of a science, which the study of nature already has entered. Science aims at knowledge of phenomena. Natural science aims at knowledge of empirical phenomena as a system of objectively existing regularities between events. Legal science aims at knowledge of legal phenomena as a system of objectively valid norms. 'To know an object and to recognize it as a unity means the same thing', Kelsen says.[56] The normative material, which is the peculiar object of legal science, forms a unity of norms; that is to say to know a norm is equivalent to recognizing it as part of a valid legal order, about which we can all be got to agree.

Law, as presented in section 1, is norm, that is, the meaning of a human act of will by which a certain behaviour is commanded, permitted, or authorized. The norm has the specific meaning of ought, or prescription. Although an act of will is always necessary to introduce norms, the meaning of norm (i.e. ought) cannot be

[55] *ELMP*, 5.   [56] *GTLS*, 410.

identified with, or reduced to, the empirical act of will (is). To do so is, in Kelsen's opinion, to commit the naturalistic fallacy of deriving an ought from an is.[57] A legal norm (a prescription or an ought-sentence) is not 'psychological or sociological sentences, but is what it is, i.e. an objective legal ought, and not another thing, i.e. a subjective wish or will'. Since the meaning of the legal norm, which forms the object of a truly legal science, is unique, it follows that legal science is also a unique, that is, autonomous, science which aims at presenting a neutral account of the legal reality of norms. This is not to deny, as Kelsen insists, that legal science still has very intimate connections with other sciences, such as, sociology, psychology, and history, which also deal with law or legal norms. The subject-matter of these sciences, however, belongs to the realm of is, and can be described and explained by the principle of causality. The subject-matter of legal science belongs to the realm of ought, and can only be described and explained by the principle of imputation. Whereas the judgments offered in the sciences dealing with law as a social phenomenon are judgments to the effect that something is the case; the judgments put forward in legal science, which treats law as a purely legal phenomenon, are judgments to the effect that something ought to be the case. And there is a world of difference between judgments that something is the case, and judgments that something ought to be the case.[58]

However, it is vital to recognize, Kelsen says, that there is a difference between the word 'ought' when used in norms by legal authorities, and when used in statements by legal scientists. The legal authority is in a position to prescribe, i.e. to use 'ought' in a prescriptive way. The legal scientist is not in a similar position. He does not possess authority to issue norms, but his job consists only in describing the norms, which the legal authority introduces. In legal science, then, the word 'ought' is only used in a descriptive way. This is Kelsen's distinction, which he thinks is a very important distinction, between

(1) rule of law (in a descriptive sense), legal rule (in a

---

[57] Cf. *PTL*, 5–6, RR^2, 5—with reference to Moore, *Principia Ethica*, and Prior, *Logic and the Basis of Ethics* (not cited in the English translation). Cf. above p. 276.
[58] *PTL*, 5 f., RR^2, 5; cf. below p. 296.

descriptive sense), juristic value-judgment, objective value-judgment, or statement, and

(2) rule of law (in a prescriptive sense), legal rule (in a prescriptive sense), legal norm, objectively valid norm, anonymous command, or imperative statement.[59]

In group (1), the word 'ought' is used in a descriptive sense, in sentences related to acts of thought expressing a judgment or statement. It is quite otherwise in group (2) where the word 'ought' is used in a prescriptive sense in sentences related to acts of will expressing directions of behaviour. What is expressed by such acts constitutes norms or values. Since the basis for values is human acts of will or real acts of will, the values constituted by them are abritrary and relative values, in contrast to values which are based on acts of will of a 'suprahuman authority—from God or from a nature created by God', which constitute 'absolute' values.[60] Or as Kelsen says,

norms posited by human acts of will possess—in the true meaning of the word—an arbitrary character. Any behaviour we please, that is, can be decreed in them to be obligatory. The assumption that there must be norms which do not spring from 'arbitrary choice' leads to the concept of norms which are not the meaning of human acts of will; of norms in no way the meaning of any kind of 'acts' or thoughts, or, if they *are* the meaning of acts of will, the meaning not of human but of suprahuman volitions, in particular those of God.[61]

Now, Kelsen says that 'the object of a scientific theory of value can only be norms enacted by human will and values constituted by these norms'.[62] Since the values constituted by these norms are relative values, it follows that the object of a scientific theory of value—or the object of legal science, can only be relative values. What must be excluded, then, from the point of view of scientific cognition, is 'absolute value', because 'an absolute value can be assumed only on the basis of religious faith in the absolute and transcendent authority of a deity'.[63] Legal science, as scientific cognition, is expressed in judgments referring to legal norms and

---

[59] Cf. e.g. *GTLS*, 45, *WIJ*, 210, *ELMP*, 246, *PTL*, 71, *RR*², 73. Kelsen sometimes confuses (1) and (2), see e.g. *GTLS*, 30. Cp. below p. 300.

[60] *PTL*, 18, *RR*², 18.

[61] *ELMP*, 218, *WRS* II, 1457–8. Cf. above p. 278.

[62] *PTL*, 18, *RR*², 18; *ELMP*, 277.   [63] *PTL*, 63, *RR*², 65.

claims to give a true account of the prescriptive meaning of ought. Although the judgments are value-judgments, they are objective value-judgments, which do not imply any approval of the described legal norm. The value-judgment uses only the word 'ought' in its descriptive meaning.[64] They are objective value-judgments, because there is an objective method by which the truth or falsity of such judgments can be conclusively established. The method is an objective method, because the judgments correspond to a legal reality of norms as the objective meaning of acts of will, and these acts of will are objectively verifiable facts.

Law, on the other hand, is willing, which results in norms. In this respect Kelsen says, 'the judgment—so-called—pronounced by a judge, is no more a judgment in the logical sense of the word, than the norm he applies. That 'judgement' is instead a norm—an *individual* norm, limited in its validity to a concrete case, as distinguished from a general norm, called a "law".'[65] As norms, they cannot be true or false, but only valid or invalid. In this case there is also a method to establish whether a norm is a valid legal norm, that is, the method of tracing the validity of a norm to—ultimately—the basic norm. Kelsen's notion of the basic norm is fundamental in relation to acts of will, since only if the basic norm is presupposed is it possible for legal authorities to create valid legal norms with objective meaning. But Kelsen's use of the notion is also beset by great difficulties.

For example, Kelsen describes the basic norm as 'the typical case of a fiction in the sense of Vaihinger's *Philosophie des Als-Ob*'.[66] I believe that Kelsen's idea of the basic norm—in relation to acts of thought—can be traced further back to Kant's view of ideas of reason. According to Kant, ideas of reason 'are thought only problematically, in order that upon them (as heuristic fictions), we may base regulative principles of the systematic employment of the understanding in the field of experience'.[67] The function of ideas of reason, according to Kant, is not constitutive of what is the case, but rather regulates our mental operations. The function is regulative and amounts to the demand that our knowledge of

---

[64] Cf. *PTL*, 79, *RR*², 77; *ELMP*, 246.   [65] *PTL*, 19, *RR*², 20.

[66] 1 *Israel Law Rev.* 1, 7 (1966). Kelsen discusses Vaihinger's philosophy in an essay from 1919, 'Zur Theorie der juristischen Fiktionen', reprinted in *WRS* II, 1215 ff.

[67] *CPuR*, A 771; B 799.

what is the case be presented in a systematic form. The idea of reason 'postulates a complete unity in the knowledge obtained by the understanding, by which this knowledge is to be not a mere contingent aggregate, but a system connected according to necessary laws'.[68] Since the idea of reason only performs a regulative function, not a constitutive function, of what there is in the world, it does not provide science with any metaphysical basis. Nor is the idea of reason 'a question of methodology, since a methodology may and should be changed, if it fails to lead to desired results'.[69] What, then, does the idea of reason provide? The answer is that it lays down, as a presupposition, 'the systematic unity of nature as objectively valid and necessary'.[70] It provides the method of looking for an order in nature, 'and though not itself determining anything yet serves to make out the path towards systematic unity' of 'all possible empirical concepts'.[71] Instead of the word 'nature' one only has to substitute the word 'norm' to see that the basic norm provides 'the systematic unity of norms as objectively valid and necessary'. Further, the basic norm, according to Kelsen, does not provide legal science with any metaphysical, that is, absolute, basis. The basic norm is only a hypothetical norm, which provides the method of looking for order in social nature (i.e. norms), and though not itself determining anything yet serves to make out the path towards systematic unity of all possible legal norms. According to Kant, experience cannot establish this systematic unity 'to be necessarily inherent in the objects',[72] but this unity is rather presupposed a priori by the law of reason. In a similar way, Kelsen cannot say that the systematic unity of legal norms is 'necessarily inherent in norms'. The unity of the legal system is due to the basic norm.

Kelsen insists that values are created by acts of will, or posited by actual or real human acts of will. However, considering acts of will it is necessary to distinguish between impersonal acts of will and personal acts of will. The value of legality is related to an act of will, where the 'I will' is the 'I will' in its impersonal or objective sense. This will is the same above all for individuals. It is thus objective and universal. In legal matters, what is expressed by the

---

[68] *CPuR*, A 645; B 673; cf. Walsh, *Kant's Criticism of Metaphysics*, pp. 241 ff.
[69] Walsh, *Kant's Criticism of Metaphysics*, p. 244.
[70] *CPuR*, A 651; B 679.
[71] *CPuR*, A 668; B 696 and A 652; B 680.   [72] *CPuR*, A 651; B 679.

'I will' in this formal aspect is: realize non-contradiction.[73] Whatever act embodies a self-contradiction is illegal, that is, an act where no subjective meaning is present, and hence not capable of any objective meaning. Whatever act is self-consistent is legal, that is, an act where the subjective meaning is present as an objective meaning. Whatever act is self-consistent, and is done for the sake of realizing self-consistency, and for the sake of nothing else, embodies the legal-and-moral-value of legality or order, that is to say conformity and loyalty to norms. This value of legality corresponds to a certain social reality, which is common to all individuals, since legal norms are—by and large—obeyed by individuals, and if not obeyed by them, then applied by legal authorities. This is Kelsen's principle of effectiveness, which states 'an objectively verifiable fact'.[74] These facts constitute the legal materials, which are presented to our thinking to be subsumed under concepts in judgments, if legal knowledge is to result. The judgments about values are value-judgments concerned with the legal value of law as legality, and value-judgments concerned with the moral value of law as justice. Since legality is a formal standard, there is no connection between it and the content which is brought under it by means of the material standard of justice. The formal standard depends upon an impersonal will and expresses the meaning of an objective value, which is valuable for everybody. In contrast to the value of justice which depends upon an individual's subjective will or wish and expresses the meaning of a subjective value, which is valuable for him, but also, it is claimed, for everybody.

Kelsen's claims that legal knowledge is possible, and that this knowledge is expressed in objective value-judgments, must then be restricted to the objective value of legality, because 'the existence of the value of law is objectively verifiable', since it 'is conditioned by objectively verifiable facts'.[75] It follows that 'juristic value-judgments are judgments that can be tested objectively by the help of facts. Therefore they are admissible within a science of law. Judgments of justice cannot be tested objectively. Therefore a science of law has no room for them.'[76] By admitting judgments of legality and excluding judgments of justice within

---

[73] Compare Bradley, *Ethical Studies*, 2nd edn. (Oxford, 1927), Essay IV, especially p. 148.
[74] *WIJ*, 226. [75] *GTLS*, 49. [76] Ibid.

legal science, it seems to me that Kelsen is mistaken. Granted that the object of legal science is norms, which constitute values, it does not follow that the judgments about values are value-judgments, as Kelsen says. Granted that the object of theology is God, it does not follow that judgments about God are God's judgments, they are instead theological statements, i.e. assertions about the existence, nature, and doings of a supernatural personal being. In a similar way there are legal science statements, i.e. assertions of the existence, nature, and doings of natural personal beings, exercising legal functions, e.g. creating norms as standards of behaviour. Then Kelsen's contrast between legality and justice breaks down. Since Kelsen believes that there is a contrast between the value of legality, common to all legal systems and all forms of governments, and the value of justice, which differs from one legal system to another, he is committed to give another account for the objective meaning of human acts. This account pays no attention to psychological or sociological facts in relation to establishing the objective meaning of human acts. Instead it offers a legal definition of the objective meaning of human acts. According to this theory to say that 'a norm is a valid legal norm' is to say that 'the lawgiver so commands'.

The implication of this theory is that it is self-contradictory to say that a norm is a valid legal norm but the lawgiver has not created it. It is self-contradictory to say that this is a valid legal norm, but it ought not to be obeyed, since 'valid' simply means 'ought to be obeyed'. According to this theory, a theoretical jurist, describing the legal norms in statements, claims that though it is true to say of legal norms that they are ordered to be so by the legal authority, and true to say of them that they are right, to say this is not to make two different statements about the legal norms, but to make one and the same statement in two different ways. The theory implies that to say that an action is right (legal, lawful) just means that the legal authority has permitted it, and to say that an action is wrong (illegal, unlawful) just means that the legal authority has prohibited it. The legal authority depends upon the presupposed basic norm. The implication of this is that if one does not accept this presupposition, believing that there is no human legal authority, then one is committed to holding that nothing is legal (right, lawful) and nothing is illegal (wrong, unlawful). One is committed to holding that human acts of will have no objective meaning, for if the basic norm is not presupposed and accepted, then there will be no justification of the legal authority.

Hence the importance of stressing that the basic norm is not an arbitrary invention, but 'really exists in the juristic consciousness',[77] and manifests itself in norms (i.e. an objective ought) posited by acts of will. What is given in this way is the value of legality, which means the maintenance of a positive order—regardless of its contents—by 'conscientious application' of the norms. Legality, Kelsen claims, 'is compatible with and required by any positive legal order, be it capitalistic or communistic, democratic or autocratic'.[78] Since legality is the common and universal element of every legal order, there is room for making objective judgments about this value, in contrast to judgments about the value of justice, which is related to the contents, as opposed to the form, of legal norms. The form of legal norms is ubiquitous regardless of any human interests, the content of legal norms is variable and depends upon conflicting human interests. These conflicts 'cannot be answered on the basis of rational or scientific considerations'.[79] Quite the contrary is the case of the value of legality, questions about which can be answered on the basis of rational and scientific considerations. The basis is the law of non-contradiction, which is a presupposition of all consistent thinking, just as legality is a presupposition of all consistent willing. One cannot prove the law of non-contradiction, since this is the principle, which makes proof possible, but only show the results that one would get by denying it, that is, the denial of 'the difference between belief and knowledge, which implies the denial of any difference between religion and science'.[80] By parity of reasoning one cannot prove the value of legality but only show the results one would get by denying it, that is, anarchy or civil war. If this is so, then the value of legality cannot be, as Kelsen claims, just a relative value. It is an absolute value in the sense that it is common to all value-systems, as Kelsen also acknowledges. But again, if this is so, then Kelsen cannot maintain that he 'recognizes only relative truth and relative values'.[81] Certainly, Kelsen considers his pure theory of law to be true, not only for himself but for everybody concerned with law. And the value of legality is not relative to a particular legal system

---

[77] *GTLS*, 116, cf. *GTLS*, 395.
[78] *GTLS*, 14.   [79] *ELMP*, 6.
[80] *WIJ*, 391.   [81] *WIJ*, 199.

but holds for every legal system. Consequently, Kelsen involves himself in a self-contradiction.

V. KELSEN'S PHILOSOPHY OF JUSTICE

In Kelsen's view the pure theory of law 'leads to a division of labour between a philosophy of law and a science of positive law'.[82] As far as I can see, Kelsen offers two arguments for this division of labour. One argument is that science only deals with objects, which cannot change. Scientific knowledge must be restricted to judgments, which have the characteristics of being necessarily true. A science of positive law must then, to qualify as science, deal with objects, which cannot change, that is, the common structure underlying all positive legal norms. Knowledge of this common structure is expressed in hypothetical judgments, which have the characteristics of being necessarily true. The scientific questions of what is common for every norm, and what is common for every legal system can be 'unambiguously ascertained by an objective method'.[83] In the first place it is the status of objects, which makes the division of labour between legal science and philosophy of law necessary. Legal science is concerned with expressing judgments about norms, and norms relate of necessity to the unity of a legal system, which in turn is a necessary unity of legality. Philosophy of law, on the other hand, is concerned with the internal contents of norms, which need possess no further necessity of their own. 'Justice is primarily a possible but not a necessary property of a social order'.[84] Thus, the problem whether there is an objective criterion for deciding between different judgments of justice is left open. It may be the case that there is such a criterion, but still there are two distinct disciplines. One discipline, that is, legal science, is concerned with knowing and

---

[82] *1 Israel Law Rev.* 1, 4 (1966).

[83] *WIJ*, 229, cf. *GTLS*, 49. In both places Kelsen speaks of the 'contents' of positive law. This is, perhaps, confusing since Kelsen makes a distinction between the form and contents of positive law. Kelsen's pure theory is concerned with the form of positive law, i.e. the common character of the subject-matter of law, which depends upon principles, which are universally applicable and accepted by all jurists, in contrast to the contents of positive law, i.e. what is in fact commanded, permitted, or authorized, which depends upon the principles just mentioned *and* acts of will.

[84] *ELMP*, 1, *WIJ*, 1; cp. Rawls, *A Theory of Justice* (Oxford, 1971), p. 7.

describing its object, another discipline, that is, philosophy of law, is concerned with evaluating its object.

Kelsen's second argument for relegating questions of the justice of legal norms or legal systems to be answered by the philosophy of law is quite different. This argument is based on the method of reasoning used to justify judgments of justice, or value-judgments about the contents of legal norms. Concerning these value-judgments Kelsen claims that 'there is not, and cannot be, an objective criterion of justice, because the statement: something is just or unjust, is a judgment of value referring to an ultimate end, and these value-judgments are by their very nature subjective in character, because based on emotional elements of our mind, on our feelings and wishes. They cannot be verified by facts, as can statements about reality.'[85] Juristic value-judgments about the values of law can be verified by facts, or tested objectively, hence they are admissible within a science of law. Judgments of justice cannot be verified by facts, or tested objectively, hence they are not admissible within a science of law. Kelsen's argument is similar to Kant's argument that 'feeling lies outside our whole faculty of knowledge'.[86] Judgments of justice are, however, admissible within a philosophy of law. Judgments of justice are governed by emotional factors, and thus, Kelsen says 'highly subjective in character'.[87] Hence, Kelsen concludes 'that very different and contradictory value-judgments are possible'.[88] This is Kelsen's 'relativistic philosophy of justice', according to which the Kelsenian claim is that justice is 'a relative value, different according to different value-systems'.[89]

How is Kelsen's claim to be understood? Is it an empirical claim, which means that what different people believe to be just according to their value-system is believed by other people to be unjust in their system of value? If this is so, then it may be characterized as sociological relativism, which may be contrasted with sociological absolutism, that is, the view that there is one ultimate principle of justice underlying all the different value-systems in the world. Kelsen wants to contrast judgments of justice and judgments of legality. The former are subjective judgments, the latter are objective judgments. Concerning judgments of

[85] *WIJ*, 295, cf. *GTLS*, 49, *PTL*, 20, RR^2, 20.
[86] *CPuR*, A 801; B 829.   [87] *ELMP*, 4, *WIJ*, 4.
[88] *ELMP*, 7, *WIJ*, 7.   [89] 1 *Israel Law Rev.* 1, 4.

justice, Kelsen writes, for example, 'in view of the extraordinary diversity of what men have actually held good or bad, just or unjust, at different times and places, it is impossible to establish any element common to the contents of the various moral orders'.[90] This sociological relativism, it is often argued,[91] implies normative ethical relativism, that is, the normative claim that standards of justice are valid only in relation to a value-system which people have adopted as part of their way of life and as basis for their judgments of legal norms as being just or unjust. As a consequence the standard of what is just is identified with what people believe to be just. This contrast to normative ethical relativism is normative ethical absolutism, which makes the normative claim that there is an absolute standard or criterion of justice applicable to all legal norms or all legal systems in the world. A distinction must be maintained, it is held by the absolutist, between the word 'standard' in the sense of what people believe to be just and the word 'standard' in the sense of what is just whether people believe so or not. Normative ethical absolutism is, sometimes, considered to follow from the facts of sociological absolutism, that is to say from the empirical claim that the ultimate principle of justice does not vary from one legal system to another but only the implementation of the ultimate principle into specific rules and standards.

On the basis of these distinctions it is possible to account for Kelsen's different treatment of judgments of legality and judgments of justice. Judgments of legality—as normative judgments—are based on sociological absolutism; judgments of justice—as normative judgments—are based on sociological relativism. This is consistent with Kelsen's claim that the existence of legality can be tested objectively by referring to the facts, the facts being human acts of will, which occur in time and space. Underlying these acts of will is the ultimate principle of order or the principle of harmonizing people's conflicting interests. But in a similar way the existence of justice can be tested objectively by referring to the facts, the facts being again human acts of will occurring in time and space. The difference from legality relates to the fact that justice is concerned with the contents of norms, and there is no common core to the contents of norms. In both cases what is so verified is the acts,

[90] *ELMP*, 88.
[91] See Taylor, *Problems of Moral Philosophy*, Ch. 2, for a critical survey.

which belong to the realm of is, and what these acts express, which
belongs to the realm of ought. What the acts express is people's
beliefs about what is legal and what is just. Now, Kelsen is
adamant that 'the criterion of justice, like that of truth, is certainly
not to be found in the number of factual or value-judgments
expressed'.[92]

Further there is in Kelsen's opinion 'an irremoveable dualism
. . . such . . . that an "ought" cannot be deduced from an "is", nor
an "is" from an "ought", since neither is derivable from the
other'.[93] To be consistent, then, Kelsen cannot support his
normative claims that legality is an objective value and justice is a
relative value by reference to either sociological absolutism in case
of judgments of legality, or sociological relativism in case of
judgments of justice. If this is so, Kelsen must look for support for
his relativistic philosophy of justice elsewhere. The question is,
then, what sort of support? Kelsen's answer is:

if the history of human knowledge can teach us anything at all, it is the
futility of attempting to discover by rational means an absolutely valid
norm of just conduct, i.e., one that excludes the possibility of also
regarding the opposite conduct as just. If we can learn anything at all from
the intellectual experience of the past, it is that human reason can grasp
only relative values, and hence that the judgement in which something is
declared just can never advance any claim to exclude the possibility of an
opposite value-judgement. Absolute justice is an irrational ideal. From
the point of view of rational knowledge, there are only human interests,
and thus conflicts of interest. To solve them, there are only two methods
available: either to satisfy one interest at the expense of the other, or to
engineer a compromise between the two. It is not possible to prove that
one solution alone, and not the other, is just. If social peace is assumed to
be the highest value, the compromise solution may appear to be just. But
even the justness of peace is only a relative, not an absolute, form of
justice.[94]

Thus Kelsen's support for his normative ethical relativism is to
be found in metaethical considerations concerning the scope of
human reason or rational knowledge. Rational knowledge,
according to Kelsen, is only possible if there is an objective and
conclusive method. This method consists of the use of logical

---

[92] *ELMP*, 7–8, *WIJ*, 8.
[93] *ELMP*, 116, *WRS* I, 817; cf. *PTL*, 5 f., RR^2, 5.
[94] *ELMP*, 2, *WIJ*, 21–2.

principles and acceptance of certain self-evident principles; in law it means the acceptance of the basic norm and the principle of imputation. Using this method it is possible to say, as Kelsen says in another context, that judgments about legality 'claim to be true not only in relation to the judging subject, but to everybody, always and everywhere'.[95] Alas this method is not available concerning judgments of justice. These judgments make a similar claim to 'express an objective value. According to their meaning, the object to which they refer is valuable for everybody. They presuppose an objectively valid norm.'[96] However, there is no objectively valid norm to be found. Hence judgments of justice do not have an objective meaning independent of the psychological states of particular speakers. Instead they have only a subjective meaning. A judgment of justice is 'merely the immediate expression of his emotional attitude toward a certain object'.[97] If Kelsen's analysis of the meaning of moral terms, e.g. the word 'justice', is a true analysis, then he is also committed to a naturalistic view concerning judgments of justice. According to a naturalistic view values are one kind of fact; the meaning of moral terms can be completely analysed and defined in non-moral terms, i.e. people's emotional attitudes. It follows that Kelsen's philosophy of justice becomes a branch pf psychology, sociology, or social psychology. The existence of justice is then a fact about the standards actually adopted by an individual, a group, or a society. And then there is, indeed, no basis for denying the existence of justice. However, the existence of justice as a fact is one thing, quite another thing is the existence of justice as a value. Kelsen cannot, if he is consistent, reduce standard, in the sense of what people believe is just, to standard, in the sense of what is just. In other words it is not possible to reduce a philosophy of law to a sociology or psychology of justice. If Kelsen does this, then he commits the very fallacy of asserting that that something ought to be follows from the statement that something is.

I think that Kelsen does contradict himself. If his analysis of the meaning of moral terms is accepted, then philosophy of law is not an autonomous discipline. Kelsen thinks that it is an autonomous discipline, in which case he must reject his own analysis of the meaning of the word 'justice'. If on the other hand Kelsen accepts

---

[95] *WIJ*, 199.   [96] *GTLS*, 49.   [97] *PTL*, 20.

his own analysis of the meaning of the word 'justice', then he can
only say 'what justice is for me' (i.e. Kelsen).[98] What this amounts
to is that Kelsen feels a certain kind of emotion towards a legal
norm. That is all. That Kelsen is in a certain emotional state is a
fact about him. Why does Kelsen take all the trouble to inform
others about his emotional state of mind? Kelsen's answer is 'the
need to justify or rationalize'[99] our value-judgments as an
expression of objective values. The justification of a value-
judgment is, however, relative to the individual, or, to generalize,
the justification is relative to the society or culture in which men
live. So it is possible that the same value-judgment may be justified
by one individual, or in one society, such as the value of human
life, but not justified by another individual, or in another society.
The question of which, if any, of these relative methods of
justification does lead to objective moral knowledge is for Kelsen
logically undecidable. In the end, people's subjective feelings
about what is just or unjust are the only criteria which exist. Thus
Kelsen identifies what people feel or believe is just with what is
just. Kelsen denies that there is an absolute criterion of justice,
which is equally applicable to all men in all societies at all times.
This criterion is necessary, if there is to be any objective
knowledge of justice. Concerning this criterion Kelsen asserts that
'the criterion of justice, like that of truth, is certainly not to be
found in the number of factual or value-judgments expressed'.[1]
Since this condition is not fulfilled one cannot speak of scientific
knowledge of what is just or unjust, or the concept of justice, but
only of (unscientific) knowledge or beliefs of what is just or unjust,
or conceptions of justice. What people believe to be just in their
society is often claimed to be just in all societies. They believe not
only that there is but one true concept of justice for all mankind,
but that the one true concept is their conception of what is just.
And this often leads to intolerance and dogmatism, which Kelsen
most of all repudiates, because it leads to political absolutism,
which 'is synonymous with despotism, dictatorship, autocracy',[2]
which means, in turn, the complete lack of freedom and equality
for the individual member of society. Kelsen's assumption, then, is
that if we believe that there are absolute moral distinctions
between what is just or what is unjust, then we shall become

---

[98] *ELMP*, 24, *WIJ*,. 24.   [99] *ELMP*, 8, *WIJ*, 8.
[1] *ELMP*, 7–8, *WIJ*, 8.   [2] *WIJ*, 201.

dogmatic and authoritarian. In the light of the idea of absolute justice, we shall have reason for an authoritarian and totalitarian state, which uses this ideal in practice.

Against Kelsen's view, it may be objected that he fails to make a distinction between absolutism in the sense that there are moral norms applicable to all mankind (which may be called ethical objectivism) and absolutism in the sense that these moral norms do not admit of any exceptions. The latter version of absolutism is concerned with the contents of moral norms, the claim is that the contents of moral norms are valid 'under all possible circumstances'.[3] Kelsen's view of the objectivity of moral judgments is bound up with the belief in absolute moral norms in the latter sense of absolutism, i.e. that there is only one eternally true moral code, the provisions of which must be applied unvaryingly to all men in all societies at all times. It is this form of absolutism which Kelsen rejects. Kelsen identifies this form of absolutism with the other form of absolutism (i.e. ethical objectivism). Ethical absolutism holds that there are moral norms applicable to all men, but insists on distinguishing between making exceptions to rules on the one hand, and the quite different thing that rules themselves may have certain classes of exceptions. Since Kelsen identifies the two versions of absolutism, and since he rejects absolutism concerning the contents of moral norms, he also rejects absolutism in the sense of ethical objectivism. But this is mistaken.[4] It is logically possible to adopt ethical absolutism (in the sense of objectivism) and reject the moral view of an absolutist, who holds that moral norms do not admit of any exceptions, because he overlooks that circumstances do matter for the moral evaluation of legal norms. Still the basis for this evaluation is a common method for all men, regardless of the society in which they live. What is not logically possible is to adopt ethical absolutism (i.e. ethical objectivism) and also subscribe to the view that moral judgments in the last resort are governed only by emotional factors. The latter view implies, as Kelsen rightly stresses, that there can be no common method by which the evaluations can be established as objective in the same way that the truth of judgments about reality can be established.

[3] *PTL*, 63 f., *RR*², 65 f.
[4] See Bambrough, *Moral Scepticism and Moral Knowledge* (London, 1979), p. 32 f.

The trouble for Kelsen is that he subscribes to what he calls epistemological relativism. According to this doctrine Kelsen 'recognizes only relative truth and relative values'.[5] The consequence is, as far as I can see, that Kelsen is forced to claim that to say that a scientific judgment is true is in the last resort to say that it is accepted by the scientists of our culture, just as to say that a value-judgment is true is in the last resort to say that it is accepted by people of our culture. Thus, Kelsen cannot contrast scientific judgments and value-judgments in the way he actually does. In the end he contradicts himself. Against Kelsen's assumption that the belief in absolute moral rules implies an undemocratic government, whereas the belief in relative moral rules implies a democratic government,[6] Hume's objection applies. Hume's objection is that 'there is no method of reasoning more common, and yet none more blameable, than in philosophical debates to endeavour to refute any hypothesis by a pretext of its dangerous consequences to religion and morality. When any opinion leads us into absurdities, 'tis certainly false; but 'tis not certain an opinion is false, because 'tis of dangerous consequence'.[7] Kelsen's opinion does lead him into absurdities, because Kelsen is guilty of contradicting himself.

VI   KELSEN AS A DISGUISED ABSOLUTIST

By rejecting absolute justice as an irrational ideal in favour of the ideal of relative justice, Kelsen firmly believes that his relativism is of great advantage to solving questions of conflicts amongst contending parties with different interests. Thus, Kelsen's position is very similar to Westermarck's position. 'Could it be brought home to people', Westermarck writes, 'that there is no absolute standard in morality, they would perhaps be on the one hand more tolerant, and on the other hand more critical in their judgments'.[8] Kelsen also believes that his relativistic philosophy of justice implies the principle of tolerance. Kelsen asks the question: 'What

---

[5] *WIJ*, 199; cf. above p. 281.
[6] *GTLS*, 396, *ELMP*, 38; see note 43.
[7] Hume, *A Treatise on Human Nature*, Book II, Part III, Section II.
[8] Westermarck, *Ethical Relativity* (London, 1932), p. 59, cited Taylor, *Problems of Moral Philosophy*, p. 64; cf., for a similar view, Hägerström, *Philosophy and Religion*, 94 f.

is the morality of this relativistic philosophy of justice?'[9] His answer is that his relativistic philosophy of justice has a morality.

The moral principle underlying a relativistic theory of value, or deducible from it, is the principle of tolerance, the demand, that is, that the religious or political outlook of others should be understood in a spirit of goodwill, even if one does not share it, and indeed precisely because one does not; and hence that peaceful expression of such views should not be prevented.[10]

But Kelsen thinks that there is no rational method by which moral principles can be established as valid for everyone. If, as Kelsen claims, the principle of tolerance is the valid moral principle for a relativist, it follows that this principle cannot be valid for everyone. Kelsen accepts this, when he continues to write: 'It will be self-evident that a relativistic world-outlook engenders no right to absolute tolerance; it enjoins tolerance only within a framework of a positive legal order.'[11] But in saying this, Kelsen contradicts himself, because he then implicitly holds that the principle of tolerance has a status of greater validity than the opposite principle of intolerance. According to Kelsen's own teaching the value of the principle of tolerance is as justified as that of the principle of intolerance. To quote a remark from Kelsen, 'the question, which of these two values is the higher, cannot be answered on the basis of rational or scientific considerations'.[12] However, it is quite clear that Kelsen believes that the value of the principle of tolerance is securely founded on the methods of science. Kelsen cannot consistently say this, so he contradicts himself.

Further to say, as Kelsen does, that the principle of tolerance is 'self-evident' means, as Kelsen says in another context, that 'it is immanent in, or emanates from, reason. The concept of a directly evident norm presupposes the concept of a practical reason, that is, a norm creating reason; but this concept is untenable, as will be shown, because the function of reason is knowing and not willing, whereas the creation of norms is an act of will.'[13] Thus Kelsen's position is untenable, because he himself believes that his act of will is an act of reason. Kelsen tells us on the one hand that 'there

---

[9] *ELMP*, 22, *WIJ*, 22.   [10] *ELMP*, 23, *WIJ*, 22.
[11] *ELMP*, 23, *WIJ*, 22.
[12] *ELMP*. 6, where Kelsen deals with the values of humanity and truth.
[13] *PTL*, 196, *RR*[2], 198.

can be no such things as norms which are valid only in virtue of
their directly evident content',[14] on the other hand there is such a
thing as the principle of tolerance, which is valid only in virtue of
its directly evident content. 'It is precisely such tolerance which
distinguishes democracy from autocracy.'[15] If Kelsen is consistent
he can only say that since no moral principle is more valid than any
other principle, then let each of us advance his own principle. And
in a similar way concerning the question of the structure of
government Kelsen can only say that there are not two conflicting
views, but rather two equally valid views, democracy and
autocracy. But Kelsen is not consistent, because tolerance is to be
preferred to intolerance and democracy to be preferred to
autocracy. The preference cannot, if Kelsen's view is correct, be
based on any rational grounds, but depends upon our feelings.
Then a possible conflict between equally valid opinions about what
is a just form of institutional structure cannot be settled by
arguments or peaceful means, but 'every régime, including a
democratic one, has the right to put down by force and to prevent
by suitable means attempts to overthrow it by force'.[16] The basis
for this right is a presupposed norm, which in turn is based on a
belief in absolute values, that is, 'It is the justice of freedom, the
justice of peace, the justice of democracy, the justice of tolerance.'[17]

At the end of the day, Kelsen claims to have the right to impose
his opinion as well as his will upon the others, who are in error. In
reality, Kelsen's principle of tolerance only encompasses those
individuals who happen to agree with him. Those who do not
agree with him are not to be considered as proper residents of the
legal realm. Since they are in error, it is justifiable to correct their
mistaken views and enforce the correct view, if necessary by force.
If this is correct then Kelsen turns out to be a disguised absolutist,
because there is, after all, an absolute standard of justice. To be
sure, Kelsen tells us that he rejects absolute justice because based
on religious beliefs to adopt justice relative to a value system,
which must be based on common beliefs. Kelsen then maintains
that the question whether a valid legal norm is a just legal norm is

---

[14] Ibid.   [15] *ELMP*, 23, *WIJ*, 23.
[16] *ELMP*, 23, *WIJ*, 23; cf. the argument in Raz, *The Authority of Law*, p. 127 f,
that certain ways of peacefully granting independence to new states would become
impossible if one accepted Kelsen's doctrine that all laws belonging to one chain of
validity are part of one and the same legal system.
[17] *ELMP*, 24, *WIJ*, 24.

a legitimate question. To answer this question properly Kelsen assumes that there must be one, and only one, absolute standard of justice to which all valid legal norms must conform. Since the value system, which Kelsen adopts, is based on scientific facts Kelsen concludes that what he believes to be a valid system for him is the valid system not only for him but for all individuals, at least if they are rational. It is but a short step from this position to dogmatism and 'juristic imperialism', when 'the own state of the interpreter becomes the sole and absolute legal authority, the god in the world of law'.[18] This is Kelsen's own description of the absolutist position. The description fits Kelsen's own position. If this is correct, it must be rejected. To be sure Kelsen is a great legal philosopher, but he is not to be considered as 'the god in the world of law'.[19]

[18] *WIJ*, 203.

[19] I wish to thank the secretary of the Department of Jurisprudence, University of Aarhas, Miss Jytte Mønster, for deciphering and typing my manuscript, and Professor D. N. MacCormick of the University of Edinburgh, for reading it and correcting my linguistic errors.

CHAPTER 13

KELSEN ON JUSTICE: A CHARITABLE READING

PHILIP PETTIT

IN his paper on 'Kelsen's Theory of Law and Philosophy of Justice' Jes Bjarup brings three interesting and important objections against the so-called relativist theory of justice, and of ethical values generally, which Kelsen defended. The objections in question, and they are not the only ones raised in Bjarup's presentation[1], are all allegations of inconsistency. The first says that Kelsen's ethical relativism is inconsistent with the overall epistemological relativism that he upheld; the second that it is inconsistent with his theory of the basic norm; and the third that it is inconsistent with his proclamation of tolerance as the supreme political virtue.

So far as I understand it I am not myself much in sympathy with Kelsen's theory of law: neither with the view that legal phenomena are in a certain sense trans-empirical, nor, paradoxical though the joint reservation may seem, with the view that their identification does not call into play one's personal evaluative beliefs.[2] Surprisingly however I find that I want to come to Kelsen's defence in respect of the three objections mentioned. I am no Kelsen scholar but my inclination is to think that Bjarup may have been less than charitable in so construing Kelsen's claims that they involve the inconsistencies mentioned. My paper will be an exercise in speculative rather than scholarly interpretation. What I shall try to

---

[1] Other objections include: the allegation, based on a suspect ascription of ethical emotivism, that Kelsen cannot regard the philosophy of justice as an autonomous discipline (Bjarup 278–9); and the contention, related to the third objection considered in the text, that utimately Kelsen invokes its allegedly dangerous consequences, a factor which ought to be irrelevant, in arguing against ethical objectivism (Bjarup above, p. 300).

[2] The paradoxical appearance of this dual denial should be dissolved by the discussion in Macdonald and Pettit, *Semantics and Social Science* (London, 1981), Ch. 4.

establish is that it is possible to understand Kelsen's claims in such a way that the inconsistencies do not arise; whether it is plausible to do so I leave to the scholars to decide.

This account of what I shall attempt is the only professionally respectable one, since my knowledge of Kelsen's work is limited. I may admit in parenthesis however that the account is a little disingenuous. The fact is that I do, in an unscholarly way, have my own views about what Kelsen actually meant to claim and in putting forward my charitable interpretations I cannot see myself just as involved in abstract conjecture. For the record, I believe that the construals which would undermine the first two objections are highly plausible but that the reading which would disarm the third involves recasting Kelsen's views in the light of a distinction which probably never struck him. In what follows I shall pander to my prejudices about what Kelsen actually meant by occasionally quoting from certain articles of his, all but one of them collected under the title *What is Justice*? I hope that such self-indulgence may be forgiven and that it will not turn attention from the main, speculative thrust of the paper.

Jes Bjarup's first objection to Kelsen is nicely summarized in the following passage.

The trouble for Kelsen is that he subscribes to what he calls epistemological relativism. According to this doctrine Kelsen 'recognizes only relative truth and relative values'. The consequence is, as far as I can see, that Kelsen is forced to claim that to say that a scientific judgment is true is in the last resort to say that it is accepted by the scientists of our culture, just as to say that a value-judgment is true is in the last resort to say that it is accepted by people of our culture. Thus, Kelsen cannot contrast scientific judgments and value-judgments in the way he actually does. In the end he contradicts himself.[3]

When someone simultaneously proclaims epistemological and ethical relativism it is uncharitable, to say the least, to assume that relativism is understood in the same sense within the two proclamations. If it is understood in the same sense then of course the epistemological doctrine will undercut the ethical. The only point in ethical relativism is to draw a certain contrast in respect of relativity between ethical and non-ethical judgments. If all judgments are equally relative, and all are relative only in the

---

[3] Bjarup, 300; cf. 281–2 and 284.

sense in which they are equally so, then it is indeed the case that there is no contrast for ethical relativism to draw.

Relativism may mean many things, depending on what the judgments of which it is asserted are relativized to. Epistemological relativism will not undercut ethical relativism if that to which the epistemological doctrine says that all judgments are relative differs in a certain way from that to which the ethical doctrine says that ethical judgments are specifically so. One might be an. epistemological relativist in thinking that cognition is always species relative, that truth is always truth-for-man: this in the sense that one finds no substance in the thought that at most one can be true of a number of competing theories between which no humanly available evidence can decide. Being such a species relativist about epistemological matters generally, one could still think that ethical judgments were distinctively relative, being relativized not just to the species but to the individual subject or to the members of the individual culture. Holding this one would assert at least the following: that there is no substance in the thought that at most one can be true of a number of conflicting ethical judgments which are defended by different people or cultures.[4]

I propose that in all charity we should ask whether Kelsen's relativist doctrines do not bear the relationship described before we endorse Bjarup's charge of inconsistency. I conjecture that Kelsen may well have held a pair of doctrines such as those characterized and not the self-defeating combination implicitly ascribed by Bjarup. I now put that conjecture to the scholars for their adjudication, the judgment required being beyond any competence that I can claim.

Pandering to my interpretative prejudices however, I may be allowed to record my hunch that Kelsen did in fact maintain a pair of relativist doctrines of the kind of question. I would like to quote two passages in support of my hunch, both from papers published in 1948. The first is this.

Freedom of the knowing subject is a fundamental prerequisite of the relativistic theory of knowledge . . . The subject is not absolutely free in the process of cognition. There are laws governing this process in which the chaos of sensual perceptions is transformed into a meaningful kosmos.

---

[4] There are great difficulties in persuasively, and even coherently, formulating relativist doctrines, epistemological or ethical. These I presume to ignore.

In complying with these laws, rational cognition of reality—in contra-distinction to evaluation based on subjective emotions—has an objective character.[5]

Here Kelsen explicitly says that the freedom of the knowing subject which he thinks that epistemological relativism involves is not so absolute that the distinctive relativity of ethical judgments is lost. The point is made even more forcefully in the second passage.

Even if we accept a philosophy of radical subjectivism and admit that the universe exists only in the mind of man, we must nevertheless maintain the difference which exists between value judgments and statements about reality. The difference may be relative only as a difference between degrees of subjectivity ('objective' meaning the lowest possible degree of subjectivity).[6]

If my hunch is right and relativism means different things to Kelsen, depending on whether epistemological or ethical matters are in question, it is natural to wonder how Bjarup could have come to misinterpret him: and this, despite the fact of showing an awareness of the sources from which I have quoted. I suggest that the reason Bjarup goes wrong is that he has a conception of relativism whereby it always relativizes judgments to the individual subject and never merely to the species. Of all forms of epistemological relativism that associated with Kant would seem most obviously not to allow the individual subject cognitive freedom and yet Bjarup writes as follows. 'Kelsen thinks that the Kantian view implies epistemological relativism. Epistemological relativism is the doctrine that the individual's beliefs and statements are relative to his freely chosen perspective or conceptual framework.'[7] The epistemological perspective to which Kant and Kelsen relativize judgments is anything but freely chosen.

Bjarup's second charge of inconsistency concludes, [c]onsequently, Kelsen involves himself in a self-contradiction.'[8] The argument on which the conclusion is based is presented in a long and complex discussion of Kelsen on the basic norm and it will be necessary here to consider it in a reconstructed form. I am not convinced that the reconstruction is absolutely faithful to the line of Bjarup's thinking but I hope that it may in any case be of some interest in its own right.

---

[5] *WIJ*, 200; cf. 201.   [6] *WIJ*, 296.
[7] Bjarup, 284.   [8] Bjarup, 293.

The reconstructed argument moves in three stages to its conclusion.

(1) 'The legal authority depends upon the presupposed basic norm. The implication of this is that if one does not accept this presupposition, believing that there is no human legal authority, then one is committed to holding that nothing is legal (right, lawful) and nothing is illegal (wrong, unlawful).'[9]

(2) Making the presupposition of the basic norm goes hand in hand with proclaiming the value of legality, i.e. the value of having some recognized legal norms: notice that this is different from legality in the sense of the value belonging to each of the recognized legal norms, although the distinction is not clearly drawn by Bjarup. 'What is given in this way is the value of legality, which means the maintenance of a positive order—regardless of its contents—by "conscientious application" of the norms.'[10]

(3) The legality in question is proclaimed, moreover, as a non-relative or absolute value. 'It is an absolute value in the sense that it is common to all value-systems. . .'[11]

(4) Thus in making the presupposition of the basic norm Kelsen proclaims a certain absolute value and takes up a stance inconsistent with his ethical relativism.

Presented with such an argument my speculative response, tutored by whatever charity I possess, is to ask whether Kelsen does really presuppose the basic norm in the sense in which this would force him, assuming the truth of (1), (2), and (3), to proclaim the absolute value of legality. It is charitable to open up this possibility, not just because it would save Kelsen from contradicting his ethical relativism but also because it would prevent him from denying his much more loudly protested positivism. If Kelsen is said to presuppose the basic norm in a given legal order which he is studying as a legal scientist, and if that presupposition is tied to the recognition of a value, whether or not an absolute value, then legal science is not value-free as positivism would have it.

Presented just with the material given in (1) to (4), how might we most charitably construe Kelsen's claims? The most obvious possibility would be to suggest that for Kelsen it may not be the

[9] Bjarup, 291.   [10] Bjarup, 292.   [11] Bjarup, 292.

legal scientist studying a given order, but the legal agents within that order, who are said to presuppose the basic norm. This slight shift of interpretation would save both Kelsen's ethical relativism and his legal positivism. If the legal scientist does not have to make the presupposition of the basic norm himself, if his only job is to record that presupposition on the part of the agents he is studying, then *qua* legal scientist Kelsen will not be forced into the damaging proclamation of the value of legality.[12]

I believe that the suggested interpretation of Kelsen actually fits but before showing something of the sources of that prejudice I would like to mention in passing a possibility which I shall not further examine. The legality which Bjarup says is tied up with the presupposition of the basic norm is the value of having some recognized legal norms. This is a substantive social value and might be referred to as the value of orderliness. The possibility which I would just like to open is that Kelsen may not regard the presupposition of the basic norm as being tied up with the recognition of such a value but rather as being connected with the countenancing of a very much less substantial value that also goes under the name of legality. This is the value, mentioned in the presentation of (2) above, which each norm that is recognized in a legal system has: the value, as we might call it, of orderedness. Unlike orderliness, orderedness does not have any content independently of the systems with which it is associated and if this is all that the presupposition of the basic norm involved one in recognizing, then it would not matter for Kelsen even if the presupposition had to be made by the legal scientist.

To return to my suggestion that it is legal agents, not legal scientists, who presuppose the basic norm, I would like to quote two passages from Kelsen. The first is from an article of 1942.

The norm which confers validity upon a constitution may be a previous constitution in accordance with the provisions of which the new

---

[12] By (3), of course, he will have to admit that legal agents universally acknowledge the value of legality. That is something which he is free to do however, while himself denying the objective, and in that sense non-relative, nature of the value. He writes against an opponent: 'the fact that many individuals utter the identical value judgment cannot change the character of the judgment. Mr. Bergman confuses the objectivity of a judgment with the frequency of the act of judgment' (*WIJ*, 391). It must be admitted on the other hand that one of the grounds for Kelsen's ethical relativism is the belief in the variety of ethical opinion and this ground is somewhat compromised by (3). See Bjarup 294–5.

constitution was established. In such a series of constitutions one must historically be first. And the norm giving the 'fathers' of this first constitution their authority, that is, a norm according to which one ought to behave in conformity with their decisions, cannot itself be a positive legal norm created by any legislative act. It is a norm presupposed by those who consider the establishment of the first constitution and the acts performed in conformity with it as law-creating acts. The science of law reveals this presupposition by an analysis of juristic thinking.[13]

The important point in this passage is that the science of law is said to reveal the presupposition of the basic norm rather than to make the presupposition itself. The point is echoed sharply in an article published many years later, in 1966.

A legal order is not an aggregate of legal norms coordinated on the same level, but a hierarchy of norms on the top of which stands the basic norm. As a norm the basic norm must be the meaning of an act of will. Hence it is not the science of law which presupposes the basic norm. The science of law, which is a function of cognition not of will, only ascertains the fact: that if men consider a coercive order established by acts of will of human beings and by and large effective as an objectively valid order, they, in their juristic thinking, presuppose the basic norm as the meaning of an act of will.[14]

The third objection which Bjarup brings against Kelsen is that his ethical relativism is inconsistent with his proclamation of the value of tolerance. The charge of inconsistency is particularly sharp because Kelsen claims that it is the relativist nature of ethical values which forces on one the recognition that tolerance is a virtue. In a quotation given by Bjarup, he writes as follows.

The moral principle underlying a relativistic theory of value, or deducible from it, is the principle of tolerance, the demand, that is, that the religious or political outlook of others should be understood in a spirit of goodwill, even if one does not share it, and indeed precisely because one does not; and hence that peaceful expression of such views should not be prevented.[15]

In maintaining the view summarized here, Bjarup says that Kelsen is guilty of the most blatant self-contradiction.

---

[13] *WIJ*, 221.
[14] 'On the Pure Theory of Law', 1 *Israel Law Rev.* 1, 6 (1966). I am grateful to Jes Bjarup for drawing this article to my attention.
[15] Quoted by Bjarup, 301. See *WIJ*, 28.

According to Kelsen's own teaching the value of the principle of tolerance is as justified as that of the principle of intolerance. . . . However, it is quite clear that Kelsen believes that the value of the principle of tolerance is securely founded on the methods of science. Kelsen cannot consistently say this, so he contradicts himself.[16]

Taken in any strict sense I am inclined to agree with Bjarup that Kelsen's claims involve him in an inconsistency. If ethical values are all subject-relative, this means that there is no substance in the thought that at most one can be true of a number of conflicting ethical judgments which are defended by different people. Kelsen must be aware that where he asserts the value of tolerance, others will wish to deny it, and his ethical relativism ought therefore to inhibit him from presenting tolerance as a universally binding value: as a value which the objective truth of the relativist doctrine forces one to countenance.

In a passage quoted by Bjarup, Kelsen tries to make out that tolerance is defended by him only as a relative value but his comment is a manifest fudge. 'It will be self-evident', he says, 'that a relativistic world-outlook engenders no right to absolute tolerance; it enjoins tolerance only within a framework of a positive legal order.'[17] The fudge comes in the fact that the relativity here acknowledged in the value of tolerance has nothing to do with the damaging sort of relativity to which ethical relativism would commit one. All that relativity is allowed to mean within the remark is something quite innocuous; it is taken to consist in the fact that tolerance is always interpreted within the framework of a positive legal order, an order which presumably sets out the respects in which tolerance is and is not due. Pushing interpretation further, what may also be suggested is that tolerance always has to be balanced against other values which may occasionally outweigh it. In any case however the relativity granted is very different from the relativity to which Kelsen is committed.

In the remainder of this paper what I would like to do is raise the question whether we can envisage any modification of Kelsen's claims whereby he might be enabled to evade Bjarup's third charge of inconsistency. Is there any amendment imaginable whereby it would become possible for Kelsen at once to deny that there are universal ethical standards and to recommend the denial

[16] Bjarup, 301.   [17] Quoted by Bjarup, 301. See *WIJ*, 22–3.

for the tolerance it encourages? I believe that such an amendment is conceivable and that it is philosophically worthwhile exploring the possibility.

As we have already mentioned, to be an ethical relativist is to hold that there is no substance in the thought that at most one can be true of a number of conflicting ethical judgments which are defended by different people. The point on which my proposed amendment turns is that it is possible to distinguish between two different sorts of ethical judgments, two different statements of value. The one sort I describe as evaluations, the other as prescriptions.[18] The difference between the two classes of value statement is that whereas prescriptions present the courses of action on which they bear as, all things considered, what must be done or avoided, evaluations depict the corresponding projects only as prima facie desirable or undesirable. The prescription depicts a particular action, or any action of a certain class, as good or bad *simpliciter*, the evaluation pictures it as good or bad *secundum quid*, good or bad in a certain respect.[19]

Whether a value statement is an evaluation or a prescription is sometimes, but not always, clear from its linguistic form. Statements which employ concepts such as 'is kind', 'is generous', 'is fun', are reasonably taken as always just evaluations: they specify a respect in which an action is desirable or undesirable without suggesting that the action is so *simpliciter*. On the other hand statements which say that an action represents the best course possible, that it is absolutely obligatory, or that it must be done, certainly have the force of prescriptions: the comment they make on the action is not relative to a particular respect but is taken to carry under any description of the behaviour. However between these two clearcut classes we find value ascriptions which do not show in their linguistic form whether they are evaluations or prescriptions. These are statements which use such evaluative notions as 'good'

[18] The distinction is discussed in my paper 'Evaluative "Realism" and Interpretation', in Holtzman and Leitch, eds., *Wittgenstein: To Follow a Rule* (London, 1981).
[19] The difference between judgments of value *simpliciter* and judgments of value *secundum quid* is discussed in Davidson, 'Intending' in Yovel, ed., *Philosophy of History and Action* (Dordrecht, 1978). Wiggins in 'Truth, Invention and the Meaning of Life', 62 *Proceedings of the British Academy* 331 (1976) draws a distinction similar to that drawn here between evaluations and prescriptions. Notice that it is often unclear whether 'moral' realism is meant to be evaluative or prescriptive realism.

and 'bad', 'right' and 'wrong', 'ought' and 'ought not', and so on. The trouble with them is that it is not clear just from the words used whether what is characterized in one of these terms is said to be unconditionally desirable or undesirable, or desirable or undesirable only in a certain respect. 'Good' may mean 'good absolutely' or only 'good as such', and so on for the other terms.[20]

There are two useful tests for deciding whether an ambiguous value ascription is a prescription or an evaluation. The first has to do with the connection between the ascription and action. With a prescription the failure of an agent to act in accordance with it counts as powerful evidence against his having endorsed the judgment in the first place. Even if he publicly claimed to endorse the judgment, his behavioural failure will give us reason to think that he was insincere or self-deceived; if it does not lead us to that conclusion, this will be because we accept some special explanation of the failure in terms of weakness of the will or psychological incapacity. With an evaluation on the other hand it is more or less unsurprising that an agent who accepts it should still fail to act accordingly. Since the evaluation bears on an action only under a particular aspect, we can understand why it should fail to move the agent: we naturally take it that other aspects of the action engaged contrary evaluations in the agent and that these prevailed over the original one in question.

The second test for whether an ambiguous value statement is a prescription or an evaluation has to do with the effect of what we may call internal negation: this involves putting a 'not' before a value predicate such as 'good' or after a value expression such as 'ought', as distinct from negating the statement as a whole, say by the use of a prefix such as 'It is not the case that . . .' To negate a proposition as a whole is always to produce a statement which is inconsistent with it, assuming that the meaning of the terms within the proposition remains the same. The difference in the effect of internal negation on prescriptive and evaluative statements using ambiguous value concepts is that in the first case it produces an incompatible statement, in the second it does not. The reason for

---

[20] This point is well made in Graham, 'Moral Notions and Moral Misconceptions', *Analysis* 65 (1975); he distinguishes between an action's being generally right or wrong and its being right or wrong decisively. Evaluations which use ambiguous notions may be regarded as surrogates for evaluations in which the operative respect is spelled out. Thus the later discussions in this paper are carried on as if there were only evaluations of the latter sort.

the difference is that if the prescription says that an action is good *simpliciter* then a statement which says that it is not good *simpliciter* is bound to be incompatible with the original, whereas if the evaluation says that it is good *secundum quid*, i.e. in a certain respect, then a statement which says that it is not good *secundum quid* need not conflict with the first claim, the respect in which it is said not to be good being a different one. Thus it cannot be at once that I must take a certain line of action and that I must not take it, while it may be that one and the same project can be said to be good and not good, something that I ought to do and something I ought not to do.[21]

If we grant the distinction between evaluations and prescriptions, the question arises whether Kelsen means to be an ethical relativist in respect of just one sort or of both. Since he did not draw the distinction at issue, at least not to my knowledge, we must say both. However what I would now like to point out is that were we to amend his position slightly and cast him as a relativist only in respect of prescriptions, then it would not necessarily be vulnerable to Bjarup's third charge of inconsistency.

One might hold that while evaluations deserve to be seen in a non-relativist light, prescriptions do not. This would be to say that, subject perhaps to a general epistemological relativism, at most one of any number of conflicting evaluations is true, whereas this is not always the case with prescriptions: at least some sets of conflicting prescriptions, which are upheld by different people or cultures, do not allow us to say that at most one member is true. Such a mixture of evaluative non-relativism and prescriptive relativism would not be outlandish, since evaluations provide the grounds on which prescriptions are formulated and the *entrée* for prescriptive relativism might be that in some cases, such as moral dilemmas, the grounds are so ambivalent that no single prescription is indicated as the true one. Were we now to cast Kelsen as an evaluative non-relativist and a prescriptive relativist, we could take his claim about tolerance to be this: that being a relativist about prescriptions, the evaluation of attitudes and actions as tolerant becomes a salient and weighty one, an evaluation which

[21] On the two ways of negating judgments of value see Williams, 'Consistency and Realism' and 'Ethical Consistency', reprinted in *Problems of the Self* (Cambridge, 1973). Wiggins in 'Truth, Invention and the Meaning of Life', p. 367 points out that 'must' and 'must not' are incompatible, being contraries.

one is naturally led to take seriously in the determination of one's own conduct. Such a claim would not involve any inconsistency and would enable Kelsen to evade Bjarup's third objection.

Finally, indulging my interpretative prejudices in regard to Kelsen, I would like to suggest that the mixed doctrine just described may be more faithful to the spirit of his thought than the comprehensive relativism that would undermine his proclamation of the value of tolerance. There are three grounds on which I make the suggestion: the first bears on his analysis of ethical judgments, the second on his conception of what they enjoin and the third on one of his methods of arguing for ethical relativism.

Jes Bjarup ascribes to Kelsen an emotivist analysis of ethical judgments, according to which each such judgment amounts to the expression of a feeling and has no more cognitive significance than banging on the table.[22] This is not the analysis which is defended by Kelsen in the writings with which I am familiar. Rather, what he maintains in those writings is that the ethical judgment, like the normative legal judgment, asserts a relation between the object valued and a norm: a norm which is the meaning of an act of will and which is expressed by use of an 'ought' sentence.

The statement that a legal institution, for instance slavery or private property, is just or unjust, does not mean that somebody has an interest in this institution or in its opposite. The interest theory does not give a correct analysis of what a statement of this sort intends to express. Such a statement means that the institution in question corresponds or does not correspond to a norm whose validity is presupposed by the person making the statement.[23]

According to Kelsen the difference between the normative legal judgment and the ethical one comes from the fact that there are no universally valid ethical norms, in particular no norms of justice. 'The norms which are actually used as standards of justice vary from individual to individual and are often mutually irreconcilable.'[24] And what is it that makes the difference between ethical norms and legal ones? Simply the fact that agreement is attainable in respect of the latter, but not in respect of the former.

---

[22] Bjarup, 297.
[23] *WIJ*, 228. The quotation is from a paper of 1942. If Kelsen seems to go for an interest theory in remarks from a piece of 1948 (*WIJ*, 295) this impression will be revised in the light of comments from 1951 (*WIJ*, 353).
[24] *WIJ*, 228.

To the norms of positive law there corresponds a certain social reality, but not so to the norms of justice. In this sense the value of law is objective, while the value of justice is subjective. And this holds true even though sometimes a great number of people have the same ideal of justice . . . Juristic value judgments are judgments that can be tested objectively by facts . . . Judgments of justice cannot be tested objectively.[25]

From our point of view the important thing about Kelsen's analysis of ethical judgments is that it suggests that what he is thinking of in the main are prescriptions. This is not incompatible with his citing judgments of justice as examples for while justice may appear to be merely one aspect making for the desirability of a social arrangement, it may also be taken to refer us to the unconditional desirability of the matter in question. The reason that Kelsen's analysis seems to bear on prescriptions rather than evaluations is that it has all ethical judgments invoke norms and norms have an unconditionally prescriptive force. 'A rule prescribing or forbidding a certain behaviour, we call "norm"'.[26] It is hard to see how Kelsen could have been thinking of mere evaluations when he put forward the analysis in question.

A second reason why Kelsen may be taken to have regarded only prescriptions as ethical judgments proper, in particular as judgments subject to his relativistic strictures, is mentioned by Jes Bjarup. This is that, as Bjarup points out, Kelsen took ethical judgments to be meant as exceptionless injunctions to behave or not to behave in a certain way.[27] Only if he was thinking exclusively of prescriptions could he have taken them in this way. No one could characterize an evaluation as exceptionless in what it recommends.

The third and last reason for taking Kelsen to have reduced ethical judgments to prescriptions is provided by the nature of one of his favourite arguments in defence of ethical relativism. This argument is that ethical judgments are often made on the basis of conflicting values and they cannot be assigned truth in a non-relative sense because such value-conflicts may be irresolvable. The argument clearly does not apply to evaluations and it strongly suggests that for Kelsen it was only prescriptions which were held to be relative.

Ultimate value judgments are mostly acts of preference; they indicate

---

[25] *WIJ*, 229.   [26] *WIJ*, 210.   [27] Bjarup, 299.

what is better rather than what is good; they imply the choice between two conflicting values, as for instance the choice between freedom and security . . . There are individuals who prefer freedom to security because they feel happy only if they are free, and hence prefer a social system and consider it just only if it guarantees individual freedom. But others prefer security because they feel happy only if they are economically secure, and hence consider a social system just only if it guarantees economic security. Their judgments about the value of freedom and security and hence their idea of justice are ultimately based on nothing but their feelings. No objective verification of their respective value judgments is possible.[28]

This must bring our ruminations to a close. I hope to have shown in the preceding that Kelsen may be read somewhat more charitably than Bjarup reads him and that a charitable construal of his position may render it proof against Bjarup's complaints about inconsistency. I would like to emphasize in conclusion that although I have been at pains to defend Kelsen's point of view I am not particularly sympathetic to what he has to say. It need not be surprising that I have taken his part, for my avowed motive was charity and charity is not a virtue which one reserves for one's friends.

[28] *WIJ*, 296. The values mentioned in the second last sentence I take to be the relative values of freedom and security.

PART SIX

INTERNATIONAL LAW

CHAPTER 14

HANS KELSEN AND INTERNATIONAL LAW

HEDLEY BULL

HANS Kelsen is the only one of the major figures of modern analytical jurisprudence to have had a great deal to say about international law. Neither Hobbes (although he is the principal author of the modern International Relationist's scepticism about international law) nor Bentham (who is commonly credited with having invented the term international law) nor Austin (notwithstanding his famous view that international law is not law properly so-called) nor Hart (who has put forward some suggestive ideas about international law) expresses himself at length on the subject. Kelsen, however, apart from the sections dealing with international law in the *Allgemeine Rechtslehre* of 1925, the *Reine Rechtslehre* of 1960, and other general works, left us *Das Problem der Souveränität und die Theorie des Völkerrechts*, 1928; *The Legal Process in International Order*, 1935, to me his most interesting work; *Legal Techniques in International Law*, 1939, a book on revision of the League Covenant; *Law and Peace in International Relations*, 1942, his Oliver Wendell Holmes lectures at Harvard; *Peace through Law*, 1944, advocating a new League of Nations based on compulsory jurisdiction and individual responsibility; *The Law of the United Nations*, 1950, followed by a supplement taking account of the 'Uniting for Peace' Resolution and other developments arising out of the Korean War, *Recent Trends in the Law of the United Nations*, 1951; and finally his summa, *Principles of International Law*, 1952.

It is sometimes said that Kelsen's main concepts were already contained in the *Hauptprobleme der Staatsrechtslehre* of 1911. His thinking about international relations, however, is essentially the product of the 1930s and 1940s, the era of the collapse of hopes for the League and of high hopes for the United Nations, at least on the part of international lawyers in Western countries. It embodies

the assumptions and shares the limitations of much of the work
done in that period. I propose to comment on five major themes
with which Kelsen seeks to deal: the question whether or not
international law is truly law; the relationship between force and
international law; positivism in international law; change in
international law; and the relationship of international law to
power politics.

I   THE CLAIMS OF INTERNATIONAL LAW TO BE LAW

The question whether or not international law is truly law,
infuriating as it is to professional international lawyers, is one that
is still worth asking, and to which the answer is by no means clear.
There are, indeed, strong practical grounds for dismissing the
sceptical view out of hand. To doubt the genuinely legal character
of what is called international law is to weaken its force and to
circumscribe the role it may play in international relations. There
is in fact a profession of legal specialists who advise governments,
pronounce judgments in courts of law, and write textbooks about
the rules of international law, whether it is properly so-called or
not, and to this extent the question seems an idle one. But the
theoretical issue remains. The view ordinary people often take,
that what is called international law is so different from the
domestic law of a modern state that it ought not to be called by the
same name (because it 'cannot be enforced', it can be disregarded,
it lacks authoritative rules of recognition, adjudication, and
change etc.) raises questions that deserve answers.

The core of the sceptical position is the Hobbesian view that
there can be no law in the absence of government, and that
relations between sovereign princes or states take place in a state
of nature which is a state of war. Austin's position is a refinement
of that of Hobbes: that since law is 'the command of the sovereign'
and there is no common sovereign standing over states in their
relations with one another, what is improperly called international
law is merely 'positive international morality', or 'opinions or
sentiments current among nations generally.'[1] On the one hand,
the Hobbesian view helps to lay the foundations of the Realist
school of interpretation of international relations as an arena of

---

[1] Austin, *The Province of Jurisprudence Determined* (London, 1954; first
published 1832), pp. 127, 141-2.

conflict in which states jostle for power and position in a legal or normative vacuum. On the other hand, it is also central to the outlook of advocates of a world state or central authority, who accept that relations among states do in fact take place in a Hobbesian state of nature, but draw the conclusion from this that it is only by establishing a supreme government over the world as a whole, that law in relations between different communities can be made to prevail.

In between these extremes there is the Grotian tradition which rejects the description of international relations as a Hobbesian state of nature, and contends that states form together an anarchical society without government, more akin to the state of nature as it is depicted by Locke. The society of states or international society, in the account of the Grotians, is a primitive or imperfect one, but it is still a society, and the rules by which its members are bound in their relations with one another, include rules of law. Most professional expositors of modern international law belong at least in a loose sense to the Grotian tradition, although in the writings of late nineteenth-century positivist international lawyers the elements of a Realist outlook are sometimes strong.

Kelsen's approach to the matter presents something of a paradox. On the one hand he is an international lawyer, clearly within the Grotian tradition and firmly committed to the view that international law is truly law. But on the other hand he is also committed to the proposition that law is inseparable from coercion. His own approach to the problem of the definition of law, although it breaks with Hobbes and with Austin in vital respects, takes as its starting-point the idea that law is 'a coercive order'.

A common way in which expositors of international law seek to defend the claims of their subject to be law is to question definitions of law that make enforcement or sanctions a necessary part of it, and to set out the case for some other definition. Hart's definition of law as 'the union of primary with secondary rules', for example, allows us to separate the idea of law from that of coercion or enforcement.[2] So does McDougal's concept of law as 'a social process of decision-making that is both authoritative and

---

[2] See Hart, *The Concept of Law* (Oxford, 1961).

effective'.[3] Kelsen, however, does not question the definition of law as necessarily bound up with coercion, but instead argues that international law is no less a coercive order than is domestic law. He argues, that is to say, that international law has precisely the feature that its denigrators say it lacks.

Kelsen does, of course, depart from Austin's view that law is 'the command of the sovereign', and excludes the relationship of political superiors to political inferiors from his definition of law. A system of law, as Kelsen tells us, is characterized by the subordination of men not to other men, but to legal rules: *non sub homine sed sub lege*.[4] This does, indeed, eliminate one of the alleged contrasts between international and domestic law, and enables Kelsen to say that it is no less true of the latter than of the former that its essence is to subordinate men to rules rather than to one another. The concept of the basic norm, moreover, enables Kelsen to give an account of the unity or coherence of a legal system in terms that enable him likewise to dispense with the notion of 'the command of the sovereign' and to show that international law may constitute a legal system in the same sense as does domestic law.

But what is distinctive about law, Kelsen tells us, is that it is a coercive order; by contrast with other forms of social order, such as those that are based upon religious sanctions or on moral sanctions, law is 'a system of compulsion'. International law is not without this element of compulsion; indeed, 'there could be no question of international law without such compulsion'.[5] A legal rule is a hypothetical judgment which makes a sanction or threatened evil the consequence of a delict. This applies as much to international law as to domestic law (or, as Kelsen calls it, 'national law'). What is distinctive about the former is not the absence of sanctions, but the fact that the sanctions involved are decentralized rather than centralized.

Whereas in domestic law, the compulsion is supplied by a central authority, in international law it is supplied by the member states of international society, operating under a system of self-

---

[3] See McDougal *et al.*, *Studies in World Public Order* (New Haven, 1960).

[4] See e.g. *Law and Peace in International Relations: The Oliver Wendell Holmes Lectures* (Cambridge, Mass., 1942), p. 66 (henceforth, *Law and Peace*).

[5] *The Legal Process and International Order* (London, 1935), p. 11 (henceforth, *The Legal Process*).

help. Positive international law, he wrote in 1935, provides for two such sanctions to be administered by states under the system of self-help: reprisals and war. The contrast between the centralized enforcement mechanism operating in domestic society and the decentralized mechanism characteristic of international society, according to Kelsen, is relative rather than absolute. In domestic law there is provision for decentralized sanctions, inasmuch as the individual person retains certain basic rights of self-defence, despite the existence of a centralized enforcement mechanism. In international law, moreover, the collective security mechanisms of the League of Nations and the United Nations have provided the framework of a centralized system of compulsion. The difference is that in domestic society it is the centralized mechanism that is primary, while in international society the decentralized mechanism is primary.

Kelsen recognizes that the system of compulsion provided by decentralized sanctions is imperfect, and inferior to that which is available when the sanctions are centralized. It is a primitive system of law, a 'vendetta system'.[6] The individual members of the society, to whom the business of enforcement is entrusted, are judges in their own cause. There is no guarantee that when those who have committed delicts are confronted by the law-enforcers, the latter will prevail over the former. But it is Kelsen's argument that the contrast between a primitive coercive order and no coercive order is greater than the contrast between a coercive order that is decentralized and one that is centralized.[7] This is the heart of the case for treating domestic law and so-called international law as both examples of law in the same sense.

Kelsen believed that international law was evolving from a less to a more centralized system of sanctions. The domestic or national legal system, centralized though it was, had evolved from a decentralized system; international law was evolving in a parallel fashion. There was an early stage of complete decentralization, in which each state made its own decision as to the existence of a delict and the sanctions that were to be implemented in response to it; an intermediate stage in which these functions were taken over by a central tribunal, which decided on the existence of a delict and authorized states to engage in enforcement actions; and

---

[6] Ibid., p. 15.   [7] Ibid., p. 56.

a final stage of complete centralization.[8] Kelsen saw in the League and later in the United Nations the attempt to move from the early to the intermediate stage.

The notion that international society is a primitive or rudimentary society, and international law a form of primitive law, has a long ancestry in modern thinking about international relations. So has the idea that enforcement in the form of self-help or 'the hue and cry', provides a set of sanctions that help to bring about the efficacy of international law. Even today, when it is widely asserted by interpreters of international law that states no longer have any general right of self-help in enforcing their rights, but only a right of self-defence (and, indeed, that this right of self-defence is limited to defence against attacks on a state's territorial integrity and political independence), it may still be argued that the efficacy of the international legal system still rests in substantial measure on acts of law-enforcement carried out by individual states.

But Kelsen's approach to the question whether international law is law, leaves him vulnerable. As we have seen, the thesis that international law is truly law may be defended by questioning the Hobbesian or Austinian approach to law, which defines it as a coercive order. Kelsen, however, himself defines law as a coercive order, and makes the coercive character of international law the central part of his argument. This, as Hobbes and Austin saw, is implausible. Force does not have the same relationship to international law as it has to domestic law.

II   THE RELATION BETWEEN FORCE AND INTERNATIONAL LAW

The fact of war, or more broadly of the use of force in international relations, presents a challenge to the idea that states form together an international society. When states resort to war, or to the use or threat of force against one another, surely this shows that they are not part of the same society?

The Grotian theorist seeks to show that war and international society are not contradictory of one another. He does so by distinguishing between just and unjust wars. On the one hand,

---

[8] *The Legal Process*, p. 16.

international society must seek to limit, or contain war, which is antithetical to the very nature of international society. But on the other hand international society cannot be opposed to all war, because war, or more broadly, the use of force, is an instrumentality which international society must harness to enforce its rules.[9] Thus Grotius himself set about adapting the ancient and medieval tradition of just war theory to the needs of a modern and secular society of states. On the one hand, he sought to show that the law of nations excluded certain unjust causes of war, and that it required war to be fought in a just way. On the other hand he sought to show that it permitted states to resort to war to enforce certain of their rights, when these were injured by others. This has been the path of modern international law. In Grotius's own conception the distinctions between just and unjust causes of war and between just and unjust ways of waging it rested on a variety of normative principles, including those of natural law. Later these distinctions came to be written into positive international law.

This is the kind of ground on which Kelsen takes his stand. Force and law, he tells us, are not in fact opposites. Force indeed, so far from being the opposite of law, is the essence of law. It is wrong to imagine that law guarantees peace; because it deprives only the individual not the community of the right to use force, it guarantees only 'relative peace'. Where there is law, if there is a resort to force, this must be either a delict or a sanction, a violation of the law or an attempt to enforce it. Thus law is characterized by 'the force monopoly of the community'.

All this applies to international law. Without force, international law is inconceivable. 'War and counter-war are in the same reciprocal relation as murder and capital punishment'.[10] Reprisals, or acts of limited interference in the affairs of other states, may be sanctions; so may wars be acts of unlimited interference. Where there is international law, then when force occurs, it must be either a delict or a sanction. International law, too, establishes 'the force monopoly of the community'.

Kelsen's insistence on the place of force in international law was not merely a matter of theory, but also in some measure a matter

---

[9] This is set out at greater length in Bull, *The Anarchical Society. A Study in Order in World Politics* (London, 1977).

[10] *The Principles of International Law* (New York, 1952), p. 28 (henceforth, *Principles*).

of policy. He was in fact a strong advocate of collective security measures as a means to the maintenance of peace, both in the League and in the United Nations period. He said in his Harvard Lectures that there is no prospect of total or partial disarmament before the creation of a centralized executive power.[11] He notes that in the course of the twentieth century, the idea that force in international relations must be either a delict or a sanction has been written into positive international law, by virtue of the Versailles Treaty, the League Covenant, the Kellog-Briand Pact, and the United Nations Charter. The League Covenant, he thinks, takes us beyond the traditional just war doctrine of a *right* of all states to assist victims of a delict by measures of self-help, to the idea that they have a *duty* to provide such assistance. The United Nations Charter in Chapter VII establishes in the Security Council an authority competent to determine the existence of a delict, and to order a war of sanctions to take place; it establishes—or did until this was undone by the Uniting for Peace Resolution of 1950—a 'force monopoly of the Security Council'.[12]

Here again, Kelsen's argument for the existence of a system of decentralized sanctions is stated in evolutionist or progressivist terms. He believes that international society is bound to pass through the same stages of evolution that were experienced in the case of domestic society. He suggests a programme for further steps of centralization. The first stage is not the centralization of sanctions themselves, but the establishment of a centralized tribunal which will take away from particular states the power to determine the existence of a delict, and to authorize a war of sanctions. This formed the basis of the proposal he advanced in 1939 for the reform of the League of Nations; and it is the great advance which the United Nations Charter marks over the League Covenant, at least partially. The case for the existence of a system of dencentralized enforcement is partly that it is a centralized system *in statu nascendi*.[13]

Kelsen strikes a certain note of uncertainty, even of apology, in advancing his theory of an international 'force monopoly of the community'. He notes that there is always a strong sense in international society that war should not be resorted to without an

[11] *Law and Peace*, pp. 155–6.
[12] *The Law of the United Nations* (New York, 1966; first published 1950), p. 970.
[13] *Law and Peace*, p. 51.

acceptable justification, and that this was just as true in the period when international law proclaimed the sovereign right of all states to resort to war, as it has been since legal restrictions have been placed on this right. 'Never yet has a government declared that it was resorting to war only because it felt at liberty to do so, or because such a step seemed advantageous.'[14] But he admits that it is more controversial to claim that a war may be a sanction.

Kelsen, indeed, sometimes speaks as if the theory that international law establishes a force monopoly of the community, and the theory that it does not, were both consistent with the evidence, and the choice between one and the other a subjective one: 'The situation is characterized by the possibility of a double interpretation', he wrote in 1947. 'It is not a scientific, but a political decision which gives preference to the *bellum justum* theory . . . We choose this interpretation hoping to have recognised the beginning of a development of the future, and with the intention of strengthening as far as possible all the elements of presentday international law which tend to justify this interpretation, and promote the evolution we desire.'[15]

Kelsen's doctrine that in international society there is a 'force monopoly of the community' strains against the facts. It is one of the most salient features of the modern international system that in it force is the monopoly not of the community but of the sovereign states of which it is made up. Kelsen's approach, like so much that was written by experts on international law and organization in that period, was the product of wishful thinking.

Kelsen's theory of sanctions, as he recognized, involves a paradox: the coercive measure is of exactly the same sort as the act it seeks to prevent. 'Force is employed to prevent the employment of force', he wrote in 1935. 'This seems to be an antinomy, and the effort to avoid the social antinomy leads to the doctrine of absolute anarchism, which proscribes force even as a sanction.'[16]

The fact is, however, that in international relations it is not the exceptional, but the normal case that there is no general agreement in treating acts of force as either a delict or a sanction. It is not the case that there is normally agreement in international society as to which side in an international armed conflict represents the law-breaker and which the law-enforcer. There is

---

[14] Ibid., p. 37.   [15] *Law and Peace*, p. 54–5.   [16] Ibid., p. 11.

commonly disagreement on this matter, or there is agreement that the conflict should be regarded as a political one in which each side is asserting its interests, and its rights as it sees them, and neither can be said to represent international society as a whole. Kelsen's doctrine excludes the category of wars that are neither delicts nor sanctions, the category in which neither side has a just cause, and the category in which both have just causes.

In *Principles of International Law* Kelsen considers three objections to the *bellum justum* theory: that there is no objective authority competent to decide whether a war is illegal; that sanctions can be successful only if there is superior power; and that the function of war is not only to enforce existing law, but also to modify it, war playing in this respect a role in relation to international law like that of revolution in relation to national law. These objections are perhaps fatal to the prospects of effective application of Kelsen's doctrine of 'the force monopoly of the community', which presupposes a consensus in international society about the grounds for resort to force much greater than that which now obtains.

The force monopoly of which Kelsen speaks, it is true, is a monopoly in law, not in political fact; and he held, rightly, that international law should be viewed in dynamic terms, not static, so that a force monopoly might be recognized to be in process of becoming, even if it was not a present reality. But a legal system has to be built upon political facts, and not merely constitute a protest against them; and aspirations are not enough by themselves to bring changes about. Kelsen's approach, like the wider twentieth-century solidarist or neo-Grotian school of which it is part, is at best premature.[17]

III   POSITIVISM AND INTERNATIONAL LAW

Kelsen is, above all, a positivist. He was a lifelong opponent of attempts to bring natural law or sociological jurisprudence into the exposition of the law, being insistent that law is a scientific and technical discipline. He was a critic of reductionist doctrines that sought to deny law a distinct character, and treat it as a reflection

---

[17] See Bull: 'The Grotian Conception of International Society', in Butterfield & Wight eds., *Diplomatic Investigations* (London, 1966).

of something else; his account of the logic of the law, of *imputation*, was one of his most original contributions.

He carried these attitudes into his account of international law. The concepts of the basic norm and of the hierarchy of norms, for example, are applied in relation to the international legal system. He argues that there is no scientific way of determining whether international law or domestic law is superior, given his monist view of the relationship that subsists between them.[18] He maintains that consent is the foundation of international law, and holds that 'general' international law consists only of customary law, and that even the Charter of the United Nations is no more than 'particular law'.[19]

In this century, positivism in international law has been under considerable attack: on the one hand from writers like Brierly and Lauterpacht, who have sought to revive natural law, and on the other hand from exponents of a 'sociological' or 'policy-oriented' approach to international law, that asserts the legitimacy of moral, social, and political considerations in international legal decision-making—natural law, as it were, through the back door.

Legal positivism is the doctrine that legal issues should be separated from other normative issues, and that law is a distinct science that should not be confused with morals, sociology, or politics. Since these issues are in fact separate, and law is a distinct science or it is nothing, legal positivism is a correct doctrine. It serves the purpose of safeguarding legal science and legal technique against the inroads made upon it by extraneous subjects. It does, indeed, restrict the scope of legal specialists, confining them within their professional preserve and requiring them to stick to their lasts. But it does not imply that moral, social, and political questions are unimportant or should not be pursued.

The great onslaught on positivism in international law in the last generation has come from the school of sociological jurisprudence, and especially from the Yale law school, centred upon the work of Myres S. McDougal and his colleagues. At the centre of their position there is the doctrine that law is not a body of rules, but 'a process of decision that is both authoritative and effective'.[20] It is indeed the case, as is argued by writers of this school, that law is

---

[18] See *Das Problem der Souveränität und die Theorie des Völkerrechts* (Tübingen, 1928).
[19] *Principles*, pp. 247 ff. [20] See Note 3 above.

inter alia a social process; that moral, social, and political considerations do influence legal decision-making; and that legal decision-makers (judges, legal advisers, academic experts) do sometimes have to take positions on matters on which the rules themselves do not provide guidance.

But the distinctive feature of law as a social process is that it is one in which decisions are made authoritative because they derive from technically expert interpretations of agreed rules; if we once lose sight of these rules and the techniques for interpreting them, there is nothing to distinguish the law from other processes of decision. It is true that legal decision-makers are in fact influenced by extraneous considerations, but it is only to the extent to which they reach their decisions on strictly legal, non-extraneous grounds that they partake of a legal profession at all. It may be desirable that when judges, legal advisers, and legal scholars find it essential to come to a decision on an issue over which the law has no guidance to offer, they should make the best analysis possible of the moral, social or political issues at stake. But if they fail to give priority to the objective, technical study of the legal issues themselves, they are derelict in their duty as specialists in the law. Kelsen's defence of the integrity of international law provides a strong riposte to these false and fashionable doctrines.

But while the law is itself and not another thing, we must go beyond the law if we are to provide a moral appraisal of it, to explain its role in society or to make it the servant of policy. International ethics, the sociology of international law, and international 'policy science' are valid subjects in themselves, and international law does not encompass them. Kelsen does not in fact confine himself to international law, but strays into these other fields. We have seen that he had a strong commitment to peace through collective security; that in his analysis of this subject he allowed himself to be influenced by political preference; and that he even acknowledged that his position was based on political rather than on scientific considerations. He also went beyond strict positivism in international law in dealing with the subject of change.

IV CHANGE IN INTERNATIONAL LAW

It is a difficulty of the strict positivist approach to international law that it does not easily accommodate change. The traditional international law tells us that treaties may be changed by consent, and that customary law changes with the practice of states. But the consent of states to revision of treaties is not always forthcoming, and customary law changes only slowly. The sharp lines drawn by the positivists between what is law and what is not appear to inhibit legal change.

In the interwar period, when much of Kelsen's thinking about international relations was done, the issue of change was brought to the fore by the revisionist states, which threatened to change the 1919 peace settlement by war if the *status quo* powers would not agree to change it by peaceful means. This led to great interest in the subject of 'peaceful change'; if war was to be abolished, how would change come about? Article 19 of the League Covenant empowered the Assembly to discuss the revision of treaties, and this was invoked not only by Germany and the other revisionist states, but also by China and other non-European states in relation to so-called 'unequal treaties'. But the kind of peaceful change that actually came about in the 1930s (the kind celebrated by E. H. Carr in *The Twenty Years' Crisis*, 1939) was brought about not by the League of Nations but by the threat of force.

Kelsen is not unconscious that international law has to provide for change. He argues strongly against the idea that war is an unacceptable agent of change, seeking especially to combat the idea that war is to international law what revolution is to municipal law: wars, he says, unlike revolutions, are fought for subjective interests, not reforming principles.[21] His strong commitment to the development of collective security, moreover, led him to advocate reform of the League of Nations, and, under the impact of the Korean War, of the United Nations.

The United States, unable during the Korean conflict because of the Soviet veto to control the Security Council, but able along with its allies to command favourable majorities in the General Assembly, sought to assert new powers for the latter in matters of peace and security, especially through the 'Uniting for Peace' Resolution of 3 November 1950. Kelsen, in his book published in 1951, argues that change in the law of the Charter was possible not only by formal amendments but also by interpretation, even if it was not in conformity with the ascertainable intentions of the

[21] *Principles*, p. 36.

authors. The rule of unanimity among the permanent members of the Security Council, he argued, had paralysed the collective security system of the Charter, and change by interpretation was called for. Certain acts might be considered unconstitutional, Kelsen wrote, but 'directing our view towards the future, we may see them as the first steps in the development of a new law of the United Nations . . . There are cases where a new law originates in the violation of an old law.'[22] Here Kelsen speaks for change, but his voice is not that of a strict positivist.

In the 1960s and later the path of Charter revision through command of the General Assembly, pioneered by the United States in the 1950s, has been followed by the states of the Third World. The entry into international society of 100 or so new member states, and the coalescence of these states into Afro-Asian, non-aligned, and other groupings brought demands for change in international law. It was asserted that the old international law reflected the special interests of European or Western states, and that it had been made without the consent of the Third World states. There were suggestions that the latter were in some sense ranged against the international legal system itself, and might be forced to create some alternative or rival system.

In fact what has happened is that the Third World states have remained within the international legal order, but have brought about sweeping changes in its rules, for example, with regard to the use of force; the legitimacy of colonial rule and of rule by white racial minorities; the rights of states to permanent sovereignty over their natural resources; the relative importance of customary law and treaty law (where they have reversed the priority upheld by Kelsen); the validity of treaties agreed under duress; and the law with regard to human rights. This process by which Third World states have been absorbed within the international legal order is one that has done violence to international law as it was expounded by strict positivists. General Assembly resolutions owe their impact to a blurring of the lines between what is legal and what is not. There has been a departure from Kelsen's concept that even near universal treaties are still only particular treaties, and to embrace the idea that they are a form of legislation. We have seen the development of the idea that consensus rather than

[22] *Recent Trends in the Law of the United Nations* (London, 1951), p. 912.

consent is the basis for changing international law and the emergence of what is called 'soft law', that is to say, of rules that are not clearly either legal or non-legal.

The positivist might reply that all these developments have been at a great price, as yet unreckoned. There has been a decline of legality. What is seen as the construction of new 'soft' law is also the disintegration of old 'hard' law; we are now *without* firm rules that we had before. This disintegration of old law is storing up problems for the future that both the Western and Third World countries will have to face; the Third World countries themselves have a great need of firm legal rules in their relations with one another. All this may be true, but it has to be weighted against the likelihood that a rigid insistence on strict standards of positive law might have alienated many of the new states from the system altogether.

Kelsen, as we have seen, himself stood for Charter revision. But in doing so he was acting contrary to the spirit of his own strict positivist doctrines. These doctrines, moreover, preclude the vast changes in international law, or in what is taken to be international law, which in the last two decades have made it possible for international society to absorb the new states of the Third World without bursting apart at the seams.

V INTERNATIONAL LAW AND POWER POLITICS

The effectiveness or efficacy of international law is notoriously limited by power politics: the historical record shows that where considerations of power are uppermost, states disregard the imperatives of international law. Exponents of international law have sometimes responded to this by seeking to compromise with power politics. Some, for example, consign power politics to a separate sphere of international life that is not regulated by international law. Others seek to make international law conform to power politics, by defining its rules in such a way that they permit power politics (the approach often attributed to Vattel, for example). The response to the twentieth-century neo-Grotians or solidarists, however, has been to set up international law in opposition to power politics, to promulgate rules that contradict it.

This is the approach of Kelsen. He presents war as a contest between the law-breakers and the law-enforcers, but takes no account of the possibility that the latter will not have might on their side. His conception of international law as 'the force monopoly of the community' makes no concessions to the fact that force is the monopoly of states and that the international community is without force. His discussion of the maintenance of peace and security by measures of collective security takes no account of the distribution of power among states.

Kelsen's only references to power are made in the course of his discussion of the efficacy of law. The validity of law, he tells us, does not depend on its efficacy, although the validity of the legal system as a whole is dependent on its efficacy. The efficacy of the legal system, however, in Kelsen's view, does not depend on the power of the state, standing behind it: 'If the relationship of superiority essential to law is power, then this power is only the effectiveness of the norms establishing the coercive measures . . . As a power, the state is the effectiveness of the legal order, and as an order, it is this legal order itself.'[23] The state as entity exerting power, in disregard of the legal order, engaged both domestically and internationally in contests for power that take no account of law, is thus defined out of existence.

The 'pure theory of law' recognizes that law has its own logic and legal reasoning its own integrity, which non-legal considerations must impugn. Legal logic, however, will not help us to understand the place of international law in international relations, nor to prescribe the conditions of peace and security: this requires a study of international political realities. Kelsen, as we have seen, was not a consistent positivist in his discussion of international law and did not confine himself to a scientific exposition of legal rules. We have also to say that having strayed from the province of international law and ventured into the territory of international political science, his understanding was confined by the idealist or progressivist assumptions so common in that period.

[23] *Law and Peace*, pp. 69–70.

INDEX

1. Most references are to Kelsen, his theories and writings, unless otherwise stated.
2. Sub-entries are alphabetically arranged except where chronological order is significant.